The Cambridge Companion to Schumann

This *Companion* is an accessible, up-to-date introduction to Schumann: his time, his temperament, his style and his œuvre. An international team of scholars explores the cultural context, musical and poetic fabric, sources of inspiration, and interpretative reach of key works from the Schumann repertoire, ranging from his famous Lieder and piano pieces to chamber, orchestral and dramatic works. Additional chapters address Schumann's presence in nineteenth- and twentieth-century composition, and the fascinating reception history of his late works. Tables, illustrations, a detailed chronology and advice on further reading make it an ideally informative handbook for both the Schumann connoisseur and the music-lover. An excellent textbook for the university student of courses on key composers of nineteenth century Western Classical music, it is an invaluable guide for all who are interested in the thought, aesthetics and affective power of one of the most intriguing figures of a culturally rich and formative period.

The Cambridge Companion to
SCHUMANN

....

EDITED BY
Beate Perrey
University of Liverpool

CAMBRIDGE UNIVERSITY PRESS
Cambridge, New York, Melbourne, Madrid, Cape Town, Singapore, São Paulo

Cambridge University Press
The Edinburgh Building, Cambridge CB2 8RU, UK

Published in the United States of America by Cambridge University Press, New York

www.cambridge.org
Information on this title: www.cambridge.org/9780521789509

© Cambridge University Press 2007

This publication is in copyright. Subject to statutory exception
and to the provisions of relevant collective licensing agreements,
no reproduction of any part may take place without
the written permission of Cambridge University Press.

First published 2007

Printed in the United Kingdom at the University Press, Cambridge

A catalogue record for this publication is available from the British Library

ISBN 978-0-521-78341-5 hardback
ISBN 978-0-521-78950-9 paperback

Cambridge University Press has no responsibility for the persistence or accuracy of URLs for external or third-party internet websites referred to in this publication, and does not guarantee that any content on such websites is, or will remain, accurate or appropriate.

Contents

List of illustrations [page vi]
Notes on the contributors [vii]
Preface [ix]
Acknowledgements [x]
Chronology [xi]

Part I • Contexts

1 Schumann's lives, and afterlives: an introduction *Beate Perrey* [3]
2 Life and literature, poetry and philosophy: Robert Schumann's aesthetics of music *Ulrich Tadday* [38]
3 Schumann's heroes: Schubert, Beethoven, Bach *Nicholas Marston* [48]

Part II • Works

4 Piano works I: a world of images *John Daverio* [65]
5 Piano works II: afterimages *Laura Tunbridge* [86]
6 Why sing? Lieder and song cycles *Jonathan Dunsby* [102]
7 The chamber music *Linda Correll Roesner* [123]
8 Novel symphonies and dramatic overtures *Scott Burnham* [148]
9 The concertos *Joseph Kerman* [173]
10 Dramatic stage and choral works *Elizabeth Paley* [195]

Part III • Reception

11 Schumann in his time and since *Reinhard Kapp* [223]
12 The compositional reception of Schumann's music since 1950 *Jörn Peter Hiekel* [252]
13 Songs of dawn and dusk: coming to terms with the late music *John Daverio* [268]

Select bibliography [292]
Index [295]

Illustrations

1.1 Schumann's travel notebook. Reproduced with kind permission of the Robert-Schumann-Haus Zwickau, archive-nr. 12336-B3. [9]

1.2 Logier's 'Chiroplast' (lithograph after a sketch by Emile Beau from *L'anatomie de la main* (Paris, 1846)). [12]

1.3 Robert Schumann (lithograph by Joseph Kriehuber, Vienna, 1839). Reproduced with kind permission of the Robert-Schumann-Haus Zwickau, archive-nr. 96.65-B2. [15]

1.4 Clara Wieck, 1838 (lithograph by Andres Staub Vienna, 1838). Reproduced with kind permission of the Robert-Schumann-Haus Zwickau, archive-nr. 10054-B2. [17]

1.5 Robert and Clara Schumann's children, 1854. Reproduced with kind permission of the Robert-Schumann-Haus Zwickau, archive-nr. 2713-B2. [20]

1.6 Robert Schumann, 1850 (daguerreotype by Anton Völlner). Reproduced with kind permission of the Robert-Schumann-Haus Zwickau, archive-nr. 12526-B2. [29]

1.7 Johannes Brahms (photograph, *c.* 1855). Reproduced with kind permission of the Robert-Schumann-Haus Zwickau, without archive-nr. [32]

Notes on the contributors

Scott Burnham Professor of Music and Chair of the Music Department at Princeton University, is the author of *Beethoven Hero* (Princeton, 1995); translator of A. B. Marx, *Musical Form in the Age of Beethoven* (Cambridge, 1997); and co-editor of *Beethoven and His World* (Princeton, 2000). Other writings include 'Schubert and the sound of memory' (*Musical Quarterly*, 2001), 'On the beautiful in Mozart' (*Music and the Aesthetics of Modernity*, ed. K. Berger and A. Newcomb (Harvard, 2005)) and 'Haydn and humour' (*The Cambridge Companion to Haydn*, ed. C. Clark (Cambridge, 2005)).

John Daverio was Professor of Music, Chairman of the Musicology Department and Director ad interim of the School of Music at Boston University. A renowned specialist in German Romantic music and Schumann in particular, he is the author of *Crossing Paths: Schubert, Schumann, and Brahms* (New York, 2002), *Robert Schumann: Herald of a 'New Poetic Age'* (New York, 1997), *Nineteenth-Century Music and the German Romantic Ideology* (New York, 1993) and many articles, including the comprehensive article on the life and works of Robert Schumann in the second edition of the *New Grove Dictionary of Music and Musicians*. John Daverio died in 2003.

Jonathan Dunsby is Slee Professor of Music Theory at SUNY Buffalo, a prize-winning pianist and an experienced professional accompanist. He was founding editor of the international journal *Music Analysis* and has published numerous articles on the music of recent decades. He is author of *Performing Music: Shared Concerns* (Oxford, 1995). In 2004, two books appeared: his translation from the French for Oxford University Press of Jean-Jacques Nattiez's *The Battle of Chronos and Orpheus: Essays in Applied Musical Semiology* (Oxford, 2004), and his own study *Making Words Sing: Nineteenth- and Twentieth-Century Song* (Cambridge, 2004).

Jörn Peter Hiekel's writings have focussed on the music of the twentieth and twenty-first centuries. Before joining the Hochschule für Musik Carl Maria von Weber in Dresden, he was editor for the music publisher Breitkopf & Härtel, and has been director of the composers' seminars at the Darmstädter Ferienkurse since 2002 as well as co-director of the Institut für Neue Musik und Musikerziehung in Darmstadt. He is author of *Bernd Alois Zimmermanns 'Requiem für einen jungen Dichter'* (Stuttgart, 1995), and editor of Hans Zender, *Die Sinne denken. Schriften zur Musik 1965–2003* (Wiesbaden, 2004) and of forthcoming books on Helmut Lachenmann, Wilfried Krätzschmar, and Schumann's *'Welten'* (Dresden, 2006).

Reinhard Kapp is Professor of Music at the Vienna Hochschule für Musik und Darstellende Künste. He formerly taught at the Freie Universität Berlin and the Gesamthochschule Kassel, and has worked for the Richard Wagner Gesamtausgabe. He is author of *Studien zum Spätwerk Robert Schumanns* (Tutzing, 1984) and co-editor of *Darmstadt-Gespräche: Die Internationalen Ferienkurse für Neue Musik in Wien* (1998), as well as *Die Lehre von der Musikalischen Aufführung in* *der Wiener Schule* (2002). His main interests are Schumann, Wagner, the Second Viennese School and the history and theory of performance.

Joseph Kerman is a professor emeritus at the University of California at Berkeley. He has written on the concertos of Mozart and Beethoven and on the genre as a whole, in *Concerto Conversations* (1998). He is not an expert on Schumann, but gained broad knowledge of his and other music of his time as editor of the influential journal *Nineteenth Century Music* from 1977 to 1986.

Nicholas Marston is University Reader in Music Theory and Analysis in the University of Cambridge, and concurrently Fellow and Director of Studies in Music at King's College. He has published widely on the music of Beethoven and Schumann, including the Cambridge Music Handbook on Schumann's *Fantasie*, Op. 17 (Cambridge, 1992). He chairs the Editorial Board of *Music Analysis*, and takes up the position of Editor-in-Chief of *Beethoven Forum* in 2006. His next book will be on Heinrich Schenker and Beethoven's *Hammerklavier* Sonata.

Elizabeth Paley earned a doctorate in music theory from the University of Wisconsin-Madison and is currently an organist, pianist and freelance writer living in Durham, North Carolina. She has served on the faculty at the University of Kansas and Duke University, where her research focussed on music narratology, feminist theory, and intersections of music and the supernatural in melodrama. Her publications have appeared in *Nineteenth Century Music*, *South Atlantic Quarterly* and (under a pseudonym) *The Chronicle for Higher Education*.

Beate Perrey is Senior Lecturer in Critical Musicology and Analysis at the University of Liverpool and co-director of the research project *New Languages for Criticism: Cross-Currents and Resistances* at the Centre for Research in the Arts, Social Sciences and Humanities (CRASSH) at the University of Cambridge. She studied at Munich, Harvard and Cambridge where she held research fellowships at Trinity and Christ's Colleges, and was Visiting Professor in musicology at the Ecole Normale Supérieure in Paris during 2003–4. She is author of *Schumann's 'Dichterliebe' and Early Romantic Poetics: Fragmentation of Desire* (Cambridge, 2002).

Linda Correll Roesner's writings have focussed on the sources for the music of Schumann and Brahms. She is the editor of Schumann's Symphony No. 3 in E flat major, Op. 97 (*Robert Schumann: Neue Ausgabe sämtlicher Werke* (Mainz, 1995)) and co-editor of Brahms's Violin Concerto in D Major, Op. 77 (*Johannes Brahms: Neue Ausgabe sämtlicher Werke* (Munich, 2004)), and has also prepared miniature-score editions of the four Schumann symphonies (London, 1986–97). In 1998 she was awarded the *Robert Schumann Preis der Stadt Zwickau*.

Ulrich Tadday, Professor of Music History and Chair of the Music Department at the University of Bremen in Germany, is the author of *Das Schöne Unendliche, Ästhetik, Kritik, Geschichte der romantischen Musikanschauung* (Stuttgart–Weimar, 1999). He is the editor of *Musik-Konzepte* (Neue Folge) and has written extensively on the history and aesthetics of music in the eighteenth to twentieth centuries.

Laura Tunbridge is Lecturer in Music Analysis and Critical Theory at the University of Manchester, having previously taught at the University of Reading. She studied at Oxford, Nottingham and Princeton. Her publications include 'Schumann's *Manfred* in the mental theatre' (*Cambridge Opera Journal*, 2003). She is completing a book about Schumann's late style.

Preface

The Cambridge Companion to Schumann is an accessible, up-to-date introduction to Schumann's music, life and times. It provides information for the general listener – the music-lover who, while having an aural familiarity with the canonical works, may want to explore the historical background and cultural context of the works – as well as the specialist. It can also be used as an introductory textbook for university students, providing them with sound information about the Schumann repertoire as well as historical and aesthetic issues necessary for understanding Schumann's œuvre.

A team of top international scholars explores the contemporary cultural context, the musical and poetic fabric, and the multiple sources of inspiration and interpretative reach of masterpieces from the Schumann repertoire. Contributors include both first-rank Schumann specialists such as John Daverio, Reinhard Kapp, Nicolas Marston, Laura Tunbridge, Linda Roesner and Ulrich Tadday, as well as scholars who, while not Schumann specialists, are high-calibre scholars in their own fields, including Scott Burnham, Jonathan Dunsby, Jörn Peter Hiekel and Joseph Kerman. These 'non-specialists' have been recruited in the belief that they will be able to contribute to those chapters that address the essential, broad themes, without getting bogged down in the detailed problems that can sometimes beset Schumann scholarship. As can be seen in this volume, they have new and perceptive things to say precisely because the perspective from which to view Schumann's work is different from the set of values within which Schumann studies may sometimes have found themselves enclosed.

Part I of the Companion explores Schumann's personality, his time and temperament, as well as the literary, philosophical and compositional influences on the composer. Part II explores the various different genres of Schumann's compositional output, ranging from his famous Lieder and piano works to chamber, orchestral and dramatic repertoire. In addition, Part III offers chapters discussing Schumann's influence on works of some of today's leading composers, and the problem of Schumann's late works. Tables and illustrations, and guidance on further reading in the English language, make this volume an ideally informative handbook for both the Schumann connoisseur and the music-lover. It is an invaluable guide for all who are interested in the thought, aesthetics and affective power of the most intriguing figure of a culturally rich and formative period.

Acknowledgements

Thanks go above all to the contributors to this volume for their enthusiasm, unfailing cooperation and patience throughout the long process of bringing the project to fruition. Further I should like to thank the curators and experts who granted permission to reproduce material housed in their archives, as well as for many other acts of kindness and assistance during the preparation of this book: Anette Müller and Gerd Nauhaus of the Robert-Schumann-Haus in Zwickau; the staff of the libraries at the University of Cambridge, the British Library in London, the Ecole Normale Supérieure, the Bibliothèque Nationale in Paris, and the Bayerische Staatsbibliothek in Munich. At Cambridge University Press, my thanks go to Penny Souster and Vicki Cooper, my editors; and Rebecca Jones, assistant editor, for providing help whenever needed. Thanks also go to three anonymous readers for their encouraging and perceptive comments; to Richard Cornell at Boston University and Mario Lorenzo, Paris, for expertly preparing musical examples; to Mary Whittall for translating Chapters 2 and 11, and to Andrew Brown, Nicolas Cox and Jonathan Dunsby for their kind assistance in tricky cases of translation. The index has been prepared by Margaret Christie. Two institutions deserve special thanks: Christ's College, Cambridge, where this volume was first conceived during my time there as a research fellow, and the University of Liverpool for granting me research leave to take up a visiting professorship at the Ecole Normale Supérieure in Paris, during which period this book was beginning to take its final shape. Finally, I owe gratitude to those friends and colleagues whose willingness to read and discuss parts of the manuscript and share their ideas has been a source of inspiration: Gillian Beer, Esteban Buch, Jonathan Dunsby, Martin Kaltenecker and Donald Lee.

Our colleague, the great Schumann expert John Daverio, was not to live to see this book come into being. It is dedicated to his memory.

Chronology

Note: unless specified otherwise, selected musical works are dated according to completion of composition, rather than of publication. Literary works appear according to year of publication. Opus, WoO (works without opus number) and *Anhang* numbers throughout correspond to Margit L. McCorkle, *Thematisch-bibliographisches Werkverzeichnis* (Munich, 2003).

Developments in music, literature and philosophy	Schumann's life and selected compositions
1810 Chopin born	Robert Schumann born 8 June in Zwickau
1811 Liszt and Ferdinand Hiller born; première of Beethoven's Fifth Piano Concerto; Schubert writes his first Lieder	
1812 Sigismond Thalberg born	
1813 Verdi and Wagner born	
1815 Schubert: *Erlkönig*	
1816 William Sterndale Bennett born	
Schubert: Fifth Symphony	
Beethoven: *An die ferne Geliebte*	
1817 Niels Gade born; Weber appointed Kapellmeister in Dresden; E. T. A. Hoffmann: *Nachtstücke*	Enters primary school in Zwickau; first piano lessons with local organist J. G. Kuntzsch
1818 Beethoven: *Hammerklavier* Sonata	
1819 Clara Wieck born	Hears the piano virtuoso Ignaz Moscheles play
Jacques Offenbach born	
Schubert: *Trout* Quintet; Louis Spohr: *Faust*	
E. T. A. Hoffmann: *Die Serapionsbrüder*	
Goethe: *West-Östlicher Divan*	
1820 Pianos with metal frames produced	Enters secondary school in Zwickau

(*cont.*)

Developments in music, literature and philosophy	Schumann's life and selected compositions
1821 Weber: *Der Freischütz*	
Beethoven: Piano Sonatas, Opp. 110–11	
E. T. A. Hoffmann: *Lebensansichten des Katers Murr* (The life and opinions of the Tomcat Murr)	
Wilhelm Müller: *Die schöne Müllerin*	
1822 E. T. A. Hoffmann dies	
César Franck born	
Joseph Wasielewski, Schumann's first biographer, born	
1823 Beethoven completes *Diabelli Variations* and begins work on his last string quartets	
1824 Lord Byron dies; Bruckner and Smetana born	*Le Psaume cent cinquantième* [Psalm 150] for choir, piano and orchestra, Op. 1, begun 1821/22 (Anhang I10)
Premières of Beethoven's Ninth Symphony and *Missa Solemnis*	
Wilhelm Müller: *Die Winterreise*	
Schubert: *Die schöne Müllerin*	
1825 Eduard Hanslick born; Jean Paul dies	Founds a student literary club
Schubert: 'Great' C major Symphony	His sister Emilie commits suicide
1826 Weber dies	Schumann's father dies of a 'nervous condition'
Première of Weber's *Oberon*	
1827 Beethoven dies; Schubert: *Winterreise* and two piano trios; Heine: *Buch der Lieder* and *Reisebilder*	First songs, literary pieces and diaries
1828 Schubert: String Quartet in C and last three piano sonatas; dies in Vienna	Graduates and travels to Bayreuth, Nuremberg, Augsburg and Munich; meets Heinrich Heine
	Moves to Leipzig, matriculates as a law student and takes piano lessons with Friedrich Wieck; meets Wieck's daughter Clara
1829 Anton Rubinstein born; Friedrich Schlegel dies	Transfers to Heidelberg to attend lectures by the aesthetician A. F. J. Thibaut

xiii Chronology

Developments in music, literature and philosophy	Schumann's life and selected compositions
Felix Mendelssohn conducts the first performance of Bach's *St Matthew Passion* since Bach's death and begins composition of *Lieder ohne Worte* (finished 1845); Chopin: Piano Concerto in F minor, Op. 21; Clara Wieck (Schumann's future wife) begins her first composition, *Quatre Polonaises*, for four-hand piano, Op. 1, published 1831–3	Trip to Switzerland and Northern Italy where he hears Rossini's *La gazza ladra* at La Scala in Milan
1830 Berlioz: *Symphonie fantastique* Felix Mendelssohn: *Reformation Symphony*; Chopin: Piano Concerto in E minor, Op. 11; piano virtuoso Thalberg begins composition of virtuosic piano 'fantasias' on melodies by Weber, Rossini, Meyerbeer, Bellini, Donizetti, Mozart and Verdi; piano virtuoso Hiller begins writing piano pieces	Hears Niccolò Paganini play, moves back to Leipzig into Wieck's house, and commits himself to becoming a concert pianist under Wieck's guidance; begins experimenting with the Chiroplast, a hand-training apparatus; onset of paralysis of the right hand Finishes *Abegg-Variationen*, Op. 1 (begun 1829)
1831 Hegel dies; Achim von Arnim, co-author (together with Clemens Brentano) of *Des Knaben Wunderhorn*, dies; Joseph Joachim born Liszt begins composition of *Bravourstudien* for piano after Paganini's *Caprices* for violin, (first version published 1838) Goethe completes *Faust II*	Intensive piano studies with Wieck, composition with Heinrich Dorn (until 1832)
1832 Goethe dies	Paralysis of his right hand persists; gives up on the idea of a career as a performer and begins composing in earnest *Papillons*, Op. 2; *Studien für das Pianoforte nach Capricen von Paganini*, Op. 3; *Intermezzi*, Op. 4; *Impromptus sur une romance de Clara Wieck*, Op. 5 Works on G minor Symphony

(cont.)

Developments in music, literature and philosophy	Schumann's life and selected compositions
1833 Brahms born; Borodin born Mendelssohn: 'Italian' Symphony Mendelssohn takes up post of Music Director in Düsseldorf	Founds the semi-fictional *Davidsbündler* league Increase in compositional activity Brother Julius dies Schumann's sister-in-law, Rosalie, dies Close friendship with Ludwig Schunke *Toccata* in C major, Op. 7
1834 Liszt composes *Harmonies poétiques et réligieuses* and begins *Années de Pélerinage* (parts I and II published 1858); Berlioz: *Harold in Italy* Symphony First issue of *Neue Zeitschrift für Musik* (*NZfM*) published	Ludwig Schunke dies Liaison with and secret engagement to Ernestine von Fricken
1835 Saint-Saëns born; Bellini dies Donizetti: *Lucia di Lammermoor* Mendelssohn appointed conductor of the Leipzig Gewandhaus Orchestra Chopin: Polonaises, Op. 26, the first Scherzo, Op. 20 and the first Ballade, Op. 23	Engagement to Ernestine von Fricken dissolved Growing liaison with and secret engagement to Clara Wieck, end of 1835 Meets Mendelssohn, Chopin and Moscheles Becomes editor of the *NZfM* *Carnaval*, Op. 9; Sonata in F sharp minor, Op. 11 Critical essay on Berlioz' *Symphonie fantastique*
1836 Meyerbeer: *Les Huguenots*	Schumann's mother dies; eighteen months of separation from Clara Meets Sterndale Bennett *Concert sans orchestre*, or Sonata in F minor, Op. 14
1837 Field and Hummel die; Balakirev born Liszt: *12 Grandes Etudes* Chopin: 12 Etudes, Op. 25 (begun 1835); begins B flat minor Sonata, Op. 35	Engagement to Clara Wieck without her father's consent *Davidsbündlertänze*, Op. 6; *Fantasiestücke*, Op. 12; première of *Etudes symphoniques*, Op. 13, by Clara Wieck in the Gewandhaus Leipzig

Developments in music, literature and philosophy	Schumann's life and selected compositions
1838 Bizet and Bruch born	Visits Vienna for eight months to explore possibilities of settling there with Clara
Jeanne Louise Farrenc: piano quintets (finished 1839), Opp. 30 and 31	
Eduard Mörike: *Gedichte*	Visits Schubert's brother and discovers a number of Schubert manuscripts including the 'Great' C major Symphony
	Kinderszenen, Op. 15; C major *Phantasie*, Op. 17; *Kreisleriana*, Op. 16; *Novelletten*, Op. 21; G minor Sonata, Op. 22
1839 Musorgsky born	Brother Eduard dies
Berlioz: *Roméo et Juliette* Symphony	Returns to Leipzig
Spohr: *Historische Symphonie*, Op. 39	Takes legal action against Clara's father, Friedrich Wieck, to gain right to marry Clara
Chopin finishes the remaining three movements of the B flat minor Sonata, Op. 35; Mazurkas, Op. 41, *24 Préludes*, Op. 28 (begun 1838); Carl Czerny, publication of his *Complete Theoretico-practical School for the Pianoforte*, Op. 500	Schumann's sponsor Henriette Voigt dies
	Arabeske, Op. 18; *Blumenstück*, Op. 19; *Humoreske*, Op. 20; *Drei Romanzen*, Op. 28
1840 Tchaikovsky born; Paganini dies	Receives honorary doctorate from the University of Jena for his services as composer and music critic
	Wins court case against Clara's father and marries Clara in September
	'Year of Song': Heine *Liederkreis*, Op. 24; *Myrthen*, Op. 25; *Zwölf Gedichte von Justinus Kerner*, Op. 35; Eichendorff *Liederkreis*, Op. 39; *Frauenliebe und -leben*, Op. 42; *Dichterliebe*, Op. 48; for solo piano: *Nachtstücke*, Op. 23; *Faschingsschwank aus Wien*, Op. 26
	Meets Liszt
1841 Dvořák born	First daughter Marie born in September

(*cont.*)

Developments in music, literature and philosophy	Schumann's life and selected compositions
Felix Mendelssohn: *Variations sérieuses*, Op. 54 Chopin: *Nocturnes*, Op. 48, Ballade in A flat major, Op. 47 and the F minor Fantasy, Op. 49	First Symphony ('Spring') in B flat, Op. 38; begins Second Symphony in D minor, Op. 120 (revised 1851 as no. 4); *Ouvertüre, Scherzo und Finale*, Op. 52; *Phantasie* for piano and orchestra in A minor (first movement of Piano Concerto in A minor, Op. 54)
1842 Massenet and Sullivan born; Clemens Brentano dies Wagner: *Rienzi*; Verdi: *Nabucco*; Mendelssohn: *Scottish* Symphony; Niels Gade: First Symphony Chopin: Mazurkas, Op. 50; A major Polonaise, Op. 53; F minor Ballade, Op. 52; and the E major Scherzo, Op. 54	Accompanies Clara on a tour to Bremen, Oldenburg and Hamburg Study of quartets by Mozart, Haydn and Beethoven Three String Quartets, Op. 41; Piano Quintet, Op. 44; Piano Quartet, Op. 47; *Phantasiestücke* for piano trio, Op. 88
1843 Grieg born; Hölderlin dies Brahms' first public piano recitals Wagner: *Der fliegende Holländer* Opening of the Leipzig Conservatoire under Mendelssohn's leadership Mendelssohn's Overture *A Midsummer Night's Dream*	Second daughter Elise born Nominated by Mendelssohn as piano and composition teacher at the Leipzig Conservatoire Meets Berlioz *Das Paradies und die Peri*, Op. 50, of which he conducts the première
1844 Nikolaus Lenau dies; Nietzsche, Rimsky-Korsakov born; Mendelssohn: Violin Concerto	Accompanies Clara on five-month tour to Russia; bad health Retires as editor of his journal, the *NZfM* Begins work on *Szenen aus Goethes Faust* (WoO3) The Schumanns move to Dresden
1845 Fauré born; August Wilhelm Schlegel dies; Wagner: *Tannhäuser*	Third daughter Julie born Health deteriorates *Romanzen und Balladen*, Op. 53 (begun 1840, resumed 1843); Piano Concerto in A minor, Op. 54 (begun 1841, resumed 1843); *Sechs Studien*, Op. 56 and *Vier Skizzen*, Op. 58, both for pedal piano; *Vier Fugen*, Op. 72

Developments in music, literature and philosophy	Schumann's life and selected compositions
1846 Berlioz: *The Damnation of Faust*; Mendelssohn: *Elijah*; Fanny Mendelssohn: Piano Trio, Op. 11	First son (fourth child) Emil born
	Concert tour to Vienna and visit to Berlin
	Second Symphony in C, Op. 61
1847 Fanny and Felix Mendelssohn die	Emil dies
	Becomes conductor of the Dresden choral association *Liedertafel*
	Lieder und Gesänge, Op. 27; First Piano Trio in D minor, Op. 63; *Romanzen und Balladen*, Op. 64 (begun 1841)
1848 Donizetti dies; Duparc born	Second son (fifth child) Ludwig born
Revolution: uprisings all over Europe, all suppressed except in Paris; abdication of Ferdinand I, succeeded by Franz Joseph	Founds the *Verein für Chorgesang* in Dresden
	Bilder aus dem Osten for four-hand piano, Op. 66; *Album für die Jugend* for solo piano, Op. 68; opera *Genoveva*, Op. 81; *Manfred*, Op. 115
	Schumann's last brother Karl dies
1849 Chopin, Kalkbrenner, Nicolai, Johann Strauss the elder die	Third son (sixth child) Ferdinand born
	Collects, revises and puts in order much of his compositional output
1849 Revolution, uprisings all over Europe	His, in Schumann's own words, 'most fruitful year' includes numerous vocal works such as Opp. 51, 67, 69, 71, 75, 91, 98a/b; *Phantasiestücke* for clarinet (violin or cello) and piano, Op. 73; *Spanisches Liederspiel*, Op. 74; *Lieder-Album für die Jugend*, Op. 79; Second Piano Trio no. 2 in F Major, Op. 80; *Concertstück* for four horns and orchestra in F Major, Op. 86; *Introduction und Allegro appassionato* for piano and orchestra, Op. 92; *Drei Romanzen* for oboe (clarinet or violin) and piano, Op. 94; *Fünf Stücke im Volkston* for cello (violin) and piano, Op. 102.
Berlioz: *Te Deum*; Bruckner: Requiem in D Minor	

(*cont.*)

Developments in music, literature and philosophy	Schumann's life and selected compositions
1850 Lenau dies; Wagner: *Lohengrin*; Liszt: First Symphonic Poem Brahms' first chamber music compositions	Premiere of *Genoveva* Moves to Düsseldorf to take up post of Music Director *Lieder und Gesänge*, Op. 77 (begun 1840); *Waldszenen*, Op. 82 (begun 1848); *Sechs Gedichte von N. Lenau und Requiem*, Op. 90; *Lieder und Gesänge*, Op. 96; Third Symphony ('Rhenish') in E flat major, Op. 97; Cello Concerto in A minor, Op. 129; numerous other vocal works.
1851 D'Indy born, Liszt's first *Hungarian Rhapsodies* begin to appear Verdi: *Rigoletto*; Wagner completes *Opera and Drama*; Breitkopf & Härtel and the Leipzig Bach Gesellschaft embark on the first complete Bach edition (completed 1899) and publish its first volume	Fourth daughter (seventh child) Eugenie born Travels up the Rhine, Heidelberg, into Switzerland, Brussels and Antwerp Increasingly conflictual relations between Schumann as Music Director and his Düsseldorf colleagues Compositions include *Mädchenlieder* and *Sieben Lieder* after poems by Elisabeth Kulmann, Opp. 103 and 104; First Violin Sonata in A minor, Op. 105; Third Piano Trio in G minor, Op. 110; *Drei Fantasiestücke*, Op. 111; *Der Rose Pilgerfahrt*, Op. 112; *Märchenbilder*, for viola (violin) and piano, Op. 113; Fourth Symphony in D minor, Op. 120 (begun 1841); and numerous additional vocal works
1852 London's New Philharmonic Society founded Brahms composes his First Sonata in C major and Second Sonata in F sharp minor	Trip to Leipzig for performance of *Der Rose Pilgerfahrt* Serious health problems; others stand in for Schumann to conduct; first attempts to persuade Schumann to resign from his post in Düsseldorf Second version of the *Etudes Symphoniques*, Op. 13; Second Violin Sonata in D minor, Op. 121 (begun 1851); *Gedichte der Königin*

Developments in music, literature and philosophy	Schumann's life and selected compositions
	Maria Stuart, Op. 135; Overture for *Hermann and Dorothea*, Op. 136; and numerous vocal works including the Requiem in D flat major, Op. 148
1853 Ludwig Tieck dies; Liszt: B minor Piano Sonata dedicated to Schumann; première of Verdi's *La Traviata*; Clara Schumann composes her last works, *Variationen über eine Thema von Robert Schumann*, Op. 20, *Drei Romanzen*, Op. 21, both for piano, and *Drei Romanzen* for piano and violin, Op. 22; Wagner begins *Der Ring des Nibelungen*; Brahms composes his Third Sonata in F minor	Further deterioration of his health; meets Brahms, followed by intense compositional activity; resigns from his post in October; accompanies Clara on her tour to the Netherlands Compositions include, besides many vocal works, Piano Sonata in F minor, Op. 14 (second version of *Concert sans orchestre*, 1836); *Drei Klaviersonaten für die Jugend*, Op. 118; *Sieben Klavierstücke in Fughettenform*, Op. 126; Violin Concerto in D minor (WoO1) and *Phantasie* for violin and orchestra, Op. 131; *Vier Märchenerzählungen* for clarinet (violin), viola and piano, Op. 132; *Gesänge der Frühe* for solo piano, Op. 133; *Konzert-Allegro mit Introduction* for piano and orchestra, Op. 134; Third Violin Sonata in A minor (WoO2); *Szenen aus Göthe's Faust* (WoO3); piano accompaniment for J. S. Bach's Violin Sonatas and Partitas BWV 1001–6 (WoO8) and for the Suites for unaccompanied cello BWV 1007–12 (all lost except for no. 3, *Anhang* O2), and for Paganini's 24 Capricen for solo violin Op. 1, continued into 1855 (*Anhang* O8)
1854 Humperdinck and Janáček born; Friedrich Wilhelm Schelling dies; Hanslick: *Vom Musikalisch-Schönen*; Liszt: *Faust* Symphony; Wagner: *Das Rheingold*; Berlioz: *L'Enfance du Christ* (1850–4)	The Schumanns' last joint trip to visit Joseph Joachim in Hanover; 27 February: Schumann attempts suicide, is rescued and admitted to the mental institution in Endenich near Bonn

(cont.)

Developments in music, literature and philosophy	Schumann's life and selected compositions
	Brahms travels to Düsseldorf to stay with Clara Schumann until July 1856
	Fourth son (eighth child) Felix born
	Composition of *Variationen über ein eigenes Thema* in E flat major, the so-called 'Ghost Variations' for piano (*Anhang* F39)
1855 Chausson born	From Endenich, correspondence with Clara, Brahms and other colleagues
Eduard Mörike: *Mozart auf der Reise nach Prag*	Finishes piano accompaniment for Paganini's *24 Capricen* for solo violin, begun 1853 (*Anhang* O8)
1856 Heine dies; Sigmund Freud born	Schumann dies 29 July
Liszt: *Dante* Symphony; Wagner; *Die Walküre*	
First Steinway grand piano produced	
1858 First Schumann biography by Wasielewski appears	

PART I

Contexts

1 Schumann's lives, and afterlives: an introduction

BEATE PERREY

The basic facts of Schumann's life suggest a life in disarray. Born into the *Sehnsucht*-driven world of German Romanticism, he is torn between disciplines. He begins the study of law out of a sense of filial duty but then follows his instinct when he turns to music, though never letting go of two other great passions, literature and poetry. Even as a committed musician, however, he veers between the roles of performer, composer and critic. It is to take a self-inflicted hand injury to free him to compose in earnest, and all urgency. Although endowed with an astonishing capacity to produce very great quantities of music in very short spans of time, he suffers periods of total or near-total creative standstill. These extremes of feverish, splendidly productive activity and exhausted, self-doubting arrest testify to a creative modus operandi that is not only intense, impulsive and at times difficult to live with, but which later observers have felt inclined to identify as 'manic-depressive'. Some critics have also noted that Schumann's works themselves evince these characteristics, and his highly contrastive compositional style still incites puzzlement, if not consternation. Structurally speaking, Schumann cultivated with his seeming free-associated pieces the musically relatively new and disorientating art of brevity, discontinuity and contradiction. They develop from eccentric, spectral and 'poetic' early works to more conventional but nonetheless intricate and introvert late works. This perceived inconsistency in Schumann's nature as well as his compositional style is, however, conspicuously absent when it comes to what is probably the most widely known and possibly most popular aspect of Schumann's life – his passionate wooing and hard-fought winning of Clara Wieck, herself the first woman virtuoso able to break into and succeed in the male-dominated world of nineteenth-century solo performance. Clara's own musical career, long preceding Schumann's own years of public recognition, is a shared source of inspiration as much as it made for years of conflict. Their marriage is an intense and intensely committed one, as well as rather unsettled, enriched and encumbered by many children, and disrupted over and over by extensive travelling and frequent relocations. Like his work, Schumann the man is famous for his extravagant emotional scale. Tempted and capable of going to extremes, he lives through the human passions with alarming flexibility, passing from euphoric states to melancholic lethargy, from instances of aphasia to moments of rage and violence, culminating in his famous suicide attempt, which leads to confinement in a mental hospital for the last two-and-a-half years of his life. And it is this end, Schumann's madness, and death in madness, that seems emblematic of a life not only out of the ordinary, but also, possibly, out of control. It suggests that there was a quality to this life that was not only excessive, chaotic and incomprehensible, but also irritating, frightening and tragic.

Biography is usually supposed to make sense of a life's chaos, or at least is expected to want to do so. Certainly the writing of a life (as opposed to the casual contemplating, or ignoring of, or being puzzled by one), be it academic or novelistic, might appear, by virtue of using language, capable of capturing a life reasonably well and in reasonable terms. Through writing, one attempts to join the disparate pieces together, align them as a lifeline, create a narrative – a story. And no doubt there is satisfaction to be had and respectability to be gained in rendering a life coherent, however remote, fragmented or incomprehensible it may have been, no matter how distant (historically, culturally, temperamentally) its agent may appear. Yet, it is only with hindsight, the biographer's singular prerogative, that a life can be somehow comprehended at all – or so one would think. Looked at through the retrospective lens of the detached biographer, a life's events tend to line up before our eyes and seem to show why or how one thing led to another. Indeed, not being in the thick of things, a life can be reconstructed rather well, far away from the urgent, the humdrum, the haphazard, that may have meant the living of it. This very urgency, however, still hanging in the air, and the fascination with a related degree of chaos and madness, may become the motor for wanting to revisit a life in the first place, whether out of sheer curiosity, or in the attempt to understand it at long last. Comfortably entrenched behind their writing tools, then, both biographer and autobiographer write up the minutes of a war that is long over.

Schumann's life has inspired a whole range of different types of biographical story-writing, from academic accounts to novels, poems, plays and films. And on these all is embossed, *en filigrane*, the watermark image of one 'Robert Schumann', a great legend, perhaps the legend most powerfully evocative of the nineteenth century's myth of the artist. Interestingly, it tends to begin at the end, with Schumann's decline into madness, and invariably includes his enduring love for Clara. It is this legend, a story of love and madness, and of art and death, that will forever haunt the reception of his work. But there can be no doubt that Schumann himself helped, unknowingly or otherwise, to create it. A self-declared poet-composer, he wrote incessantly, not only music and about music, but also for himself and about himself. Schumann was his own most meticulous analyst and chronicler and lived a lifetime under the relentless, inquisitive gaze of his own self-searching eyes, screening, scrutinizing and minutely describing every move and every thought, all inner and outer events, all of them, all of the time. A tireless filler of diaries and notebooks and diligent keeper of lists, Schumann has provided his critics with more than one might perhaps ever have wished to know: endless data and detailed description, from meetings with friends and colleagues and visits of places to income and outgoing expenses, future compositional projects and performances, literary extracts, frequency of sexual intercourse, hours of sleep and much more beyond.[1] Taken together with Schumann's autobiographical sketches as well as his vast correspondence with colleagues, friends, family, and especially Clara, these written documents, rich in both quantity and quality, are the fuel that propels biographical research. Whether as the active manipulator of his public image as the Romantic artist-as-genius constructed by himself and his admirers, Schumann is a composer about whom stories always have and always will be told. Yet, such stories may tell us more about the needs of a modern society to keep them alive than, realistically, about a composer in his endeavours to shape or control them.

One story that has influenced our image of Schumann more than any other is the story of Schumann the madman. Much thought and speculation has gone into what nevertheless remains the most darkly mysterious facet of this life. What is of interest is that those biographers who had a particular investment in Schumann's madness inevitably ended up reading Schumann's life backwards. When reading about Schumann's life in the extensive secondary literature based on the equally extensive autograph archive, it is endlessly intriguing to note how Schumann's future – his death, his madness – comes to shadow his past: how this end is seen to have shaped his whole life, and made to explain his beginnings, his being and his becoming. Biography is thus tempted to make Schumann into a figure in the image of universally shared fears and ideals, into a man who is at once one of the great Romantic heroes, and a lost soul. And yet, either one of these versions consistently show us a man amidst the disarray of his solitude. In this brief and necessarily cursory biographical sketch, as well as revisiting the main landmarks of Schumann's life, I shall try to avoid the proleptic approach. Instead, I shall focus in some detail on a few moments of this life that invite a more multi-textured reading of events, events often infused with precisely this kind of indeterminacy, full of contradictions, ambiguities and loose ends. That Schumann's life, or 'personality', may appear to have contained 'problems', hardly needs acknowledgement. These need neither muffling nor continued commemorating, nor, indeed, elaborate justification. Instead, the significance of Schumann's life may lie elsewhere: it may lie not only in the ways in which it was lived, with, without or indeed despite problems; but rather in the ways in which it was a driven life, forward-flung and animated by a singular imaginative energy channelled into the kind of transformative powers to which his music, characterized by openness and unpredictability, is resounding testimony. This is clearly to be heard in his music still: an astonishing voice articulating the endlessly changing shapes of an inner and outer world, sharply perceived, essentially, as opportunity – for constant reinvention.

The early years

Unsurprisingly, there is nothing in Schumann's early life that gives any hints of who he was to become. Notably, Schumann was not a musical prodigy. Born in the Saxon town of Zwickau in 1810 into an affluent middle-class family, he is the youngest of five children. Off and on, from age three to five-and-a-half he is placed in a foster home, as his mother had contracted typhus.[2] Generations of his ancestors had been farmers until his grandfather became a pastor, and his father a publisher and writer of sorts. The Schumann Brothers Publishing Company, 'the first to call the attention of the German people to the best European writers', produced, in addition to encyclopedic and reference works, pocket editions of Byron, Cervantes, Goethe, Schiller and Scott, authors whom Schumann would come to cherish and who would significantly influence his work. At the age of seven, Schumann begins piano lessons with the local organist. More formal pianistic training does not take place until his move, aged eighteen, to Leipzig, where he commits himself to music with a view to becoming a concert pianist. Sometime in his eighth or ninth year, as the result of a number of musical experiences, the most decisive of which was hearing Mozart's *Die Zauberflöte*, he decides to make music his profession in one way or another, uncertain whether as performer or composer. He is certainly enthusiastic about live performance: as a nine-year-old, he organizes his school-friends into a theatre troupe and between his eleventh and eighteenth years he appears as a pianist, poet and orator in a series of performances. When Robert is fifteen, his father even contacts Carl Maria von Weber to arrange composition lessons for his son, but nothing comes of it as Weber dies in the same year. Lacking rigorous training on the musical side, Schumann was, in effect, an autodidact, studying musical scores and textbooks on his own, who would at certain points throughout his life return to solitary learning. On the literary side, however, he recruits those who will actively share his interests by founding a *Literarischen Schülerverein*, a literary club, the aim of which is to introduce its members to the works of major European authors, to read biographies of celebrated literati and to discover freshly written works by aspiring ones – the club's own members. It is some indication of Schumann's drive and zeal, above and beyond adolescent enthusiasm, that the group met no fewer than thirty times a year between 1825 and 1828. As his close school-friend Emil Flechsig would later recall, Schumann was already at this time convinced that he would 'eventually become a famous man'.[3]

Then, his sister commits suicide; his father dies of a 'nervous condition'. Schumann is sixteen years old.

Clearly precocious on the literary side, Schumann the adolescent reads his way through Schiller, Goethe, Wieland, Herder and Jean Paul, among others, but also commercially produces serialized romances and ghost stories: the type of writing eagerly devoured by the emergent reading classes of the late eighteenth and early nineteenth centuries. It is Jean Paul, above all, with his challengingly wayward tales and theories about discontinuity and fantasy life, who will nourish Schumann's imagination most lastingly. These and other writers introduce him to the Gothic, the figure of the *Doppelgänger*, the characters of the *commedia dell'arte*, magnetism, the uncanny, travesty, carnival, and the fourth dimension, among many of the more obvious topoi, all of which are forms of representation of otherworldly experience, of otherness, or a heightened perception of the self. They are sought out and consumed by Schumann throughout his life – as rich sources of invention during his twenties; as somewhat less but still powerfully fecund resources in his thirties; and as renewed, though less benign forces of inspiration towards the end of his life. I shall return to this.

If literature, poetry and drama were one side of Schumann's developing identity, music was the other. While his father had become a successful self-made man of letters with a degree of talent, determination, and resilience, Schumann was the first in the family to become an artist. This made him an outsider to his art, with an outsider's impatience, and critical acuity, to innovate. Given these conditions, it is interesting to observe how Schumann's compositions make rather generous use of, or allusions to, literature and poetry (through direct quotation, mottos, titles and various narrative techniques), while accommodating comparatively little musical material from other composers. Where there are instances of musical quotation, they are predominantly of his own compositions, as for example in several of his symphonic works of 1841, where he quotes, directly and indirectly, material from his earlier songs and piano pieces. There are, of course, some notable exceptions: for instance, he recalls Beethoven's melody from the song cycle *An die ferne Geliebte*, Op. 98, in his *Fantasie*, Op. 17 (1836–8), as again in the song cycle *Frauenliebe und -leben*, Op. 42 (1840), and again in his Second Symphony, Op. 61 (1845–6); in a rather different register of reference, he cites the *Marseillaise* in his *Faschingsschwank aus Wien*, Op. 26 (1839–40).[4] And there are other examples. Whether from his own works or that of others, the use of quotation is among the most salient characteristics of Schumann's compositional habits. What are we to make of it? Perhaps it means, among other things, that there are moments during his writing when he feels the need or desire to hand it all over, to have someone else write some of it, a co-author. In the case of musical self-quotation, the co-author is obviously still Schumann himself, even though it is a different Schumann, reappearing from earlier times, and in this sense, then, a stranger after all. In the case of quoting from others, a truly distinct voice enters the compositional scene, unannounced and unacknowledged. What is clear in either case, though, is that Schumann, once in a while, enjoys taking a break from himself, and that he is seeing to it that he is properly replaced in the meantime.

Schumann's use of received musical material, forms and expressions – that side of his compositional idiom that incorporates, through quotation or imitation, imported items and standard formulae (say, for example, passages redolent of Bach chorales and baroque counterpoint, Haydnesque passages and Beethovenian allusions in the chamber music, Wagnerian open-endedness in his dramatic music) – generates a particularly rich inter-textual fabric, albeit the self-conscious distancing. But his taste for extensive historical reference does not occur simply in a historicizing spirit, a preoccupation of his generation with recalling and rekindling what was perceived as its heritage. Instead, Schumann's frequent phases in which he studied Bach's *Das Wohltempierte Klavier* closely; the regular recurrence of his deployment of counterpoint in 1836, 1838, 1842 and again in 1845; his periodic attraction to composing by rule-based decision-making – all this shows a need for control and order and, by implication, a level of the possibility of losing these, as has sometimes been suggested. It is also the case, however, that the early-to-mid nineteenth century was in significant places a 'neo-Baroque' period, emblematically (if not entirely accurately) represented by Mendelssohn's revival of Bach, for example, or by the fact that Brahms's first planned piano opus was a 'Baroque Suite'. Some of Schumann's most poignant pieces – say, certain textural enhancements in *Kreisleriana*, Op. 16 (1838) for piano solo, the uncanny medieval resonances and progressions in songs such as the extraordinary 'Auf einer Burg' from the *Eichendorff Liederkreis*, Op. 39, or 'Ich grolle nicht' from *Dichterliebe*, Op. 48 (both 1840) – bespeak a whole Zeitgeist and evoke the archaeological tendencies and nostalgia for a Golden Age that animated many of that generation of 1810 that included Chopin, Liszt and Wagner.

Once freed from school, Schumann moves, reluctantly, in obedience to his mother's wishes, to Leipzig to study law. But before beginning his studies, he takes the opportunity of a *Bildungsreise*, or cultural tour, of

9 *Schumann's lives, and afterlives: an introduction*

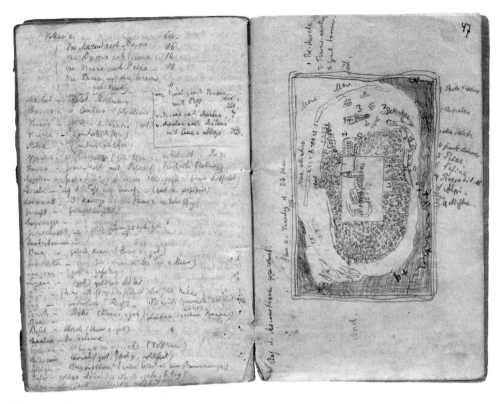

Figure 1.1 Schumann's travel notebook

Bayreuth, Nuremberg, Augsburg and Munich. In the last city he manages to introduce himself to Heinrich Heine, author of the then bestselling *Buch der Lieder* (*Book of Songs*, 1827), which Schumann would later use for some of his most famous song compositions. Once at Leipzig, he attends few, if any, classes in law, but instead enthusiastically explores the city's musical scene, then one of the liveliest in Germany. Very quickly, he finds his way into the more intimately public arena of musical soirées where he mixes with the local musical elite, at once testing and showing off his abilities as a performer and improviser. At this point he begins to compose more seriously, after a few intermittent attempts in his adolescence. He writes mainly Lieder, and continues to write his personal journal, begun the year before, as well as working in a novelistic vein, in a manner inspired by Jean Paul. One of the remarkable things about Schumann's personal writings, already fully present at this time, is his ability to compress lived experience into a single word or phrase, adding one impression, thought or idea after another, connectionless, thus creating an exhilarating succession of events through rows of isolated words. Schumann, in his diaries, as later in his compositions, is a master of brevity and spontaneity. While these diaries are clearly the reflections of a self-obsessed young man, they are also, however, the most fascinating material for a period study, and tell us, among many other things, how Schumann during this period is up-to-date with all the important literary events of the time and fully informed about the musical scene that he hopes to break into.

The pianistic phase

During his first year in Leipzig, 1828–9, Schumann takes piano lessons with Friedrich Wieck, owner of a music shop and, thanks to his nine-year-old daughter's astonishing pianistic accomplishments, considered one of the world's leading pedagogues. Wieck is impressed and enchanted by Schumann's talent and energy, but already a year later Schumann escapes to Heidelberg to study with the music aesthetician A. F. J. Thibaut, author of the influential *Über die Reinheit der Tonkunst* (*On Purity in Musical Art*). But he quickly tires of what he discovers as Thibaut's pedantry and returns to Leipzig in the autumn of 1830. From this point, he resolves to make his life as a pianist and at last stands up against his mother's requests. He resumes lessons with Wieck, whose pedagogic regime requires him to practise six to eight hours a day in addition to daily lessons. In 1831–2, Schumann also takes composition and counterpoint lessons with Heinrich Dorn, a conductor and composer and, apart from Wieck, the only professional practitioner of music ever to teach him. On his own, Schumann studies counterpoint, mainly Bach's *Das Wohltempierte Klavier* and Italian church music.

It is in Wieck's house, one filled with music and the noise of musical practising, that Schumann gradually falls in love with Clara, Wieck's only daughter, raised and educated by him alone after he separated from his wife when the girl was five years old. Wieck has but a single goal in mind: to turn his daughter into a great pianist. Whether or not aware of the premeditation in her destiny, Clara is an enthusiastic accomplice. By 1828, aged nine, she is already a celebrity, performing at the renowned Leipzig Gewandhaus, and touring, under the watchful eye of her father, all over Germany, Austria and Paris. Wieck, once aware of the growing liaison between his daughter and Schumann, is enraged. Both are soon informed by this austere and solitary man that Schumann is not acceptable as a suitor, a move that inaugurates the beginning of an intensely acrimonious battle between two very dissimilar men over the woman of their hearts: the daughter of one, the beloved of the other.

The hand injury

Schumann's famous hand injury, brought on between 1829 and 1832, shows how much he is prepared to lose in order to fulfil his destiny. Wieck is confident of being able to make Schumann 'within three years into one of the greatest living pianists, who will play more warmly and ingeniously than Moscheles, and more grandly than Hummel'.[5] Spurred on in this way, Schumann is determined to catch up on the technical prowess that, under the influence of Paganini, is then considered the sine qua non of performance: 'I now know for certain that, with much hard work, patience and a good teacher, I will be able to compete with any pianist within six years, for playing the piano is pure mechanics and know-how', he writes to his mother.[6] To speed up his progress and strengthen his right hand, he trusts the promised miracles of Johann Bernard Logier's 'Chiroplast', a contraption designed to give each individual finger greater power by briskly pulling to an extreme degree the finger inserted into the mechanism towards the back of the hand.[7]

Wieck strongly objects (while selling similar instruments in his own shop) but the recommendations of star pianists like Thalberg motivate Schumann to persist.[8] That Schumann continues with the Chiroplast treatment even in the face of its dubious effectiveness is not only proof of his determination but also an example of his capacity to go to extremes. It shows him seeking out and submitting to a slow but thorough-going form of brutality that eventually results in lasting, debilitating injury. But what this episode also shows is Schumann's total commitment to music while destroying his ability to perform it. Caught within a curious dynamic exchange of self-harm and self-realization, Schumann felt compelled to disappear as a pianist in order to reappear, or appear more fully, as a composer. He had to stop himself performing in order to let others perform him. Within weeks of being 'completely resigned' to the ruin of his hand, which by May 1832 he deems 'incurable',[9] he throws himself into composition, producing, apart from a great number of sketches to be turned into finished compositions in later years, the *Studien nach Capricen von Paganini*, Op. 3 (1832); two complete first movements and sketches for two last movements of a G minor symphony, *Auh.* A3 (1832–3); the *Abegg-Variationen*, Op. 1 (1830); *Papillons*, Op. 2 (1829–32); *Six Intermezzi*, Op. 4 (1832); *Toccata in C*, Op. 7 (1829–33); *Carnaval*, Op. 9 (1834–5); and his first Sonata in F sharp minor, Op. 11 (1833–5). Schumann needed the failure in order to have the success.

On a more private level, Schumann's hand paralysis is perhaps even less what it may seem at first sight: an instance of failure or a tendency to give up. One notes that the moment he is prepared to risk the injury, 1829–31, coincides with two increasingly urgent concerns: to establish a public

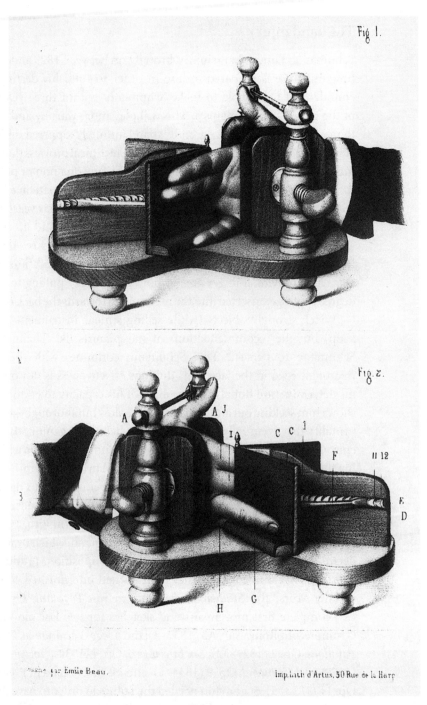

Figure 1.2 Logier's 'Chiroplast', a finger-training apparatus (Lithograph after a sketch by Emile Beau)

life, and to create a private one with Clara. In both directions, the hand injury strikes one as a daunting manoeuvre in his feverish quest to find himself. It shows him willing to inflict pain where it most matters, increasing pain to its limits, and finally going beyond those limits. Emerging on the other side of pain, he finds an unknown territory now lying before him, and the potentialities of a new and unexplored self. Schumann's transgression thus happens in the pursuit of greater self-knowledge. Once incapacitated, his hands are freed to compose; and above all for Clara, his pianist wife-to-be, whom he now can offer something to play, as well as someone to play with. Captured by her, he ensures that he will keep her captured in turn: 'Clara . . . I have never heard her play as she did today – everything was masterful, everything beautiful. The *Papillons* were almost yet more beautiful than yesterday . . . She played them just right and with fire . . . and the old Wieck pointed out the advantages: "Madame", he said to Rosalie [Schumann's sister-in-law], "isn't Clara a good substitute for Robert" . . . At home I played and continued composing the *Intermezzi*. I want to dedicate them to Clara.'[10] The highly productive exchange between him and Clara, between his composing and her performing, becomes his source of self-fulfilment: 'You make me complete as a composer as I complete you. Every one of your thoughts comes from my soul, as all my music is only thanks to you.'[11]

Multiplication and mobility of the self

In July 1831 Schumann writes: 'Completely new personae are entering my diary today – two of my best friends whom, nevertheless, I have never seen before. They are Florestan and Eusebius.'[12] A few weeks earlier he had already talked about his 'idea about the "Wunderkinder"; I do not lack of characters and personae, but stories [*Handlungen*] and the connection between the threads'.[13] Elaborating a highly individualized adaptation of the literary *Doppelgänger* motif, that ubiquitous nineteenth-century trope, Schumann soon expands his imaginary circle with yet more characters, all inspired by members of his immediate circle: Clara becomes *Cilia, Zilia, Caecilia, Chiara* or *Chiarinea*; Wieck *Meister Raro*; Mendelssohn *F. Meritis*; his teacher Dorn *Musikdirektor*; and his close friend Flechsig, significantly, the *Jüngling Echomein*. These personae promise new identities and Schumann from now on is free-floatingly attentive to whomever he wants to turn himself into. He is understandably euphoric about the endless possibilities of shaping and re-shaping what we are in the habit of calling someone's 'personality', and begins using these new voices in all his writings: personal, journalistic and compositional alike. Indeed, Schumann's *Davidsbündler*, the imaginary group of artists he invents for the music journal *Neue Zeitschrift für Musik*

(*New Newspaper for Music, NZfM*, founded by him in 1834), become the main agency behind a new art of criticism that combines technically accurate information about music with commentary that makes full use of the expressive possibilities of literature and poetry and their respective rhetoric and narrative strategies, including dialogue. In Schumann's critical writings, mixed in with excerpts taken from literature and poetry, the alternating and contrasting voices of the *Davidsbündler* articulate in direct speech, first person singular, Schumann's own voice, speaking as it were through various masks.[14]

Such proliferation of identity had already been elaborated upon and celebrated by two of Schumann's favourite novelists: Jean Paul in his *Flegeljahre* (1804) and E. T. A. Hoffmann in his *Kreisleriana* (1815), a collection of essays and stories, and his novel *Lebensansichten des Katers Murr* (*The Life and Opinions of the Tomcat Murr*, 1820–2). These works operate through highly prospective and volatile mental manoeuvres to re-create, via literary means, the dynamics of the multiplication and mobility of the self. In the 1854 introduction to his *Gesammelte Schriften über Musik und Musiker* (*Collected Writings on Music and Musicians*), bringing together his earlier writings for the *NZfM*, Schumann comments revealingly on the *Davidsbündler*: they are 'more than a secret society' made up of artist-characters, their spirit 'running like a red thread' through the pages of the *NZfM*, combining 'Wahrheit und Dichtung' (truth and invention).[15] He thus sees fictional multiplicity as the means for an artistic quest for truth at the very core of his vocation as a critic. The same dialogical dynamics animate his music, above all in the *Davidsbündlertänze*, Op. 6 (1837), eighteen short piano pieces, each bearing the signature 'F.', 'E.' or 'F. und E.' to designate the extrovert Florestan and the more introvert Eusebius and which, in the first edition, received additional commentaries such as 'Here Florestan kept silent, but his lips were quivering with emotion' or 'Eusebius had the following afterthought: at the same time his eyes were full of happiness.' What we have here is a composer-writer constantly changing his identity. Thanks to the *Davidsbündler*, Schumann is many. But that he sought and found names for himself in this way, and considering what these names were and what they represented, tells us much about what Schumann tried intermittently to make himself into. From this time and throughout his life, Schumann took delight in becoming others, and in creating a network of voices speaking to, against and for each other, but always *through and in* him. And this bold move would also lead to his becoming part of the general representation of schizophrenia.

Indeed, in Schumann's case, the conflation of work and life is tempting and it is easy to suspect his music of articulating the dynamics of an otherwise disturbing personality disorder – a temptation that remained widely

15 *Schumann's lives, and afterlives: an introduction*

Figure 1.3 Robert Schumann (lithograph by Joseph Kriehuber, Vienna, 1839)

unresisted by critics of his late work, who regarded the compositions of the 1850s especially as mental echo-chambers of the composer's looming madness.[16] Yet, works such as the *Davidsbündlertänze* are more than a mere representation of Schumann's mood swings and a correspondingly dissociated inner nature, for they seem to be not only as if *peopled* with characters, but rather as if entirely imbued with them: as if created by them from within, and so as if becoming, in and of themselves, new and wholly independent figures in their own right. In other words, Schumann, seen as a fantasist with a disordered self, was able to explore in moments of creativity the many forms and faces, the sphinx-like inner texture and essential opacity, of the isolated human self. To escape a unified author-authority his self multiplied, became mobile and fluid, as well as fragmented – but most of all, alive. And whole aspects of Schumann's self may be split off and put on display here to generate a highly animated as much as bewildering plurality of narrating selves. In this sense, the creative Schumann is full of possibility. 'To assume', in the memorable words of Adam Phillips, 'that there is an unconscious is to believe that there really are other people, other voices, inside and outside oneself (that if there is a mind it has a mind of its own).'[17] Such a mind of its own, constantly in movement and changing its mind, is what we hear at work in Schumann's music.

Uncertainties

For much of the 1830s Schumann is fairly directionless. He lives at the mercy of spells of intense anxiety and panic attacks that at once generate and result in his tentative approach to life. His performing career as a pianist has turned to dust with the hand injury, and, although he now runs his own journal, he still has not created a stable source of income. Throughout the decade, however, he composes, although comparatively little is published, let alone widely performed. Thus virtually unknown as a composer, he is nevertheless sitting on a goldmine of completed piano music the like of which the world has never before seen: the *Abegg-Variationen*, Op. 1 (1830); *Papillons*, Op. 2 (1829–32); *Toccata in C*, Op. 7 (first version 1829–30, second version (1833); the *Paganini Etudes*, Op. 3 (1832); *Intermezzi*, Op. 4 (1832); *Symphonic Etudes*, Op. 13 (1834–5); *Carnaval*, Op. 9 (1834–5); Piano Sonata, Op. 11 (1833–5); *Concert sans orchestre*, Op. 14 (1836); *Phantasie*, Op. 17 (1836); *Davidsbündlertänze*, Op. 6 (1837); *Fantasiestücke*, Op. 12 (1837); *Kinderszenen*, Op. 15 (1838); *Noveletten*, Op. 21 (1838); the second Piano Sonata, Op. 22 (1833–5, 1838); and *Faschingsschwank aus Wien*, Op. 26 (1839–40). His letters to Clara reveal a magnificent confidence about his work, and it is obvious that he now knows that his future lies in composition. The only question is, when? The lack of a solid professional grounding, in terms of recognition as much as remuneration, also mirrors a more private lack of grounding: Clara, since his mother's death in 1836 the centre of his universe, appears more unattainable than ever. Her father's bitter attacks on their relationship exasperates his daughter and incenses her lover. Between 1836 and 1837 Wieck manages to separate the couple for eighteen months during a concert tour for Clara – the first of several lengthy separations to come. But Clara and Schumann write to each other daily, sometimes two or three times. By 1838 Wieck's agitations take the form of semi-public hate-campaigns. He distributes defamatory texts among friends and colleagues, spreading rumours about Schumann's mental health and moral fitness as

17 *Schumann's lives, and afterlives: an introduction*

Figure 1.4 Clara Wieck, 1838

citizen and husband, blackening his character as an incipient alcoholic and a social misfit. Wieck also insists that Schumann show proof of financial competence and solvency as a condition of marriage. In the absence of Clara, and with her father's shadow looming large, the situation weakens Schumann's impulse to compose, and his hopes of marrying Clara. Searching for escape routes, he decides in the autumn of 1838 to visit Vienna to explore the possibilities of starting a new life there for the two of them. After six months he returns to Leipzig, unsuccessful. Clara still is far away. At this moment, when Schumann is most at a loss, he finally takes the initiative. With Clara's consent, he decides to take recourse to the law, and Wieck and the whole affair before the court, to obtain the right to marry Clara. His diaries reveal little of his thoughts on the subject during this most embattled period, but he is suddenly all-consumed by composition: the period just prior to the court's decision propels him into a whole new creative phase: the immensely productive *Liederjahr*, the Year of Song. Indeed, with Clara his real *ferne Geliebte*, there is no better time to break into song. He composes over 125 Lieder in 1840 alone, among them the cycles *Dichterliebe*, Op. 48; *Liederkreis*, Op. 24 – both on poems by Heinrich Heine – and the *Liederkreis*, Op. 39 on poems by Joseph von Eichendorff; and goes on to set texts by many of the leading European poets: Goethe, H. C. Andersen, Shakespeare, Burns, Byron and Moore, among others. On 7 July 1840 he laconically notes 'the end of the court case', and on 4 September 1840: 'Clara, from now on forever with me'.[18] His wedding present to her is the song cycle *Myrthen*, Op. 25, containing the hauntingly beautiful 'Du bist wie eine Blume'.[19]

No doubt, Robert Schumann is a complicated man. As a potential husband he is an uncertain proposition. The son of a widowed and uninfluential middle-class mother, embarking on what is to this day considered a profession fraught with insecurities, he is also the son of a reportedly unstable father and the brother to a sister who committed suicide. From his twenties he is a man prey to anguish, to depression, to hypochondria, with a tendency to drink. His diaries are replete with observations of his changing states of mind and body. A late developer in his own eyes, he is anxious, if not panic-stricken by a deeply felt need to catch up, to make his mark, to establish a name for himself at last. Clara, his junior by almost a decade, is nevertheless strongly drawn to him and embraces him and his insecurities, as well as the real personal and artistic capacities that these tend to mask and immobilize. She embarks wholeheartedly on what has since become the most fêted romantic love story in the history of Western music. A year into their marriage, the Schumanns have their first child, Marie. Clara is to give birth to a further seven children in the course of their fourteen-year marriage.

By way of premières, Clara also gives birth to virtually all of her husband's piano compositions and carefully nurtures these throughout her long career.[20] Many of Schumann's orchestral works were given their debuts in concerts in which she performed as a soloist. After Schumann's death, during the four long decades of her widowhood, she devotes herself to her husband's memory, preparing editions of the piano works, editing his *Jugendbriefe* and, assisted by Johannes Brahms, labouring over what will become the thirty-one-volume *Gesamtausgabe*.[21] In short, as both are carried by music in their being, the courtship and marriage between Clara and Schumann seems to render real the Romantic dream of bringing together two human beings through the magically communicative power of music alone, itself in no need of words, yet capable of operating on the deepest emotional level. Nineteenth-century Germany was in awe of its music. And so it was when it came to a union made in its name.

No doubt, Schumann's own attraction to Clara was manifold. Seeing her, young, confident, and well-prepared, embark on an international career as if it were a matter of course, no doubt gave Schumann occasion to reflect on certainty. He himself has had a delayed start, has swerved and stumbled, failed or stopped himself, and continues to fear the future, constantly caught between doubt and hope. By 1839 he has still not found his way; Clara has what Schumann seeks but cannot find. She inhabits it, like a birthright: a place in the world of music and in the world at large. This tension between Schumann and Clara, between his private conviction and lack of public success, and her inner confidence and public success, is to persist throughout their marriage, and is one of which Schumann remains acutely aware: in 1838, for instance, he notes in his diary: 'My Clara has been appointed Kammermusikerin – this is news I expected, and yet it does not give me any real joy. But why? Because I am so meagre in comparison to this angel.'[22] In his acceptance of his persistent feeling of worthlessness, of which we find proof again and again in the diaries and letters, Schumann senses well, however, in a way that he feels he can't quite formulate, that there is actually something quite undermining, concerning himself of course, but also others. He writes to Clara shortly before their marriage

> I want to confide to you a few things about myself and my character, given how difficult it is to figure me out, how I often respond to the most tender signs of love with coldness and rejection and how I insult and ignore especially those who mean it so well with me. So many times have I asked myself why this is and have blamed myself, for in my most inner self I am grateful for the smallest gift. I understand every move of the eye, every slightest movement in the heart of others. And yet I still so often fail in words and gestures in response. But you will know how to take me, and you will surely forgive me. Because I am not bad at heart; and I love from the depth of my soul all which is good and beautiful.[23]

In his diaries and letters Schumann speaks repeatedly, indirectly and directly, about what he sharply perceives as his predicament and what, by the time of his internment in the mental hospital, has finally ripened into a feeling that finds its least embellished expression in the image of the one who is God-forsaken: he believes he is 'a sinner, who doesn't deserve the love

Figure 1.5 Robert and Clara Schumann's children, 1854

of people', as Wilhelm Wasielewski, one of Schumann's direct acquaintances and first biographer, reports.[24] About Schumann's way of interacting with his children, Wasielewski recalls:

> He did not love his children less affectionately than his wife, even though he didn't possess the gift to occupy himself with them either continuously or deeply. If he coincidentally met them on the street, he certainly stopped, took out his lorgnette, and looked at them for a moment, while amicably remarking, in pursing his lips: 'Well well, you darlings?' Then his previous facial expression took back over and he carried on, as if nothing had happened.[25]

Diaries, letters

In common with many nineteenth-century bourgeois couples, the Schumanns keep a marriage diary. Published, interestingly, as part of Schumann's personal diary, these *Ehetagebücher* provide a true record of their self-fashioning as husband and wife. The first volume, a present from Schumann to Clara on her twenty-first birthday, 13 September 1840, coinciding by a day with their wedding, is reserved for 'everything that touches us mutually in our household and our marriage; in it we will record our wishes and our hopes; it should also be a little book of requests directed at one another when speech is insufficient'.[26] The statutes, drawn up by Schumann, further specify that they are to 'exchange secretarial duties' once a week, to write a minimum of one page per week, to accept an unspecified penalty if failing to do so, and to read in each other's company the other's entry either out loud or silently, depending on content. As well as detailing the events of their professional lives, a further objective is 'carefully to evaluate the course of the whole week, whether it had been an honourable and industrious one, whether we grow inside and outside in our well-being, whether we are perfecting ourselves more and more in our beloved art'[27] and, finally, to record 'all the joys and sorrows of married life as true history'.[28] Three things are worthwhile to note about this enterprise. First, it shows Schumann's hope for the durability of his union with Clara; second, it shows his belief that such durability could be secured, or ensured, via the written word; and third, it shows his wish to establish and keep a record of this hoped-for durability. In view of the measure of insecurity that marked their courtship, and Schumann's anxiety in particular as to whether it was ever to come to a marriage at all, his desire to retain written proof of its achievement is not entirely surprising. Nevertheless, given the many other opportunities for writing that Schumann ingeniously invented for himself, from diaries to notebooks, lists, letters, reviews, novels, poems and so forth, it also may simply show the need that Schumann felt for the written word.

The marriage diaries also signify continuity. They are an attempt to prolong the couple's earlier written correspondence by which they had been able to seek and find each other, sustaining them during many months' separation over many years. As 'speech' is felt to be 'insufficient', even, or perhaps especially, at times of togetherness, this project of a shared diary demonstrates the tremendous faith both have in what the written word may be capable of achieving which the spoken word would, or could not. Another aspect to which the marriage diaries bear witness is the Enlightenment ideal of self-improvement and its stated assumption of personal perfectibility. Under Schumann's direction, we see the couple go through the musical classics, Bach fugues and Beethoven sonatas in particular, along with a good number of literary works. Clara willingly enters into what is, in effect, a programme of higher education devised by her husband. Under his guidance, she now composes regularly, writing Lieder and fugues as well as poems. One cannot fail to notice, however, that she has moved from the hands of a teacher-father into the hands of a teacher-husband.

The Schumann who emerges from these documents does not appear a consistently charming man. Patronizing and self-aggrandizing, he is avid for Clara's admiration and ready to induce it by force. Clara, on her part, colludes with her husband's notions of himself, sometimes featuring in ways that twenty-first-century sensibilities can hardly credit in a woman who, in so many ways, and to so many, seems a feminist *avant la lettre*. She encourages polarization: 'My request to you, my dear Robert, is that you may have patience with me and may forgive me when I have said stupid things here and there, of which there will be no lack.' Schumann: 'We fought once about your conception of my compositions. But you are wrong, little Clara. The composer, and only the composer, knows how to present his compositions. If you think you could do it better, that would be as if a painter, for example, wanted to make a tree better than God had done.'[29]

The correspondence between Clara and Robert Schumann has been the object of much curiosity ever since the first partial edition, prepared by Clara, appeared in 1895.[30] Infused with the intensity of the couple's shared passions and concerns – music, of course, and each other – their heightened, still separate lives find here a declarative mode of expression that bespeaks their desire to meet and to merge, and shows them seizing every half-chance to do so. The intimacy in tone and content leaves the reader, unsolicited interloper into the densely woven textual cocoon of this amorous exchange, by turns intrigued, amused, wincing, fatigued. Nonetheless, reading about Clara's and Schumann's differently remarkable ways of responding to and resisting Wieck's rage, for example, is instructive. Schumann first hesitates to take it up with the man he long considered to be something of a surrogate father. Then, attempting to meet Wieck's requirements, a task rendered impossible by the simple fact that Schumann – or, one imagines, any suitor – was per se unacceptable, he finally follows his instinct, counter-attacks and wins. Clara, now fallen from grace in her father's eyes, likewise shows strength of character when she agrees to take legal action against her own father. Faced with this conflict, she opts for the future, and for herself. Over the five years of their beleaguered courtship in hundreds of letters written between 1835 and 1840, Schumann and Clara appear as two people not only victorious in their pursuit to live their desires against fierce opposition from the outside, but strengthened in their conviction to belong with each other.

Schumann's declared desire to be one with Clara, to be her, and for her to be him, is the theme of a great number of his letters and other writings.

23 *Schumann's lives, and afterlives: an introduction*

Contemplating Clara's portrait of 1838 (see above the lithograph of Clara made in 1838 by Andreas Staub, figure 1.4), he writes 'But now to your picture – what can I say! I've almost kissed it to pieces', and 'I dare not look at your picture often; it agitates me too much. It often wakes me in the night, so that I have to light the lamp – and now I am sinking into it, thinking no more, becoming one with it.'[31] In 1833, seven years before their marriage, he writes to her:

> Since no chain of sparks draws us together now or even reminds us of each other, I have a suggestion. Tomorrow at precisely 11 o'clock I shall play the adagio from Chopin's *Variations* and will intensely think of you, indeed only of you. Now I ask you do the same so that we can see each other and meet in spirits. Our Doppelgängers will probably meet above the small gate of the Thomaskirche[32]

Clara signs one of her following letters with 'Clara Wieck/Clara Wieck/Doppelgänger'.[33] The mirroring or folding into each other also leads to joint compositions such as, in 1841, the *Zwölf Gedichte aus Rückerts Liebesfrühling*, a song cycle of duets consisting of nine pieces by Schumann and three by Clara, published as Op. 37 and Op. 12 respectively. In June 1839, Schumann already explains to Clara:

> I didn't get to compose much . . . But once you are mine, you will certainly sometimes get to hear some new works. I think you will much inspire me, and nothing but to be able to hear some of my compositions played will lift my spirits . . . We will also publish a certain amount in *both of our names*; posterity should regard us as one heart and soul, and be unable to tell what is by you and what is by me. How happy I am.[34]

Not surprisingly, Clara's direct or indirect influence on Schumann's compositions has been the object of a considerable amount of recent scholarly research.[35]

Sonorous *tableaux vivants*

The Schumann of the 1830s was a young man in his twenties. The music that made him famous was largely written during this period. Mostly written for the piano, each piece and each collection of pieces represents a new, highly idiosyncratic compositional approach, and today's world of pianism would be unthinkable without them where they remain at the core of the so-called Classical repertoire. What makes these works special?

The main trend of Schumann studies today is to see Schumann's piano works and song cycles up to 1840 as what one might call constellations of musico-poetic fragments. The term 'fragment' entered the descriptive and conceptual vocabulary through the writings of the early Romantics. They also used the term 'ensemble', which complements conceptually and historically the later, more modernistic notion of 'montage',[36] a particularly fitting term John Daverio uses on one occasion to define Schumann's compositional habit of constructing what are, in essence, not works at all, but curious and complex *Gebilde* made of several, mainly independent smaller parts. One is tempted to consider 'collage' as a term that most nearly approaches a description of Schumann's compositional procedures and that shows how his methods adumbrated formal preoccupations of twentieth-century art, including music. The Romantic fragment results from a relatively spontaneous act of composition followed by a play with form and forms, mixing the contrasting individual and often open-ended parts in a seemingly random manner until the 'non-work' eventually, after some experimentation, all seems to fall into place.[37] A similarly improvisational way of arranging separate smaller pieces into larger multi-movement forms obtains for some of the Lieder cycles, *Dichterliebe*, Op. 48, above all.[38] This practice has launched a whole polemic among musicologists about the nature of musical narrative, of the presence or absence of inherent organic structure and structural coherence. To a nineteenth-century audience, certainly, Schumann's piano works were not easily heard or understood. Clara, writing in 1839, sums up the problem: 'Listen Robert, couldn't you just once compose something brilliant, easily understandable, and without inscriptions – a completely coherent piece, not too long and not too short? I'd so much like to have something of yours to play that's specifically intended for the public. Obviously a genius will find this degrading, but politics demand it every now and again.'[39]

In giving shape through sound to the various imaginary individuals of the *Davidsbündler*, Schumann was endowed with a remarkable capacity to reproduce the dynamics of affective movements, with a rare sense of rhythm and harmony and a gift for hallucinated vision. His description of the music of Franz Schubert, a composer he admired all his life,[40] gives some idea of his own compositional aspirations:

> Apart from Schubert's there exists no music that is so psychologically unusual in the course and connection of its ideas, and in the ostensible logic of its discontinuities ... What for others was a diary in which to set down momentary feelings was for Schubert a sheet of music paper to which he entrusted his every mood, so that his thoroughly musical soul wrote notes when others wrote words.[41]

Theodor W. Adorno, reflecting on Schumann's late style after a performance of 'Schumann's blind, desperately lonely cello concerto, which the Frankfurt cellist Schuyler was intellectually and spiritually not up to', raises one of the most intriguing questions about Schumann's development as a composer:

> By the way: since Draeske's venomous phrase that Schumann had begun as a genius but ended up as a talent, people have grown fat repeating the assertion about the waning of his creative powers. But it would be much more worthwhile to ask whether the regressive circularity of his forms, crudely criticized as formlessness; the fleeting inconspicuousness of melodic construction behind which one may feel that creative weakness lurks; and his whole late style with its vacillations between the clumsy and the hackneyed; are not all in fact significantly related to his whole inner nature, to his tragically dissociated inwardness.[42]

One first response to the catchphrase about promise left unfulfilled (the story of a Schumann who 'had begun as a genius but ended up as a talent') is to recall to memory, in view of his late style, the sheer energy and forcefulness of the piano works of the early period, the 1830s, and the impression they make on the listener. Written as if there were no tomorrow, not only in terms of the speed with which most of them had been conceived, drafted, penned, completed – many seemingly at one go – but even more so in terms of their unusual expressive intensity and waywardness, these pieces are sonorous reflections of breathless, urgent flights of ideas, changing direction as quickly as thoughts and mental images, moving fast and without transition between exuberantly vigorous, and more mellow, lyric, moods and emotions. As performer, listener, analyst or historian, one simply does not get here a strong sense of real, fundamental development. Even if the Moscheles- and Paganini-inspired virtuosity and ebullience of a few early pieces is eventually absorbed into a yet more concentrated, contrastive mode of expression, especially of course in his Lieder, one cannot speak of substantial, let alone paradigmatic changes with regard to Schumann's overall aesthetic or compositional procedures. Development seems, at least until the 1840s and his late work, as foreign to Schumann's imagination as it was fundamental to Beethoven's.

Another point of Adorno's comment is to consider what resonates beneath the story of Schumann's diminishing powers with his coming of age. For it seems that behind the overt admiration, behind the admission of Schumann as a genius, a basic kind of puzzlement enters the epistemological scene as part of an effort to find answers for what is essentially perceived as a difficult case, *both* in terms of his early *and* his late work. No doubt the eminently visceral quality of the early work, that special kind of 'formlessness' to which Adorno refers, is what made Schumann irresistible.[43] For the sensual magnetism of his music written for the pianist – hands forming bodies of sound, creating rhythms and counter rhythms as they move in an endlessly animated stream of a wordless kind of communication suspended in time – is what characterizes these works. But such modern choreography of sonorous bodies and their rhythmic interplay is also what lies beyond traditional frameworks of classification. His piano pieces are frenzied, fragmentary moments of improvisational pianism, juxtaposing the 'fleeting inconspicuousness of melodic construction', as Adorno puts it, with unorthodox harmonies that weaken the structural order and dramatic efficiency of clear-cut tonal conflict. This unreconciled coexistence of extreme opposites clearly defies the Classical ideal of *telos* and well-groundedness and lies, analytically speaking, beyond the sonata form in particular. And here, Schumann's so-called 'manic-depressive disorder', or the suspected schizophrenic part of his personality leading to madness, may appear a logical consequence; for such boundless imagination and energy had to lead, sooner or later, to creative burn-out or mental overdrive which, in turn, may then explain a 'whole late style with its vacillations between the clumsy and the hackneyed'. This kind of interpretative construction by inference, however, which confounds individual artistic creativity – in compositional style as well as mode of production – with general representations of mental illness, merely repeats the overly reassuring myth of genius. Rehearsed over and over again in cases before and after Schumann, it has here remained a particularly tenacious idea. It suggests, in the words of Paul Möbius, one of many to preoccupy himself with Schumann's 'case', that 'we see here an excellent example of how great talent is paid for by illness'.[44]

Schumann's madness, its symptoms, causes and possible names have, ever since the composer's death in the mental asylum, been a matter of intense debate. Today's ever-growing public interest both in biography and in the more specialized sub-genre of 'case history' writing or psychobiography has, with Schumann certainly, taken on yet another dimension that might be worthwhile thinking about. Why, one might ask, are we interested in Schumann's mental illness at all? What might this interest take care of or promise an answer for? Why, in other words, do we want Schumann to be not only the composer of extraordinary music, but also the sufferer of an intriguing illness? These are the kinds of questions that an assertion such as the one made by Möbius raises, rather than answers.

Critical writings

Schumann's contribution to music criticism is immense. Already in 1830, unamused by what he calls a 'very dry' musical scene and its similarly uncreative critical counterpart,[45] he feels that a new journal could make a difference. To challenge the influential and established *Allgemeine musikalische*

Zeitung, run, in his eyes, by a group of complacently respectable Philistines, Schumann instigates in 1834 the *NZfM*, which he runs more or less singlehandedly for a decade, writing most of the articles himself. In the name of a 'new, poetic future'[46] Schumann conducts a searching interrogation of music through 'theoretical and practical articles', 'belletristic pieces', 'critiques' of contemporary compositions and significant musical events, providing coverage of the concert scene in Europe and abroad. Unlike other music-critical papers of the day, Schumann's has no obligations vis-à-vis a sponsoring publishing house, and is therefore able to report impartially on the developments of the international musical scene, using correspondents in Berlin, Vienna, Paris, London, Naples and St Petersburg, and further afield in Poland, Belgium, and North and South America. Schumann's criticism is driven by a real degree of vigour, acuity, humour and exuberance, not just because this is Schumann's temperament but because his whole journalistic enterprise emerges from, and speaks to, a historical crisis in music writing. Schumann's ambition was to create 'that highest order of criticism that leaves an impression on its own account, similar to the impression produced by the original'.[47] The idea here was to make critical writing itself a creative act, an art form, an idea developed and perfected by the early Romantics,[48] where the quality of the critical writing is to equal the object analysed or discussed.

As in his musical compositions, Schumann's prime writing strategy in his critical work is role exchange and the development of 'fantasy-people'.[49] By using pseudonyms and aliases such as 'Eusebius', 'Florestan', 'Raro' and so on, he turns the endless multiplicity of interpretative possibilities into an applied art by refusing to speak in a single unified voice. Here we find Schumann the critic, like Schumann the composer, not one but many. This is nowhere more evident than in his reviews of Schubert's C major Symphony and of Berlioz's *Symphonie fantastique*, both now classics of the genre. These writings are so well-known and so often quoted that they seem to represent definitive music criticism. What tends to be overlooked, however, as these reviews have turned into classics, is their real contemporaneous novelty: both Schubert and Berlioz were virtually unknown in the musical 'canon'. The technical and aesthetic criteria by which Schumann judged these symphonies have themselves become canonical in music criticism. And Schumann's critical essays have the crucial ingredient of any worthwhile criticism – intellectual urgency. Yet, while it is clear that Schumann involved himself in music criticism partly, or even mainly, to create a source of income, to top up meagre fees from compositions with a view to freeing himself for composition, it is true too that Schumann was barely capable of hack work. Indeed, his critical writings are luminous, whatever he or we think his overt motivations may have been. A forerunner of a few other isolated, extraordinary composer-critics such as Liszt, Berlioz and Wagner, Schumann set the tone against a whole age of music-critical misanthropists.

Midlife

With a more ordered life came a new order in compositional enterprise, with social establishment the aim to master all established Classical forms. Over the following years, from his thirties to early forties, Schumann sets out to explore all major musical genres: piano music (1833–9), song (1840), symphonic music (1841), chamber music (1842–3), oratorio (1843), contrapuntal music (1845), incidental music and opera (1847–8) and religious music (1852). At the same time he composes a substantial contribution to each category.[50] At the same time, he still has no stable source of income, and in December 1844, following his rejection as Mendelssohn's successor as Director of the Leipzig Gewandhaus, the Schumanns leave Leipzig for Dresden, capital of Saxony, in the hope of better prospects. On arrival, however, Schumann's health deteriorates dramatically – never to be fully restored. As always when in crisis, he fills his diaries with close observations of his anxiety and depression, watchful and weary of their potential to overthrow him. But this is also a time when he turns to contrapuntal studies. Routine and rigour in his working hours as well as in compositional style, focussing his attention on polyphonic and fugal forms, restores a sense of security. Throughout 1845 Schumann produces a whole series of works emulating J. S. Bach and Palestrina. He also manages to finish his Second Symphony in December 1845. Relatively unproductive in 1846, which also brings the death of the Schumanns' youngest child and first son Emil on 22 June, the following year sees the composition of the bulk of *Faust*, a series of dramatic scenes based on Goethe's celebrated play, and a number of choral and chamber works, as well as work on his first opera, *Genoveva*, Op. 81, a tale of medieval romance, which he completes in August 1849. Then he moves on to write incidental music for Byron's verse drama *Manfred*, Op. 115, for which he invents an unusual formal design, combining spoken dialogues with vocal and instrumental numbers. The year 1848, when Europe is convulsed by political eruption and uprisings, turns out to be his 'most fruitful year'. While the revolution rages through Dresden, the Schumanns retreat to the countryside, little inclined to support a political agenda to which, a priori, they are not actually hostile. Rather, what one sees in this kind of engaged non-engagement with the events of 1848 is symptomatic of the behaviour of a whole generation, and generations to come, namely the obscure mixture of a certain degree of political awareness and sympathy for political change leading to a vaguely pro-democratic stance that was,

Figure 1.6 Robert Schumann, 1850 (daguerreotype by Anton Völlner, Hamburg, 1850)

however, in the end, and in reality, not sincerely felt, or not sincerely enough. Highly conscious, however, of the facilitating quality that the surrounding political disarray has for him artistically, Schumann later writes 'I worked hard in all this time – it has been my most fruitful year – as if the outer storms compelled people to turn inward.'[51] He composes some forty works, including the piano fragments *Waldszenen*, Op. 82, and *Fantasiestücke* for clarinet and piano, Op. 73, and increases his income four-fold.[52]

In 1850, Schumann, now 40, accepts the post of Music Director for the city of Düsseldorf and finally has a regular income, conducting subscription concerts and the summer festival. A few weeks after arrival in the Rhineland town in September he composes his Cello Concerto, Op. 129 (in less than two weeks), as well as finishing his new symphony, the 'Rhenish', Op. 97. In

1851, he composes three overtures; some songs; the famous *Märchenbilder*, Op. 113, for viola and piano; two sonatas for violin and piano, Opp. 105 and 121; and the G minor Trio, Op. 110, each of these in less than a week. By the end of 1851 he rewrites and finishes his last symphony, Op. 120, originally begun in 1841, and an overture to Goethe's *Hermann und Dorothea*. During the first half of 1852 he writes, among other things, his Mass, Op. 147, and the *Requiem*, Op. 148, while the second half of the year is devoted to the preparation of his *Collected Writings on Music and Musicians*. But by 1853 relations between him and members of the orchestra lead to major confrontations. One witness describes Schumann's conducting as 'completely oblivious to the public, paying little attention even to the orchestral musicians, he lived only in his music...'[53] This way of being with music intensifies over the next months. In a concert in October 1853, Schumann is seen to continue to wave the baton after the music has stopped. Throughout the ensuing 'impertinent effronteries'[54] with the orchestra and its management, Schumann remains in stiff denial, refusing to take any responsibility, and knows that he can count on Clara's support. Schumann's position as director of the orchestra continues to be challenged, however, and he resigns in November 1853.

Part of Schumann's debacle in Düsseldorf, his tendency to be wholly caught up in music, seems linked to a life-long inclination to silence. Numerous contemporaries describe how little he spoke and how, when addressed in company for example, Clara often answered on his behalf. There are occasions when his refusal to speak is seen as a provocation: 'After an almost silent greeting, I sat with him for a quarter of an hour. He didn't speak and just stared at me. I was also silent, to test how long this would last. He didn't open his mouth. That's when I jumped up from my chair in desperation', the poet Friedrich Hebbel reports.[55] Similar experiences are described by the critic Franz Brendel,[56] and the influential Austrian music critic Eduard Hanslick: 'After a few hopeless efforts to entertain Schumann with news from the musical scene in Prague, I began to feel uncomfortable [in my role] as soliloquist [*Soloredner*]. I feared he meant to silence me away [*fortschweigen*].'[57] As early as 1837, Schumann himself writes: 'I have nothing to offer. I hardly speak at all, somewhat more in the evening, and most at the piano.'[58] Yet, ceasing to speak, preferring music to words, and to continue hearing music after the music has stopped, seems, after all, a rather sensible thing to do for a composer. But towards the end of his life, this introverted way of experiencing music takes on a whole new significance, both magic and portentous, for Schumann. After he suffers internal 'intolerable aural disturbances'[59] immediately following the conflict with the orchestra, these soon turn into 'music so magnificent, [played] with such splendidly sounding instruments as one had never heard here on earth'.[60] A whole new phase of his life is about to begin, adumbrating the beginning of the end of the composer's sanity.

But first, in September 1853, a few months prior to Schumann's final downfall, Clara and Robert Schumann receive the visit of Johannes Brahms, twenty years old, and coming to them on the recommendation of the renowned violinist and composer Joseph Joachim. About this young, radiant musician-composer Schumann has but one thing to say: 'Brahms's visit (a genius)'.[61] Brahms plays for them, among other things, his F sharp minor piano sonata (Op. 2), which Schumann calls 'veiled symphonies – Lieder whose poetry one would understand without knowing the words, while a deep vocal melody runs through all of them'. Schumann describes some of the other, shorter pieces as 'of partly daemonic nature'. 'A young eagle', he writes to Joachim, 'a true apostle who will inscribe revelations that many Pharisees . . . will not decipher for centuries to come'.[62] For the first time in more than a decade, Schumann picks up the critic's pen and, under the title 'Neue Bahnen' (New paths), he bestows in the October 1853 issue of the *NZfM*, Elijah's mantle on the 'chosen youth'. His praise is limitless – 'He who was destined to come, springing forth, fully armed, like Athena from the head of Zeus (. . .) a young man over whose cradle Graces and Heroes have stood watch'[63] – as he entrusts Brahms, son-like, to carry the torch for a new *Davidsbündler* generation.[64] Whether or not accepting his appointed role, Brahms now visits the couple almost daily. All three are strongly drawn to each other, each of them, in their own different ways, intertwined via music. Indeed, Brahms will remain faithful to Clara and Robert Schumann all his life, attempting at once to reconcile and consume his love for both by proposing marriage to their first child Marie – an attempt that fails. Brahms will remain unmarried as well as childless all his life.

Towards the end of 1853, after Brahms's visit, Schumann becomes increasingly agitated and fears himself turning violent. Clara, however, does not allow herself to criticize her husband and adopts as much as possible her husband's views, interpreting the symptoms as signs of his genius: as voices from higher regions speaking through him. Just as Schumann himself takes these voices at face value – 'Friday 17th, shortly after going to bed, Robert got up again and wrote down a theme which, as he insisted, had been sung to him by angels; once it was written down, he lay down again and phantasized all night, with his eyes open and looking up at the sky. He firmly believed himself to be surrounded by angels who offered him the most magnificent revelations, all in the form of wonderful music'[65] – Clara chooses to see them as reflections of an illness that 'is almost entirely of a religious nature'.[66] This reading, however, generously accommodates the malignant nature of some of Schumann's other inner voices, for soon the angels are to turn into demons, offering 'hideous music', announcing 'that he was

Figure 1.7 Johannes Brahms, c. 1855

a sinner' and – in voices now coming from 'tigers and hyenas' – 'hurling him into hell'.[67] Alternately persecuted by voices of evil one moment, then soothed by those of angels the next, Schumann writes down his last composition, the *Geistervariationen*, five 'ghost variations' (*Anh.* F39) for solo piano, which he dedicates to Clara. With this composition, Schumann has truly become one of the chosen ones, visited by divinities and demons alike, speaking with their authority. And it is this interpretation of his personality that his wife endorses all the way – at least as long as the voices remain angelic, dictating a 'beautifully moving and devout theme' such as that of the *Geistervariationen*.[68] Through Clara's seeing him to be guided as well as driven by voices that are always nobler or viler than simply human, and never truly his own, Schumann the man – living with but also against others, and himself – is conveniently absorbed into the image of the artist who remains forever beyond reach, beyond reproach and, notably, beyond human vulnerability or failure. And in case one were not inclined to embrace the answers offered by mysticism, one question remains: if Schumann was indeed spoken through by angels, who, then, was behind the occasional malignancy? In other words, if the voices in Schumann weren't his own, if he was not responsible for them, who was?

The last three years

Some fifteen years earlier, in July 1838, Schumann wrote in his diary: 'Haven't slept a wink with the most terrifying thoughts and eternally torturing music – God help me that I will not one day die like this.'[69] The arrow through time made by this glimpse of his own end is chilling. Having spent 'almost half of this year (1952) lying very ill with a deep nervous condition (*tiefen Nervenverstimmung*)',[70] Schumann nevertheless produces during the last part of 1853, precisely during the time of Brahms's visit, a number of major works, and in very short periods of time: among them the rarely performed *Violinphantasie*, Op. 131 (in a week), and his Violin Concerto, WoO1 (in less than two); the better-known *Märchenerzählungen*, Op. 132, in three days; the little-known *Gesänge der Frühe*, Op. 133, in four; the Third Violin Sonata (WoO2) in A minor in ten; and the *Fünf Romanzen* for cello and piano (*Anh.* E7) in three.[71] By the beginning of 1854, however, he is once again plagued by severe insomnia, aural disturbances and menacing hallucinations. On 27 February 1854, he tries to kill himself by throwing himself into the Rhine, but is rescued. Having requested that he be institutionalized several times earlier – 'He always spoke about being a criminal . . . and [said] that he needed to go to a mental asylum, for he no longer had control over himself and wasn't sure what he might end up doing during the night'[72] – he is finally admitted to a private mental hospital in Endenich near Bonn, where he remains for the next two-and-a-half years until his death. After Schumann's internment, Brahms moves to Düsseldorf and takes on the role of *pater familias* in the Schumann household. In August 1855, when Clara moves to a new flat, Brahms takes up residence under the same roof. He departs in July 1856. As for Clara, to whom Schumann had confessed himself on the day of his suicide attempt 'to be unworthy of her love',[73] she does not visit her husband in Endenich until 27–9 July 1856. Leaving him briefly to fetch, together with Brahms, Joachim at the Endenich train station, she returns to the hospital to find her husband dead: 'I saw him only half an hour later . . . I stood by his corpse, my ardently beloved husband, and was quiet; all my thoughts went up to God with thanks that he was finally free.

And as I knelt at his bed . . . it seemed as if a magnificent spirit was hovering over me – ah, if only he had taken me along.'[74]

During the first part of his stay in Endenich, Schumann is not allowed to have much personal contact with other people apart from his doctor and his round-the-clock attendant. While daily reports on the patient's changing states of mind and body are composed with exactitude – this is the age of scientific observation and experiment – the idea of his having a life, or of having had one prior to his breakdown, and his wanting to be in touch with it, is considered perilous to his stability. Steps are thus taken to ensure undisturbed calm and visitors are kept at a distance. Forbidden to meet and speak to him directly, they observe Schumann through a small window in the wall of his cell. Thought to bring with them all the excitement of a life of which for Schumann, it is assumed, there had already been rather too much, his visitors themselves are protected from the spectacle that the composer's over-excited life has now turned into.[75] As if peeping through a keyhole, they take a glimpse at what goes on behind closed doors and get to see fragments of a scene that is, while clearly 'off limits', intriguing, enigmatic and utterly irresistible. Then they, too, go on and write 'reports', even if in the form of letters. Ten months of solitary confinement will pass until Schumann receives his first visitors; Joachim, Brahms and others follow, but few and far between. In April 1856 Brahms reports:

> We sat down, it became increasingly painful for me, his eyes were moist, he spoke continuously, but I understood nothing . . . Often he just blabbered, sort of bababa-dadada. While questioning him at length I understood the names of Marie, Julie, Berlin, Vienna, England, not much more . . . Richarz says that Schumann's brain is decidedly exhausted . . . He will remain, at best, in this significantly apathetic state; in one or two months only supportive care will probably be necessary.[76]

In Endenich, Schumann's activities until at least mid 1855 include much of what he used to do: playing the piano, composing, writing, keeping up correspondence, making lists, even taking walks in the surroundings of Endenich with his ever-present attendant. The medical reports provide much detail about his behaviour and states of mind – 'suffers from hallucinations', 'shouted for hours', 'his body seized by convulsions', 'attacked the attendant', 'refuses food for it were poison',[77] – as well as about the treatment he receives, consisting of acts of benevolence and brutality alike. Despite the hospital's policy of following the – at this time innovative – 'no restraint' method,[78] there is mention of the use of a straitjacket, apart from other contemporary means of tranquillization. When he is too agitated, 'all of his writings, books and writing utensils are removed' from him immediately[79] since his 'deterioration' is seen to be caused by a general 'overexertion' (*Überanstrengung*), and more specifically in the composer's 'immoderate mental, especially artistic, productivity'.[80] When attacking his doctors or guards, he is repeatedly detained in the '*Unruhigenabteilung*', a section for the unruly and disruptive. All in all, the various personal testimonies, and the no less disconcerting medical reports about Schumann's last years in Endenich, leave us with a feeling of pity. In view of the altogether still rather hesitant and reserved reception of his late work, and in view of the exceptional vehemence and passion with which one sees the value of this part of his work defended – and the mere fact that such defence is felt to be needed – we are left with the vague but insistent feeling that the 'late' Schumann as we have come to know him was perhaps not only one of the unstable or 'weak', but also one of the abused and defenceless: one of those, in other words, who may never be forgiven their suffering.

Schumann dies, alone, aged forty-six, on 29 July 1856.

Notes

1. Nauhaus calls Schumann a *Sonderfall*, a special case, whose critical nature (*Bedenklichkeit*), psychologically speaking, should not be ignored: "How do we explain that an artist of such high rank would have, over many years, written down even the most insignificant facts of his life, from the temperature of the air and water during a spa visit to the ever-unchanging cost for his daily cigar ration?" See preface by Gerd Nauhaus in *Robert Schumann Tagebücher*, ed. Georg Eismann and Gerd Nauhaus, 4 vols. (Leipzig: VEB Deutscher Verlag für Musik, 1971–82), vol. III, *Haushaltsbücher Teil I 1837–1847*, p. 21.
2. John Daverio, *Robert Schumann: Herald of a 'New Poetic Age'* (New York: Oxford University Press, 1997), p. 21. My account of the most widely known events of Schumann's life is based on information provided in Daverio's excellent biography.
3. Quoted after Eismann in Daverio, *Robert Schumann*, pp. 22–3.
4. I am providing dates of composition, rather than of publication.
5. Georg Eismann, *Robert Schumann: Ein Quellenwerk über sein Leben und Schaffen*, 2 vols. (Leipzig: Breitkopf & Härtel, 1956), vol. I, pp. 64–5.
6. Schumann to his mother in a letter dated 30 July 1830, quoted in Ernst Burger, *Robert Schumann: A Chronicle of His Life in Pictures and Documents*, Robert Schumann New Edition of the Complete Works, series VIII, supplements, vol. I (Mainz: Schott, 1998), p. 86.
7. Although he seems to have injured mainly his third finger, Schumann's concern, apart from a general weakness of the hand, may well have been the notoriously weak fourth finger. The fourth finger, linked to the third by the hand's inner bone structure, is dependent on the third finger and thus less mobile.
8. See Burger, *Robert Schumann*, p. 105.
9. Robert Schumann, *Jugendbriefe von Robert Schumann*, after the originals communicated by Clara Schumann (Leipzig: Breitkopf & Härtel, 1885), p. 194.
10. *Robert Schumann Tagebücher*, vol. I, ed. Eismann and Nauhaus, pp. 386, 397.
11. Quoted (without details of date) in Wolfgang Held, *Clara und Robert Schumann* (Frankfurt: Insel, 2001), p. 58.
12. *Robert Schumann Tagebücher*, vol. I, ed. Eismann and Nauhaus, p. 344.
13. *Robert Schumann Tagebücher*, vol. I, ed. Eismann and Nauhaus, p. 342.
14. Daverio, *Robert Schumann*, p. 113.
15. *Neue Zeitschrift für Musik* (*NZfM*), reprint, Breitkopf & Härtel, Wiesbaden 1985, v.
16. For a critical account of the problematic reception of Schumann's late work, see John Daverio's 'Songs of dawn and dusk: coming to terms with the late music' in this volume, pp. 268–91.
17. Adam Phillips, preface to Sigmund Freud, *Wild Analysis* (London: Penguin, 2002), p. viii.

18. *Robert Schumann Tagebücher*, vol. II, ed. Eismann and Nauhaus, p. 97. For a full account, see Daverio, *Robert Schumann*, pp. 182–96.
19. For a detailed discussion of this song, see the chapter on songs in this volume, pp. 118–19.
20. See Nancy Reich, 'Clara Schumann and Johannes Brahms', *Brahms and His World* (Princeton: Princeton University Press, 1990), p. 40.
21. *Robert Schumanns Werke*, ed. C. Schumann (Leipzig 1881–93), ser. 114 (31 vols.). See Nancy Reich, *Clara Schumann: The Artist and the Woman* (Ithaca, NY: Cornell University Press, 1985, revised edn February, 2001) for an account of Clara Schumann's life.
22. Diary entry of March 1838, *Robert Schumann Tagebücher*, vol. I, ed. Eismann and Nauhaus, p. 52.
23. Wilhelm Wasielewski, *Robert Schumann: Eine Biographie*, enlarged edn (Leipzig: Breitkopf & Härtel, 1906), pp. 502–3. My translation.
24. *Ibid.*, p. 493.
25. *Ibid.*, p. 502.
26. *Robert Schumann Tagebücher*, vol. II, ed. Eismann and Nauhaus, p. 99, quoted in Daverio, *Robert Schumann*, p. 196.
27. *Robert Schumann Tagebücher*, vol. II, ed. Eismann and Nauhaus, pp. 99–100.
28. *Ibid.*, 'treue Geschichte', p. 100.
29. *Robert Schumann Tagebücher*, vol. II, ed. Eismann and Nauhaus, pp. 106–7.
30. A complete edition is available as *Clara und Robert Schumann: Briefwechsel*, 3 vols., ed. Eva Weissweiler (Basel/Frankfurt am Main: vol. 1 (1984), 2 (1987) and 3 (2001)).
31. *Clara und Robert Schumann Briefwechsel*, ed. Weissweiler, vol. I, letter no. 49 (13 April 1838) p. 133 and (same letter continued over several days, here 20 April 1838) p. 153.
32. *Clara und Robert Schumann Briefwechsel*, ed. Weissweiler, vol. I, letter no. 4 (13 July 1833), p. 7.
33. Letter of 8 June 1834, *Clara and Robert Schumann: Briefe einer Liebe*, ed. Hans-Joseph Ortheil (Königstein: Athenäum, 1982), p. 21.
34. *Clara und Robert Schumann Briefwechsel*, ed. Weissweiler, vol. II, p. 571. Emphasis original.
35. For a detailed study of such influence, see the chapter 'Piano II: afterimages' in this volume, pp. 86–101.
36. Daverio, *Robert Schumann*, p. 220.
37. *Ibid.*, pp. 132–4.
38. See Beate Perrey, *Schumann's 'Dichterliebe' and Early Romantic Poetics. Fragmentation of Desire* (Cambridge: Cambridge University Press, 2002).
39. Berthold Litzmann, *Clara Schumann: Ein Künstlerleben*, 3 vols., vol. I (Leipzig: Breitkopf & Härtel, 1903), p. 311.
40. See Marie Luise Maintz, *Franz Schubert in der Rezeption Robert Schumanns: Studien zur Ästhetik und Instrumentalmusik* (Kassel: Bärenreiter, 1995).
41. Quoted in Daverio, *Robert Schumann*, p. 48.
42. Theodor W. Adorno, *Gesammelte Schriften*, 20 vols., ed. Rolf Tiedemann *et al.* (Frankfurt am Main: Suhrkamp, 1970–86), vol. XIX, Musikalische Schriften, VI, p. 33.
43. See Roland Barthes' essay 'Loving Schumann', in *The Responsibility of Form: Critical Essays on Music, Art, and Representation*, trans. Richard Howard (New York: Hill and Wang, 1985), pp. 287–98.
44. Paul Möbius, *Über Robert Schumanns Krankheit* (Halle: Marchold, 1906), p 1. For a comprehensive historical overview of what has rightly been called a 'problem of diagnosis', see Peter Ostwald's study *Schumann: The Inner Voices of a Musical Genius* (Boston: Northeastern University Press, 1985), pp. 295–307.
45. See *NZfM*, no. 33, 1836.
46. Robert Schumann, *Gesammelte Schriften über Musik und Musiker* (Leipzig: Breitkopf & Härtel, 1854); reprinted with epilogue by Gerd Nauhaus, 2 vols. (Wiesbaden: Breitkopf & Härtel, 1985), vol. I, p. 60.
47. Robert Schumann, *Gesammelte Schriften über Musik und Musiker*, 2 vols., rev. 5th edn, ed. Martin Kreisig (Leipzig: Breitkopf & Härtel, 1914), vol. I, p. 44.
48. See John Daverio, *Nineteenth-Century Music and the German Romantic Ideology* (New York: Schirmer, 1993), pp. 1–88, and Perrey, *Schumann's 'Dichterliebe'*, pp. 13–46.
49. *Robert Schumann Tagebücher*, vol. I, ed. Eismann and Nauhaus, p. 371.
50. Discussed in the respective chapters in this volume. For a particularly nuanced discussion of Schumann's apparent 'system' of genres, see also Daverio, *Robert Schumann*, pp. 218–21.
51. Letter to Friedrich Hiller, 10 April 1849, *Robert Schumanns Briefe: Neue Folge*, ed. F. Gustav Jansen (Leipzig: Breitkopf & Härtel, 1904), p. 302.

52. See Daverio, 'Robert Schumann', in *The New Grove Dictionary of Music and Musicians*, 2nd edn (London: Macmillan, 2000), p. 782.
53. Richard Pohl, 'Erinnerungen an Schumann', *Deutsche Revue*, 1878, p. 309, quoted in Reinhard Kapp, 'Das Orchester Schumanns', *Musik-Konzepte Sonderband Robert Schumann II*, ed. Heinz-Klaus Metzger and Rainer Riehn (Munich: Edition Text und Kritik, December 1982), p. 198.
54. *Robert Schumann Tagebücher*, vol. III/2, ed. Eismann and Nauhaus, p. 641.
55. Quoted in Burger, *Robert Schumann*, p. 292.
56. Cf. *ibid.*, p. 292.
57. See Eduard Hanslick, *Aus meinem Leben*, 3rd edn, vol. I (Berlin: Verein für deutsche Litteratur, 1894), pp. 66–7.
58. Hermann Erler, *Robert Schumanns Leben aus seinen Briefen geschildert* (Berlin: n.p., 1887), p. 109.
59. *Robert Schumann Tagebücher*, vol. II, ed. Eismann and Nauhaus, p. 441.
60. Litzmann, *Clara Schumann*, vol. II (Leipzig: Breitkopf & Härtel, 1905), p. 298. See also Daverio, *Robert Schumann*, p. 457 and Wasielewski, *Robert Schumann*, p. 492.
61. *Robert Schumann Tagebücher*, vol. III/2, ed. Eismann and Nauhaus, p. 637.
62. Letter of 8 October 1853, *Robert Schumanns Briefe. Neue Folge*, ed. Jansen, p. 379.
63. English translation in Robert Schumann, *On Music and Musicians*, ed. Konrad Woolff, trans. Paul Rosenfeld (London: Dennis Dobson, 1947), pp. 252–4.
64. See Daverio, *Robert Schumann*, p. 454 for detailed discussion.
65. Quoted in Eismann, *Robert Schumann*, vol. I, pp. 190–1.
66. Litzmann, *Clara Schumann*, vol. II (Leipzig: Breitkopf & Härtel, 1905), p. 298.
67. *Ibid.*, p. 298. See also Daverio, *Robert Schumann*, p. 458.
68. Litzmann, *Clara Schumann*, vol. II, p. 298.
69. *Robert Schumann Tagebücher*, vol. II, ed. Eismann and Nauhaus, p. 61. *Robert Schumann in Endenich (1854–1856): Krankenakten, Briefzeugnisse und zeitgenössische Berichte*, ed. Bernhard Appel, Schumann Forschungen, vol. 11 (Mainz, 2006) appeared too late for consideration in this chapter.
70. *Robert Schumanns Briefe. Neue Folge*, ed. Jansen, p. 364.
71. See Michael Struck, *Die umstrittenen späten Instrumentalwerke Schumanns* (Hamburg: Wagner, 1984). See also John Daverio's chapter in this volume, pp. 268–91.
72. Litzmann, *Clara Schumann*, vol. II, p. 299.
73. *Ibid.*, p. 300.
74. Berthold Litzmann, *Clara Schumann, Ein Künstlerleben*, 7th edn, 3 vols. (Leipzig: Breitkopf & Härtel, 1925), vol. II, p. 415.
75. Note Litzmann's evaluation that Schumann had been 'sick' almost throughout his entire life and that his illness had 'manifested itself to varying degrees and in changing forms, with long intervals of quiescence but gruesome regularity, and always in overexcitement'. Litzmann, *Clara Schumann*, 7th edn, 3 vols. (Leipzig: Breitkopf & Härtel, 1925), vol. II, p. 138.
76. Quoted in Ostward, *Schumann: The Inner Voices*, p. 291.
77. These and following quotations from 'Auszüge aus Dr. Franz Richartz' Verlaufsbericht 1854–56', in *Robert Schumanns letzte Lebensjahre. Protokoll einer Krankheit*, Archiv-blätter, 1 (Stiftung Archiv der Akademie der Künste, Berlin, März 1994), pp. 17–24.
78. Franz Hermann Franken, 'Robert Schumann in der Irrenanstalt Endenich', in *Robert Schumanns letzte Lebensjahre*, p. 9.
79. *Ibid.*, p. 21.
80. Franz Richarz, 'Über Robert Schumanns Krankheit', *Signale für die Musikalische Welt*, 40 (1873), pp. 625–9.

2 Life and literature, poetry and philosophy: Robert Schumann's aesthetics of music

ULRICH TADDAY

Robert Schumann's music is not romantic and irrational *Träumerei*; the history of the aesthetics of genius in the Romantic era is not the history of Schumann's Romantic music or aesthetics. The latter history begins in the literature Schumann read all his life, and continues in his music. To understand the history of Schumann's music, however, we need to approach it through the life, the literature, the poetry and the philosophy.

The literature in the life

Robert Schumann's aesthetics needs to be understood as a process of enculturation within an educated and cultured bourgeoisie, in terms of social history, and – as one of lifelong appropriation and reification of art, literature and music – in terms of developmental psychology. The premises of the former are to be found partly in the protestant ethic that Schumann inherited first and foremost from his father and grandfather. Schumann's father, himself the son of an evangelical (Lutheran) clergyman, was a businesslike and hardworking publisher-bookseller and an author of scholarly and bellettristic works, with a reputation that went beyond the bounds of Zwickau or Saxony. Friedrich August Gottlob Schumann was a member of what had at last come to be recognized in Germany from the 1790s onwards as the educated, cultivated middle classes, comprising government officials; judges; university professors; schoolteachers; private tutors; protestant clergy; and university-educated professionals such as physicians, pharmacists, advocates and notaries; as well as self-employed artists, writers and journalists. In sum, a community of discourse, enjoying a certain social privilege but lacking closer social integration, defined by the educational standing that distinguished it from both the less privileged and the more privileged strata of the population. Their education (or *Bildung*: the word implies a process of formation – shaping and polishing – in addition to literacy and numeracy) enabled members of these classes and professions to claim familiarity with literature, music and painting as genuinely middle-class terrain, that is, to define the arts as integral elements of middle-class identity. For these educated and cultivated middle-class people, culture was the medium in which they found a reflection and a realization of the meaning and the reality of life and of society: Friedrich August Gottlob Schumann found them in the medium of literature, and his son Robert found them in the medium of music.

The reason that Robert Schumann's musical aesthetics had literary roots is not only sociocultural, or familial, in that his father's cultural preoccupations necessarily influenced him, but stemmed from his individual development as well: he was still a schoolboy when he began to show an interest in literature that was well above the average. His classmate Emil Flechsig recalled that after a period of enthusiasm for Latin and Greek literature:

> we got into German poetry and stopped there, and he showed a decided talent for writing verse and composing German prose, as anyone can see from the collected edition of his musical writings. We had unlimited opportunities to find out about literature: the whole Schumann house was crammed with the classics, and we were allowed to help ourselves to the soiled copies – I still have some of them.
>
> It was a special treat when Schumann senior, who doted on his son, allowed us to go into his private library, which was normally kept locked, and where he had stored away all the treasures of the world's literature.[1]

Schumann's early love of literature led him to found a 'literary society' in 1825, with ten school friends. As president, Schumann wrote the constitution himself: 'It is the duty of every cultivated person', wrote the fifteen-year-old:

> to know the literature of his own country, so it is likewise a duty for us, who already yearn to attain to higher cultivation, not to neglect German literature but to strive with might and main to acquaint ourselves with it. The aim of this society, therefore, shall be understood to be an initiation into German literature, which has so much rich material to offer us in every field of knowledge, but of which some of us, whether through neglect or through lack of means, know very little as yet.[2]

Schumann was also responsible for keeping a record of the reading matter the society discussed in the course of thirty meetings, up to the beginning of 1828: the list in the 'Protocoll zum litterarischen Verein' includes works by such authors as Collin, Gleim, Kosegarten, Ernst Schulze, Zacharias Werner and – not least – all the plays of Schiller except *Wallenstein*. Another notebook from a later period of Schumann's life, the *Lektürebüchlein*, lists many of the books he read between 1845 and 1852. At the time of the founding of the *Litterarischer Verein* he began to collect quotations from the books he read. By 1852 he had accumulated a file of some 274 pages with no fewer than 1,229 excerpts, which has survived under the title *Mottosammlung*.[3]

Schumann used some of these 'mottos' in the *Neue Zeitschrift für Musik*, but the collection as a whole has a private character. In compiling the *Dichtergarten* of 1853–4, on the other hand, a 750-page anthology of quotations about music, taken from the sweep of world literature from Classical antiquity to the present, Schumann intended publication.

The picture of Schumann's receptiveness to literature would be incomplete if it did not include his own literary productivity. He began to write as a schoolboy: the collection of bellettristic pieces *Blätter und Blümchen aus der goldenen Aue, gesammelt und zusammengebunden von Robert Schumann* (1823) and the poems *Allerley aus der Feder Roberts an der Mulde* (1825–30) were the most substantial products. From the standpoint of musical aesthetics, the most noteworthy of his early experiments are *Juniusabende und Julytage, Die Tonwelt* and *Ueber Genial- Knill- Original- und andere itäten*.[4] These testaments to the young Schumann's literary ambitions remain largely unexplored by researchers, but his *Tage- und Haushaltsbücher*, presenting a supercharged view of his thinking and his milieu, have appeared in a scholarly edition.[5] In the end, however, it was his writing about music that brought Schumann recognition – even a degree of fame – as a writer, not his essays or verse. He collected the criticism and other articles he had written between 1833 and 1844, while editor of the periodical he himself had founded, the *Neue Zeitschrift für Musik*, and republished them in 1854 as his *Gesammelte Schriften über Musik und Musiker*.[6]

Together with what can be learned from his letters,[7] not least his correspondence with his wife,[8] the examples given above demonstrate that the process of enculturation within an educated and cultured bourgeoisie was one of 'lifelong learning', actively pursued by Schumann, assiduous in both reading and writing from his childhood on. The importance of literature in his life was recalled by Franz Brendel, writing in 1858 that he was 'constantly occupied with reading, carried books with him wherever he went, read poetry on walks and wherever he was alone'.[9]

The Jean Paul of music

Of all the books Schumann read in his life, none had greater significance for him than those of Jean Paul, as he himself recognized as early as 1828. He wrote in his diary:

> I often asked myself where I would be if I had not known Jean Paul: because he seems to be intertwined with me, on one side at least. For I sensed him earlier: perhaps I would write exactly as I do now, but I would not avoid the society of men as much, and I would dream less. I cannot really imagine exactly what I would be like. It's a question I cannot answer.[10]

Schumann appears to have been about seventeen when he discovered the writer Johann Paul Friedrich Richter (1763–1825), universally known as Jean Paul. A school essay of around that time cites the novel *Titan* in the course of considering aesthetic issues raised by the question of 'why people are so much more upset by disparagement of their taste than by any other kind of criticism'.[11] As well as *Titan* (1803), Schumann of course read all Jean Paul's great novels: *Die unsichtbare Loge, Hesperus* (1895), *Siebenkäs* (1797) and *Flegeljahre* (1805), to name only the most important. Jean Paul's prose style, which cast its spell over Schumann, was aptly described by Carlyle as 'a wild complicated Arabesque'.[12] Reviewing a biography of the German writer in the *Edinburgh Review* in 1827, Carlyle explained:

> Not that he [Jean Paul] is ignorant of grammar, or disdains the sciences of spelling and parsing; but he exercises both in a certain latitudinarian spirit; deals with astonishing liberality in parentheses, dashes, and subsidiary clauses; invents hundreds of new words, alters old ones, or by hyphens chains and pairs and packs them together into most jarring combination; in short, produces sentences of the most heterogeneous, lumbering, interminable kind. Figures without limit; indeed the whole is one tissue of metaphors, and similes, and allusions to all the provinces of Earth, Sea and Air; interlaced with epigrammatic breaks, vehement bursts, or sardonic turns, interjections, quips, puns and even oaths! A perfect Indian jungle it seems; a boundless, unparalleled imbroglio; nothing on all sides but darkness, dissonance, confusion worse confounded![13]

Although Schumann himself admitted that there was a programmatic relationship between *Papillons*, Op. 2, and the end of *Flegeljahre*,[14] it was in matters of form – that is, structure, rather than content – that literature in general, and the writing of Jean Paul in particular, left its mark on his early musical compositions. In general, 'narrative episodes, rhetorical emphases, digressions, flashbacks, declamatory gestures, epigrammatic distillations and aphorisms [are] the structural forms acquired from his reading that Schumann converted to compositional ends'.[15] In particular, Jean Paul's influence on Schumann's compositions of the 1830s is manifested in: '1. The propensity for brief, almost aphoristic musical statements . . . 2. A love for mystery and concealed meaning . . . 3. The quotation of thematic material from previous compositions in new ones . . . 4. The often abrupt juxtaposition of grotesque humor with elements of profound sentiment'.[16]

Romantic Humour and (no) Irony

Of all the influences Jean Paul exercised on Schumann, in the early and the late works alike, humour was the most important. Schumann did not just discover Jean Paul's humour by reading his novels; he also pursued it in his *Vorschule der Ästhetik* (1804). There Jean Paul defines humour as a central category of philosophical aesthetics:

> Humour, as the sublime inverted, destroys not the individual but the finite by the contrast with the Idea . . . it humbles greatness, but (unlike parody) in order to set it at the side of littleness, and it raises up littleness, but (unlike irony) in order to set it at the side of greatness and thus makes both naught, because everything is equal, and naught, in the sight of infinity.[17]

This definition of philosophical humour is the key, aesthetically, to the structure of most of Schumann's works. But – as the definition quoted above should make clear – Jean Paul's type of humour must not be confused or equated with the so-called Romantic irony of Friedrich Schlegel, whom Jean Paul numbered among the 'poetic nihilists'.[18] Jean Paul's humour is a corrective to Schlegel's Romantic irony: it does not lose itself in the void of infinite reflection but reveals itself amenably in sentimental sensuousness. Schumann, too, made a substantial distinction between humour and irony. In terms of theory, he adopted the distinction only at second hand, above all from Jean Paul's *Vorschule der Ästhetik*, for he did not read the philosophical writings of August and Friedrich Schlegel, Novalis or Karl Wilhelm Ferdinand Solger, but he practised the distinction in his criticism. He spoke out plainly, for instance, against the ironic, sarcastic 'Heinism' that he heard in *L'aimable Roué*, the divertissement by his one-time composition teacher, Heinrich Dorn (1836): 'But if irony once insinuates itself into our art, then we must indeed fear that it really is as near its end as some believe, if little comical comets have the power to overthrow the order of the greater solar system.'[19] As an advocate of humour, Schumann was prepared to allow that there was a time and a place for Romantic irony, but at the heart of his own understanding of music he rejected it:

> If one set out to oppose the whole trend of the spirit of our time, which tolerates a burlesque Dies irae, one would have to repeat what has been said and written for years against Byron, Heine, Victor Hugo, Grabbe and others like them. At some moments in eternity Poetry puts on the mask of irony, so as not to let her anguished face be seen; perhaps the kindly hand [of a genius] will remove it.'[20]

The process of poetic reflection

Though Schumann's humour is to be understood as a formal category in aesthetic terms, rather than one of content, that is not to say that his music should be viewed purely in terms of formal aesthetics. Certainly, as various statements testify, he did not think instrumental music should be interpreted programmatically. There is the notorious verdict he pronounced in 1835 on Berlioz's *Symphonie fantastique*: 'So much for the programme. All Germany will wish him joy of it: there is always something unworthy, a whiff of the charlatan, about such signposts.'[21] But the comment does not mean that Schumann renounced the poetic principle of music, for he went on to say:

> Many people worry too much about the difficult question of how far instrumental music can be allowed to go in representing thoughts and events. They are certainly mistaken if they think that composers put pen to paper with the paltry intention of expressing, depicting, painting this or that. But the importance of fortuitous influences or external impressions should not be underrated. There is often an idea at work unconsciously alongside the musical imagination, the eye alongside the ear, and amid all the sounds and notes the eye, this ever-active organ, holds fast certain outlines that may solidify and take distinct shape as the music advances. So the more elements related to the music convey ideas or shapes that were generated with the notes, the more poetic or plastic in expression the composition will be – and the more imaginative or keen the composer's intrinsic power to conceive, the more his music will elevate or excite. Why should the thought of immortality not have struck a Beethoven as his fancy soared? Why should memories of a great, fallen hero not have inspired him to a piece of music? Why should the recollection of bygone happiness not similarly inspire another? Must we be ungrateful to Shakespeare for having drawn forth a work worthy of himself from the breast of a young composer? Or ungrateful to nature, and deny that we have borrowed some of her beauty and sublimity for our own works? Italy, the Alps, the sea, the dawn of a spring day – would anyone claim that music has never related any of these? No, even smaller, more specific images can lend music so charmingly precise a character that its ability to express such traits amazes us . . . Let us leave open the question of whether there are many poetic moments in the programme of Berlioz's symphony. The central concern remains, whether the music amounts to anything in itself, with or without text and explication, and, more importantly, whether spirit dwells within.[22]

In other words, Schumann objected not only to the particular programme of the *Symphonie fantastique* but to programmes generally, because they restrict the listener's imagination. For the same reason he chose for his own music only titles 'that suggest the mood of the piece as a whole'.[23] Titles such as those of the pieces in *Kinderszenen*, Op.15, 'came into existence later, of course, and are really nothing but more precise pointers for performance and comprehension'.[24] This remark of Schumann's risks being misinterpreted, insofar as it suggests that the titles are fortuitous extras lacking any connection with the musical substance of the pieces. Quite the reverse: the titles are important components of the compositions, and have as much connection with the music as titles have with poems. 'If poets do it', Schumann wrote in a review of Ignaz Moscheles's *Charakteristische Studien*, Op. 95, 'if they seek to wrap [*verhüllen*] the meaning of the whole poem in a title, why should musicians not do it too? Only let such indication through words be done sensitively and cleverly: it is the very thing that will reveal the musician's cultivation.'[25] For Schumann, therefore, poetic titles fulfil the same function in music and in poetry. By indicating the composer's intention, they awaken the recipient's interest in a piece of music that promises to be more than a fugue or a sonata, which their titles signal as pure forms. At the same time, by connotation and association, titles direct the recipient's interest in a specifically unspecific direction, that is, they lend wings to a player's or a listener's imagination, without restricting its freedom. So when Schumann writes that musicians, like poets, 'seek to wrap the meaning of the whole poem in a title', his meaning is deliberately ambivalent: titles simultaneously unwrap and wrap the meaning and content of a composition, titles allow listeners and players to discover the meaning of the music by covering it and vice versa, titles present the recipient with a Romantic puzzle to solve.

The aesthetic function of the titles is important because the poetic principle of Schumann's understanding of music is essential to the titles: they stand detached from the music, as a kind of *tertium comparationis*, and denote a process of reflection that starts in the composer's thoughts and emotions and crosses over into the responding thoughts and feelings of the recipients. This open-ended reflection process widens the boundaries of the piece of music, in that it dialectically mediates between the composer's creation and the responsive re-creation of the listener.[26] Schumann himself described the process of reflection on the part of the re-creating – and post-creating – listener in his essay on Schubert's C major Symphony.

> Often, when I looked down on [Vienna] from the mountains, it occurred to me that Beethoven's eyes may well have wandered at times searching for the distant Alps, that Mozart may often have dreamily followed the course of the Danube, which seems to disappear into the trees and shrubs at every bend, and that Papa Haydn will often have gazed at the spire of St Stephen's, shaking his head at its dizzy height. The images of the Danube, St Stephen's spire and the distant Alps, compressed into one with a faint Catholic aroma of incense lying thereover, and we have an image of Vienna itself; and if the whole enchanting landscape lies spread out before us, then surely strings stir within us that would never have sounded otherwise. With Schubert's symphony, and the bright, burgeoning, romantic life within it, the city springs up before me today, clearer than ever, and again I understand how this is the setting in which such works can be born. I will not try to give the symphony a foil, different generations choose too differently among the underlying texts and images . . . But if we only want to, it is easy to believe that the exterior world, bright today and darkening tomorrow, often touches the inner being of poets and musicians; and if we want to acknowledge that

more lies hidden in this symphony than a beautiful song, more than merely sorrow and joy such as music has expressed hundreds of times before – that it leads us, rather, into a region where we cannot remember ever having been before, then we need only listen to this same symphony. Quite apart from the masterly musical technique of the composition, here also is life in every fibre, colours in all their finest gradations, meaning everywhere, the keenest expression of the individual, and finally, a romanticism poured out over the whole such as we already know from elsewhere in Franz Schubert. And the heavenly length of this symphony, like a fat, four-decker novel, perhaps by Jean Paul, which can never end, and for the best of reasons, namely to let the reader continue with creating it afterwards . . . Everywhere, you feel that the composer was in control, and that you will surely come to understand in time how it all coheres. The impression of certainty is conveyed immediately by the magnificent romantic introduction, even though as yet everything still seems wrapped in mystery.[27]

Eessentially, this review of Schubert's Great C major Symphony contains the kernel of Schumann's understanding of music; it describes the production and reception of music as a cohesive process, and rejects the formalist view of a supposedly 'absolute music' as a delusion. The open-ended process described by Schumann, emanating from the creating composer to be continued by the post-creating listener, is of course not restricted to the meaning or interpretation of titles and headings. The process of reflection may begin with them but it does not end there. As Schumann's music criticism clearly states, music, if it is poetic, creates opportunities enough to give the recipient's imagination wings. If it fails to do so, perhaps because it exhausts itself in empty virtuosity, as in the piano works of Kalkbrenner, Herz and Hünten, for example, it is not poetic but prosaic. 'Prosaic' was Schumann's verdict on the music about which much was written in the early 1830s, in the pages of the Leipzig *Allgemeine Musikalische Zeitung*, although there was nothing more to say about it than that it had nothing to say. That was the reason why Schumann founded a 'new journal for music', the *Neue Zeitschrift für Musik*, in 1833, to champion the poetic music of the time, the music that would help to usher in 'a young, poetic future at last'[28] – or, 'a new poetic age at last'.[29]

Schumann's rejection of the culture of the prosaic was a critique of a society that trivialized and commercialized music by treating it as a commodity, an entertainment medium. His proclamation of a culture of the poetic was socially utopian, for it entailed an alteration in the role and position of music that would require an alteration in society. Schumann's dream, then, was of a new musical mythology, of a society that would define its identity, among other ways, by means of musical discourse, in that it would have the spirit and the time to realize an *advance* in the spirit of the time. In this sense, Schumann's aesthetics of music is Romantic and revolutionary.

Notes

1. Emil Flechsig, *Erinnerungen an Schumann, um 1875*, quoted after Ernst Burger, *Robert Schumann: Eine Lebenschronik in Bildern und Dokumenten*, in collaboration with Gerd Nauhaus and the Robert-Schumann-Haus Zwickau (Mainz, 1999), pp. 36. Emil Flechsig, 'Erinnerungen an Robert Schumann, aus dem Manuskript erstmalig vollständig veröffentlicht vor seiner Urenkelin Hilde Wendler', in *Neue Zeitschrift für Musik*, 117 Jg., Heft 7/8, pp. 392–6 (392).
2. Robert Schumann, Heinrich Rothe *et al.* 'Protocoll zum litterarischen Verein', in Martin Schoppe, *Schumanns 'Litterarischer Verein'*, in *Robert Schumann und die Dichter: Ein Musiker als Leser*, Katalog zur Ausstellung des Heinrich-Heine-Instituts in Verbindung mit dem Robert-Schumann-Haus Zwickau und der Robert-Schumann-Forschungsstelle e.V. in Düsseldorf, prepared by Bernhard R. Appel and Inge Hermstrüwer (Düsseldorf, 1991), pp. 21f.
3. Leander Hotaki, *Robert Schumanns Mottosammlung: Übertragung, Kommentar*, Einführung. Rombach Wissenschaften: Reihe Litterae; Band 59 (Freiburg im Breisgau, 1998).
4. Frauke Otto, *Robert Schumann als Jean Paul Leser* (Frankfurt am Main, 1984), pp. 25–43, 66–75, 109–14.
5. *Robert Schumann Tagebücher*, 4 vols. vol. I: 1827–38, ed. Georg Eismann (Leipzig, 1971; Basel and Frankfurt am Main, n.d). Vol. II: 1836–54, ed. Gerd Nauhaus (Leipzig, 1987; Basel and Frankfurt am Main, n.d). Vol. III: *Haushaltbücher, Teil. I*, 1837–47, ed. Gerd Nauhaus (Leipzig, 1982; Basel and Frankfurt am Main, n.d); *Haushaltbücher, Teil. II*, 1847–56, ed. Gerd Nauhaus (Leipzig, 1982; Basel and Frankfurt am Main, n.d).
6. Robert Schumann, *Gesammelte Schriften über Musik und Musiker*, 2 vols., ed. Gerd Nauhaus, reprint of the 1854 Leipzig edn (Wiesbaden, 1985).
7. Robert Schumann, *Jugendbriefe von Robert Schumann*, after the originals communicated by Clara Schumann (Leipzig, 1885). Robert Schumann, *Robert Schumanns Briefe. Neue Folge*, ed. F. Gustav Jansen, 2nd improved edn (Leipzig, 1904).
8. Clara Schumann, *The Complete Correspondence of Clara and Robert Schumann: Critical Edition*, ed. E. Weissweiler, trans. H. Fritsch and R. Crawford (New York, 1994).
9. Franz Brendel, '"R. Schumann" Biographie von J. W. v. Wasielewski, Zweite Besprechung', *Neue Zeitschrift für Musik*, 25 (1858), 139.
10. *Robert Schumann Tagebücher*, vol. I, ed. Eismann, p. 82.
11. Quoted after Kristin R. M. Krahe, 'Robert Schumanns Schulaufsatz: "Warum erbittert uns Tadel in Sachen des Geschmakes mehr, als in andern Dingen?" ', in *Robert Schumann und die Dichter*, pp. 36ff. Translation by Mary Whittall.
12. Thomas Carlyle, 'Jean Paul Friedrich Richter', in *The Works of Thomas Carlyle in Thirty Volumes*, 30 vols., vol. XXVI: *Critical and Miscellaneous Essays I* (London, 1899), p. 19. [1827 originally published in *Edinburgh Review*, no. 91, 'Jean Paul Friedrich Richter's Leben, nebst Characteristic seiner Werke, von Heinrich Döring, Jean Paul Friedrich Richter's Life, with a Sketch of his Works, by Heinrich Döring, Gotha, 1826']
13. *Ibid.*, p. 12.
14. Robert Schumann, Brief an die Familie vom 17.4.1832, in *Jugendbriefe*, pp. 166ff. Translation by Mary Whittall.
15. Bernhard R. Appel, 'Robert Schumann als Leser', in *Robert Schumann und die Dichter*, p. 13.
16. Eric Frederick Jensen, 'Explicating Jean Paul: Robert Schumann's program for Papillons, Op. 2', *Nineteenth Century Music*, XXII/2 (autumn 1998), 133f. Erika Reiman, *Schumann's Piano Cycles and the Novels of Jean Paul* (Rochester, 2004).
17. Jean Paul, *Vorschule der Ästhetik*, ed. Norbert Miller (Munich, 1974), p. 125.
18. *Ibid.*, pp. 31ff.
19. Robert Schumann, 'H. Dorn, "L'aimable Roué", Divertissement (C-majeur) oe. 17', *Gesammelte Schriften über Musik und Musiker von Robert Schumann*, ed. Martin Kreisig, 2 vols., vol. I, 5th edn (Leipzig: Breitkopf & Härtel, 1914), p. 185.
20. Schumann, 'Sinfonie von H. Berlioz', in *Gesammelte Schriften. Ibid.*, p. 85.
21. *Ibid.*, p. 83.
22. *Ibid.*, pp. 84f.
23. Robert Schumann, 'Ferdinand Hillers Etuden', in *Gesammelte Schriften*, p. 49.
24. Robert Schumann, 'Brief an Heinrich Dorn vom 5.9.1839', in *Robert Schumanns Briefe*, ed. Jansen, p. 170.
25. Robert Schumann, 'Charakteristische Studien für das Pianoforte von I. Moscheles', in *Gesammelte Schriften*, p. 361.

26. Ulrike Kranefeld, *Der nachschaffende Hörer: Rezeptionsästhetische Studien zur Musik Robert Schumanns* (Stuttgart–Weimar, 2000).
27. Robert Schumann, 'C-dur-Sinfonie von Franz Schubert', in *Gesammelte Schriften*, pp. 462ff.
28. '... endlich eine junge, dichterische Zukunft': from the original version of Schumann's article 'Zur Eröffnung des Jahrganges 1835', *Neue Zeitschrift für Musik*, 2 (1835), 3.
29. '... endlich eine neue poetische Zeit': from the revised version of 'Zur Eröffnung des Jahrganges 1835', published in Schumann, *Gesammelte Schriften*, and adopted by Martin Kreisig in the fifth edition (1914).

3 Schumann's heroes: Schubert, Beethoven, Bach

NICHOLAS MARSTON

> In all Schumann's compositions for the piano one can sense a constant striving for originality – originality of both form and content ... One cannot fail to note the powerful, lasting impressions that the study of classical models, such as Sebastian Bach or Beethoven, made on Schumann; on occasion the listener can even identify more recent composers, for example, Franz Schubert, Felix Mendelssohn Bartholdy, or Chopin.
>
> It goes almost without saying that one must speak, in this case, not of actual reminiscences or intentional, slavish imitation but rather of works created in a similar tone and a related spirit.   Carl Koßmaly[1]

As a largely self-taught composer who for the first part of his career was equally if not more active as a critic, Schumann was intensely aware of his own and his contemporaries' historical moment. Studying Wilhelm Christian Müller's *Aesthetisch-historische Einleitung in die Wissenschaft der Tonkunst* around 1834, he would have encountered the view that the period 1800–30 marked the highpoint – indeed, the perfection (*Vollendung*) – of musical history.[2] But for Schumann the past mattered above all to the extent that it paved the way for a future music that it was the duty of his generation to cultivate. In his editorial for the first 1835 issue of the *Neue Zeitschrift für Musik* (*NZfM*) he set out his critical position as being 'to keep emphatically in mind the former age and its works, to draw attention to the fact that only at such a pure source can new artistic beauties be invigorated – and thereby to resist the immediate past as inartistic, bent only on the enhancement of superficial virtuosity – and finally to prepare and hasten the coming of a new poetic age'.[3] Later that year, in a review of Ferdinand Hiller's Etudes, Op. 15, he judged their composer to be prominent among a young generation,

> whose destiny it seems to be to free from chains an age that is still hanging on to the old century by a thousand links. With one hand they go on working to unloose the chains, with the other they are already pointing to a

---

For detailed study and documentation of Schumann's reception of the three composers discussed in this chapter the reader is referred to Marie Luise Maintz, *Franz Schubert in der Rezeption Robert Schumanns: Studien zur Ästhetik und Instrumentalmusik* (Kassel, 1995); Bodo Bischoff, *Monument für Beethoven: Die Entwicklung der Beethoven-Rezeption Robert Schumanns* (Köln-Rheinkassel, 1994); and Bodo Bischoff, 'Das Bach-Bild Robert Schumanns', in *Bach und die Nachwelt, Band 1: 1750–1850*, ed. Michael Heinemann and Hans-Joachim Hinrichsen (Laaber, 1997), pp. 421–99.

future in which they will command a new kingdom which ... conceals deep within itself things strange and as yet unseen, of which Beethoven's prophetic spirit now and then gave report, and which the noble youth Franz Schubert retold in his childlike, gifted, fairytale-like manner. For just as with the poetic art of Jean Paul, who, after he had been laid in the earth, gushed forth like a life-saving spring in a ravine, until two youths whom I need not name led him back into the sunlight and, inspired, proclaimed all too passionately 'let a new age begin' – so it was with the music of Beethoven.[4]

Schumann's formulation here not only makes plain his estimation of Beethoven's and Schubert's works as the foundations upon which the 'new poetic age' must be built but also neatly expresses his perception of these two great forebears vis-à-vis one another. Beethoven is characterized as the (ancient) seer and prophet, his foresight taking on an almost divine quality, while Schubert is positioned as an *epigone* or *ephebe*: younger, less forbidding, more human.[5] These terms of comparison would persist: in a review of the 1837–8 winter concert series in Leipzig, Schubert would be described as 'Beethoven's first-born [son]'; and in an 1838 review of the posthumous Grand Duo, D. 812, and the Piano Sonatas, D. 958–60, musing on the relationship between age and musical preferences, Schumann stated that 'Schubert will always remain the favourite of [youth].'[6] There was a strong autobiographical element in this judgement; for although by 1838 Schumann had achieved a degree of critical (and compositional) distance from Schubert's music, it was to this composer rather than to Beethoven that he had first been particularly attracted as a youth in the later 1820s. Significantly, perhaps, we know nothing of the sixteen-year-old Schumann's reaction to Beethoven's death on 26 March 1827; but when he heard of Schubert's death just twenty months later, on 19 November 1828, Schumann reportedly was heard sobbing throughout the whole night.[7]

By his own admission, Schumann first encountered Schubert's music around 1827, in the form of 'Erlkönig', D. 328; the Piano Sonata in A minor, D. 845; and a Lied identified only as 'in G flat' (thus either 'Der Du von dem Himmel bist', D. 224, or 'Nähe des Geliebten', D. 162).[8] Subsequently, during his period of piano tuition with Friedrich Wieck in Leipzig in 1828–9, he was to get to know some of the four-hand piano music, including the Variations on a Theme from Herold's *Marie*, D. 908; some Polonaises – whether those of D. 824 or D. 599 is unclear – and the Rondo in A, D. 951. This latter work, which had been published in 1828 or 1829 as Op. 107, is specifically mentioned in a much-quoted letter to Wieck dated 6 November 1829, in which Schumann describes in some detail the effect that Schubert's music has on him, and makes a characteristic analogy between music and literature:

> Schubert is still my 'one and only Schubert' . . . when I play Schubert, it's as if I were reading a novel 'composed' by Jean Paul. Recently I played his four-hand Rondeau, Op. 107, which I count among his best compositions, unless you can give me something to compare with the tranquil sultriness, and with the colossal, still, *constrained, lyrical* madness, and with the full, deep, gentle ethereal melancholy that hovers over this whole *authentic-whole* [*Wahrhaft-ganze*] . . . Apart from Schubert's, no music is so *psychologically* curious in the *course* and *connection* of its *ideas* and in its *apparently* logical discontinuities [scheinbar *logischen Sprüngen*] and how few [composers] have been able to *express* as well as he a unique individuality [from] *an abundance of* such varying *tone-pictures*.[9]

Schumann was five months into his nineteenth year when he penned these remarks, and one should perhaps resist the temptation to measure Schubert's music against them too closely; in particular, it is not easy to understand what fundamental 'discontinuities' masquerading as logically connected sequences of ideas – if that is indeed the sense of what Schumann meant to convey – he might have heard in the A major Rondo. But as for his diagnosis of a music whose 'logic' is that of the discontinuous, whose coherence is to be apprehended at the psychological level rather than being susceptible of 'musicological' demonstration: again, if this is something of what Schumann's words mean to comport, then his remarks to Wieck are remarkably prescient of many of his own early piano compositions, particularly *Papillons*, Op. 2 and *Carnaval*, Op. 9 (in the latter work, consider especially the sequence 'Florestan–Coquette–Réplique', where the identity of the individual pieces is compromised by cross-reference and formal and tonal open-endedness).

Other works that Schumann studied with Wieck included the 'Wanderer' Fantasy, D. 760, and – an especial favourite – the Piano Trio in E flat, D. 929; comparing it in 1836 to the Trio in B flat, D. 898, which was published posthumously that year,[10] Schumann resorted to a gendered comparison, describing the E flat work as the more 'active, masculine, dramatic', while the B flat was 'passive, feminine, lyrical'.[11] This particular binary opposition was one on which he would draw, in addition to that of the child versus the giant, as another means of positioning Schubert and Beethoven in relation to one another, in the 1838 review of posthumous keyboard works noted above:

> Thus anyone with some degree of feeling and cultivation will recognize and distinguish Beethoven and Schubert from their opening pages. Schubert is a maidenly character compared to the other, far more talkative, softer, broader; he compares to the other as a child who plays, carefree, beneath the giants. Such is the relationship of these symphony movements to those of

Beethoven, and such is their inwardness that they could have been imagined by none other than Schubert. To be sure, he too brings in his powerful passages, and summons up massed forces; but it is always a case as of woman versus man, who commands where she pleads and persuades. All this, though, in comparison only to Beethoven; compared to others [Schubert] is man enough, and indeed the boldest and most freethinking of modern musicians.[12]

The 'symphony movements' referred to here are the movements of the Grand Duo, which Schumann was at pains to promote as the keyboard transcription of an intended symphony, not least in order to shield the work against the charge of being unidiomatic in terms of its piano writing. 'If we take it thus, we are one symphony richer,' suggested Schumann.[13] That was in 1838; his words may have come back to haunt him the following year during a visit to Schubert's brother Ferdinand in Vienna, when a genuine 'new' symphony by his deceased idol came into his hands. This was the 'Great' C major, D. 944, which Schumann subsequently had premièred under Mendelssohn's baton in Leipzig on 21 March (Bach's birthday), and published by Breitkopf & Härtel the following year. Schumann's March 1840 review of the publication was almost the last major essay on Schubert's music that he published (a review of choral and vocal works appeared in July the same year); in his now-famous description of the 'heavenly length' of the Symphony, Schumann once again reached back to Jean Paul for comparison, imagining the Symphony in terms of a fat, four-volume novel by that author 'who also can never end, and for the best reasons, [namely] in order to leave the reader to go on creating afterwards'.[14]

If it seems surprising that Schumann should have concentrated his critical attention on Schubert's instrumental compositions – in addition to the works already mentioned, he reviewed the Piano Sonatas, D. 845, 850, 894, and D. 617 in late 1835, and also lavished praise on the String Quartet in D minor ('Der Tod und das Mädchen'), D. 810 – rather than on the lieder, it is also symptomatic of his deeply ingrained sense of musical values.[15] Despite his acknowledgement, in 1843, that the Lied was perhaps the only musical genre in which genuinely significant progress had been made since Beethoven,[16] Schumann insisted again and again that it was the duty of the composers of his generation to cultivate the 'large forms': in effect, the instrumental legacy of Beethoven and Schubert. The immediate and direct impact of Schubert's four-hand keyboard and chamber music on the youthful Schumann is obvious in two compositions of 1828–9, the *VIII Polonaises . . . Op. III* (*Anh.* G1), material from which was later used in *Papillons*, Op. 2, and the ambitious Piano Quartet in C minor (*Anh.* E1), designated as his Op. 5 and influenced by the Schubert E flat Trio.[17] Schubert was again his source and inspiration in 1833, when he composed the (unpublished) *Sehnsuchtswalzer Variationen: Scènes musicales sur un thême connu* (*Anh*. F24): the '*thême*' derives from Schubert's D. 365, No. 2 and D. 972, No. 2, and the whole project formed a stage in the genesis of what was to become *Carnaval*. And as John Daverio has suggested, Schumann's breakthrough as a symphonic composer in the early 1840s was achieved in part through his finding a means to fuse Schubert's expansive style (his 'heavenly length') with a goal-directed sense of motion learned principally from Beethoven.[18] Recounting his delight at hearing the 'Great' C major in rehearsal in December 1839, he wrote to Clara that 'I was totally happy, and wished only that you should be my wife and that I also could write such symphonies.'[19] The discovery of this hitherto unknown major work by Schubert was decisive for Schumann the symphonist.

A decade earlier, Schumann had already gained first-hand experience of another symphony on the grand scale: he is known to have played Beethoven's 'Eroica' in a four-hand arrangement, probably between 1827 and 1828. This was apparently the only Beethoven score that he owned prior to 1830, and knowledge of his familiarity with Beethoven's music prior to the composer's death is scanty.[20] His intensive engagement with it dates essentially from 1830, following his move from Heidelberg to Leipzig, where, in addition to familiarizing himself with this music through his own and others' performances, Schumann furthered his close study of Beethoven's symphonic works by making piano reductions of the third *Leonore* overture and parts of the Second, Fourth, Fifth and Ninth Symphonies.[21]

But the most palpable effect of his initial response to this music is to be found in two compositions of his own: the *Etüden in Form freier Variationen über ein Thema von Beethoven*, *Anh*. F25 (1833–5); and the Symphony in G minor, *Anh*. A3 (1832–3). The slow movement of the Seventh Symphony was the source for the theme of Schumann's 'free variations', a work which he twice revised extensively, cutting the original eleven variations to nine and then seven, including various newly composed pieces along the way. This was not his first variation work: his 'Abegg' Variations had been published as his Op. 1 in 1831, and he had made various other experiments in the genre. Comparison of the three versions of the Beethoven set suggests that Schumann was at pains to play down the virtuosic conception of some of his initial ideas, although the third version remains technically very demanding. There are parallels, too, with the later *Etudes symphoniques*, Op. 13 (1837; the title of the revised [1852] version – *Etudes en forme de variations* – immediately recalls the title of *Anh*. F25), most notably in the textures of the third Beethoven variation (in the third version), and with Op. 13, Etude VI. The overall conception of Op. 13 as a rounded totality that is more than the mere sum of its individual parts considerably outstrips that of the Beethoven set, however. Only one variation (the fifth from the second version) was ever published, as 'Leides Ahnung' from *Albumblätter*, Op. 124 (1854); earlier, in 1838, Schumann had written off the whole work as an 'ungrateful idea'. The definitive final variation alludes additionally to the opening of the Ninth Symphony, and quotes from the first movement of the Seventh in a manner reminiscent of the reference to *Papillons*, Op. 2, in 'Florestan' from *Carnaval*. There are allusions to other symphonies also, making this work an important witness to Schumann's reception of Beethoven's symphonies in the early 1830s.

The Symphony in G minor remained unfinished: only the first two movements were completed, though the first was performed twice by itself, in 1832 and 1833. Incorporating elements from an earlier projected E flat major overture or symphony, the first movement opens with what appear to be clear references to the 'Eroica' (for example, the strongly triadic opening that is disrupted by an early chromatic turn in the bass at bar 5, coordinated with the introduction of a syncopated figure in the first violins); and its generous proportions, including a substantial coda following a condensed recapitulation, also suggest a concerted effort to emulate this great symphonic ancestor. The second movement, in the unexpected (and Schubertian!) key of B minor, is more original in its formal layout. A foreground ABA' design is realized in terms of an *Andantino assai Allegretto–Intermezzo quasi Scherzo–Tempo I dell' Andantino* sequence, effectively combining slow-movement and scherzo functions into a single, continuous design. The framing *Andantino* sections, however, relate to one another much as do a sonata-form exposition and recapitulation; and inasmuch as the Intermezzo takes its main thematic material from a subsidiary idea first stated by clarinets and bassoons beginning in bar 61 of the *Andantino*, it takes on a developmental function while not losing its character as an essentially separate movement.

Unfinished though it is, the Symphony in G minor readily articulates a difficulty that is fundamental to the topic of this chapter: how to discern responsibly the presence of 'influence' between one composer's works and those of another. Koßmaly had already addressed the issue shrewdly in his 1844 review: 'It goes almost without saying that one must speak, in this case, not of actual reminiscences or intentional, slavish imitation but rather of works created in a similar tone and a related spirit.' Schumann's critical writings suggest that he generally regarded 'reminiscences', where not intended as actual quotations (as, for instance in his Beethoven *Etüden*) as a sign of creative weakness; thus, the tracing of Beethoven's influence through the presence, real or imagined, of thematic allusion or reminiscence in Schumann's own compositions, may risk missing the point.[22] The apparent reference to the opening of the 'Eroica' in the Symphony in G minor may be supplemented by many other examples, notably the slow movement of the String Quartet in A, Op. 41, No. 1, with its seeming reference to the parallel movement of Beethoven's Ninth Symphony.[23] More significant, though, may be the fusing of movement-types and the thematic transformation found in the second movement of the Symphony. Schumann would have encountered both these techniques in Schubert's 'Wanderer' Fantasy, of course; but the former is also typical of several of Beethoven's late slow movements, notably those of the Ninth Symphony (which Schumann heard and was transfixed by in a performance at the Leipzig Gewandhaus on 2 April 1829)[24] and the String Quartet in A minor, Op. 132, as well as of the first movements of this quartet and its companion, Op. 130 in B flat. Schumann was an early champion of Beethoven's late music (though his writings contain unfortunately little detailed discussion of it): for example, the late quartets in E flat, Op. 127, and C sharp minor, Op. 131, struck him as works 'for whose greatness no words can be found', and which seemed to probe the furthest limits yet attained by musical art and imagination.[25] The Beethoven slow movements just noted bear comparison with Schumann's procedure in examples such as the slow movements of his Piano Quartet, Op. 47, and Piano Trio in F, Op. 80;[26] and the Beethovenian techniques of thematic transformation, concatenation of movements, and end-weighted multi-movement structures are also basic to the Second and Fourth Symphonies, among other orchestral and chamber works. Finally, one might hazard the claim that Beethoven's late music, more so than that of Schubert, would readily have furnished Schumann with rich examples of those '*apparently* logical discontinuities' of which he wrote in 1829.[27] It is in respects such as these that a Beethovenian 'tone' and 'spirit' may be heard in Schumann's music.

The work that more than any other invites us to contemplate the nature of Schumann's response to Beethoven and its modes of musical expression is his *Fantasie*, Op. 17 (1836; published 1839), with its celebrated apparent reference, at the culmination (see bars 295ff.) of the first movement, to the opening of the final song in Beethoven's song cycle *An die ferne Geliebte*.[28] Whatever the real status of this reference (Schumann never authenticated it), it is only one factor by means of which the *Fantasie* takes its place in musical history by acknowledging its debt to the past precisely in demonstrating how that past might be carried forward creatively, 'not [by] actual reminiscences or intentional, slavish imitation . . .' Reviewing a series of piano sonatas in 1839, Schumann had suggested that 'it looks as if this form has run its course, which is indeed in the nature of things[;] we should not repeat the same thing century after century and also have an eye to the new. So, write sonatas, or fantasies (what's in a name!), only let not music be forgotten meanwhile.'[29] The injunction was not so much against sonata composition per se but rather against an unthinking, mechanical adherence to outmoded formulae. The *Fantasie*, Op. 17 (it was originally to be entitled 'Sonate für Beethoven', as Schumann's contribution to the Bonn Beethoven memorial project), fully bears out this programme.

The *Fantasie* defies the usual single-movement convention for such works by being cast in three separate movements, which, however, do not follow the sequence expected of a three-movement sonata either; there are echoes here not only of Beethoven's Op. 27 sonatas *quasi una fantasia*, which likewise forgo conventional sonata sequences, and approach single-movement status by means of *attacca* directives and other inter-movement continuity devices, but also of Schubert's 'Wanderer' Fantasy, which, conversely, is a single movement whose four sections nevertheless mimic both the four-movement design of a symphony and the component sections of a sonata-form movement. In his own first movement, in which sonata-form procedures are paradoxically as obvious as they are problematic in their working-out, Schumann also demonstrates his ability to handle thematic transformation of the kind evinced in the 'Wanderer', though with the signal difference that the fundamental form of the thematic material seems to emerge only at the end of the movement, in the Beethoven allusion. Schumann thus achieves a kind of reverse teleology whereby the goal that is striven for proves to be a displaced beginning rather than a true end. And if we accept the origin of this beginning in Beethoven's song cycle of 1816, then the movement may come to seem a musical representation of Schumann's sense of music history.[30]

In considering Schumann's reception of his major precursors it is easy to forget that the state of musical scholarship in relation to their music was quite different from that of today: and 'scholarship' here includes the editing and publication of much of the actual music as well as critical writing about it. As already noted, Schumann himself was directly involved in the first performance and publication of Schubert's 'Great' C major Symphony; and it was the posthumous publication of major works such as the last three sonatas and the Impromptus, D. 935, that provided the impetus for his critical assessments of them.[31] While the availability of Beethoven's major works was much less of an issue, it was only during the 1830s that now-standard biographical materials such as Seyfried's edition of Beethoven's studies in figured bass and counterpoint (1832), the *Biographische Notizen* of Wegeler and Ries (1838) or the biography by Anton Schindler (1840) were published.[32] As for Bach, Mendelssohn's famous performance of the *Matthäus-Passion* in Berlin in March 1829 may be regarded as one of the most crucial events in the so-called 'Bach revival' of the early nineteenth century; it was a revival in which Schumann, too, played his part.

It was only in 1829, in fact, that the qualities of Bach's music began to dawn on Schumann; up to that point he had, by his own admission, been unreceptive to both Bach and Goethe.[33] Thereafter his reverence for Bach never faltered. In a brief biographical sketch, published in 1834, he remarked that 'this was a man through and through. For that reason we find in him no half measures, but rather everything whole, written for eternity'; writing of an organ recital by Mendelssohn in 1840, he considered 'how one is never finished with Bach, how he becomes ever more profound the more one listens to him'; and in his *Musikalische Haus- und Lebensregeln* written in 1848 and intended to accompany the *Album für die Jugend*, Op. 68, he admonished the young to 'be industrious in playing fugues by great masters, above all J. S. Bach. Let the "Well-tempered Klavier" be your daily bread.'[34] In addition to studying Bach's music intensively, and using it as teaching material, Schumann was instrumental in the formation of the Bach-Gesellschaft and (along with Mendelssohn) campaigned vigorously for the inauguration of a complete edition of Bach's music. During his years as conductor of the Dresden Verein für Chorgesang (1848–50) and subsequently the Düsseldorf Musikverein (1851–2) he rehearsed and performed the *Johannes-Passion* and parts of the B minor Mass and *Matthäus-Passion*, as well as other little-known choral works by Bach.[35]

After his initial study of Bach's counterpoint, first with his composition teacher Heinrich Dorn in 1831–2 and subsequently on his own initiative, Schumann would return to similarly intense activity at various stages in later life. In 1837–8 he copied out *Die Kunst der Fuge*, Anh. P3, and studied Bach's organ chorale preludes. Then, following their marriage in September 1840, he and Clara embarked on a systematic study of the '48' (they had already undertaken four-hand playing of the fugues in the early 1830s); a similar period of self-immersion in contrapuntal study began in 1845. Finally, in 1853, he busied himself with composing piano accompaniments to the sonatas and partitas for solo violin and the solo cello suites: works that were little known at the time, but which Schumann had learnt in the mid 1830s through his friendship with Ferdinand David and Karl Uhlrich. He regarded them as a 'hidden treasure' that he wished to help reveal through the addition of what he described as 'harmonic support straps'.[36]

The consequences of all this for Schumann's own music were considerable, though as always he was interested not in 'slavish imitation' but rather in the extent to which what he found in Bach could be reinterpreted for his own time.[37] He admitted that his first enthusiasm for Bach was the impetus for his *Impromptus sur une romance de Clara Wieck*, Op. 5 (1833), although these could be seen 'rather as a new form of variation'.[38] The most obvious outcome of his later Bach studies is to be seen in three keyboard works of 1845: the *Vier Fugen*, Op. 72, the *Sechs Fugen über den Namen: B. A. C. H.*,

Op. 60, for organ or pedal piano (which he considered, erroneously, might prove to be his most lasting composition), and the six canonic *Studien für den Pedal-Flügel*, Op. 56; while compositions such as the fourth movement of the 'Rhenish' Symphony or the second song, 'Stirb, Lieb' und Freud'!', from the Kerner *Liederreihe*, Op. 35, are self-conscious pastiches of the *stile antico*. But it is in the delicate handling of inner voices in character pieces such as the well-known 'Träumerei' from *Kinderszenen*, Op. 15, or the use of canon and the evocation of French overture style in numbers 4 and 8 of the *Etudes symphoniques*, Op. 13, for example, that Schumann's understanding of the continuing and enriching relevance of the contrapuntal idiom of Bach and the Baroque to a keyboard composer of the mid nineteenth century may perhaps be better gauged.[39]

That Schumann himself saw no contradiction between the genres of fugue and character piece – indeed, that he evidently viewed fugue as a genre or a compositional technique rather than as a form – is made clear in his comments (dating from 1838, the year in which *Kinderszenen* was composed) on Czerny's edition of the '48'. He approved Czerny's addition of performance indications, especially since these might help to militate against monotonous performances shaped only by emphatic marking of thematic entries. 'Most of Bach's fugues are in fact *Characterstücke* of the most superior kind,' he wrote, 'some of them genuine poetic pictures, each requiring its individual expression, its particular lights and shades.'[40] But naively to trace the use of Baroque compositional techniques and styles in Schumann's own music may yet be to pursue the wrong quarry. In an article on Schumann and the music of Bach published in 1957, Georg von Dadelsen observed that the encounter between new composition and earlier music 'has often been most powerfully and successfully effective in those cases where it remains externally hidden, where the finished composition appears to conceal it'.[41] And while citing Schumann's claim concerning the *Characterstück* qualities of Bach's fugues, as well as his remark, in a letter to Gustav Adolph Keferstein, that 'the combinatorial density, poetry, and humour of new music originate primarily in Bach',[42] von Dadelsen admits that the search for explicit Bachian or Baroque models in Schumann's piano compositions of the 1830s is largely fruitless (the Gigue, Op. 32, No. 2 being an obvious exception): what Schumann found in Bach (and Beethoven) was the expression of the 'poetic', of those 'rare conditions of the soul' of which Romantic music was, for him, the supreme mouthpiece.[43] The Schumann *Characterstück* is, as it were, a 'metapoetic' expression of the poetic qualities found in Bach;[44] the relationship is one that is more felt than literally demonstrable. But while Schumann emphasized the uniqueness and individuality of every Bach fugue, a somewhat different aesthetic bearing on his own cycles of *Characterstücke* may inhere in his response in 1852–3 to Bach's solo violin sonatas and partitas (WoO8). Although the initial project to compose piano accompaniments evidently involved only a selection of movements from these works, Schumann treated them all, telling the publisher Härtel that 'on the whole the individual movements of the sonatas cohere so intimately that omissions would only mar the original'.[45] Although an unspoken desire to maximize his financial gain ought not be disallowed here, this remark has potential implications for Schumann's own collections or cycles of sharply characterized and individuated miniatures.

'The most important form of influence is that which provokes the most original and most personal work.'[46] Thus has Charles Rosen restated von Dadelsen's view, noted above. Indeed, what is perhaps most remarkable about Schumann's relationship to his three great forebears is his seeming unconcern about any 'anxiety of influence'; such anxiety as has been manifested has largely been the prerogative of an earlier generation of critics who, for example, preferred to sustain a myth of Schumann's imperfect mastery of Classical sonata form rather than confront his creative engagement with its principles.[47] Influence there surely was; but while many composers would feel oppressed and even inhibited by the perceived challenge posed by a musical heritage of such range and quality – recall Brahms's gloomy evocation of that 'giant' (Beethoven) marching along behind him[48] – Schumann appears to have revelled in the imperative to engage with it as a precondition for progress and the creation of 'the most original and most personal work'. We may speak of 'Schumann the traditionalist' if, with Stravinsky, we understand that 'far from implying the repetition of what has been, tradition presupposes the reality of what endures. It appears as an heirloom, a heritage that one receives on condition of making it bear fruit before passing it on to one's descendants.'[49] Or, as Schumann himself had put it already in 1831, 'the future should be the higher echo of the past'.[50]

Notes

1. Carl Koßmaly, 'On Robert Schumann's piano compositions (1844)', trans. Susan Gillespie, in *Schumann and His World*, ed. R. Larry Todd (Princeton: Princeton University Press, 1994), pp. 307–8. The original appeared in 'Ueber Robert Schumann's Claviercompositionen', *Allgemeine musikalische Zeitung*, 46 (1844), col. 17.
2. Müller's book was published in Leipzig in two volumes, in 1830. On Schumann's familiarity with it, see Bischoff, *Monument*, pp. 246ff. For an English-language summary of Schumann's view of music history, see John Daverio, *Robert Schumann: Herald of a 'New Poetic Age'* (New York and Oxford, 1997), pp. 118–30.
3. Robert Schumann, 'Zur Eröffnung des Jahrganges 1835', in Robert Schumann, *Gesammelte Schriften über Musik und Musiker*, ed. Gerd Nauhaus (hereafter *GS*) (Wiesbaden, 1985), vol. I, p. 60; unless otherwise indicated, this and all further translations are mine. The original, slightly different text, appears in *Neue Zeitschrift für Musik* (*NZfM*), 2 (1835), p. 3.
4. *GS*, I, pp. 69–70.

5. Schumann's 'es beginne eine neue Zeit' resonates with God's 'es werde Licht!' (Genesis 1:3), as also with 'Siehe, ich mache alles neu' (Revelation, 21:5).
6. *GS*, III, p. 53; II, p. 236.
7. The story was reported by Schumann's friend Emil Flechsig: see Ernst Burger, *Robert Schumann: Eine Lebenschronik in Bildern und Dokumenten* (Mainz, 1999), p. 64.
8. References to these works are found in Schumann's autobiographical sketches 'Materialien zu einem Lebenslauf' and 'Älteste musikalische Erinnerungen', both preserved at the Robert-Schumann-Haus, Zwickau; see Burger, *Schumann*, p. 52, and Maintz, *Franz Schubert*, pp. 17–19.
9. Burger, *Schumann*, p. 78. Schumann was very fond of (not necessarily consistent) analogies between composers and authors, and music and literature, at this time: for example, see also Robert Schumann, *Tagebücher* (hereafter *TB*), vol. I: 1827–38, ed. Georg Eismann (Basel and Frankfurt am Main, 1971), pp. 95–7.
10. For a detailed study of Schumann's reception of the Trio in E flat, see John Daverio, *Crossing Paths: Schubert, Schumann, and Brahms* (New York, 2002), Chapter 1.
11. *GS*, I, p. 303.
12. *Ibid.*, II, p. 238.
13. *Ibid.*
14. *GS*, III, p. 201; for the subsequent review of choral and vocal works see *Gesammelte Schriften über Musik und Musiker von Robert Schumann*, ed. Martin Kreisig (Leipzig, 1914) (hereafter Kreisig), vol. II, pp. 336–7.
15. For the sonatas, see *GS*, I, pp. 202–7; for D. 810, see *GS*, II, p. 236 and III, p. 53.
16. *GS*, IV, p. 263.
17. In mid 1846 Schumann recalled the Trio of the third movement of the Piano Quartet as including a passage which in 1828 had struck him as 'Romantic, in which a spirit different from that of earlier music revealed itself, a new poetic life seemed to open up to me': *TB*, vol. II: 1836–54, ed. Gerd Nauhaus (Basel and Frankfurt am Main, 1987), p. 402; for an opinion as to the passage in question see Daverio, *Schumann*, p. 54.
18. Daverio, *Schumann*, pp. 226–8.
19. Robert und Clara Schumann, *Briefwechsel: kritische Gesamtausgabe*, ed. Eva Weissweiler, vol. II (Basel and Frankfurt am Main, 1987), p. 826.
20. Bischoff, *Monument*, pp. 40–4, and 415–72, where an exhaustive catalogue of Schumann's encounters with Beethoven's works is provided. Bischoff also notes (p. 86) Schumann's playing of the 'Archduke' Trio, Op. 97, and the Piano Trios, Op. 1, in 1829, and argues for a limited influence of these works on Schumann's Piano Quartet in C minor.
21. Anh. P4–9. See the facsimile reproductions in Bischoff, *Monument*, pp. 488–504, and the associated discussion on pp. 143–8.
22. See, for example, Schumann's review of Louis Hetsch's *Grosses Duo*, Op. 13, in *GS*, IV, pp. 275–6, where the resemblance between the main theme of the first movement and that of Beethoven's 'Emperor' Concerto is 'excusable' thanks to the composer's overall warm treatment of it. On a related point, it may be noted that Schumann evidently regarded overt inter-movement thematic relationships within a composition as an aesthetic deficiency: see his remarks on Loewe's *Grande Sonate brillante*, Op. 41, in *GS*, I, pp. 93–7.
23. On the general issue, see R. Larry Todd, 'On quotation in Schumann's music', in *Schumann and His World*, ed. R. Larry Todd (Princeton, 1994), pp. 80–112; Christopher Alan Reynolds, *Motives for Allusion: Context and Content in Nineteenth-Century Music* (Cambridge, MA, and London, 2003); and Charles Rosen, 'Influence: plagiarism and inspiration', *Nineteenth Century Music*, 4 (1980), 87–100.
24. *TB*, I, p. 185 and p. 453, n. 178.
25. *GS*, III, p. 53. Schumann's enthusiasm for Beethoven's late quartets is also evidenced by his publication in 1839, in the *NZfM*, of a series of articles on the quartets written by Herrmann Hirschbach: for details and further references, see my article 'Schumann's monument to Beethoven', *Nineteenth Century Music*, 14 (1991), 249. Particularly telling in the present context is Schumann's evident fascination with the formal novelty of Hirschbach's quartets, as witness his letter to Clara of 13 July 1838, cited here.
26. Schenker noted the kinship of the slow movement of Op. 47 to that of the Ninth Symphony in his monograph on the latter work: see Heinrich Schenker, *Beethoven's Ninth Symphony: A Portrayal of Its Musical Content*, trans. and ed. John Rothgeb (New Haven and London, 1992), pp. 192–6.

27. The relevant literature on late Beethoven is extensive. Beyond Joseph Kerman's insistence on 'dissociation', particularly in relation to the String Quartet, Op. 130 (Kerman, *The Beethoven Quartets* (London, 1967), pp. 303–25), may be cited Daniel K. L. Chua, *The 'Galitzin' Quartets of Beethoven* (Princeton, NJ, 1995) and Theodor W. Adorno, *Beethoven: The Philosophy of Music*, trans. Edmund Jephcott (Cambridge, 1998), esp. pp. 123–37 and 154–61, on 'The late style'. Schumann's 1829 remarks on Schubert might bear further scrutiny in relation to Adorno's claim (p. 13) that 'the Beethovenian form is an integral whole, in which each individual moment is determined by its function within that whole only to the extent that these individual moments contradict and cancel each other, yet are preserved on a higher level within the whole'.

28. For a full discussion of this work, which obviates extended discussion here, see Nicholas Marston, *Schumann: 'Fantasie'*, Op. 17 (Cambridge, 1992); also Berthold Hoeckner, 'Schumann and Romantic distance', *JAMS*, 50 (1997), 55–132, subsequently incorporated into the same author's *Programming the Absolute: Nineteenth-Century German Music and the Hermeneutics of the Moment* (Princeton and Oxford, 2002), Chapter 2.

29. *GS*, III, p. 80.

30. Daverio, *Schumann*, p. 103, notes the formal similarity between the second movement of the Symphony in G minor and the first of the *Fantasie*.

31. On Schumann's response to the Impromptus, D. 935, see Daverio, *Crossing Paths*, Chapter 2.

32. Schumann owned copies of all three books; for more on Schumann's reception of Beethoven literature, see Bischoff, *Monument*, pp. 242–62.

33. See Bodo Bischoff, 'Das Bach-Bild Robert Schumanns', in *Bach und die Nachwelt*, ed. Michael Heinemann and Hans-Joachim Hinrichsen, vol.I, 1750–1850 (Laaber, 1997), pp. 421–99 for relevant quotations from Schumann's *Selbstbiographische Notizen* (*c.* 1840), facsimile, ed. Martin Schoppe (Zwickau, n. d.).

34. Kreisig, II, p. 201; I, p. 492 (also *GS*, III, p. 256); II, p. 166. On the *Album*, see Bernhard R. Appel, '"Actually, taken directly from family life": Robert Schumann's *Album für die Jugend*', in *Schumann and His World*, ed. Todd, pp. 171–202, where Appel notes (p. 176) Schumann's intention at one stage to include arrangements of works by Bach, Handel, Gluck, Haydn, Mozart, Beethoven, Weber and Mendelssohn so as to form 'a kind of representative tour through the historical progression of great composers'.

35. See Bischoff, 'Das Bach-Bild Robert Schumanns', pp. 475–9 for full details.

36. Letter to Hermann Härtel, 17 January 1853: see Robert Schumann, *Robert Schumanns Briefe. Neue Folge*, ed. F. Gustav Jansen (Leipzig, 1904), p. 480.

37. Commentators have inevitably trawled Schumann's music for quotations and references to specific works by Bach: the second of the *Vier Fugen*, Op. 72 seems clearly enough to relate to the subject of the Fugue in B flat minor from Book 1 of the '48', for example; and Susan Wollenberg has drawn attention to the 'modelling' relationship of the Piano Quintet to the Prelude in E flat from the same book: Susan Wollenberg, 'Schumann's Piano Quintet in E flat: The Bach legacy', *The Music Review*, 52 (1991), 299–305. The coda to the finale of the Quintet is of course a celebrated example of Schumann's contrapuntal artifice that owes as much to the corresponding part of Mozart's 'Jupiter' Symphony as it does to its apparent Bach model.

38. *Selbstbiographische Notizen*, quoted in Bischoff, 'Das Bach-Bild Robert Schumanns', p. 428. The combination in Op. 5 of two themes, one a basso ostinato and the other a melody, recalls Beethoven's 'Prometheus' Variations, Op. 35, though it is not certain that Schumann would have known this work at this stage.

39. The slow movement of the F major Piano Trio, Op. 80, again bears mention here, as an example of unobtrusive strict canonic writing between cello and piano left hand (see bars 1–7) in a thoroughly non-Baroque context.

40. *GS*, III, p. 5.

41. Georg von Dadelsen, 'Robert Schumann und die Musik Bachs', *Archiv für Musikwissenschaft*, 14 (1957), 46.

42. Letter of 31 January 1841: see *Briefe*, ed. Jansen, pp. 177f.

43. *GS*, II, pp. 263–4.

44. Comparing the Gigue from Op. 32 with *Kreisleriana*, No. 8, von Dadelsen ('Robert Schumann', p. 51) remarks that 'nur ein traumhaftes Phantasiebild an die "Stimmung", die "Seelenzustände", die das Vorbild hervorrief, bleibt zurück', and refers to a process of 'Weiterdichten'.

45. Letter to Härtel, 17 January 1853 (see *Briefe*, ed. Jansen, p. 479).

46. Rosen, 'Influence', p. 88.

47. Two important revisionist texts are Linda Correll Roesner, 'Schumann's "parallel" forms', *Nineteenth Century Music*, 14 (1991), 265–78, and Joel Lester, 'Robert Schumann and sonata forms', *Nineteenth Century Music*, 18 (1995), 189–210.

48. In a remark to the conductor Hermann Levi made in the early 1870s, see Max Kalbeck, *Johannes Brahms*, vol. I (Berlin: Deutsche Brahms-Gesellschaft m. b. H., 1908), p. 165. It was Schumann, of course, who in his famous article 'Neue Bahnen' (*NZfM*, 39 (1853), 185–6) hailed Brahms in frankly messianic terms as the true inheritor of the legacy of German instrumental composition. On the relationship of both Schumann and Brahms to the Beethovenian symphonic tradition, see Mark Evan Bonds, *After Beethoven: Imperatives of Originality in the Symphony* (Cambridge, MA and London, 1996).

49. Igor Stravinsky, *Poetics of Music: In the Form of Six Lessons*, trans. Arthur Knodel and Ingolf Dahl (Cambridge, MA, 1970), p. 75.

50. *TB*, I, p. 304.

PART II

Works

4 Piano works I: a world of images

JOHN DAVERIO

I

'In the dizzying realm of the intermezzo'

Schumann's name has been and probably always will be inextricably linked with the piano. When in July 1830, at the age of twenty, he decided once and for all to pursue a career in music, it was as a pianist that he hoped to make his mark. In accordance with what had long been the case among performing artists, this entailed the production of a substantial portion of the repertory that he would be presenting in both private and public venues. During the course of the previous years Schumann had already tried his hand at composing for a variety of media. The breadth of his early forays into composition is evident in the pieces, not all of them completed, to which the young and largely untrained composer assigned the opus numbers 'I' through 'V': a setting of Psalm 150 for vocal soloists, piano and orchestra (Op. I, 1822) (*Anh.* I10); eleven Lieder, some on texts by Schumann himself (Op. II, 1827–8) (*Anh.* M2); a set of eight polonaises for piano, four hands, conceived under the spell of Schubert (Op. III, 1828) (*Anh.* G1); a fragmentary set of variations for piano on a theme by the musically gifted Prince Louis Ferdinand of Prussia (Op. IV, 1828) (*Anh.* G2); and a piano quartet in C minor (Op. V, 1828–9) (*Anh.* E1).

Once Schumann had firmly resolved to master the piano, however, that instrument became the touchstone of his creative efforts. Indeed, in the decade from 1829 to 1839, he composed almost exclusively for solo piano. Granted, during that period he aspired to write for larger and more imposing forces, a tendency to which the drafts for a piano concerto in F (1830) (*Anh.* B3), the sketches for a 'Hamlet' symphony (1831–2) (*Anh.* A2) and the unfinished Symphony in G minor (1832–3) (*Anh.* A3) bear witness.[1] But just as we do a disservice to Schumann's later symphonic output by viewing it as piano music writ large, so too the early keyboard music represents more than a sublimation of his urge to write for orchestra. Even after it became evident to him in 1832 that, owing to a curious malady in the middle finger of his right hand, he would have to abandon his dream of a performing career, the keyboard remained the principal conduit for his creative energy for some time to come.

Table 4.1 *Schumann's keyboard music, 1827–36*

Piano Concerto in E minor (*Anh.* B1)
- preliminary sketches, 1827

Eight Polonaises for piano, four hands, 'Op. III' (*Anh.* G1)
- comp. 1828; publ. 1933
- portions from Nos. 4 and 7 reused in *Papillons*, Nos. 11 and 5

Variations on a Theme by Prince Louis Ferdinand of Prussia for piano, four hands, 'Op. IV' (*Anh.* G2)
- fragment, comp. 1828

Piano Concerto in E Flat (*Anh.* B2)
- preliminary sketches, 1828

Thème sur le nom Abegg varié pour le Pianoforte et dedié à Mademoiselle Pauline Comtesse d'Abegg, Op. 1
- comp. 1829–30; publ. 1831
- projected version for piano and orchestra

Toccata, Op. 7
- first version comp. 1829–30
- second version comp. 1833; publ. 1834
- orig. titles: *Etude fantastique en double-sons*; *Exercice fantastique*

Papillons, Op. 2
- comp. 1830–1; publ. 1831
- draws on *8 Polonaises* (1828) and six waltzes (1829–30)

Andantino
- comp. 1830; based on Lied *Im Herbste* (1828) (*Anh.* M2)
- used later in Piano Sonata in G minor, Op. 22

Piano Concerto in F (*Anh.* B3)
- unfinished; comp. 1830

Allegro, Op. 8
- comp. 1831; publ. 1835
- orig. intended for a piano sonata in B minor

Etudes in the form of free variations on a theme by Beethoven (*Anh.* F25)
- based on second movement (*Allegretto*) of Beethoven, Symphony No. 7, Op. 92
- first version comp. 1831; second and third versions comp. 1833–5; first and second versions publ. 1976

Variations on the Zigeunermarsch from Weber's Preziosa (*Anh.* F9)
- unfinished; comp. 1831–2

Variations on an original theme in G (*Anh.* F7)
- unfinished; comp. 1831–2

Etudes pour le pianoforte d'après les Caprices de Paganini, Op. 3
- comp. 1832; publ. 1832

Intermezzi, Op. 4
- comp. 1832; publ. 1833
- No. 4 draws on Lied *Hirtenknabe* (1828)

Impromptu, Op. 124, No. 1; *Leides Ahnung*, Op. 124, No. 2; *Scherzino*, Op. 124, No. 3; *Burla*, Op. 124, No. 12; *Larghetto*, Op. 124, No. 13; *Walzer*, Op. 124, No. 15
- comp. 1832; publ. 1853 in *Albumblätter*, Op. 124

Fandango in F minor (*Anh.* F15)
- comp. 1832
- reworked as first movement of Sonata in F sharp minor, Op. 11

Canon on 'An Alexis send' Ich Dich' (*Anh.* F19)
- comp. 1832; publ. 1858

Impromptus sur une Romance de Clara Wieck, Op. 5
- comp. 1833; publ. 1833
- second version publ. 1850
- based on Clara Wieck, *Romance varié*, Op. 3

Six Etudes de concert pour le pianoforte d'après des Caprices de Paganini, Op. 10
- comp. 1833; publ. 1835
- orig. publ. 'Op. X'

Pianoforte-Sonate. Clara zugeeignet von Florestan und Eusebius [Sonata in F sharp minor], Op. 11
- comp. 1833–6; publ. 1836
- first movement based on *Fandango* (1832)
- second movement based on Lied *An Anna II* (1828)

Table 4.1 (cont.)

Sonata in G minor, Op. 22
- comp. 1833–5, 1838; publ. 1839
- second movement (*Andantino*) comp. 1830
- new finale (*Rondo: Presto*) comp. 1838
- orig. finale (*Presto passionato*) publ. 1866

Variations on a Nocturne by Chopin (Anh. F26)
- unfinished; comp. 1835–1836
- based on Chopin, *Nocturne*, Op. 15, No. 3

Variations on Schubert's Sehnsuchtswalzer (Anh. F24)
- unfinished; comp. 1833
- opening reused in *Préambule* of *Carnaval*

Carnaval: Scènes mignonnes . . . sur quatre notes, Op. 9
- comp. 1834–5; publ. 1837

XII Etudes symphoniques, Op. 13
- comp. 1834–5; publ. 1837
- second version publ. 1852
- five variations rejected by Schumann publ. 1873

Concert sans orchestre, Op. 14
- comp. 1835–6; publ. 1836
- second version, with *Scherzo*, publ. 1853 as *Grande Sonate*

Walzer, Op. 124, No. 4; *Romanze*, Op. 124, No. 11; *Elfe*, Op. 124, No. 17
- comp. 1835; publ. 1853 in *Albumblätter*, Op. 124

Fantasie, Op. 17
- comp. 1836–8; publ. 1839

Albumblatt, Op. 99, No. 6
- comp. 1836; publ. 1852 in *Bunte Blätter*, Op. 99

Fantasietanz, Op. 124, No. 5; *Ländler*, Op. 124, No. 7
- comp. 1836; publ. 1853 in *Albumblätter*, Op. 124

Sonata in F minor (Anh. F28)
- unfinished; comp. 1836

Titles of published works are given as they appear in the first edition.
Abbreviations: comp. = composed; orig. = original(ly); publ. = published

As indicated in Table 4.1, by 1836 Schumann had already made significant contributions to the entire array of early nineteenth-century keyboard genres, ranging from the dance, the character piece, and the theme and variations, on one end of the generic spectrum, to the sonata and the fantasy, on the other. In his critical writings, Schumann frequently mused on the distinction between what he called the 'smaller' and the 'higher' sub-genres of piano music, and it is clear that he was in two minds about both. As early as 1834, the year in which he founded the *Neue Zeitschrift für Musik* (*NZfM*), Schumann was advising young composers (such as J. C. Kessler) to devote themselves less assiduously to 'the smallest though wittiest of artistic forms'; yet eight years later, in a review of Ludwig Berger's complete works, he noted that 'one should not underestimate the value of short pieces, for the performance as well as the enjoyment of such concentrated compositions requires heightened powers of concentration from players and listeners alike'.[2] Similarly, although in a review-essay of 1839 he commented wistfully on the sonata's having 'run its life course', he conceded in the same breath that 'this is indeed in the order of things, since we cannot repeat ourselves for centuries, but rather should think about producing what is genuinely new'.³

To a certain extent, these critical observations reflected issues that Schumann had already confronted in his own compositions. Among the more notable features of his earlier keyboard music is its generic fluidity, its straddling of the boundaries between strictly segregated musical types. The fine line between dance and character piece, for instance, is evident from the compositional history of *Papillons*, which includes materials from the *Eight polonaises* of 1828 and a set of six waltzes drafted soon thereafter. Few if any of Schumann's keyboard pieces evince an unequivocal generic profile, displaying instead what Friedrich Schlegel, perhaps the leading voice of early German Romanticism, called the 'Romantic imperative', the demand for a 'mixture of all poetic types'.⁴ Schumann's tendencies in this direction are particularly evident in his sets of variations, which combine that form with a wide variety of other markers, including the dance and the virtuoso showpiece (*Abegg* Variations), the étude and the contrapuntal study (*Etuden in Form freier Variationen über ein Beethovensches Thema*), and the character piece and fugue (*Impromptus*). In a stunning realization of the 'Romantic imperative', nearly all of these genres – variation, dance, character piece, étude, virtuoso show-stopper, contrapuntal tour de force – are fused in the *Etudes symphoniques*.

The tension between 'smaller' and 'higher' forms distinguishes a large proportion of this repertory as well. In his early cycles of character pieces (*Papillons, Intermezzi, Carnaval*), Schumann staged a rapprochement between the requirements of both types, though here the accent admittedly falls on the striking details projected by the miniature forms in the series. (This quality did not exactly ingratiate Schumann with mid-nineteenth-century listeners; what Carl Koßmaly wrote of the *Davidsbündlertänze* – that the pieces in the cycle were 'dashed off more like sketches than fully executed character pieces'⁵ – might just as easily have been said of *Papillons* or *Carnaval*.) Conversely, Schumann's keyboard works in the 'higher' forms bear palpable traces of the small-scale genres. The slow movements of both the Sonata in F sharp minor and the Sonata in G minor, for example, are based on songs composed in 1828: *An Anna II* (the source for the *Aria* of the former sonata) and *Im Herbste* (reworked in the *Andantino* of the latter). The most obvious manifestation of the dialectic between small- and large-scale composition occurs in the first movement of the *Fantasie*, which, as Nicholas Marston has proven almost beyond the shadow of a doubt, was first conceived as an independent fantasy-movement called *Ruines* in June 1836.⁶ Just past the midpoint of the movement, Schumann interrupts what has been proceeding as an unusual but still recognizable sonata-form design with a quasi-independent character piece in C minor – *Im Legendenton* – of almost a hundred bars in length. Entitled *Romanza* in the autograph score (and perhaps drafted initially as a separate work), the *Im Legendenton* represents an incursion of a 'small though witty artform' into the realm of the 'higher forms'. The contrast in the *Fantasie* between two quite distinct worlds – the sentimental, 'artless' world of the *Im Legendenton* and the 'artful' world of the surrounding sonata-form frame – has further parallels in Schumann's attempts to establish common ground between lyrical expression and contrapuntal rigour in the *Impromptus* and the *Etudes symphoniques*.

While these issues of form and genre are vital for an understanding of Schumann's art, there are other, equally crucial factors that cut across the various sub-genres exemplified by his early keyboard music. Taking their cue from nineteenth-century critical strategies, a number of recent writers (the present one included) have emphasized the 'poetic' element in Schumann's piano music – an element that played a decisive role in his approach to both the smaller and larger forms. The eccentric prose of his favourite author, Jean Paul, affected not only his variation sets and cycles of miniatures (the *Abegg* Variations, the *Intermezzi* and *Carnaval* all owe something to the masked ball, a typically Jean-Paulian motif), but also his essays in the more extended forms (the Sonata in F sharp minor was 'dedicated' to Clara Wieck by 'Florestan and Eusebius', imaginary alter egos modelled in part on the twin-brother protagonists of Jean Paul's *Flegeljahre*, Vult and Walt).[8]

To a degree that is difficult to measure with precision, this music is also an embodiment of lived experience – above all, the experience of being in love. If at some level the *Etudes symphoniques* and *Carnaval* reflect Schumann's feelings for Ernestine von Fricken (his fiancée from the autumn of 1834 until about a year later), then the *Impromptus*, the Sonata in F sharp minor, the *Concert sans orchestre* and the *Fantasie* were even more intimately bound up with the joys and sorrows occasioned by the quest for the love of his life: Clara Wieck. At the time that his passion for Clara came to full bloom, Schumann's professional life was revolving increasingly around his editorship of the *NZfM*, an activity that was not without consequences for his compositional efforts. Indeed, there was a striking reciprocity between his critical and his creative pursuits. In reading Schumann's criticism, one often has the impression that he is not projecting his remarks outward, to an audience of readers, but inward, to himself. Schumann's frequent exhortations that young composers tackle the 'higher' forms, for instance, invite an interpretation of this kind. Moreover, his piano works sometimes bore surprising traces of his experience as a critic. To cite a telling example: the indications *Fortsetzung* and *Fortsetzung und Schluß* in the eighth and last of the *Novelletten*, Op. 21, composed in the later 1830s, derive directly from journalistic practice, lending to the music the appearance of an essay or long review published in serial format. In an even broader sense, Schumann's earlier compositions might well be considered as critiques, though purely in sound, of the contemporaneous trends he analysed so astutely in the pages of the *NZfM*.

In sum, literature, autobiography and criticism all offer potent lenses through which to view Schumann's keyboard music. Furthermore, any number of passages from his critical writings, correspondence and diaries can be adduced in support of all these approaches. Another avenue of inquiry, also hinted at by Schumann himself, is worthy of closer consideration. While discussing the pros and cons of programme music in his 1835 review of Berlioz's *Symphonie fantastique*, Schumann made some suggestive remarks on the relationship between aural and visual modes of understanding:

> It is certainly an error to think that composers take up pen and paper with the miserable intention of expressing, depicting or portraying [*malen*] this or that. Yet one should not underestimate the importance of fortuitous influences and external impressions. While the musical imagination is at work, so too, though often unconsciously, the eye is just as active as the ear, seizing powerfully upon certain contours amidst the sounds and tones than can condense and develop into distinct shapes as the music proceeds. The more that the musically related elements embody thoughts or images engendered along with the tones, the more poetic or plastic the expression of the composition will be.[9]

Although this passage deals chiefly with the role of visual factors in the genesis and perception of musical works, it also implies that, in certain cases, music may actually take on the structure of an image. As some of Schumann's contemporaries observed, though not always with approval, his own music was notable for its embodiment of visual properties in this immanent sense. In the opinion of Ignaz Moscheles, for example, the opening movement of the Sonata in F sharp minor 'is rich in images, in so far as each period possesses its own colours and contours, but they recur unchanged, without forming a single bouquet, and without blending into the whole'.[10] More recent writers, among them the critic and consummate Schumann-lover Roland Barthes, have been more indulgent. In Barthes's view, Schumann fashioned an imaginative world in which 'nothing lasts long', where 'each movement interrupts the next'. Invoking a metaphor drawn from Schumann's own fund of genre designations, he situates the composer's output in 'the realm of the intermezzo, a rather dizzying notion when it extends to all of music'.[11] In another essay, Barthes related these observations to the imagistic essence of Schumann's music: 'The sequence of intermezzi has as its function not to make contrasts speak but rather to fulfil a radiant writing, which is then recognizable much closer to painted space than to the spoken chain. Music, in short, at this level, is an image, not a language.'[12] Put another way, the discursive model for much of

Schumann's music is less the continuous unfolding of events in a narrative than the discontinuous succession of frames in a film. And while, in the passage just quoted, Barthes is primarily concerned with *Kreisleriana*, his comments resonate with earlier keyboard cycles such as *Papillons*, the *Intermezzi* and *Carnaval*.

In the following discussion, we will explore more fully the significance of the image – both as generative stimulus and immanent structure – in Schumann's early piano music. As we will see, the composer's world of images was informed, in equal parts, by humour, mystery and profound feeling.

II

Playful images

With the *Abegg* Variations, Op. 1, the first work completed after he decided to devote himself full-time to music, Schumann made his official debut as a composer. As Alfred Einstein once noted, the 'Opus 1 is always the work with which a musician is intent upon introducing himself to the public, with which he wishes to prove his legitimate claims'.[13] How did Schumann introduce himself to the world and what sorts of claims did he make in his Opus 1?

If we accept Schumann's view of the dance as the genre of 'modern' music in which art 'is most sensuously and blatantly allied with life', then in the *Abegg* Variations – a set of three strict variations and an improvisatory *Cantabile* on a waltz-like theme, capped off by an extended *Finale alla Fantasia* – he appears as a mediator between these two realms.[14] In modelling his work on Moscheles's flashy Variations on *La Marche d'Alexandre*, Op. 32, which Schumann had performed in Heidelberg to great applause in January 1830, Schumann also lays claim to entry into the ranks of virtuoso pianist-composers, whose main representatives then included (apart from Moscheles) J. N. Hummel, John Field and Henri Herz.[15]

Above all, however, the composer of the *Abegg* Variations entered the public arena as something of a prankster. The Countess Pauline d'Abegg – whose last name, 'translated' into musical pitches, provided the point of departure for Schumann's theme – was almost surely a fabrication. According to Anton Töpken, a friend from his Heidelberg days, Schumann identified Pauline d'Abegg as a young aristocrat from Mannheim and the inamorata of another, unnamed friend, though Töpken knew nothing of a close relationship between the youthful composer and the countess. Furthermore, her name does not appear on the list of over forty family members, friends and colleagues to whom Schumann planned to send copies of the printed opus. It is odd, to say the least, that he would have failed to arrange for a copy of his Opus 1 to be sent to its noble dedicatee (for the full title and dedication of the first edition of the *Abegg* Variations, issued by the Leipzig publisher Friedrich Kistner, see Table 4.1) – unless, that is, she never existed in the first place.[16]

A further element of play in Schumann's Opus 1 is evident in his approach to the variation principle. The theme itself is the product of a number of variation techniques (including sequence and melodic inversion) applied to the five-note cell, A–B–E–G–G, which serves as the work's opening gesture. Of course, the practice of deriving a musical idea from the letters in a name was hardly new. Traceable to the *sogetti cavati* of Renaissance vocal polyphony, it emerged again in the fairly large body of contrapuntal works from the late eighteenth and nineteenth centuries based on the pitch-cell B♭–A–C–B, the musical equivalent of 'Bach'.[17] Jean Paul underscored the sportive quality of the technique in a scene from *Flegeljahre*, the young Schumann's favourite novel. While Walt Harnisch is tuning one of the B flat strings on the ramshackle piano in the home of the bookbinder Paßvogel, three of its other strings (A, C and B) snap simultaneously. The startled onlookers exclaim 'Ach!' in unison, prompting Paßvogel to add: 'Aus dem Ach wird ja ein Bach' ('Indeed, every "Ach" becomes a "Bach"').[18] That Schumann too would have understood the practice of musical encipherment as an essentially playful enterprise is made explicit in a letter to Moscheles of 23 August 1837. Commenting on his recently published *Carnaval*, Schumann predicted that 'deciphering my masked ball will be a real game for you'.[19]

Based on a series of musical analogues for the name 'Asch' (Ernestine von Fricken's home town), *Carnaval* amplifies the generative principles of the *Abegg* Variations in striking and unusual ways. Schumann calls the cycle's basic pitch-cells 'Sphinxes', and although he presents three of them in archaic, breve notation between the eighth and ninth character pieces – (1) E♭–C–B–A = SCHA; (2) A♭–C–B = AsCH; (3) A–E♭–C–B = ASCH – only the latter two play a constructive role in the work as a whole.[20] In equating the decipherment of his 'masked ball' with a game, Schumann invoked two colourful metaphors for the aesthetic experience embodied in what is perhaps the most Jean-Paulian of his cycles of character pieces. The 'maskers' are primarily members of his semi-fictional *Davidsbund* (Band of David) – Eusebius, Florestan, Chiarina (i.e. Clara) – some of whom arrive in costume as *commedia dell'arte* figures: Pierrot, Arlequin, Pantalon and Colombine. Chopin and Paganini put in appearances as well, and the musical portraits of the entire company of revellers alternate with stylized dances in which the waltz clearly dominates. Furthermore, the little pieces in Schumann's *Carnaval* constitute a 'game' for the player (or listener) and the composer alike. While the former is engaged in the act of decipherment, the latter approaches the process of encipherment as if it, too, were a kind of game. Like all games, this one has rules, the most important of which might be formulated as follows:

(1) Select, as the basis of your cycle, a name whose letters can be readily 'translated' into pitches.
(2) Begin every piece in the cycle with one of the basic (i.e. untransposed or otherwise varied) forms of the enciphered word. (In *Carnaval*, there are only two exceptions: *Pierrot* and *Paganini*.)
(3) The basic form may be associated with any rhythm, articulation or dynamic level, but note repetitions are to be avoided, unless the generating name includes repeated letters (e.g. 'Abegg').
(4) Generally, the basic form should appear first in the upper part.
(5) The piece should employ the basic form more than any other.
(6) When the basic form or one of its derivatives appears within the body of a piece, it should be placed at the beginning of a phrase.
(7) The pitch material of the basic form may be varied in several ways. It may appear transposed, in sequence, in inversion, or in retrograde; it may initiate longer melodies; individual pitches from the basic form may be chromatically altered; the basic form may be embedded in a longer phrase; its pitches may be permuted; finally, derivatives of the basic form may be contrapuntally combined.

Schumann's exploration of the correspondences between pitches and letters of the alphabet in the *Abegg* Variations, *Carnaval* and other pieces large and small[21] has fed into the popular belief that he often approached his art as a kind of cryptography in tones. We will consider Eric Sams's theories to that effect in the final section of this chapter. For now, suffice it to say that the *Abegg* Variations and *Carnaval* offer little evidence of interest, on Schumann's part, in cryptographic methods. Derived from two Greek words, *krúvo* (hide) and *gráfo* (write), cryptography is the practice of encoding texts in such a way that only those who possess a key to the code (or can deduce it) will be able to understand the enciphered text. According to Johann Klüber, author of a comprehensive manual on the subject published in 1809: 'The art of secret writing, also known as cryptography or stenography, shows us how to inscribe thoughts so that what has been written, or its actual contents, will remain a secret.'[22] By this standard, Schumann was a singularly inept cryptographer, for the invariable tendency in his pieces built from musical 'ciphers' is to reveal, not to conceal. In his Opus 1, he boldly announces the 'secret' message in the title: *Thème sur le nom Abegg*. Similarly, the full title of *Carnaval* indicates that the cycle is based 'sur quatre notes' ('on four notes'), which Schumann obligingly lays out in the 'Sphinxes' and whose meaning can be easily inferred from the tenth piece, entitled *A.S.C.H.- S.C.H.A. (Lettres dansantes)*. In other words, Schumann behaves less like a cryptographer than an excitable child who gives himself away during a game of hide-and-seek by giggling from behind the sofa or under the table.

This brings us to our central point. Schumann and his contemporaries would not have thought of, let's say, the 'Sphinxes' in *Carnaval* as bona fide ciphers, but rather as *rebuses*, the picture puzzles that found an especially receptive home in the children's books of the early and mid nineteenth century. There can be little doubt that Schumann was familiar with this literature. Indeed, it is hardly a coincidence that he called upon a figure such as Johann Peter Lyser to design the title page of *Carnaval*.[23] A member of the circle of *Davidsbündler* whose discussions led to the founding of the *NZfM* in 1834, Lyser was not only a gifted critic, but also a skilled graphic artist whose credits as an illustrator included the coloured lithographs in A. L. Grimm's *Fabelbuch* (1827), one of the most widely circulated children's books of the period. Telling is his *Musikalische Bilder: ABC zum Lesenlernen der Noten, Vorzeichen und Schlüssel* (*Musical Images: Alphabet Book for Learning to Read Notes, Key Signatures and Clefs*). Published in the early 1840s, and grounded in a tradition of long standing, this volume introduces the child to the fundamentals of musical notation by way of a fanciful mixture of notes and letters that yield humorous sentences, often coupled with equally droll illustrations. Picture puzzles also found an audience among adults. As the Leipzig publisher J. J. Weber put it in the preface to his *Rebus-Almanach* of 1845, the puzzles in this collection 'occupy the imagination, sharpen the wit, and when they are well understood and put to good use, they are very well suited to provide the spirit with amusement'.[24] Much the same could be said of the games enacted in Schumann's *Carnaval*, a vehicle for adult musicians that is at the same time deeply informed by motifs drawn from the world of children's books.

Schumann explicitly affirmed the identity between musical substitution ciphers and picture puzzles in a diminutive piano piece entitled *Rebus*. Written in the autumn of 1848 as one of many training pieces for his seven-year-old daughter Marie, it was originally intended for inclusion in a *musical* book for children, Schumann's *Album für die Jugend*, Op. 68. A mere eight bars in length, the composition consists of a chorale-style harmonization of a melody whose pitches are generated from the letters in the phrase: '(L)ass das Fade, fass das Ächte' ('Leave trifles aside; seize only what's genuine').[25] Although this piece post-dates the period we are considering by more than a decade, there is every reason to believe that its underlying premises were firmly entrenched in Schumann's mind even before he wrote his Opus 1. In order to unriddle a rebus, the viewer must perform a simple operation: he or she calls an image by its name. This, in turn, is precisely what Schumann demands of readers of scores such as the *Abegg* Variations and *Carnaval*, where the 'images' the riddle comprises are individual musical pitches. Schumann emphasizes the fundamentally imagistic nature of the enterprise in his layout of the 'Sphinxes' in *Carnaval*; meant to be seen and not played (much as children were supposed to be seen and not heard), they

Example 4.1 From Schumann, 'Bericht an Jeanquirit in Augsburg über den letzten kunsthistorischen Ball beim Redacteur', *NZ fM* (19 May 1837), p. 161.

gape at the beholder of the score like the eyes of a fantastic beast: the Sphinx. One of Schumann's most intriguing musical rebuses is also his shortest: a series of four chords appended to an 1837 review – presented in the guise of a story by 'Florestan' about an 'art-historical ball' – of dance collections by Chopin, Liszt and others.[26] As shown in Ex. 4.1, the top line of the chordal texture consists of the pitches B♭–E–D–A, thus spelling out 'Beda', the name of a young lady who enchants the other guests at the ball with her piano-playing. Placed near the end of the review, just above a brief postscript, the chords form an unusual cadence on D. In other words, this little cadential tag is a rebus for the designation 'Finis' that one is apt to encounter at the conclusion of plays, novels or short stories. In the 'Beda' cadence, as in the *Abegg* Variations and *Carnaval*, Schumann appears to us not as a cryptographer but as a drafter of musical picture puzzles, an explorer of the imagistic potential of musical notation.

III

Magical images

On 11 April 1830, Schumann heard Niccolò Paganini in concert in Frankfurt am Main. The event, as described in his diary, made an extraordinary impact on the impressionable young man. Although he had 'doubts about [Paganini's] artistic ideals', suspecting that the Italian virtuoso lacked 'the great, noble, priestly serenity of a true artist', he was nonetheless overcome by an 'incredible enchantment' in the wake of the performance, so that after drifting off to sleep later that night he 'dreamt gentle dreams'.[27] The pieces Schumann heard on that unforgettable evening no doubt included *La campanella*, the rondo finale of Paganini's Violin Concerto No. 2 in B minor, and a staple of his repertory while on tour in France, central Europe and Great Britain between 1828 and 1834. A little over a year after first hearing Paganini, Schumann made sketches for a set of variations for piano and orchestra on the *Campanella* tune, which he must have taken down from memory, since Paganini's showpiece did not appear in print until 1851. While this project was left incomplete, materials from the sketches would re-surface in several of Schumann's keyboard works, including the *Allegro*,

Op. 8 (like *La campanella*, in B minor), the sixth of the *Intermezzi*, and No. 3 of the *Davidsbündlertänze*.[28]

The most significant of Schumann's Paganini-inspired efforts, however, grew out of a plan to 'make his caprices into studies for pianists who want to develop their technique further'. Schumann entered this phrase into his diary on 20 April 1832, and within two months he had finished at least a half dozen arrangements – or 'elaborations' (*Bearbeitungen*), as he preferred to call them – of Paganini's *Twenty-four Caprices for Violin Solo*, Op. 1.[29] During the following year, Schumann transcribed another group of caprices for piano, making twelve in all, published as the *Etudes pour le pianoforte*, Op. 3 (1832) and the *Six Etudes de Concert*, Op. X (1835). The designation of the second set as 'Op. X' (and not as 'Op. 10') was in accordance with Schumann's express wishes, for as he explained, the letter 'X' was a 'symbol of the unknown quantity' and hence a perfect symbol for Paganini's captivating skills as both performer and composer.[30] As it turned out, the captivating powers of an image played a decisive role in the genesis of the earlier set.

While working on his elaboration of Paganini's Caprice No. 16 in G minor, Schumann noted in his diary on 4 June 1832: 'The day before yesterday I saw a picture that made a shocking impression – Paganini in a magic circle [*Zauberkreis*] – the murdered wife – dancing skeletons and an entourage of magnetic, misty spirits . . . As I was transcribing the *Presto* in G minor it often hovered before me, and I think that the coda [of the transcription] calls it to mind.'[31] The picture that prompted this reaction was, in all probability, a caricature by his fellow *Davidsbündler* J. P. Lyser, whose visual portrayal of the leading motifs in the Paganini legend – namely, the violinist's murder of his wife and his collusion with evil forces – was inspired by Paganini's Viennese concerts of 1828.[32] In the years to come, the 'magic circle' would serve Schumann the critic as a pliable metaphor for the defining features of Paganini's multi-faceted artistry: its incomparable brilliance, its fusion of supreme technical command with genuine expression, its ability to induce a trance-like state in those who experienced it – in short, its whole range of magical properties.[33] In the present context, it will be useful to reflect on some of the ways in which the image of Paganini 'in a magic circle' left its imprint on Schumann's own artistic sensibility.

Paganini's Caprice No. 16 is an acrobatic *moto perpetuo* characterized by catapulting arpeggios, unexpected leaps, contrasting types of patterned figuration in rapid succession and, as a foil to its steady semiquaver motion, a fair amount of what the theorist Harald Krebs calls 'metrical dissonance'. According to Krebs, the latter takes two principal forms: 'grouping' dissonance, where the configuration of pulses suggested by the time signature gives way to alternate patterns, and 'displacement' dissonance, where the metric accent is shifted one or more pulses forward or backward.[34] The

Example 4.2a Paganini, Caprice no. 16 in G minor for violin solo, bar 1

Example 4.2b Paganini, Caprice no. 16, bars 45–53

G minor Caprice is rich in both types. Grouping dissonance appears already in the first bar, the *f* on the third semiquaver of the second beat transforming the 3 × 4 patterns indicated by the time signature into 2 × 6 (see Ex. 4.2a). Paganini in turn makes use of registral leaps and accents in the closing bars of the caprice to destabilize the metric flow, the result being displacements by either one semiquaver (bars 46–9) or two (bars 50–1) (see Ex. 4.2b). In his elaboration of the opening section of the caprice, Schumann transposed the original violin line down an octave, combining it with a passionate counter-melody in the right hand of the piano. After restoring the *moto perpetuo* to its original register (bars 13–46), he allows it to plunge back into the lower reaches of the keyboard during the coda, and it is significant that here – at just the spot where he claimed to have been haunted by a vision of Paganini 'in a magic circle' – he not only highlighted the metric dissonances in the original, but actually intensified them. In bars 49–51 (see Ex. 4.2c), the *sforzandi* in the right-hand counterline displace the metric accent by one semiquaver, adding a further layer of dissonance to Paganini's displacement of the pulse by two semiquavers.[35]

It is tempting to conclude, therefore, that for Schumann the image of Paganini was closely tied to the deployment of new and unsettling rhythmic

Example 4.2c Schumann, *Etudes*, Op. 3 no. 6, bars 46–56

effects. Consider as well the movement named after Paganini in *Carnaval*. A brief *Presto* in F minor, it evokes Paganini's incredible bowing technique with rapid octave leaps, both *staccato* and *legato*, in the right hand. The figuration recalls that of Paganini's Caprice No. 12 in A flat, elaborated by Schumann as Op. X/10, No. 1; though here, in *Carnaval*, the rhythmic element is accorded special prominence owing to a conflict between the accentual pattern in the right hand and the displacement of that pattern, by one semiquaver, in the left. The point, no doubt, is to mesmerize the listener – to draw him or her into the 'magic circle' – by evoking an atmosphere charged with electrical impulses. The means toward this end, as also in the kinetic finale of the *Concert sans orchestre*, resides primarily in Schumann's treatment of rhythm. Without question, the image of Paganini inspired Schumann's cultivation of an idiosyncratic virtuoso idiom in much of his earlier keyboard music. One thinks of the incessant 'double-stopping' in the *Toccata* (originally called *Etude fantastique en double-sons*), the rhapsodic cadenzas in the *Allegro* (Op. 8), and the breathtaking chordal leaps in the coda of the second movement of the *Fantasie*. Yet at an even deeper level, it was through his absorption of Paganini's rhythmic wizardry that Schumann found a way of drawing his listeners into a magic circle.

IV

Beloved images

Of all the images that populated Schumann's figurative world, none exercised as immediate, far-reaching, and long-lasting an impact as that of Clara Wieck. Having exchanged their first kiss in November 1835 (Schumann was twenty-five and Clara sixteen at the time), they soon developed a bond powerful enough to withstand the emotional turmoil occasioned by a lengthy period of enforced separation and a protracted legal battle with Clara's father that was finally decided in their favour in August 1840. Through all this, the image of Clara was Schumann's constant companion, serving not only as a consoling presence ('your bright image pierces through the darkness,' he wrote to her soon after the death of his mother in February 1836, 'allowing me to bear my burden more lightly'),[36] but also as a spur to his creativity. As he put it in a letter of October 1837: 'there is only one thought that I would like to portray [*hinmalen*] in large letters and block chords: *Clara*'.[37] Thus, just as Schumann transformed Clara's image into a disembodied thought, he later gave material form to this thought, in the process of creation, as a musical image or portrait.

A poetic confirmation of the intimate yet ineffable connection between Schumann's art and his lived experience, this statement and others like it have been interpreted literally by Eric Sams as evidence for Schumann's invention of a musical cipher system that allowed him to utter 'Clara' in tones. According to Sams, Schumann developed this system in the early 1830s with the aid of Klüber's manual of cryptography, and although it was capable of conveying any message in code, its primary purpose was to transmit the name 'Clara' with the pitch cell D–C#–B–A#–B or one of its derivatives, the most common of which was C–B–A–G#–A.[38] While this is not the place for a detailed critique of the chain of deductions that led to Sams's 'discovery' of the putative cipher system, or of the circumstantial evidence he marshalled in support of his hypothesis, a few observations are nevertheless in order given the (cautious) acceptance of the theory by at least some students of the music of Schumann – and of Brahms, who is supposed to have adopted his mentor's methods of encipherment.[39] First, one of the premises of Sams's argument asserts that Schumann chose the names 'Eusebius' and 'Florestan' for his alter egos in order to facilitate a 'symbolic union' of his name, represented by the initials 'E' and 'F', and Clara's, represented by 'C'.[40] Quite apart from the fact that Schumann generally spelt 'Clara' with a 'K', we should recall that Florestan and Eusebius made their first appearances in Schumann's diary during the summer of 1831,[41] at which time Schumann could hardly have been contemplating a union with Clara, who was then not yet twelve years old. Second, the musical cipher system outlined in Klüber's treatise bears no relation to the technique ascribed by Sams to Schumann. In fact, the two methods are grounded in antithetical principles: while Klüber's *musique parlante* turns on the arbitrary assignment of one or more different pitches to every letter of the alphabet,[42] Schumann's putative system is based on the non-arbitrary correspondences between individual pitches and letters of the alphabet grouped in threes. Finally, all of the examples of the 'Clara' cipher that Sams culls from Schumann's works manage to violate one or more of the principles for the elaboration of musical ciphers that can be inferred from Schumann's documented practice in compositions including the *Abegg* Variations and *Carnaval* (see Nos. 2 to 7 of the 'rules' given in Section II of this chapter). In short, the evidence suggests that the putative system of encipherment has little or no bearing on Schumann's music. The invention of an overly zealous decoder, it had best be scrapped.

In all likelihood, then, Schumann's attempts to evoke the image of Clara in tones involved something quite different from tiny four- or five-note motifs. His preoccupation with Clara's image, evident in his tendency to perceive it wherever he cast his glance, can be attributed to a simple fact: he was hopelessly in love. The philosopher and cultural critic Walter Benjamin described one of the more obvious symptoms of this condition with a beautiful metaphor in his *One-Way Street* (1923–6). In a fragment entitled 'FAN', he observed that the lover:

> will find the other person's portrait in nearly every book. Indeed, the beloved will appear as both protagonist and antagonist . . . Thus it follows that the faculty of imagination is the gift of making interpolations into infinitely small spaces, of conceiving every intensity as an extensiveness, thereby discovering in it a newly compressed fullness – in short, of receiving every image as if it were that of a folded fan that only in unfolding draws breath and presents, by way of its new expanse, the features of the beloved object within.[43]

As Benjamin further pointed out in a commentary on Proust's *A la recherche du temps perdu*, the fan is not only a metaphor for the erotic experience, but also for the process of remembrance: 'He who has once begun to open the fan of memory', Benjamin wrote in his *Berlin Chronicle* (1932), 'never comes to the end of its segments. No image satisfies him, for he has seen that it can be unfolded, and only in its folds does the truth reside...'[44] Defined as 'the capacity for [making] endless interpolations into what has been', the faculty of memory is also bound up with the photographic portrait, which, to quote Benjamin one last time, reveals 'material physiognomic aspects, image worlds, which dwell in the smallest things – meaningful yet covert enough to find a hiding place in waking dreams...'[45]

This constellation of motifs – the fan, the act of remembering, and the photo portrait – can be brought to bear on Schumann's Clara-inspired keyboard pieces of the mid 1830s, helping us to explain how they bridge the seemingly unbridgeable gap between lived experience and work of art. What these pieces offer is hardly a direct translation of experience into tones, but rather a simulacrum of the *structure* of experience – a structure characterized by interpolations on the small and large scale.

Many of Schumann's early keyboard works attest to a reciprocal exchange of creative ideas between the composer and the object of his affection. As announced in the full title of the *Impromptus*, for instance, this set of variations is based on a *Romance* by Clara (*Romance varié*, Op. 3; publ. 1833). Yet the opening bars of Clara's theme bear an uncanny resemblance to a melodic idea sketched by Schumann in September 1830, indicating that he too had a hand in the theme's making.[46] The central movement of the *Concert sans orchestre* also comprises a set of variations – or quasi-variations, according to the title – on a theme by Clara. Curiously enough, the 'Andantino de Clara Wieck' that Schumann took as his point of departure cannot be found in any of the surviving sources for her music. This notwithstanding, the affective role of the theme within the context of the *Concert* as a whole is clear enough. Beginning with a plangent descent through the F minor pentachord from c'' to f', the theme is heard as a distant echo, a disembodied memory of the very opening of the *Concert*, which presents the same gesture in thundering octaves.

In two cases from the period we are considering, Schumann's allusions to Clara's music take the form of interpolations, thus making the imagistic quality of the structure all the more apparent. The interpolations in Schumann's keyboard works fall into two broad types depending on whether they disturb the musical flow (generally through episodic asides of varying lengths), or proceed simultaneously with it (merely adding another layer to the texture). The first, episodic type is aptly represented in the opening movement of the Sonata in F sharp minor, a reworking of a *Fandango* in F sharp minor drafted in 1832. In converting the earlier character piece into a sonata movement, Schumann added an impassioned slow introduction that ends with the falling fifth from C# to F#$_1$. This gesture, transposed up a fifth and drummed out in staccato quavers, then becomes the basis for the motto that initiates the ensuing *Allegro vivace*, at first serving as preface to the fandango theme, and subsequently employed as a humorous – if rather explosive – commentary on both statements of the theme. (Considerably gentler references to the same figure also punctuate the slow movement of the sonata.) Perceived as an intruder in the musical argument, the percussive motto was almost surely derived from one of Clara's ideas: the opening gesture of her *Scene fantastique: le ballet des revenants*, No. 4 of the *Quatre pièces caractéristiques* (composed in 1833 and published three years later). Thus, both in terms of its genesis and its ultimate effect, the first movement of Schumann's sonata betrays the composer's knack for 'making interpolations into infinitely small spaces', and in this way imparts to the music the surface texture of a folded fan in whose interstices we catch fleeting glimpses of Clara's image.

Schumann's interpolative strategies would fulfil an altogether more serious function in the first movement of the *Fantasie*, Op. 17. As we have already seen, Schumann probably drafted this movement in June 1836 as an independent composition entitled *Ruines*. Conceived as a 'deep lament' for Clara – from whom he had been separated since January – the single-movement fantasy grew into a three-movement work by December, at which point it was associated in Schumann's mind with the effort to raise funds for the construction of a Beethoven monument in Bonn, hence the title on the autograph: *Ruinen, Trophaeen, Palmen. Große Sonate für das Pianoforte für Beethovens Monument von Florestan u[nd] Eusebius*.[47] The first movement, however, would retain unmistakable traces of Clara's image in the form of interpolations of both the episodic and layered variety. During the course of the transition between the first and second thematic groups (bars 33–41), an idea emerges from an inner voice of the texture that transforms the affirmative head-motif of Clara's *Romance varié* into a pathetic *cri de cœur*.[48] An emblem of yearning, this layered interpolation then recurs, transformed, as the main theme for what is surely the most extravagant of Schumann's episodic interpolations: the *Im Legendenton* section, a fully elaborated character piece in its own right, which intrudes on the reprise of materials from the first thematic group. Pointing backward in time to the earlier allusion to Clara's *Romance*, and forward as well to the movement's lyrical coda (heard by many listeners as a reference to the final song of Beethoven's *An die ferne Geliebte*), the *Im Legendenton* is thus a site of both pastness and futurity, reminiscence and premonition. Furthermore, Schumann's designation of this section in the autograph as a *Romanza* at once underscores the music's bittersweet blend of melancholy and romantic ardour (as a lyric verse form, the *romance* relates a tragic or amorous event),[49] and links those sentiments directly with Schumann's own beloved (by echoing the title of

Clara's *Romance varié*). Wedged between the recurrence of two phrases that had proceeded without a break earlier in the movement, the *Im Legendenton* section occupies a tiny fold in the design that 'in unfolding draws breath and presents . . . the features of the beloved object within'. And of course, that beloved object is Clara.

The rationale for the extended digression in the first movement of the *Fantasie* is not difficult to determine. A dreamy prolongation of a single point in time, the *Im Legendenton* section represents an attempt to hold fast to a fleeting moment – the moment of erotic fulfilment, a complex alloy of bliss and melancholy, recollection and anticipation – thereby preserving it for eternity.[50] Hence it is noteworthy that Schumann's essays in the art of making musical interpolations were almost precisely coterminous with the experiments that led to the invention of photography. This is not to say that Schumann was somehow influenced by the efforts of the Frenchmen Nicéphore Nipce and Louis-Jacques-Mandé Daguerre to develop a process of photographic reproduction in the late 1820s and early 1830s. The point is rather to suggest that both endeavours, the musical and the technological, were motivated by the same urge: the desire to accord permanence to the ephemeral. In this, however, the photograph may ultimately fail. As Roland Barthes reminds us, the photographic image provides a 'certain but fugitive testimony'. A perishable entity, the image recorded by the camera at first fades, then vanishes entirely.[51] How ironic, then, that music, the most intangible mode of artistic expression, became a medium for the creation of durable images in the hands of Robert Schumann.

Notes

1. On Schumann's life-long preoccupation with the larger forms, especially those involving orchestra, see Akio Mayeda, *Robert Schumanns Weg zur Symphonie* (Zurich, 1992), and Reinhard Kapp, *Studien zum Spätwerk Robert Schumanns* (Tutzing, 1984).
2. See *Neue Zeitschrift für Musik* (hereafter *NZ fM*), 1 (10 July 1834), pp. 113–14, and *NZ fM*, 16 (31 May 1842), pp. 173–4.
3. *Ibid.*, 10 (26 April 1839), p. 134.
4. Friedrich Schlegel, *Fragmente zur Litteratur und Poesie*, no. 586, in *Kritische Friedrich Schlegel Ausgabe*, vol. XVI, ed. Hans Eichner (Munich, 1981), p. 134.
5. Carl Koßmaly, 'Über Robert Schumann's Claviercompositionen', *Allgemeine Musikalische Zeitung*, 46 (1844), col. 20.
6. See Nicholas Marston, *Schumann: Fantasie, Op. 17* (Cambridge, 1992), p. 8.
7. For a discussion of the autograph of the *Fantasie* and a transcription of the sketches for the *Im Legendenton/Romanza*, see *Ibid.*, pp. 7–17.
8. On the Jean-Paulian overtones in Schumann's early keyboard music, see my *Robert Schumann: Herald of a 'New Poetic Age'* (New York and London, 1997), pp. 79–87.
9. *NZ fM*, 3 (14 August 1835), p. 50.
10. *Ibid.*, 5 (25 October 1836), p. 137.
11. Roland Barthes, 'Loving Schumann', in *The Responsibility of Forms: Critical Essays on Music, Art, and Representation*, trans. Richard Howard (New York, 1985), p. 295.
12. Barthes, 'Rasch', in *The Responsibility of Forms*, pp. 301–2.
13. Alfred Einstein, 'Opus I', in *Essays on Music* (New York, 1956), p. 41.

14. *NZ fM*, 2 (12 May 1835), p. 153. In a diary entry of 22 February 1830, Schumann refers to the *Abegg* Variations as the 'Abegg Waltz'. See Robert Schumann, *Tagebücher*, vol. I: 1827–38, ed. Georg Eismann (Leipzig, 1971), p. 228.
15. Like Moscheles's *Alexandre* Variations, and any number of other variation sets from the period, Schumann's *Abegg* Variations were perhaps first conceived for piano and orchestra. Wolfgang Boetticher provides a transcription of the forty-bar sketch for an orchestral introduction to the variations in *Robert Schumanns Klavierwerke – Neue biographische und textkritische Untersuchungen, Teil I, Opus 1–6* (Wilhelmshaven, 1976), pp. 37–9. Although Boetticher dates this sketch to the autumn of 1829, Claudia Macdonald places it in the summer of 1831, nearly a year after the solo piano version of the *Abegg* Variations appeared in print. See Claudia Macdonald, 'Schumann's earliest compositions and performances', *Journal of Musicological Research*, 7 (1987), p. 282, n. 101.
16. Töpken's remarks on the Countess d'Abegg come from a letter of 30 September 1856 to Schumann's biographer Wilhelm Joseph von Wasielewski; see Georg Eismann, *Robert Schumann: Ein Quellenwerk über sein Leben und Schaffen* (Leipzig, 1956), vol. 1, p. 70. Schumann listed the names of those who were to receive copies – both 'ordinary' and 'deluxe' – of his Opus 1 in a diary entry of 18 November 1831; see Schumann, *Tagebücher*, I, pp. 377–8. It is worth noting that while Schumann was studying law in Heidelberg he made the acquaintance of a pair of brothers (August and Otto) whose last name was 'Abegg'. For references to the Abegg brothers, see Schumann *Tagebücher*, I, pp. 225, 227, 233 and 295.
17. Schumann contributed to this repertory in his *Sechs Fugen über den Namen BACH* for organ or pedal piano, Op. 60, of 1845.
18. Jean Paul, *Werke*, vol. II, ed. Gustav Lohmann (Munich, 1959), p. 713. Paßvogel's little rhyme also makes a pun on 'Bach', meaning 'brook' in German.
19. *Robert Schumanns Briefe. Neue Folge*, ed. F. Gustav Jansen, 2nd edn (Leipzig, 1904), p. 92. Similarly, in a review of Liszt's appearances in Dresden and Leipzig during the 1840 concert season, Schumann referred to *Carnaval* as a kind of musical *Spielerei* (i.e. amusement or frivolous diversion). See *NZ fM*, 12 (10 April 1840), p. 120.
20. In order to understand Schumann's generation of these and other cells, it is necessary to keep in mind the German designations for musical pitches: A flat = 'As'; B flat = 'B'; B = 'H'; E flat = 'Es' or 'S'. For a penetrating analysis of the relationships between the 'Sphinxes' and the overall tonal and melodic organization of *Carnaval*, see Peter Kaminsky, 'Principles of formal structure in Schumann's early piano cycles', *Music Theory Spectrum* 11/2 (1989), 211–16.
21. These include the *Sechs Fugen über den Namen BACH*, Op. 60; the *Nordisches Lied* (on 'Gade') from the *Album für die Jugend*, Op. 68; and Schumann's *Intermezzo* and *Finale* for the F. A. E. Sonata (on 'froh aber einsam') dedicated to Joachim.
22. Johann Ludwig Klüber, *Kryptographik: Lehrbuch der Geheimschreibekunst (Chiffrir- und Dechiffrirkunst) in Staats- und Privatgeschäften* (Tübingen, 1809), p. 3.
23. Schumann's letter of 20 December 1836 to Lyser is discussed in Bernhard Appel, *Robert Schumanns 'Album für die Jugend'* (Zurich, 1998), p. 70. Apparently, Lyser did not accept the assignment.
24. Quoted in *ibid.*, p. 69. A number of the rebuses in Weber's collection touch on musical topics. For instance, the solution to rebus No. 14 – 'Die Schwestern Therese und Marie Milanollo' ('The sisters Therese and Marie Milanollo') – names two well-known child prodigies. Likewise, the picture puzzles in Tobias Haslinger's *Rebus aus dem Gebiete der Musik* (c. 1840) employ musical symbols (mainly pitches) to yield sentences or phrases dealing with music. For a reproduction of the rebus from that volume whose solution reads 'Das Studium des Generalbasses und des einfachen und doppelten Contrapunktes ist nicht zu vermeiden' ('The study of figured bass and of simple and double counterpoint should not be avoided'), see *ibid.*, p. 68.
25. The piece remained unpublished during Schumann's lifetime. For a transcription and discussion of its role in the genesis of the *Album für die Jugend*, see *ibid.*, pp. 64–7, 318. 'Das Ächte' ('the genuine') refers to the arrangements of melodies by famous masters – Handel, Bach, Mozart, Beethoven, Weber, Schubert – that Schumann initially planned to include in the *Album für die Jugend*. In his *Rebus*, Schumann renders the letter 't' (in 'Ächte') as the pitch 'D'.
26. 'Bericht an Jeanquirit in Augsburg über den letzten kunsthistorischen Ball beim Redacteur', *NZ fM*, 6 (19 May 1837), pp. 159–61.
27. Schumann *Tagebücher*, I, pp. 282–3.
28. See Boetticher, *Robert Schumanns Klavierwerke, Teil I*, pp. 124–5, 169–70; and Boetticher, *Robert Schumanns Klavierwerke – Neue biographische und textkritische Untersuchungen, Teil II, Opus 7–13* (Wilhelmshaven, 1984), p. 56.

29. Schumann *Tagebücher*, I, pp. 379, 405–6.
30. *NZ fM*, 4 (1836), p. 134. On his *Handexemplar* of the *VI Etudes de Concert*, Schumann added 'No. 2' after the opus number 'X'. This, together with Schumann's notation of 'Op. X, No. 1' on his *Handexemplar* of Op. 3, led Boetticher to conclude that the contents of both sets were conceived as a unit in 1832 (see Boetticher, *Schumanns Klavierwerke, Teil I*, pp. 93–4). As Kurt Hofmann points out, however, both *Handexemplare* date from no earlier than 1835. See Kurt Hofmann, *Die Erstdruckte der Werke von Robert Schumann* (Tutzing, 1979), p. 7. Furthermore, entries in Schumann's *Projektenbuch* clearly date the first volume to 1832, and the second to 1833. See Eismann, *Schumann: Quellenwerk*, vol. I, p. 82. In other words, it was only in 1835 or thereabouts that Schumann came to view the pair of collections as two instalments in his confrontation with the 'unknown quantity'.
31. Schumann, *Tagebücher*, I, p. 404.
32. *Ibid.*, p. 404.
33. See, for instance, Schumann's account of his first hearing of Paganini in an 1834 review of a concert given by the violinist Henri Vieuxtemps in Leipzig: 'As [Paganini] cast his magnetic chains casually and almost invisibly into the audience, the listeners swayed from side to side. Then the coils became . . . more tightly entwined and the people pressed more closely together; finally, Paganini . . . fused them into a single mass.' *NZ fM*, 1 (28 April 1834), p. 31.
34. See Harald Krebs, *Fantasy Pieces: Metrical Dissonance in the Music of Robert Schumann* (New York and Oxford, 1999).
35. It is interesting to observe how Schumann approached the same passage in the piano accompaniment he wrote for this caprice – as he did for all of Paganini's twenty-four – in the mid 1850s. Here too he heightened the metrical dissonance in the violin part, coupling it with a sarabande rhythm in the piano accompaniment that displaces the accent to the second beat of the bar.
36. Letter of 13 February 1836, in Robert Schumann, *Jugendbriefe*, 2nd edn, ed. Clara Schumann (Leipzig, 1886), p. 268.
37. *The Complete Correspondence of Clara and Robert Schumann*, ed. Eva Weissweiler, trans. Hildegard Fritsch and Ronald L. Crawford (New York, 1994), vol. I, pp. 31–2.
38. See, in particular, Eric Sams, 'Did Schumann use ciphers?' *Musical Times*, 106 (1965), 584–91; 'The Schumann ciphers', *Musical Times*, 107 (1966), 392–400; 'Why Florestan and Eusebius?' *Musical Times*, 108 (1967), 131–43; 'The Tonal analogue in Schumann's music', *Proceedings of the Royal Musical Association*, 96 (1969–70), 112–14; 'A Schumann primer?' *Musical Times*, 111 (1970), 1096–7; and 'Schumann and the tonal analogue', in *Robert Schumann: The Man and His Music*, ed. Alan Walker (London, 1972), pp. 398–401.
39. I offer a more complete analysis of Sams's theory in Chapters 3 and 4 of my *Crossing Paths: Schubert, Schumann, and Brahms* (Oxford, 2002).
40. Sams, 'Why Florestan and Eusebius?'
41. Schumann, *Tagebücher*, I, pp. 342–4.
42. Klüber, *Kryptographik*, pp. 264–75.
43. Walter Benjamin, *Einbahnstraße*, in *Gesammelte Schriften* IV/i, ed. Tilman Rexroth (Frankfurt am Main, 1972), p. 117.
44. Walter Benjamin, *Selected Writings, Volume 2: 1927–1934*, trans. Rodney Livingstone *et al.*, ed. Michael W. Jennings, Howard Eiland and Gary Smith (Cambridge, MA and London, 1999), p. 597.
45. 'Little history of photography' (1931), in *ibid.*, p. 512.
46. Schumann notated the sketch in his diary; see Schumann, *Tagebücher*, I, p. 321.
47. See Marston, *Schumann: Fantasie, Op. 17*, pp. 7–8.
48. Berthold Hoeckner draws interesting conclusions from this observation in 'Schumann and Romantic distance', *Journal of the American Musicological Society*, 50/1 (1997), 121–3.
49. For a sensitive account of the implications of the title *Romanza* for an understanding of the first movement of the *Fantasie*, see Nicholas Marston, ' "Im Legendenton": Schumann's "unsung voice" ', *Nineteenth Century Music* 16/3 (1993), 227–41.
50. Stephen Downes offers an eloquent and imaginative discussion of the erotic connotations of another passage from the movement – a phrase from the second thematic group that Schumann quoted in a letter to Clara of 9 June 1839 – in 'Kierkegaard, a Kiss, and Schumann's *Fantasie*', *Nineteenth Century Music* 22/3 (1999), 268–80.
51. Roland Barthes, *Camera Lucida: Reflections on Photography*, trans. Richard Howard (New York, 1981), p. 93.

5 Piano works II: afterimages

LAURA TUNBRIDGE

Faces, not masks: Schumann's comparison of the *Davidsbündlertänze* to *Carnaval* suggests that his later piano works explore a different musical territory from the ciphers, rebuses and radiant texts discussed in the previous chapter.[1] No longer are the members of the *Davidsbund* dressed as *commedia dell'arte* figures, or is Paganini seen in a magic circle; but while the images of the later music are less artificial – the mask is dropped – they are somehow also less immediate, haunting the listener as does a distant memory. The technical reasons for the change are complex. It certainly involves an altered use of quotations, both from Schumann's own works and Clara's; developments in his harmonic, melodic and rhythmic language; and his occasional evocation of music and voices 'aus der Ferne' (from the distance).

The first of the *Davidsbündlertänze* took its musical motto from a mazurka in Clara's *Soirées musicales*, Op. 6, which Schumann had reviewed in the *Neue Zeitschrift für Musik* on 12 September 1837 (signed 'Florestan und Eusebius'), the day before Clara's eighteenth birthday, when she had consented that he might ask for her hand.[2] The *Davidsbündlertänze*, perhaps more than any other of Schumann's works, express love and hope for their union.[3] What is more, Clara's influence over Schumann's piano music cannot be overestimated, either as creative muse or as performer.[4] His greater emotional stability (particularly once her father's objections to their marriage had been overturned by the courts) encouraged him to be productive, while his increased personal responsibilities seemed to have inspired a different approach to composition; he became more concerned with public success, something that manifested itself most obviously in his turn to larger forms such as symphony and oratorio, but that also influenced the manner of his solo piano works – alongside the difficult *Kreisleriana*, for example, he wrote the more accessible *Kinderszenen*. In the *Davidsbündlertänze* it is clear that even if Schumann still felt an outsider at the masked ball, he now at least had the emotional confidence to be able to enjoy his own – undanceable – dances.

The *Davidsbündlertänze* were published in two volumes in 1838. In this edition each movement was signed 'F.' or 'E.', continuing Schumann's use of Florestan and Eusebius as alter egos from his criticism (in contrast to *Carnaval*, which titled movements 'Florestan' and 'Eusebius', these are not so much portraits of their characters as their supposed compositions). The last numbers of each volume bore enigmatic inscriptions: at the close of No. 9, 'Here Florestan stopped, and his lips trembled sorrowfully'; for No. 18, 'Quite redundantly Eusebius added the following; but great happiness shone in his eyes all the while.' Not for the first or last time, Schumann invokes extra-musical associations to remark on and in some ways explain peculiar musical features – in this instance, Florestan's and Eusebius's interjections correspond with each volume unexpectedly ending in C major, while the basic tonality of the cycle has been B minor; the unexpected tonal close might be thought the result of their poetic additions. The two characters have certain stylistic and affective traits: as in the *Fantasiestücke*, Eusebius was linked with the marking *innig* (intimate) and Florestan with *rasch* (quick or hasty). Florestan's signature in the *Davidsbündlertänze* was often associated with the designation *mit Humor*; the verse originally included by Schumann at the head of the collection referred to *Lust und Leid*, laughter and sorrow, a juxtaposition of moods that runs throughout the dances, and which forecasts the affective changes of pieces like *Kreisleriana* and the *Humoreske* – the latter Schumann described as his most melancholy composition.[5]

Clara's motto is the first of many quotations embedded in the eighteen movements of the *Davidsbündlertänze*, some of which are taken from Schumann's earlier works: 'Promenade' from *Carnaval* and a sketch from the abandoned variations on a theme from Paganini's *La Campanella* appear in No. 3, and *Papillons* in no. 17 (bars 35–6). Unlike quotations in the *Impromptus* and the *Concert sans orchestre* these citations tend not to come across as interpolations (there is one notable exception, to which I will return), but as integral to the musical texture and structure. Clara's motto, for example, is not left to stand alone, but is extended to propel the work's opening gesture and, as Charles Rosen has discussed, becomes a continuous presence of which listeners are barely aware.[6] The distinctive scalic ascent of the first movement of *Papillons* is not remarked on in writing in the score as it was in 'Florestan' from *Carnaval*, but is transferred into a bass-line and coincides with the resolution of chromatic voice-leading (bar 35).[7] In other words, quotes are not simply framed; they are integral to the movement's structure, our awareness of which is enhanced by their recognizability.

Quotation also functions as a large-scale, inter-movement structural marker; for example, the literal return of material from the second movement at bar 51 of the penultimate movement (No. 17) has been thought to assert the cyclic organization of the *Davidsbündlertänze*.[8] Its placement, however, is unusual: typically, material from the very beginning would be expected to reappear at the very end. Perhaps as a result of its preemptory position, though, the quotation from the second movement is far from a

Example 5.1

consolidation of what has gone before. Movement 16 – Florestan's 'Mit gutem Humor' – is the only dance that does not reach a formal close. Following its initial quaver-driven scherzo in an unstable G major (that keeps lurching towards E minor), the somewhat slower B minor trio is diverted off course, never returning to the first section, instead drifting into the next movement. The diversion begins, ironically, by what seems to be an attempt at quotation, or at least cross-reference: the trio takes its initial rhythm and three *forte* quavers from the upbeat to bars 3–4.[9] Unlike the scherzo, whose dynamic flourish marks a cadence, the trio's *forte* does not: the three quavers ring out an octave F sharp, apparently determined to prevent the music from making its way back to the tonic (Ex. 5.1). This strange arrest in the harmonic movement seems to affect the rhythmic impulse, for the quavers smudge into syncopated crotchets, sinking through the register to an F sharp pedal that continues into movement 17. This penultimate dance is marked *Wie aus der Ferne* (as if from the distance). A sense of space and depth is suggested by the lack of a frame between movements, by the permanently lifted dampers (a device Schumann also used in the third of the *Nachtstücke*) and by the imitation of the soprano melody in the bass, as if an echo (bars 1–16). Berthold Hoeckner, taking his cue from Franz Brendel's description of the *Fantasiestücke* (Op. 12) as landscape painting (especially 'Des Abends' and 'In der Nacht'), describes 'Wie aus der Ferne' as 'a landscape with a blurred harmonic background against which melodic shapes stand out like sunlit objects'.[10] The sun's light seems strongest on the reprise of the second movement from bar 51, with its change of key to B minor and remembered melody. This extended passage is more of an interpolation than Schumann's other quotations in the *Davidsbündlertänze*; the recalled music appears in its complete form, now with repeats. Notably, the one aspect missing from

Example 5.2

its otherwise exact return is the marking *innig*. Recast as a 'sunlit object', the music loses its intimacy – we watch it, we hear it, from a distance. Yet the memory continues to haunt the cycle; the B of the final chord becomes the soprano voice of the next movement in C major, a move that means that the piece in which the conclusion of the cycle seemed most likely to occur is left open-ended. The actual final movement seems in this context like a tonal bookend, providing outside support for the inner movements but with little content of its own beyond reasserting the 'official' tonic of the cycle – as mentioned, Eusebius added it 'quite redundantly'.

Another distant voice, another quotation, is heard in the last of Schumann's *Novelletten*, Op. 21. Again, this collection of pieces was associated with his prospective happiness with Clara: he told her she appeared throughout, 'in all possible places and situations'.[11] In the final movement he quotes another of her pieces from *Soirées musicales*, 'Notturno', marking it *Stimme aus der Ferne* (voice from the distance; Ex. 5.2). Hoeckner and Daverio have discussed how Schumann's interlocking of two previously composed Novellettes sets up the voice from afar: the dotted pedal of the second trio (originally a D major Novellette) grows quieter to usher in Clara's languorous melody, which is brought closer to the surrounding music on being absorbed into the next section in a more lyrical incarnation.[12] The Notturno reappears in the movement's conclusion, augmented but at its original pitch (in F major, starting on A); perhaps significantly, its slightly varied ending is marked *innig*, as though the distant voice has been internalized. As mentioned in the previous chapter, the final sections are marked *Fortsetzung* (continuation) and *Fortsetzung und Schluss* (continuation and conclusion), terms probably borrowed from serializations of articles in journals such as Schumann's own *Neue Zeitschrift für Musik*. The composer's use of them here might have been intended to draw attention to the process by which he treated Clara's *Soirées musicales*: first reviewed in words, then quoted in music, then edited or recomposed and brought to what was perhaps a conclusion different from what she intended. Liszt described Schumann as having 'turned musical criticism into a literary object'; it seems as if, here, he turned it into music itself.[13]

Schumann's playful approach to form in the *Novelletten* derived, according to Erika Reiman, from the narrative strategies of Jean Paul.[14] A darker world-view and even more unorthodox musical composition seems to have been encouraged by another of the composer's favourite authors, E. T. A. Hoffmann. The *Fantasiestücke* of 1837, *Kreisleriana* of 1838 and the *Nachtstücke* of 1839 all respond to Hoffmann texts, both in terms of their subject matter and structurally. The *Fantasiestücke* inaugurated Schumann's use of poetic cycles, and in its establishment of tonal coherence between movements through less traditional harmonic relationships – here, by pairing keys related by a third (a practice continued in subsequent works) – might have referred to Hoffmann's unusual means of connecting sections of his texts. *Kreisleriana* took its movement titles from the same book on which the *Fantasiestücke* were based, Hoffmann's *Fantasiestücke in Callots Manier*. But it also seems to have been inspired by Hoffmann's *Lebensansichten des Katers Murr: nebst fragmentarischer Biographie des Kapellmeisters Johannes Kreisler in zufälligen Makulaturblättern*: a novel that randomly intersplices the memoires of the tomcat Murr with the biography of his master, the musician Kreisler.[15] The musical structures in *Kreisleriana* seem to owe something to the novel's narrative form, not only, as in the earlier works, abruptly changing affect between movements, but also doing so within them.[16] The transitions between sections are often violent ('sometimes your music actually frightens me', Clara told Schumann on first seeing the score): a particular figuration will be established, primarily by repetition, and then suddenly switch to another, whose relationship to the former is not always obvious.[17] In the seventh movement, *Sehr rasch*, tumbling semiquavers in the right hand, accompanied by accented onbeat broken chords in the left, dominate the first 41 bars, and are then displaced by a semiquaver theme that begins in the bass and gradually moves upwards, supported by a quaver figure that is varied, becoming legato and syncopated, between bars 54 and 70. The subsequent return to a variation of bar 9 onwards, at an even faster tempo, suggests a kind of ternary form, but suddenly a chorale enters, *piano*, slower and, perhaps most surprisingly, cadencing on to B flat. Its melody bears a skeletal resemblance to the opening, tempestuous C minor

Example 5.3

Example 5.4

theme; as if to confirm its distant relation (and perhaps grant it redemption), on its repeat, the chorale shifts up a fourth to C minor's relative major E flat, the key in which the movement ends (Ex. 5.3). The seventh movement's harmonic open-endedness interrupts the cycle's tonal pattern: after the D minor opening, it alternates agitated G minor movements (3, 5, 8) with slow ones in B flat major (2, 4, 6).

Rhythm drives the music of *Kreisleriana*, but just as its harmonies disrupt rather than define the underlying structure, the blows on the body (which Roland Barthes famously wrote about) are not the regular throb of a dance but jolts that throw the listener and performer off balance.[18] In the last movement, the bass does not support the burbling top line by giving it a firm beat, and so sense of metre, but gently displaces it; the effect is not so much of playfulness, as the movement's designation implies, but of anxiety or teasing (Ex. 5.4).[19] Even in the second section (bars 25–49), where the bass has a melody in common duple time and a relatively regular rhythm, it is made to struggle against its simplicity by having to break its parallel octaves, despite its being easy for the performer to play the notes in unison. The melody of bars 74–113 is submerged between bass and treble lines, and the pedalling in particular obliges the performer to use maximum strength to extract the tune (perhaps that was what Schumann meant by the marking

Mit aller Kraft – with all your strength!). On the opening's return, in bar 114, the wayward bass line seems to have become still more reticent, dropping out entirely in bar 125. The extent to which the metre is displaced can be gauged by observing that it is difficult to remember after hearing the piece – or even between sections – where the rhythmic blows fell: all we have are the aural bruises that change colour with time, eventually fading into normality.

Against the emotional and structural complexity of *Kreisleriana*, Schumann's most popular work, *Kinderszenen*, strikes a radical contrast. Debates as to whether this music is for or about children seem best solved by Liszt, who imagined the pieces as stories to be read to children; they are probably too hard for them to play.[20] Schumann pursued many of the same musical and poetic features as in his other piano works: movements 1 and 4, and 2 and 6, are connected motivically; the last three movements revolve around the tonal dualism of E minor and G major; and vigorous, repeated rhythmic patterns drive movements such as 'Hasche-Mann' and 'Wichtige Begebenheit', while 'Bittendes Kind' and 'Kind im Einschlummern' entwine melodic and accompanimental figuration almost as much as movements from *Kreisleriana*. As in the *Davidsbündlertänze* and the *Novelletten*, towards the end of the cycle a voice enters – in this case, that of 'the poet'. If we follow Liszt's interpretation, and consider the final movement as the poet's attempt to speak directly to the children rather than tell them a story, we also have to admit that while this music is the hardest to understand, it is because it seems the least – not the most – profound communication. Having happily told tales, the music seems to struggle to find its own voice: beginning in chorale fashion, none of its opening phrases finds its way to the tonic G major: starting from a V7d chord, bar 4 cadences on to the dominant, D; the next bars seem to move on to a chord of A major, but there is no root until the perfect cadence on to A two bars later (Ex. 5.5). Bars 9–12 slip into conventional lyrical piano figuration, with a sustained melody accompanied by falling quavers, pausing over diminished seventh chords on F sharp. The following recitative passage is based on two implied harmonies, built on diminished seventh chords on D sharp in its first inversion, and on A sharp. While the recitative is perhaps the most overt attempt at vocal expression, its flourishes only lead back to a repetition of the chorale, which now ends in G major. What has the poet said? Somehow the borrowed, multiple, distant voices of the *Davidsbündlertänze* and the *Novelletten* seemed more convincing: we might now see the poet's face, rather than a mask; but his voice remains unclear.

Schumann briefly moved to Vienna in 1839, to investigate the feasibility of establishing a new life there with Clara, away from her father's interference. His next compositions, *Arabeske* (Op. 18) and *Blumenstück* (Op. 19), were in keeping with his determination to make a mark professionally,

Example 5.5

Example 5.6

being written in a more accessible style; he described them in a letter to Ernst Becker as 'delicate – for ladies'.[21] As with the *Kinderszenen*, the explanation is disingenuous.[22] While on the surface song-like, comparable to Mendelssohn's *Lieder ohne Worte* and the *Nocturnes* of John Field, the *Blumenstück* is in double theme and variation form. The second, A flat theme grows parasitically from the first in D flat, and soon dominates: in fact, although D flat resurfaces in sections III and IV, and at the end, the first theme never reappears. The *Arabeske* is a winsome little rondo whose coda, while not questioning the piece's tonal closure in C, opens out the ending by introducing a new arpeggiated texture and melody. In its penultimate bar the head-motto reappears, not to pursue the main theme yet again, but to blossom into the resonance of the final chord: what is quite an unassuming piece finally suggests something more – the poet speaks, perhaps (Ex. 5.6).

The idea of a piece being left open-ended, or not explaining as much as it might, has been tied to the Romantic aesthetic of the fragment.[23] According to Friedrich Schlegel's famous *Athenaeum Fragmente* 116, Romantic poetry exists in a perpetual 'state of becoming': it is work in progress.²⁴ The implication is not that Schumann's 'fragmentary' piano pieces should be thought incomplete: a piece such as 'Warum?' from the *Fantasiestücke* remains, in Vladimir Jankélévitch's words, 'eternally suspended ... forever interrogative', never expecting a musical answer.²⁵ The fragment's challenge is one of interpretation; listeners are left to make their own connections and conclusions about meaning. Carl Koßmaly, reviewing Schumann's piano works in 1844, remembered Novalis (the archetypal 'fragmentary' author) having written 'that a work is all the more interesting, and a genuine expression of personality, the more impulses it gives – the more meanings, varieties of interest, points of view, indeed the more ways it has of being understood and loved'.²⁶ A complex work such as the *Humoreske* (Op. 20) 'gradually communicates itself to the listener' and as such, Koßmaly claimed, was one of Schumann's most significant and outstanding piano compositions: 'the great variety of content and form, the continual and quick, although always natural and unforced succession of the most varied images, imaginary ideas and sentiments, fantastic and dreamlike phenomena swell and fade into one another, and not only maintain but continually increase one's interest from beginning to end'.²⁷

The varied images of the *Humoreske* might be thought a kind of photo album of Schumann's earlier keyboard styles, with snapshots of Bach-like invention pasted next to character pieces and free fantasies; the fourth movement travels from a B flat major *Innig* section to an overwrought G minor *Sehr lebhaft*, which winds back towards its relative major, concluding with a stretto, before the mock-grandiose *Mit einigem Pomp* in A flat, which is eventually diverted back towards the tonic, and an extended conclusion to the whole piece (another of Schumann's quasi-journalistic references, *Zum Beschluss*). The transitions between sections are in part guided by cross-reference and quotation; here, more than in any other of Schumann's solo piano works, the process of memory, its internalization of remembered voices and melodies, is made apparent. At the end of the first movement, we return to its opening, as if nothing has happened; a further recollection of this music then returns before the final movement's *Sehr lebhaft*. It is not an exact quotation, but it is still recognizable – to borrow Koßmaly's description, as if images in a dream. The second movement, *Hastig*, includes a middle stave marked in parenthesis *innere Stimme* (inner voice): an impossible melody, imagined to float out from amidst the surrounding figuration (Ex. 5.7). Typically thought of as *Augenmusik*, to be seen but not heard, this 'inner voice' is nonetheless a memorable presence; in bars 197–232, when the passage returns, stretched into sustained chords, no middle line is given, and we might think that we miss it.²⁸ In fact, we hear the notes it suggested (if not at pitch) on both occasions; the trick is one of visual

Example 5.7

rather than aural perception, which makes hearing the *innere Stimme* no kind of transgression, as it would be to play out loud the 'Sphinxes' from *Carnaval*.[29] After bars 9–24 have been repeated without their extra voice they do not suddenly fly off into another mood as before, but reflect on their figuration, repeating the phrase as if unsure where to go next. Not onward, for now, but to an *Adagio* reminiscent of the *Etwas lebhafter* close to the first movement's *Einfach* – a reference subtly acknowledged by the grace note tied to the final chord. Details such as this provoke the listener to forge links between sections, extending a web of associations, of memories and afterimages, over the *Humoreske* so that, as Koßmaly explained of the fragment, 'we shall not have missed the truth but instead [have] come close to it, even if in our own way'.[30]

After the death of his brother Eduard, Schumann composed a *Leichenphantasie* (Corpse fantasy), naming the movements *Trauerzug* (Funeral march), *Kuriose Gesellschaft* (Strange company), *Nächtliches Gelage* (Nocturnal revels) and *Rundgesang mit Solostimmen* (Round with solo voices).[31] It was published in June 1840 as *Nachtstücke* (Op. 23), the title after E. T. A. Hoffmann's eight tales by the same name.[32] Schumann's grief seems apparent in the musical language, which obsessively repeats rhythmic and melodic patterns, perhaps as Julia Kristeva describes the chronically depressed compulsively making the same movements over and over again.[33] The opening movement has been described as transforming 'Von fremden Ländern und Menschen' from *Kinderszenen* into a funeral march, making what might be appropriate associations with the loss of childhood (Ex. 5.8).[34] The repetitive, weary melody recurs throughout the movement; its rhythm is even more persistent, continuing in other sections, with a remnant returning in the fourth movement. Schumann's tendency to fixate on certain rhythmic configurations in works like *Kreisleriana* has already been noted, and it would become one of the defining aspects of his late style, suggesting the

Example 5.8

Nachtstücke to be both a transitional and visionary set of pieces, and one haunted by foreboding.

For most of the 1840s, Schumann concentrated on genres other than the solo piano piece, producing only a few fugues and pieces for children. But then, at the close of 1848, he began *Waldszenen* – completing a draft within a fortnight, but taking two years over revisions. Initially each movement had a fanciful title taken from the writings of Gustav Pfarrius and Heinrich Laube, but in the end only the fourth, 'Verrufene Stelle', retained its morbid motto from Hebbel's *Waldbilder*:

> Die Blumen, so hoch sie wachsen,
> Sind blass hier, wie der Tod;
> Nur eine in der Mitte
> Steht da im dunkeln Roth.
> Die hat es nicht von der Sonne:
> Nie traf sie deren Gluth;
> Sie hat es von der Erde,
> Und die trank Menschenblut.
>
> [The flowers here, grown tall, are pale as death;
> Just one amongst them is deep red.
> That one never knew the sun's glow:
> It drew its colour from the earth, which drinks human blood.][35]

We are far from the friendly, cajoling flowers of *Dichterliebe* here. Hebbel's vampyric blooms incite some of the oddest music of *Waldszenen*, combining a distant relation of the French overture – which shares its dotted rhythms, but is *pianissimo* rather than proclamatory – with a yearning sequential phrase decorated by a mordent (it is unusual to find such ornamentation in Schumann), and a semiquaver figure that slips in and out. 'Verrufene Stelle' is in D minor, the furthest the cycle strays from its guiding B flat tonality. Generally, the musical language of *Waldszenen* is much simpler than that of Schumann's earlier piano pieces. On entering the woods we are greeted by a movement that sounds like a song accompaniment without

Example 5.9

words: no longer is the absent voice heard from the distance or within. A Biedermeier sensibility of the friendly forest is appealed to by the hunters' song, the scene in the shelter or on lookout, and the artless picture of the lonely flower – apart from 'Verrufene Stelle', the one troubling moment comes in 'Vogel als Prophet'.[36] The bird's flitting around G minor is suddenly interrupted by a muscular, lyrical chorale, which glides up from G major to E flat before disappearing as quickly as it came: the bird, untroubled, continues to swoop and peck around its arpeggiated figuration (Ex. 5.9). Originally, the movement's motto was from Eichendorff's 'Zwielicht', 'Hüte dich, sei wach und munter!' (Be on your guard, be awake and alert!): Eric Jensen has interpreted the bird as a messenger of danger.[37] Christopher Reynolds extends this reading to treat the chorale as a quotation, suggesting the source in a line from the boys' chorus in Part III of Schumann's *Szenen aus Goethes Faust* that warns innocents, much as the bird might.[38] But can we really say it is the bird speaking? In the poem, a voice advises deer to beware of man; the chorale is a quintessentially human genre, more likely to issue from man than from a bird that, after all, returns immediately to its flight around the forest, as unimpressed as the fishes listening to St Anthony's sermon in *Des Knaben Wunderhorn*. A further reason for assuming the voice to be mortal will become apparent when considering Schumann's final piano work, where the chorale's melody no longer predicts the future, but is a reminder of the past.

The final version of *Waldszenen* was published as Opus 82 in 1850. Around that time, Schumann started to revise many of his solo piano works. In a letter to the publisher Friedrich Whistling he wrote that he had 'heavily revised' *Kreisleriana*, explaining that earlier he often wilfully ruined his pieces.[39] Schumann edited out the fragmentary quality of the second and fifth movements, cutting passages from and adding repeats to the former and adding a perfect cadence to the end of the latter.[40] A second edition of the *Davidsbündlertänze* was published under Schumann's direction, renamed *Davidsbündler* and omitting the references to 'F.' and 'E.' and the poetic inscriptions. As with *Kreisleriana* he attempted to 'normalize' the music: the B was no longer to be held over between the last two movements, curtailing the original's open-endedness, and repeat signs were added to the first two movements, as if to make the music more solid and balanced. Schumann's motivations have been credited to a shift in his aesthetic viewpoint, a rejection of Romanticism for *Hausmusik*, an embracing of proto-Brahmsian academic Classicism, or to a desire not to reveal his personal life to the public as do works such as the *Novelletten* and *Kreisleriana*.[41] As Rosen comments, it is understandable that a composer should lose sympathy with his earlier works; in Schumann's case, however, the situation was complicated by his medical condition.[42] As a young man, he played on ideas of insanity as a creative tool, using the eccentric texts of Jean Paul and Hoffmann as models to overturn conventional musical structures. In later years, as he became aware of his mental weaknesses, Schumann seems to have become desperate to re-establish formal stability in his music. As his 'real' madness took over he attempted to quell its imaginary predecessor – perhaps he was concerned that one had brought about the other. Today, despite modern concerns with performance practice and *Urtexte*, we tend only to hear the revised versions of the solo piano works; that they nevertheless retain something of their audacity is testament to the extent of the composer's innovation.

Schumann's solo piano works were rarely performed in public during his lifetime: the rare exceptions were Liszt's 1840 performance of *Carnaval* in Leipzig, and Clara's inclusion of some of the less complex later movements, such as a selection of the *Fantasiestücke*, in her recitals.[43] The earlier pieces were considered by the composer, his wife and their audience to be too difficult for general understanding. After Schumann's death, Clara brought *Kreisleriana, Davidsbündler, Faschingsschwank aus Wien, Humoreske* and *Kinderszenen* into her repertoire. However influential she was in bringing some of her late husband's music to the public, Clara also prevented certain works from being performed; one such was *Waldszenen*. The weaknesses

Clara claimed to feel in these pieces were possibly compounded by the sense that this was haunted music. The middle section of 'Vogel als Prophet', already discussed as a possible quotation from the *Szenen aus Goethes Faust*, bore a striking resemblance to the theme of Schumann's *Thema mit Variationen für das Pianoforte* (WoO 24) – the so-called *Geistervariationen* – supposedly a transcription of the melody dictated to the composer by angels on the evening before his 1854 suicide attempt. (It is also similar to the second movement of the 1853 Violin Concerto, WoO 23, another work Clara suppressed.) Brahms used the theme as the basis for his Op. 23 four-hand variations, dedicated to Julie Schumann.[44] In the same way that the melody seemed to have plagued Schumann – recurring in so many pieces in such significant contexts – it might have haunted his family and friends, burnt on the aural retina so even with eyes shut it remained an afterimage: the unforgettable face once glimpsed behind the mask.

Notes

1. In a letter to Clara Wieck (17 March 1838), Schumann wrote: 'I think [the *Davidsbündlertänze*] are quite different from *Carnaval*, compared to which they are what a face is to a mask.' *Robert und Clara Schumann: Briefe einer Liebe*, ed. Hans-Josef Ortheil (Königstein, 1982), p. 97.
2. Linda Correll Roesner, 'The sources for Schumann's *Davidsbündlertänze*, op. 6: composition, textual problems, and the role of the composer as editor', in *Mendelssohn and Schumann: Essays on Their Music and its Context*, ed. Jon W. Finson and R. Larry Todd (Durham, NC, 1984), pp. 53–70. Roesner suggests that Schumann's designation of the *Davidsbündlertänze* as Opus 6, outside the established number order of his works, might have been another reference to Clara's composition.
3. 'If ever I was happy at the piano, it was when I composed them', Schumann wrote. Letter of 6 February 1838, *Briefwechsel: Kritische Gesamtausgabe*, ed. Eva Weissweiler (Frankfurt, 1984), 3 vols., vol. I, p. 90.
4. On Clara's influence, see David Ferris, 'Public performance and private understanding: Clara Wieck's concerts in Berlin', *Journal of the American Musicological Society*, 56 (2003), 351–408, and Nancy B. Reich, *Clara Schumann: The Artist and the Woman* (Ithaca, NY, rev. edn, 2001), pp. 249–78.
5. Letter to Ernst Becker, 7 August 1839: *Briefe. Neue Folge*, ed. F. Gustav Jansen (Leipzig, 2nd edn, 1904), p. 166. On *Humor* in Schumann's compositions see Heinz J. Dill, 'Romantic irony in the works of Robert Schumann', *Musical Quarterly*, 73 (1989), 188, and Ulrich Tadday, 'Life and literature, poetry and philosophy: Robert Schumann's aesthetics of music', this volume, pp. 38–47.
6. Charles Rosen, *The Romantic Generation* (London, 1996), p. 235.
7. Rosen describes the quotation of *Papillons* in *Carnaval* as occurring 'with the same effect as quotation marks', in *Romantic Poets, Critics, and Other Madmen* (Cambridge, MA, 1998), p. 97. See also John Daverio, *Nineteenth-Century Music and the German Romantic Ideology* (New York, 1993), pp. 58–61.
8. Peter Kaminsky, 'Principles of formal structure in Schumann's early piano cycles', *Music Theory Spectrum*, 11 (1989), 207–25.
9. Kaminsky argues that the thrice repeated F sharps establish a 'surface motivic relation' with movement three, 'Etwas hahnbüchen'; Berthold Hoeckner connects this to the first waltz from Clara's *Valses romantiques* (Op. 4), which Schumann had already quoted in *Carnaval*. Kaminsky, *ibid.*, pp. 219–20, and Hoeckner, 'Schumann and Romantic distance', *Journal of the American Musicological Society*, 50 (1997), 101–2.
10. Hoeckner, *ibid.*, 96.
11. Letter of 30 June 1839, *Briefwechsel*, ed. Weissweiler, vol. II, 608.

12. Hoeckner, 'Schumann and Romantic distance', 102; John Daverio, *Crossing Paths: Schubert, Schumann, and Brahms* (Oxford, 2002), pp. 138–9.
13. Franz Liszt, 'Robert Schumann (1855)', trans. Christopher Anderson, in *Schumann and His World*, ed. R. Larry Todd (Princeton, 1994), p. 345.
14. Erika Reiman, *Schumann's Piano Cycles and the Novels of Jean Paul* (Rochester, NY, 2004).
15. On the structure of Hoffmann's novel see Lora Deahl, 'Robert Schumann's *Kreisleriana* and double novel structure', *International Journal of Musicology*, 5 (1996), 132–4.
16. See Daverio, *Nineteenth-Century Music*, p. 62.
17. Letter of 30 July 1838, *Briefwechsel*, ed. Weissweiler, vol. I, p. 213.
18. Roland Barthes, 'Rasch', in *The Responsibility of Forms: Critical Essays on Music, Art, and Representation*, trans. Richard Howard (Berkeley, 1991), pp. 299–312. See also Robert Samuels, 'Music as text: Mahler, Schumann and issues in analysis', in *Theory, Analysis and Meaning in Music*, ed. Anthony Pople (Cambridge, 1994), pp. 162–3.
19. On metric displacement in Schumann's music see Harald Krebs, *Fantasy Pieces: Metrical Dissonance in the Music of Robert Schumann* (New York, 1999).
20. Franz Liszt, 'Robert Schumann (1855)', p. 354. See also Daverio, *Robert Schumann*, p. 166.
21. Letter of 15 August 1839, *Briefe. Neue Folge*, ed. Jansen, p. 169.
22. See Schumann's letter to Clara 24 January 1839, *Briefwechsel*, ed. Weissweiler, vol. II, p. 365.
23. On the aesthetic of the Romantic fragment see Beate Julia Perrey, *Schumann's 'Dichterliebe' and Early Romantic Poetics: Fragmentation of Desire* (Cambridge, 2002), pp. 26–32; Philippe Lacoue-Labarthe and Jean-Luc Nancy, *The Literary Absolute: The Theory of Literature in German Romanticism*, trans. Philip Barnard and Cheryl Lester (Albany, NY, 1988), pp. 39–58; and John Daverio, 'Schumann's systems of musical fragments and *Witz*', in *Nineteenth-Century Music*, pp. 49–88.
24. See David Ferris, *Schumann's Eichendorff 'Liederkreis' and the Genre of the Romantic Cycle* (Oxford, 2000), pp. 62–6.
25. Vladimir Jankélévitch, *Music and the Ineffable*, trans. Carolyn Abbate (Princeton, 2003), p. 19.
26. Carl Koßmaly, 'On Robert Schumann's piano compositions (1844)', trans. Susan Gillespie, in *Schumann and His World*, ed. Todd, p. 312.
27. *Ibid.*
28. R. Larry Todd mentions the tendency to think of the inner voice as *Augenmusik*: 'On quotation in Schumann's music', *ibid.*, p. 80.
29. On the 'Sphinxes', see Carolyn Abbate, *In Search of Opera* (Princeton, 2001), pp. 240–2 and Slavoj Žižek, 'Robert Schumann: The Romantic Anti-Humanist', in *The Plague of Fantasies* (New York: Verso, 1997), pp. 203–6.
30. Koßmaly, 'On Robert Schumann's Piano Compositions', p. 312.
31. See Schumann's letter to Clara, 7 April 1839, *Briefwechsel*, ed. Weissweiler, vol. II, pp. 473–4.
32. On Hoffmann's influence see Christine Moraal, 'Romantische Ironie in Robert Schumanns *Nachtstücke* op. 23', *Archiv für Musikwissenschaft*, 54 (1997), 68–83.
33. Julia Kristeva, *Black Sun: Depression and Melancholia*, trans. Leon S. Roudiez (New York, 1989).
34. Moraal, 'Romantische Ironie', pp. 77–8.
35. My translation. On the mottos' sources, see Peter Jost, *Robert Schumanns 'Waldszenen' op. 82: Zum Thema 'Wald' in der romantischen Klaviermusik* (Saarbrücken, 1989), pp. 285–9.
36. On representations of the woods in literature and visual arts in nineteenth-century Germany that might have influenced Schumann, see Jost, *ibid.*, pp. 21–70.
37. Eric Frederic Jensen, 'A new manuscript of Robert Schumann's *Waldszenen*, op. 82', *The Journal of Musicology*, 3 (1984), 83–4.
38. Christopher Alan Reynolds, *Motives for Allusion: Context and Content in Nineteenth-Century Music* (Cambridge, MA, 2003), pp. 77–82. Another reference might be Schumann's setting of Hoffmann von Fallersleben's 'Frühlings Ankunft' in the *Lieder-Album für die Jugend* (Op. 79, No. 19), composed in 1849.
39. Letter of 20 November 1849, in *Robert Schumann's Leben aus seinen Briefen geschildert*, ed. Hermann Erler (Berlin, 1887), 2 vols., vol. II, p. 105.
40. See Charles Fisk, 'Performance analysis and musical imagining, Part II: Schumann's *Kreisleriana*, no. 2', *College Music Symposium*, 37 (1997), 95–108.
41. Anthony Newcomb argues that Schumann's aesthetic views had shifted towards a *Hausmusik* style in 'Schumann and the marketplace: from butterflies to *Hausmusik*', *Nineteenth-Century Piano Music*, ed. R. Larry Todd (New York, 1992), pp. 258–315.

42. Rosen, *Romantic Generation*, p. 663.
43. On Clara's performances of Schumann's music, see Martin Schoppe, 'Schumann-Interpretationen Clara Schumanns (Tageskritik und Konzertbericht)', *3. Schumann-Tage* (1979), 17–24, and Beatrix Borchard, *Robert Schumann und Clara Wieck: Bedingungen Künstlerischer Arbeit in der ersten Hälfte des 19. Jahrhunderts* (Ph.D. diss., University of Bremen, 1985).
44. See David Brodbeck, 'The Brahms–Joachim counterpoint exchange: or, Robert, Clara, and "the best harmony between Jos. and Joh."', in *Brahms Studies*, ed. Brodbeck (Lincoln, 1994), p. 72.

6 Why sing? Lieder and song cycles

JONATHAN DUNSBY

A story of decades

Song and Schumann are as inextricably linked in the public mind as they are in the minds of performers and musicologists, and this has been the case for roughly a century and a half. It is clear from the history of later nineteenth- and twentieth-century music that Schumann's songs have never gone out of fashion. They seem no more likely to do so than do Mozart's symphonies, or Debussy's piano music. When we are entranced by the experience of a Schumann song we do not need to think about all his other songs: the dominant 13th chord at the end of 'Morgens steh' ich auf' (*Liederkreis*, Op. 24, No. 1) seems to belong to a different universe from the dominant 13th at the end of 'Die alten, bösen Lieder' (*Dichterliebe*, Op. 48, No. 16); even the theorist determined to make connections in the quest for the identification of a musical 'language' will note the different context, register, key and so on – a matter of technical comparison such as will be important in the further investigations below. Instead, our cumulative experience of Schumann song is part of the trust that builds up in this repertoire, a belief common already perhaps to most readers of these words that if you happen to encounter one not encountered before, it will be time well spent in a magical world where everything is in its mysterious place. Schumann, who came to regard song as a higher form of poetry, never – or perhaps it is: rarely – faltered in his inspiration in setting words for voice and piano, as opposed to opera and other choral music, where the Midas touch never quite seemed to appear, or so a century and a half of critical reception can be taken to indicate.

It is integral to this magical world that it evokes a sense of enlarged consciousness that offers no escape from the human condition. This is not tribal music, intoxicating us in a conspiracy of belonging or individuation, and it is not popular music to which we can dance or through which we can in any way celebrate the ephemeral. It penetrates to the heart of how things are, Beckett's *Comment c'est*,[1] whoever's company we find ourselves in through Schumann's poets; wherever they place us geographically; at whatever point in the past, present or future; or, more usually, taken altogether out of time as only art can do.[2] And in the end, however many people and lands and epochs Schumann leads us through, it is not comfort we find in his song world, but a sense that there is something to think about – in our own lives of course. Beate Perrey puts this in a different, more eloquent way:

> The principal mode of speaking performed by Schumann in his songs is essentially that of soliloquy or, to remain with the Early Romantic philosophical cast, monologue. In constant self-reflective discourse, the song realizes structurally the Romantic hero's 'operation' to 'identify the low Self with the better Self' [Novalis]. This means an invocation of the *Other* in terms of an interlocutor who may fill the existential 'gap'. But this gap is also what defines the Romantic Solitary, is site and source of his hallucinations. Although there is thus always a 'voice that answers', the song, however, never truly fills the gap, but rather widens it.[3]

Schumann, that is, never meant his songs to be easy on the mind, however perfectly they continue to meet the ear. They are not, by and large, entertainment. They are, by and large, so true to life that they are beyond categories such as 'good' and 'bad'.

Schumann's emotions, like those of most educated, youngish men in love, or indeed people at any age, could well up to a point where only poetry could express them. This is just what happened in early December 1838 when he sent to his beloved Clara – a biographical story told elsewhere in this volume – 'little verses', which in fact amounted to a rather extensive 120 lines about their joint past and their prospects. 'Did you get my little verses?', he writes: 'Look, they express the way I view things. You're getting a poet for a husband, and you made me one yourself.'[4] What Clara did not know at that stage of her life, and despite the fact that Schumann was already in the European mainstream of leading composers, was that she was also going to be getting a Lied-composer as a husband, since in 1838 this aspect of his creative genius was as yet inchoate.

Schumann's early songs from a decade before (1827–9) were in 1838 inconspicuous in his output, if only on the test for example that not until 1840 was the first Schumann song in fact published. Opinion on the thirteen songs from the late 1820s (very possibly more were written and are now lost) is divided. Gerstmeier is not untypical in judging them to be 'immature experiments'.[5] The best that the characteristically positive Daverio can observe is that Schumann was to draw on this early material later, notably in the slow movements of the F sharp minor and G minor Piano Sonatas (Opp. 11 and 22 respectively, completed in 1835 and 1838; in this writer's opinion these movements are two gems among Schumann's piano output). Not only is Daverio unfailingly positive about the composer to whom he devoted his life's work in the twentieth century, but in this case it may in fact be special pleading for him to try to persuade us that the 'early lieder... occupy a special place in Schumann's output... because they represent his first extant works in a polished compositional idiom'. Yet he is certainly right that 'even in his keyboard music . . . Schumann emerges as poet and composer in one person'.[6]

Those studying Schumann's life have always been fascinated by its rhythms, and it is perhaps especially in relation to his songs that this aspect needs to be considered. He was given, as we shall certainly be contemplating later in this chapter, to bouts of intense concentration that one can call – if not necessarily in its technical, medical sense – obsessive; and as is typical of those composers who have tended to work doggedly and almost exclusively on particular issues over long periods (think only for example of Schoenberg's preoccupation in his late forties with dodecaphony), there will also be 'returnings' in their lives that are thus rather special in terms of their psychobiography (in Schoenberg, again, the quasi-tonal 2nd Chamber Symphony, Op. 38, begun in Vienna and Berlin in 1909–16, completed in Los Angeles in 1939). If there is a sense of decade-on-decade 'returning' in Schumann's song composition, the period around 1850 was to be his final opportunity, at a time of effulgent emotion that Ostwald, in the perhaps unfortunately titled *Schumann: Music and Madness*, characterized as 'Trouble on the horizon, 1849–1852'.[7] Trouble maybe, but this was a really productive return to song for Schumann. The year 1849 saw the completion of Op. 98a, the nine songs of the *Lieder und Gesänge aus Wilhelm Meister*, as well as the ambitious twenty-eight songs of the *Lieder-Album für die Jugend*, Op. 79.[8] In 1850 no fewer than twenty songs appeared, in Opp. 83, 89,[9] 90 and 96. Pohl provides us with an overview:

> The year 1850 marked an important turning point for Robert Schumann. With it, he entered the last phase of his life and creativity. Of course, he had no more presentiment of this than did his numerous friends and admirers when he left Dresden in the fall of 1850 to assume the position of municipal music director in Düsseldorf on 24 October. On the contrary, this move, occasioned by artistic activities, gave him renewed hope. He was just forty-one years old and had every reason to look forward to a long creative life.[10]

Schumann's new burst of creativity at this time is associated with one of what Jamison calls his 'manias', and certainly the quantitative measure of his output seems to show that depression (particularly around 1833 and 1844, and of course his final collapse of health in 1854) inhibited composition, while mania, if this is what we should call it, showed huge peaks in 1849–51 and, as we shall see, 1840.[11] The point here is that if this kind of mapping of Schumann's long-term ups and downs as a composer does make any kind of sense – and without our need to dwell on it in the sort of *Schadenfreude* that has been typical of Schumann historiography for a century and a half – it is without doubt that song was the composer's route into and out of these states of elevated consciousness.

And this brings us to the epiphanous Year of Song, 1840, of which Plantinga provides the following sketch:

> He unleashed a veritable torrent of Lieder for solo voice and piano: in 1840 alone he wrote over 125 of them, more than half of his entire output in the category. These include many of the most admired Lieder ever written: the collection *Myrthen*, Op. 25, the Heine *Liederkreis*, Op. 24, the *Liederkreis von Eichendorff*, Op. 39, the *Dichterliebe*, Op. 48, the *Frauenliebe und -leben*, Op. 42, and many others. Several reasons have been advanced for Schumann's about-face. It is possible that love lyrics now had for him an intensely personal significance. This was also a time when Schumann seemed to reevaluate certain of his most cherished ideals as to the progress of contemporary music as a whole. He had long taken for granted that the real future of Romantic music, founded, as he thought, by Beethoven, lay in the cultivation of Beethoven's kind of music, viz. the large instrumental forms. But as it gradually became clear to him that the sonata, symphony, and string quartet simply were not developing as he had hoped, both as composer and critic he showed a new surge of interest in the Lied.[12]

To which one might be allowed to respond, yes and no. 'Torrent' is a loaded word, if it tries to tempt us casually into thinking that Schumann was in some sort of daze, rather than a state of elevated calculation: we don't speak of 'torrents' in Mozart's astonishing output, and if the sheer concentration of effort on Schumann's part is the issue here, well, what about Wagner slaving away, rather despite himself, for years, and at incredible speed all told, on *Parsifal*? Conversely, and tellingly, 'surge of interest' is, as it were, *un*loaded, a casual moment in Plantinga's large study of Romantic music. By the evidence he offers and by the understated phrase 'surge of interest' the idea may be inferred that Schumann was, say, planning his next compositions rather as he might have planned his holidays. No. This was a burning but controlled enterprise. As far as I am aware, Schumann never subsequently expressed any amazement at the 'Year of Song' of the kind that historians kindle in their easy distortions. Imagine being in the first flush of middle age and keeping your *Dichterliebe* in your files in holograph for *four* years, as it seems the composer did. We still do not have a psychobiography of Schumann that makes him, so to speak, the person he was, in the way that Hildesheimer attempted so cunningly for Mozart.[13]

Poet's love

In the centre of this chapter we shall concentrate on two of the world's favourite song cycles, *Dichterliebe* and *Frauenliebe und -leben*, asking what it is about them that seems to be special, and of course always being in danger of sidelining their sheer beauty since, in the end, what is there to be said about an art that speaks for itself other than in words?

An immediate topic that is striking to all who contemplate this outpouring is Schumann's urge towards the epically cyclical, already well rehearsed in the majestic piano collections from *Papillons*, Op. 2, of 1832, to *Kreisleriana*, Op. 16, of 1838. The very starting point for this urge was a fund of great lyric poetry from the preceding fifty or so years. Schumann adored the lyrics of such as Goethe, Heine and Rückert, not to mention for example Anderson and Byron in translation, but not only for their poetic moment: for their successive feasts of originality, imagery, reversal, remembrance, for their virtually untranslatable quality of *Humor*. He also saw the narrative urge in these poets, the building of monodrama from a story of states, memories and expectations rather than mere historical actions. In this sense his precedents, such as Schubert's *Winterreise*, had shown both poetically and musically how to tell a storiless story.[14] Rosen finds this phenomenon quite remarkable and believes it to have been poetry-driven:

> It was the lyric poetry of landscape that was the chief inspiration in the development of the *Lied* . . . It is, in fact, the pretensions of the song cycle that make it such an extraordinary phenomenon. With it, a modest genre, intended largely for the unambitious amateur, becomes a major endeavor that in weight and seriousness rivals grand opera, the Baroque oratorio, or the Classical symphony . . . The prestige of the great song cycles is a testimony to the central role they played in the history of Romantic art. They realized one of the ideals of the period: to give the lyrical expression of Nature an epic status, a genuine monumentality, without losing the apparent simplicity of a personal expression.[15]

Let us examine this phenomenon as it appears in *Dichterliebe*, bearing in mind that we need to be on the lookout for the epically lyrical, the monumentally simple.

It is entirely appropriate that there exists a large secondary literature on *Dichterliebe*, which is by any standards one of the handful of masterpieces in Western music. No contemporaneous Lied composer came remotely close, so all commentators say or imply, to Schumann's achievement here, and among previous song cycles only Schubert's *Winterreise* of 1827 measures up to Schumann's epic consistency. No other Romantic composer was able to create a similar phenomenon. It was only in radically different cultural settings that a related genre of prolonged, emotionally overwhelming song-sequence was – perhaps ever could be – attempted successfully once more – Schoenberg's *Das Buch der hängenden Gärten* (The Book of the Hanging Gardens), Op. 15, completed in 1909, for example, and Kurtág's *Bornemisza*

Péter mondásai (The Sayings of Péter Bornemisza), Op.7, revised 1976. Such a comprehensive masterpiece as *Dichterliebe* has naturally attracted comment from many different angles – Schumann's understanding of Heine's poetic meaning; the structural coherence of the music; its reception-history, its personal significance for later performers, composers, writers. Like Beethoven's Ninth, or in literature Goethe's *Faust*, or in sculpture Rodin's *The Kiss*, it has created its own cultural history with a wake that lapped the shores of many arts at many times.

Not all of that history – far from it – is to be taken at face value, it goes without saying, but the brief critical discussion here will be restricted to two particularly interesting aspects – genesis and structure – which, as we shall see, in fact interlock. The genesis of *Dichterliebe* is partly a story of the predictable: songs in the Year of Song, for instance. Also, the construction of a substantial opus from discrete or nearly discrete items, most of which can stand alone like one perfectly cut diamond taken from a cluster of jewels (we can say the same of *Carnaval* and the other piano cycles), and the incursion by the composer into the poet's text. (Who dares to alter Heine? Well Schumann of course.)[16]; the occurrence too of certain generic types of song, a 'parlando' love song (No. 4), in the accompaniment a *moto perpetuo* (No. 5), a quasi-recitative (No. 13), a pastoral idyll (No. 15), a quasi-operatic *scena* (No. 16);[17] and – lastly in this account but not least in any list of the predictable about *Dichterliebe* – the unmistakable, architectural cyclic recurrence of piano 'codas' in Nos. 12 and 16. Yet on the other hand his poet's love is shrouded in mysteries as to its genesis. For one thing, Schumann's persona here is, compared for example with that in *Frauenliebe und -leben*, to be discussed below, almost completely occluded. There are no Sphinxes to suggest at least what the riddle is, if not always the solution;[18] no 'Clara' themes, no Beethoven quotations and the like.[19] Even Heine's text is not fully revealed in the sense, for example, that Schumann ends No. 1, a declaration of love, in the musical interrogative of a closing but inconclusive dominant harmony,[20] or that the dramatic reversal in the final lines of No. 4, 'But if you say "I love you", then I must weep bitterly', is undermined by Schumann's apparent musical emphasis – a diminished 7th chord followed by a 2–1 suspension – not on the verbally surprising second clause but on the first.[21] The greatest mystery concerning the genesis of *Dichterliebe* is, however, as profound as it is puzzling. It is in the nature of history for supposition to become 'fact' that is recurrently endowed with ever accruing significance in the unfolding of historiographical filiation, and so with *Dichterliebe*. How remarkable it seems that Schumann believed his original 1840 cycle of twenty songs could become, on publication in 1844, a considerably leaner, exquisitely economical cycle of but sixteen numbers. And how successive commentators have marvelled at this, as it were, visionary second sight on the part of our composer. Yet how wrong they have all probably been, for until the twenty-first century there has been not a single item of evidence supporting the contention that this pruning of the cycle was actually Schumann's decision. We simply do not know. Can it possibly be that Schumann excised four songs without feeling the need to revise – and we know or believe we know that they never were revised – any of the new end–beginning musical relationships thus forged? On the other hand, can it possibly be that the structure of this hallowed totem of a Romantic masterpiece is pretty much a matter of mundane happenstance? Such are the secrets that Schumann, it appears, perhaps never wanted to explain, although this need not present us with a problem in assimilating *Dichterliebe* if we can take on board its challenging aesthetic position:

> What we are really dealing with is discontinuity, rupture, thoughts and 'states' not perfectly ordered and harmoniously linked ... *Dichterliebe* points to a compositional conception that not only tolerates, but elevates the notion of the Romantic fragment system to the extent that its 'integrity' is not in jeopardy, even if parts of its text are missing or dismissed ... a masterpiece not despite, but by virtue of its disintegrative forces and open-endedness. It need not be interpreted through the lens of any hypothetical completeness.[22]

And that authoritative reminder has the potential to destabilize, in moving from genesis to structure causally rather than whimsically, a great deal of what some would call the analytical hubris surrounding this work in its attempt to understand and explain it as an integrated, 'organic' whole. Representative of the analytical current of the later twentieth century is the Norton Critical Score, in which Komar seeks to persuade us of Schumann's genius in building a work in the organic and monumental Beethoven tradition. Komar is, however – in comparison with the confidence displayed by Schenkerian analysts in particular in revealing, or some would say largely inventing, intricate connections between all levels of the voice-leading structure of a tonal masterpiece – appropriately diffident. He offers seven possible conclusions to an analysis of would-be organic 'wholeness' in *Dichterliebe*: the first four are routine, concerning (in my words) stylistic affinity, referential pitch and local continuities; but then Komar moves on to suggest, understandably as he aims to pursue the possible logic of analysis, that one might discover 'a coherent key scheme', an actual 'compositional plan' or even a single key governing the entire work, which he initially casts as implausible, yet with the characteristic urge of the music theorist, and for all his disclaimers, he cannot resist offering in his Ex. 18 a bass-line graph in Schenkerian notation showing *Dichterliebe* as a two-part structure (Songs 1–7 and 8–18) moving from I (A minor) to #III (C sharp minor) through two stepwise ascents.[23] Nor is this theoretical urge necessarily to be dismissed out of hand, for there is without doubt in *Dichterliebe* just the kind of miraculous balance of unity and diversity[24] that we find in a Schubert piano sonata or, say, a Bruckner symphony. *Dichterliebe* lies right at the heart of a compositional tradition, truly mastered by maybe two dozen composers over two centuries, stretching from Haydn to, perhaps, Webern – if we are to subscribe to the canonical picture of the 'Viennese' achievement. There is also the particular as to Schumann's highly integrated style: his careful, telling use of chromatics (those who have not analysed the harmony of this work will find it, contrary perhaps to one's overall impression, strikingly diatonic – statistically that is – and highly selective in the use of 9ths, 11ths and 13ths, particularly in the use of diminished chords, which Schumann always reserves for special poetic moments);[25] his neo-Baroque, post-Mendelssohnian, driving sequences of 7th chords over descending 5th root progressions; his ability to sustain what have often been called 'obsessive' pulsating accompaniments, best known, it may be, in 'Ich grolle nicht', the principal *Dichterliebe* song to have found an independent place in the lied repertoire, but also evident in Nos. 3, 5, 9 and to some extent elsewhere, for example in No. 16; and his elevation of the piano to the role of poet-without-words, opening and closing the cycle, 'commenting' on the individual poem in codas to every one, mostly elaborately and often completely unpredictably, and decisively even in the one case – No. 14 – where there are but three closing melody notes in the piano (the poet has forgotten what was said in a dream, and the piano reminds him, wordlessly, that it was *Ich liebe dich*).[26]

These imprints in Schumann's language of musical song, inscriptions as we might call them, are so plastic yet elemental that rather like the hieroglyphs of Ancient Egypt they can tell subtly inflected individual stories from a proven stock of musical figures. By way of transition to our second case, two comparisons between *Dichterliebe* and *Frauenliebe* are offered on matters of detail that can, it is hoped, capture something of the labile quality of Schumann's musical material. First, let us take what must be regarded as one of the most significant, 'structural' points in *Dichterliebe*, in a way its dénouement, where in the final number the poet declares that he is going to bury all his songs beneath the sea, in the mighty grave that such a mighty coffin will require – this image setting up the very final verse where the poet asks us whether we know why such a coffin is needed, and in his valedictory lines tells us it is because he is also sinking in it his love and his grief, an agonized grief, one may feel, or it may be a point that is simply raw with emotions that cannot be named or categorized, but crushingly final for all that. The music at the mention of the coffin and the grave (bars 39^4–43) is in essence the same as that at the end of verse 1 of *Frauenliebe*, No. 3, 'Ich kann's nicht fassen, nicht glauben', bars 8^2–15 (a semitone lower, and there is surely no need to defend my convenient 'in essence' against detailed analytical scrutiny, since of course each passage adapts in parametrical inflection – speed, rhythm, texture and so on – to its musical context). In the *Frauenliebe* passage we are not hearing of coffins and graves but of a woman's excitement at having been noticed by her hero – words that are foreign to the scenario of the Heine poem, true, but here a foretaste of the critical 'reading' to be examined below. The same, beautiful musical invention can serve Schumann in despair or elation, in retrospection or anticipation, and – an important point as we shall see – for the male *or* the female persona. As a second 'inscription' revealing how Schumann can carve new paths through familiar territory – just as Heine after all, and Chamisso, and Schumann's other favoured poets, can draw on a stock of vocabulary, images, verse forms, grammatical tropes, tenses, voice, expletives, punctuation – we can return to the *Ich liebe dich* motif mentioned above. Actually this 7–2–1 melodic figure over a V–I cadence is common in Schumann. In *Frauenliebe*, No. 6, it also closes the song, though here in the voice rather than the piano, and on this occasion to the words *dein Bildniss* (your image), as the singer finally confirms that she is carrying a child.[27]

A man's woman's love?

Is Schumann song so expressive but illusory that it can amount to some kind of deception, perhaps even some kind of *self*-deception on the part of the composer? Thus the ungenerous reader might infer from Solie's well-known essay 'The gendered self in Schumann's *Frauenliebe*'.[28] Solie reminds us that Chamisso's texts selected by Schumann – who excluded a ninth poem when the heroine, clearly much older than in the galloping events of love–marriage–childbirth–husband's death of Songs 1–8 as Schumann offers them, talks to her granddaughter about her earlier life, and who, as Solie will try to persuade us, thus colonized Chamisso's story as male-composer-poet – are seriously out of kilter with modern sensibilities, rendering *Frauenliebe*, which otherwise one might assume to be a consummately comfortable picture of domestic love and life, 'awkward to hear' (p. 220). Solie suggests three listening strategies in the face of this difficulty:

> One is to seek refuge in autonomism, to focus on 'the music itself' and to insist that it, on its own, carries no 'meaning'. Another is to take comfort in a kind of naïve historical relativism, to assume that 'things were like that' then, and that it is simply inappropriate to hold 1840s society to 1990s social standards. For a third, there is a thin but helpful veil of distance for us

> in the kinds of performance situations in which we encounter such songs, formal and professional, so unlike the intimate domestic *Liederabend* of their own period. (pp. 220–1)

As to the first, it is difficult to know what this amounts to. Schoenberg famously observed that he had understood the textual 'content' of Schubert's Lieder long before studying their texts, and believed this to be a general potential of great song.[29] Are we going to deny this power in Schumann, for the sensitive listener, even hearing *Frauenliebe* for the first time maybe, and even with no programme note for historical guidance, and even with no knowledge of German? Second, I wonder what is 'naïve' in any relativism in this case that we do not also need in *every* case: is *Die Zauberflöte* a routine cameo of everyday modern Western life that we absorb with unmediated sangfroid? Whether life was 'different' in 1840 is not the substantive point: *that* life is re-enacted *now*, and this is the sorcery of all art, especially the greatest art. Third, by far the most common 'encounter' with 'such songs' is not 'formal and professional' in the concert-stage sense that I am sure Solie is implying here, but resides – let us be realistic – in the highly intimate world of the sound recording which, as we all know and as has been much theorized, engages us in an extremely 'intimate' possession of singer, music and message.[30] In any case, Romantic song is of an immanently intimate character and it is difficult to imagine that 'veil' existing even for someone hearing – really hearing – such music in the largest amphitheatre.

All this is certainly not to contradict Solie's admonition to remember the distance between hearing *Frauenliebe* in 1840 and hearing it now, or to forget Kramer's important suggestion about the post-modernist, dynamic conception of the Lied as a 'locus of the dehistoricizing process',[31] which has some merit at least in inviting people, as I do in summoning the anachronistic spirit of Beckett, to take possession of Schumann now rather than in any authenticist delusion. Yet I find the idea that we cannot but marginalize the authentic – or call it *inherent* – impact of a work like *Frauenliebe* nothing more than the result of a taste for thought-experiment, a taste that cannot but seem 'neurotic' (see Solie's use of this word below) and evasive to some degree, if what it really does is call upon us to fight the shadows of our recent societal history.

Now, no one could be more sympathetic than this writer to Solie's difficulty in pinning down just what the message is in *Frauenliebe*, and I feel it is because of her totalizing mission – a demonstration of a 'gendered self' altogether too harsh and programmatic to survive Schumann's comprehensively illusory gaze – that Solie inevitably stumbles from one sinking epistemological footfall to another in this narrative quicksand. So, for example, 'our presumptive heroine's disavowals of, and distancings from, her own affective states are extraordinary' (pp. 230–1): perhaps, but we have already been informed that these disavowals and distancings are 'in fact an accurate portrayal . . . of fantasy rather than reality, of male ideology rather than female acquiescence' (p. 222), so the disavowals are sham anyway, it appears; and to be fair to Solie she has told us, to begin with, her view that these songs 'are the *impersonation* of a woman by the voices of male culture, a spurious autobiographical act' (p. 220).[32] But of what female role created by a male composer is this not true? 'This masquerade, the "he" behind the "she", is, moreover, not a symptom of aesthetic failure but a necessary part of the social message it was the cycle's job to transmit' (p. 222). Yet can it not be asked then whether it is not Schumann who with Chamisso created this supposedly demeaned heroine, but Solie herself who is in fact robbing the 'her' of her personal integrity? Is the woman's fictional love not fictionally real precisely *because* it involved a then customary degree of subjugation and self-abasement – the 'cycle's job'? And do we not hear the voice of critical cynicism or even sarcasm in the comment 'whether or not there is also *Herrenliebe* involved is a moot point' (p. 222: does Solie maybe think that the 'hero' is so impatient for marriage in No. 5 because he has in mind the high mortality rate of early nineteenth-century childbirth and is already fantasizing about his next family?!). Yes, to press home the point made above about the 'different', we could well ask on a much larger spiritual canvas than that of individual domesticity why Bach allowed Christ himself in the *Matthäus-Passion* to fail to stand up for his ultimate, basic human right not to suffer political execution – a simplistic *reductio* perhaps, and hopefully inoffensive, but this is just the kind of speculation that can happen when the synchrony of New Musicology is let loose in the diachronic museum of Western art.

Although no apology is offered for this potentially bleak picture, we can nevertheless also tease much that is purposeful out of commentaries that 'totalize' in the way discussed above. After all, no one is doubting that Schumann turns his intense *musical* attention to fundamental *conceptual* and interpersonal issues in *Frauenliebe*. Solie generalizes this point: 'Songs such as the *Frauenliebe* cycle have in their presentational character a stronger and more immediate power to convey such cultural messages than any literature could. They have, that is, considerable performative meaning' (p. 226), which sentiment White takes to imply that 'the tendency will be to treat the verbal text as a fairly easily discernible literalist statement which the musical matter "translates" in one way or another',[33] and thus, in other words, it is not that criticism and analysis are inevitably doomed to failure. If it is true that Schumann adds 'performative' meaning that can trump Chamisso's ideology with something even stronger and more powerful (in a 'higher sphere of art'),[34] we can ask, taking a lead from Solie if not following her own quarry, whether the composer could in any sense have been *more* faithful to the 'her' and the 'him' he inherited from the poet. He has internalized the poem and is making something more true of it, as only a Lied can do, because of its higher powers of evocation, of which Schumann was certain in principle. Can Schumann, then, actually appropriate for himself a woman's feelings? No, says Solie, categorically. Not everyone would agree, as we shall see.

Let us speculate meanwhile in a more musically technical way. In No. 2, we are told, at the re-transition to the reprise (my terminology) 'patriarchal rule reasserts itself; her crazy tonality is tamed and recaptured by the original, triadic motive, which pulls it into an inexorable, rule-governed circle-of-fifths progression . . . that reintroduces the "Herrlichste von Allen" [hero] in place of the neurotic, presumptuous "Würdigste" [the most worthy of women]' (p. 238). This is following 'a nihilistic frenzy' when at bar 54 (I presume) 'she has brought herself and the music to the absolute of alienation, the key of the tritone' (p. 238). This is as untrue, if in an interesting way, as a musical 'fact' ever can be untrue. At bar 54 the music is 'in' the key of D, as is demonstrated if one backtracks from the dominant V in 59 through a series of applied *dominant* chords: II in 58, VI in 57, III in 56, VII in 55 and, obviously, IV (natural IV, the dominant of D) in 54. There is no 'key' of A in this song, and if Solie has miswritten rather than – almost unbelievably – misheard, the offence remains in black and white. But why not take Solie at her word in general, in an adjusted scenario? Suppose that the patriarch joins the matriarch harmoniously as together they flirt with tonal disruption and *join* (bars 53–4) in backing off from the frightful tritone before the last tonicizing step, playing an equal part in this process of mutual musical safeguarding: where is the 'spurious' in *that* reading? Also, if this heroine really is going 'crazy' tonally in the passage leading up to this turning point, someone, other than Solie apparently, needs to explain how she carefully remembers, mid-'frenzy', to plant a V of I in bars 50–1, rather too organically, it might be thought, for one who has lost her tonal control; and, also, someone needs to point out that, although admittedly singing 'his' tune, it is 'she' who does actually restore the tonic (I always knew 'she' could do it!) in her triad-motif-embroidered II–V–I progression, bars 57–60.[35]

In sum, could we not turn the *Frauenliebe* 'problem' on its head and celebrate Schumann's virtuosic balancing of gendered *selves* – without trying to rewrite history and certainly without wishing to 'obliterate all presence of a cultural Other' (p. 240), Solie's main, thoughtful and timely complaint about what she calls 'formalism'? It is not as if people have completely failed to ponder the questions Solie rightly raises, and least of all, I suggest, Schumann himself. I do believe that even the venerable Philipp Spitta, even in the gruesome early twentieth century when middle-class Western women were almost as yoked as they had been in Schumann's day, wrote of just those questions, albeit in his own way: *Frauenliebe* 'gives us a deep insight into the most subtle and secret emotions of a pure woman's soul, *deeper indeed than could have been expected from any man,* and in fact no composer but Schumann would have been capable of it'.[36]

Inside the petals

If we have pondered some large issues so far, and issues that I believe Schumann would himself have recognized as valid – the cycle, poetic and perhaps even 'musical' gender, Schumann's plastic musical language, and the 'voice' of the piano – nevertheless there has been a resultant if necessary sense of skimming the surface that makes us thirst for the sheer intensity of intimate contact with an actual song, the intensity, as I put it at the beginning of this chapter, of 'time . . . spent in a magical world where everything is in its mysterious place'. Nowhere have successive generations of performers and listeners felt that intensity to be more acute than in some of the 1840 love songs, of which 'Du bist wie eine Blume' has always been a favourite, not least to the composer, who included it in *Myrthen,* Op. 25, a wedding gift for Clara of what were published as twenty-six songs, by seven poets as Schumann thought (though in fact one of the Burns poems was wrongly attributed at the time and there are eight different poetic voices here); and it became one of Clara's favourites.[37]

This is Heine's poem interspersed with what is nearly a word-for-word translation:

> *Du bist wie eine Blume*
> you are like a flower
> *so hold und schön und rein;*
> so lovely and beautiful and pure
> *ich schau' dich an, und Wehmut*
> I look at you and sadness
> *schleicht mir ins Herz hinein.*
> steals into my heart.
> *Mir ist, als ob ich die Hände*
> It seems to me as if my hands
> *aufs Haupt dir legen sollt',*
> on your head I should place
> *betend, daß Gott dich erhalte*
> praying that God keep you
> *so rein und schön und hold.*
> so pure and beautiful and lovely.

Without feeling the need to refer to nearly two centuries of Heine criticism and a great deal of discussion in the Schumann literature, we can say that most readers of this poem will have a pretty clear and agreed idea of what it is about. This is revealed not only in the vocabulary but also in the hint of action that this is written by a man about a woman: in the early nineteenth century men were not compared to flowers and that has probably been true across the ages and remains so today; in the early nineteenth century women did not write of their priestly laying on of hands, priests of course being men by definition (to date!), and this image is not fanciful in that the poet does refer to 'praying' and 'God', as is there for anyone to read. So what is on 'his' mind? Why does sadness steal into his heart? For Heine, we do not know, and more to the point, we are not supposed to know – he is not telling us what happened one day, but asking us, perhaps, what does this mean for you? For Schumann, we probably know rather more in that almost without doubt Schumann is taking on the role of poet and composer and Clara is the 'she': I say 'almost' because although the biographical anchoring of *Myrthen* is clear – if not necessarily as directly linked as Sams's fantasy story suggests about how Schumann might have described the set, and although it seems unlikely, to say the least, that the composer is going to make some eleven inter-textual musical references in this short setting[38] – I also believe that Schumann had a clear idea in such a song as this of the durable, the non-personal, the 'great', not least because he was one of the generation of composers who first had to assimilate Bach, Haydn, Mozart, Beethoven and Schubert, and deal with a sense of following in the footsteps of genius such as had not really happened before in modern Western music. We also know that Schumann is revising Heine, because he offers a repeated line that is not in the same order as either Heine's second or final lines. Schumann opts for beautiful/pure/lovely twice. Personally, I conjecture – and it has been said before – that he is thinking like a musician, the 'composer as poet', knowing that his setting will be playing with the delicacies of a varied strophic setting, and not wanting to allow a textual distraction that would, after all, be extremely noticeable if one were to experiment with restoring Heine's original text.[39] Bear in mind that Schumann has deliberately destroyed the rhyme between Heine's second and fourth line.[40] Why? As we shall see further below, through a little analytical work ('evidence-based', as I described the need in note 35), it is because Schumann wants this to be a song that is in the end not so much about beauty and loveliness as about what the bride (as male construct, Solie would doubtless claim) most importantly is: pure.

Rather than continuing to look at the words we shall move on to what Schumann seems to make of them musically. Obviously, he believes he has found a musico-poetic 'moment' for the opening line, in which we notice that it is perhaps especially the 2–1 suspension over II in the piano, bar 3^1,

Example 6.1

underpinning the 4–3 in the voice, that provides an unforgettable initial illumination of the sound. Equally obviously, 'sadness' moves the musical narrative onto a further plane, with a secondary dominant to the dominant, which is in fact as a B^7 chord a potential dominant to the Neapolitan of the dominant (flat VI of the tonic), and sustained throughout bar 7, which is a long time for a remote harmony shortly into an *Andante* song, and it leads to the noumenal cadence of the surprising invasion of the heart (bars 8–9), of which more below.[41] It is also clear that Schumann wants to pack a great deal of rhetorical weight into the penultimate line, after the onset of the virtually strophic reprise from bar 10: for the first time he stops the underlying semiquavers in the piano (bars 1–13) as the voice takes on a hint of prayer-like recitative in bar 14; he activates the 'voice' of the piano, which in bar 15 gives a trope of bar 14 in the voice (the trope being one

Example 6.1 (*cont.*)

of heightened intensity, an ascending 5th – to A-flat, the highest note of the song – trumping the voice's ascending 4th – C to F in bar 14, F being 'her' highest note, also heard in bars 3, 8 and 10 – and the diminished 4th A-flat to E in bar 15^2 providing the most 'dissonant' intervallic succession in this music); and the final line of text compared with its original, strictly diatonic presentation in bars 3^2–5^1 is wreathed in piano chromaticism, the supertonic note carrying its chromatic lower neighbour A and the dominant its upper neighbour F flat in the space of one beat, bar 16^1. A brief turn figure in the piano, and the song is done.

Yet that figure – which one might casually take to be an arabesque, a gentle cadential roulade, something pretty, seizing our attention just for a moment – has an uncanny, timeless presence. How can a conventional 1–7–1–2–1 figure such as any basically competent composer might write transfix us, spellbound in the feeling that we have been told some little, disguised thing that at the very same instant we realize is momentous? It is because of our capacity to hear musical transformation, indeed, to 'speak' music, as Schumann knew full well. That turn figure is a transposed, de-rhythmicized form of the melody in the 'noumenal' cadence, the central structural point in the music (tonicization of V), the central reversal of the poetic text ('schleicht mir in's Herz hinein'), where the 1–7–1–2–1 in bars 8–9^1 soars from the singer's highest register, including an exquisite moment where the voice is suspended on the tonic E flat against the leading note D in the piano at the seventh semiquaver of bar 8. So in one sense the piano at the end is reminding us of the plot of the entire song, and is restoring the turn figure to the tonic level: 'this is what it was all about, and this is how it has to end', we can almost hear in Schumann's musical farewell, if we choose to think about it. But I would maintain that through the piano at the end he is 'saying' something even more specific, for the very figure, at the very pitch of its closing appearance, first 'sang' at the half cadence that ended the first couplet of the song (see the notes A♭–B♭–A♭–G–A flat in bar 4^2, reverse them – or 'retrograde' them, to use the terminology of twentieth-century music – and you have precisely the piano's last five melody notes). Let us return, then, to the question of why Schumann has altered Heine's text. I believe a very specific intention can be discerned. By rotating *hold–schön–rein* to *schön–rein–hold* he achieves not one, but two new musico-poetic effects. First, *schön* receives a natural musical emphasis as the first, downbeat image of the second line of the first couplet. Since Schumann is going to make such a spectacular musical feature of the effects of the gaze in the next couplet, and since the proximate image of this physical gaze is presumably 'her' physical beauty above all, one strong connection is made. Secondly, however, the – as it were – subcutaneous quality of purity is seeded in the second half of bar 4, and the 'meaning' of what I called the 'noumenal' cadence thus achieves a deeper sentiment than the merely visual: in terms of surface word-setting, the *rein* will be our last emphasized image in bars 16–17, with its E flat in the voice offering the final vocal peak; and in the 'voice' of the piano, the last five notes are in and of themselves, as a result of what Schumann has created in the musico-poetic world of this song, an expression of purity, Clara's purity.

I doubt, by the way, that Schumann actually designed this set of relationships in the sense of consciously constructing them, because he did not need to. This kind of attenuated correspondence between detail and structure, and the ability to adapt musical material to the finest shades of transformation, was natural to this composer, who is certainly one of these 'two dozen composers' mentioned above to whom this kind of complete musical control came as second nature: a species of control that is hard-earned of course by constant striving and thought, but informed by an unerring instinct possessed by few in any generation of artists. The same kind of reasoning applies to the listener. Genius is given to very few, but the ability to respond to genius is something all humans have in common, and if you sense perfection in a Schumann song, you do not necessarily know why, or may not be equipped by training and familiarity to be in a position to be able to try to understand why: what I would emphasize is the simple fact that you do not need that particular knowledge and understanding. This song was a gift not only to Clara.

A short ending

If Schumann were writing these words, but for voice and piano rather than word-processor, an 'Other' would now take over: not for long, and it would leave us, above all, pensive. Of Schumann's typical Lied, Kramer coined the winsome phrase 'a "song without words" but with words',[42] which, while being potentially misleading in what it can be taken to imply about the poetry, points so neatly to the unfathomable eloquence of Schumann's piano voice, which usually does, indeed, have the last wordless word. Yet the 'Other' is the piano only at a first level of secret meaning in Schumann, as Kramer in his penetrating and fecund probings of Romantic song is well aware. All of Schumann's singers know that they are permanently situated in a separate place. In *Frauenliebe* this separate place is perhaps supremely evident, and in this sense Solie, for all my questions that may even have seemed cavils, was dead on target. Not only that, for all of us modern critics, but Schneider wags an important biographical finger in saying that 'the female voice, clearly expressing a "not-I", allows Schumann to escape from his recurrent melancholia'.[43] There is probably a general point in those wise words. Schumann claimed to have 'done' his song writing in 1840, to have finished with it, yet he could never finally resist returning from time to time to this genre that he had transformed from the entrancing (Schubert, Mendelssohn) into the profoundly, intellectually bewitching.[44]

Notes

1. Beckett's actual English title was *How It Is*. Quoting from Beckett may seem to be a truly quixotic attempt to find meaning in part of a whole that is itself deeply obscure: still, one may find an extract

that one can well imagine Schumann himself understanding and thinking about, such as 'but that in reality we are one and all from the unthinkable first to the no less unthinkable last glued together in a vast imbrication of flesh without breach or fissure', Samuel Beckett, *How It Is* (New York, 1964), p. 140.

2. On 'time' and 'art' in relation to music see Jean-Jacques Nattiez, *Le combat de Chronos et d'Orphée* (Paris, 1993).

3. Beate Julia Perrey, *Schumann's 'Dichterliebe' and Early Romantic Poetics: Fragmentation of Desire* (Cambridge, 2002), p. 6.

4. Clara Schumann, *The Complete Correspondence of Clara and Robert Schumann: Critical Edition*, ed. E. Weissweiler, trans. H. Fritsch and R. Crawford (New York, 1994), 3 vols. vol. I, no. 105, 315. Note that in Schumann's original German verses there is a free rhyme scheme (Clara Schumann, *Briefwechsel; Clara und Robert Schumann: kritische Gesamtausgabe*, ed. E. Weissweiler, Frankfurt am Main, Roter Stern, 1984, vol. 1, No. 105, 312–6), some of the rhymes being apparently awkward and forced, but some highly elegant, which probably reflects the content of a poem that seems to be partly in fun, partly in deadly earnest, and of course shot through with Romantic irony.

5. *Unreife Versuche*, August Gerstmeier, *Die Lieder Schumanns: Zur Musik des frühen 19. Jahrhunderts* (Tutzing, 1982), p. 10, n. 6.

6. John Daverio, *Robert Schumann: Herald of a 'New Poetic Age'* (Oxford, 1997), p. 33.

7. Peter Ostwald, *Schumann: Music and Madness* (London, 1985), pp. 229–50. I use the word 'unfortunately' because the subtitle tends to sensationalize what is actually the clinically qualified and musically acute work of an extremely fine writer. Ostwald's American edition has a more subdued subtitle that is fairer to both the composer and its author: *The Inner Voices of a Musical Genius* (Boston, 1985).

8. Op. 79, No. 28 and Op. 98a, No. 1 are the same, a haunting setting of 'Kennst du das Land' that stands up against Beethoven's, Schubert's, Wolf's and those of many lesser composers, in which Daverio notes that 'each of the strophes . . . is cast as a miniature recitative and aria', Daverio, *Robert Schumann*, p. 429. Sams's comment on this song that 'despite its charm the result is incongruous in its inadequacy, relying too much on the composer's instruction "with enhanced expression in the second and third verses"' seems little short of weird: Eric Sams, *The Songs of Robert Schumann*, rev. edn (London, 1993), p. 212.

9. Ulrich Mahlert senses a valedictory character in Op. 89. See 'Rückung in die Idylle: Robert Schumanns *Sechs Gesänge von Wilfried von der Neun* op. 89', in *Schumanns Werke: Text und Interpretation, 16 Studien*, ed. Akio Mayeda (London, 1987), pp. 223–8.

10. Richard Pohl, 'Reminiscences of Robert Schumann (1878)', in *Schumann and His World*, ed. R. Larry Todd (Princeton, 1994), pp. 233–67 (p. 234). It was in Pohl's account that there first appeared a touching, chiding letter to him from Schumann written on 6 February 1854, including the comment 'what you miss in my compositions, especially in the lied 'Du meine Seele' [Op. 25, No. 1], is love', p. 261.

11. Kay Redfield Jamison, *Touched with Fire: Manic-Depressive Illness and the Artistic Temperament* (New York, 1993), pp. 144–7.

12. Leon B. Plantinga, *Romantic Music: A History of Musical Style in Nineteenth-Century Europe* (New York, 1984), pp. 235–6.

13. Wolfgang Hildesheimer, *Mozart* (London, 1983).

14. See Susan Youens, *Retracing a Winter's Journey: Schubert's 'Winterreise'* (Cornell, 1991), especially pp. 50–116.

15. Charles Rosen, *The Romantic Generation* (London, 1996), p. 125.

16. Schumann's re-creation of Heine's poems operates at a much deeper level than the repetition of words or lines and so on. As Cone observes, 'Schumann's *Dichter* inhabits a different world from that of his poetic original: a world in which words give way to music as the primary vehicle of expression, in which to speak is to sing, and in which to sing is to imagine the full implications of one's melody by auralizing an elaborate accompaniment. We should therefore not expect the personality of Schumann's *Dichter* to be the same as that of his purely poetic original.' 'Poet's love or composer's love', in *Music and Text: Critical Inquiries*, ed. Steven Paul Scher (Cambridge, 1992), pp. 177–92 (p. 185).

17. Daverio uses this term to describe Schumann's 'Kennst du das Land', Op. 98a, No. 1, which attracts special mention in his *Robert Schumann*, p. 19.

18. Between the eighth and ninth pieces of *Carnaval* Schumann provides three 'Sphinxes' showing the notes from which the work's themes are mostly derived.

19. Admittedly, Cone does hear a reference to Beethoven's *Eroica* funeral march in No. 16, bars 171–2, not knowing whether we will take this 'seriously or ironically' ('Poet's love', pp. 191–2). How far do we wish to explore such conceivable, intertextual resonances? They are of course tremendously seductive: once I have thought that the opening of No. 8 may, in a moment of pleasurable fantasy, rekindle the music of the beginning of Schubert's *Tod und das Mädchen* string quartet, will I ever be able to 'unthink' this?

20. Much has been made of this device, which, however, will not have seemed so special to Schumann, as can be seen from e.g. the *Liederkreis*, Op. 24, No. 8, or in the piano works, *Kreisleriana*, Op. 16, No. 4. For a subdominant 'closing' chord, see *Kinderszenen*, Op. 15, No. 12.

21. This frequently made point is, in my view, only superficially plausible. The proximate weight is on *Ich liebe dich* (bars 13^2–14^2), of which the following five chords are a semantic and harmonic 'afterbeat', but the hidden meaning here is in the momentous, if fleeting, dominant 13th under the first syllable of *bitterlich*, a harmony that is the keystone of the entire work, as a glance at the closing bars and, say, bars 28–9 of No. 7, '*Ich grolle nicht*', will confirm.

22. Perrey, *Schumann's 'Dichterliebe'*, p. 121. See pp. 116–21 for a full discussion of the historical evidence.

23. Arthur Komar, 'The music of *Dichterliebe*', in *Robert Schumann: Dichterliebe* (New York, 1971), pp. 63–94. For Ex. 18 see p. 80.

24. A test put forward in the many writings of Hans Keller, whose important psychological approach to music analysis is formulated concisely and demonstrated lucidly in 'The chamber music', in *The Mozart Companion*, ed. H. Robbins Landon and D. Mitchell (London, 1956), pp. 90–137.

25. Barthes writes that 'Schumannian tonality is simple, robust . . . an insistence . . . the tonic is . . . endowed with a . . . massiveness which insists, imposing its solitude to the point of obsession.' Roland Barthes, 'Loving Schumann', in his *The Responsibility of Forms: Critical Essays on Music, Art, and Representation*, trans. Richard Howard (Berkeley, 1985), pp. 293–8 (296–7).

26. Compare No. 16, bars 37^4–8, and No. 4, bars 13^3–14^2, mentioned above in n. 21. See also the sixth- and fifth-to-last words this poet ever sings, *meine Liebe*, No. 16, bars 48^4–9^3. In No. 13 this motif is used for the words *Träne* ('tears', bars 8–9) and *weinte* ('cried', bars 19–20).

27. With a certain amusing touch, focussing on the piano solo passage preceding these words, one commentator writes of No. 6 that 'it takes our heroine twenty-three bars of slow tempo to tell her husband that she is going to have a baby and even then it is the piano that has to tell him': Astra Desmond, *Schumann Songs* (London, 1972), p. 33. The analytical point here is to note the different corollaries of the 'same' musical figure: in the *Frauenliebe* case the motif conveys an object rather than an action, and a third-party reference rather than an image of self, and it is a figure that is sung rather than played.

28. R. Solie, in *Music and Text*, ed. Scher, pp. 219–40. McClary called the original paper on which Solie's essay is based 'superb', in *Feminine Endings: Music, Gender, and Sexuality* (Minnesota, 1991), p. 169, n. 6, and so it was – well, conspicuous – for its time, in raising issues about a compositional attitude in Schumann that revealed a significant ideological subtext of great interest to those who claimed that 'fundamental questions concerning meaning' were being prohibited (p. 4).

29. Arnold Schoenberg, 'The relationship to the text', in *Style and Idea* (London, 1975), pp. 141–5 (144). Schoenberg's idea of 'content' is clearly from a different era and point of view from Solie's.

30. See, for example, my *Performing Music: Shared Concerns* (Oxford, 1995), p. 37.

31. Lawrence Kramer, *Classical Music and Postmodern Knowledge* (Berkeley, 1995), pp. 144–5.

32. I have made the technical point above that Schumann is well able to use the same music, in essence, for both male and female personae, although I suppose it would be open to Solie to argue that there can be no 'real' (non-impersonating?) female personae coming from the voices of male culture – a veritable counsel of cultural despair.

33. Hayden White, 'Commentary', in *Music and Text*, ed. Scher, pp. 288–319 (292).

34. See Perrey, *Schumann's 'Dichterliebe'*, pp. 52–67.

35. These comments are not designed to be carping or disrespectful, but to reinforce this writer's view that musicology, be it however new, should be first of all *evidence*-based.

36. 'Schumann', in *Grove's Dictionary of Music and Musicians*, ed. J. Fuller Maitland, 2nd ed., 5 vols., vol. V (London, 1908), pp. 346–83 (374), my emphasis.

37. Probably the most recent, sustained consideration of this song is by Susan Youens in her article '"Pure" Song: "Du bist wie eine Blume" and the Heine Juggernaut', *Nineteenth-Century Music Review*, 2006, 3/2, 3–32. The historical and literary aspects of Heine's poem, set by well over four

hundred composers, in many languages and musical styles, certainly bear the kind of close, expertly informed scrutiny offered by Youens; although her febrile account of Schumann's setting, which seems bent on supposedly reading the composer's mind, and is scattered with generalized sociological and psychological inflections, may strike one as more whimsical than paradigmatic.

38. Sams, *The Songs*, pp. 50 and 74–5 respectively.

39. For discussion of the general issues as well as the specific case, see Rufus Hallmark, 'The poet sings', in *German Lieder in the Nineteenth Century*, ed. Hallmark (New York, 1996), pp. 75–118.

40. In line with current performing practice, a 'corrected' edition is reproduced here, as also recommended by Sams, who notes how 'it seems incredible that not only the (undated) manuscript but the first and many subsequent editions have the misreading of "so schoen und rein und hold" for the second line as well as the last', *The Songs*, p. 74. Clearly, I tend to disagree with Sams's term 'misreading'.

41. Having mentioned the harmony, and further to the mention of Barthes's memorable encapsulation of 'Schumannian tonality' in n. 25, I offer to the specialist the observation that 'Du bist wie eine Blume' is at one level a study in chromaticism. For example, note how after a tonic insertion at the end of bar 18 producing an acute false relation between E and E flat, the progression halted at the third quaver of bar 18 is in fact taken up in the following bar, completing a III–[V]–VI–II–V cycle. More generally, the whole chromatic unfolding repays close study. It will come as no surprise – although there is something miraculous about it – to those who have studied chromatic completion in, for example, Mozart, that the texturally isolated E that tips the music into the second verse on the very final semiquaver of bar 9 completes the first chromatic aggregate in this song.

42. Lawrence Kramer, *Music and Poetry: The Nineteenth Century and After* (Berkeley, 1984), p. 131.

43. Michel Scheider, *La tombée du jour: Schumann* (Paris, 1989), p. 155, my translation.

44. I borrow these two adverbs from Spitta (see n. 36), p. 373.

7 The chamber music

LINDA CORRELL ROESNER

On 12 September 1851, Robert and Clara Schumann's eleventh wedding anniversary, Robert Schumann began work on a 'Duo for Pianoforte and Violin'.[1] This work, the Sonata in A minor for Pianoforte and Violin, Op. 105, was the first of an exceptional group of three chamber works to be written in a two-month period of intense creativity, the others being the Piano Trio in G minor, Op. 110 and the Sonata in D minor for Violin and Pianoforte, Op. 121. All three compositions embody the culmination of the composer's ever innovative approach to large-scale musical form, his response to the sonata structures that were the legacy of Haydn, Mozart and particularly Beethoven, and that Schumann, citing the example of Schubert, had always believed must continually be created anew if the cherished forms were to remain viable.[2]

In his reviews of contemporary music in the *Neue Zeitschrift für Musik*, Schumann had returned often to the principle of the organic unfolding of a large-scale musical work. His ideal was Beethoven's treatment of symphonic form, 'where in rapid succession the ideas appear [ever] changing and yet are linked through an inner, spiritual bond'.[3] The inner, spiritual bond among ideas is intrinsic to Schumann's earliest published compositions, the cycles of character pieces written for solo piano in the 1830s, in which 'motto' themes, fragile, intuitive melodic links, and carefully crafted tonal designs combine in each work to form a whole that is far greater than the sum of its parts.

In the 1830s Schumann also explored large-scale form in works that seem on the surface to be sonata-based, but that in reality break new ground. His experiments with 'parallel' forms[4] reveal that the traditional, hierarchical designs built on tonal conflict and resolution that governed the elaborate sonata forms of the Viennese Classical composers were of limited use to Schumann, whose musical language relished and even required tonal schemes that were artificially created and sometimes even symbolic. When he made use of Classical tonal principles, he tended to employ them as gesture and rhetoric – pointedly acknowledging the tradition – or as subterfuge.

In January 1841, four months after his marriage, Schumann began to compose a symphony: No. 1 in B flat major, Op. 38. This undertaking was enthusiastically received by Clara Schumann: 'The Symphony will soon be finished; although I haven't heard any of it yet, I am endlessly happy that Robert has finally entered the field where, with his great imagination he belongs; I think that he will also work himself to the point where he will no longer compose anything besides instrumental music.'[5] Clara refers to the fact that all of Schumann's published compositions had been for piano solo or – in 1840, the year of their marriage – for voice and piano. However, in the preceding decade Schumann had written, or planned, music for other combinations of instruments.[6] One of his projects involved string quartets.[7]

In Schumann's quest for new solutions to large-scale form, it is clear that 1841, the so-called Symphony Year, was a breakthrough. He produced two important and influential symphonic works: the B flat major ('Spring') Symphony, Op. 38, and the D minor Symphony, Op. 120. The former acknowledges the symphonic tradition while at the same time pointing in a new direction. The latter is a radical experiment in cyclic form that incorporates the unifying tendencies in Schumann's music up to that point and heralds the total unification of his late works.[8] Elsewhere I have posited that the structural achievements of the aforementioned three chamber works of autumn 1851 inspired Schumann to return to the D minor symphony, which he had set aside after its unsuccessful première in December 1841.[9] In the present essay I propose to examine aspects of the relationship between structure and musical language in Schumann's chamber music in selected works from the 'chamber-music' year of 1842, and the autumn of 1851.

1842

Schumann's three string quartets, Op. 41, were conceived at a gratifying time in the composer's career: his first published symphony (Op. 38) had been well received and he was acquiring a reputation in the musical world as a composer of instrumental music. On 14 February 1842 he wrote in his *Haushaltbuch*, the household accounts book in which he also kept an abbreviated diary, that he was continually thinking about quartets.[10] On 20 March, after returning to Leipzig from a month on tour in northern Germany, where his B flat major Symphony had been performed in Bremen and Hamburg, Schumann renewed his sporadic study of counterpoint to compensate for his 'miserable life'[11] without Clara (who had continued on to Scandinavia to fulfil concert obligations). He began to study the string quartets of Mozart on 1 April. On 28 April, two days after Clara's homecoming, Schumann turned his attention to the quartets of Beethoven, and then, on 6 May, to the quartets of Haydn. On 2 June he began quartet 'experiments' ('*Quartettversuche*'), and on 4 June began to sketch his first quartet.[12]

Schumann's string quartets are grounded in the noble tradition of the genre.[13] In some respects they are less adventuresome than either of the two symphonies of 1841. But Schumann's quartets testify to the composer's careful study of quartet texture, even though in 1842 he still composed at the piano. When the three quartets are considered as a cycle, they also illustrate a unique conception of musical form in the largest dimension.

Opus 41, Nos. 1 and 2

Schumann's entry in his *Haushaltbuch* for 4 June 1842 reads: 'Quartet in A minor begun; movement in F Major and A minor'.[14] This statement demonstrates that Schumann had planned the dual tonal nature of Op. 41, No. 1 from the very beginning. The first movement, in an unorthodox F major after a slow introduction in A minor, sets the stage for the entire quartet, over the course of which the tonal duality is maintained and never really resolved. In a sense Schumann is playing with Classical formal stereotypes. With the exception of the finale, each of the movements makes use of more-or-less 'traditional' tonal/formal schemes, even though these function only marginally in a Classical manner. A case in point is the first movement.

The sonata-form exposition of the first movement (*Allegro*) of Op. 41, No. 1 features the standard Classical keys: tonic (F major) and dominant (C major). However, Schumann's musical ideas and the way in which he presents them seem deliberately at odds with the Classical premise of tonal conflict, to all intents and purposes eliminating it. The principal area (bars 34–75) establishes the tonic, as is customary, but it does so with a lyrical, perfectly rounded 'song form' set forth as a series of regular four-bar phrases with a beginning in the tonic, a modulatory middle, and an ending in the tonic. It comes to an abrupt halt (bar 75). The rest of the exposition is built – *à la* Haydn – on permutation, variation and logical extension (see bars 99ff.) of the main thematic idea. The passages of contrapuntal texture and the modulatory sequences give the impression of a lengthy transition even though the phrase structure remains predominantly regular. The second tonal area (C major) is not reached until the very end of the exposition (first ending, bars 9ff.). Thematically it features yet another variant of the main theme. Schumann in effect negates the Classical tonal hierarchy by greatly subordinating the second (contrasting) tonal area: he denies it its own theme, preferring to emphasize the unifying aspects of a single thematic idea; he postpones its arrival until the last possible minute, again emphasizing unification. Thematic differentiation is not crucial in Classical sonata style (Haydn is famous for his 'monothematic' expositions); tonal polarity, on the other hand, is its driving force. In a prototypical

Classical sonata-form exposition, the second – conflicting – key is arrived at by means of a transitional passage from the first key, is established tonally (and often defined thematically and/or stylistically), can then be departed from temporarily, but is always returned to and confirmed toward the end of the exposition.

Schumann had his own idea of tonal structure. He did not generally employ keys for their functional properties, but used them conceptually for their referential value, almost as chess pieces in an intricate game. The 'game' of the Op. 41 quartets is the interplay of A minor, F major and A major, and their ultimate union. Schumann carries it out over the course of all three quartets. There are very few thematic links in the cycle. In keeping with the intellectual rigour of the 'noble' genre, the cyclic links are on the highest and yet the most fundamental plane, the tonal underpinnings.

The middle movements of Op. 41, No. 1 symbolize the tonal dichotomy of this quartet. The *Scherzo* is in A minor; the *Adagio* in F major. The equivocation with regard to the tonic key of the quartet then becomes the subject matter of the *Presto* finale, which begins in A minor. The exposition begins traditionally enough. The tonic key, A minor, seems to be set forth clearly: a four-bar phrase (antecedent) in the tonic, a four-bar phrase (consequent) on the dominant. The next two four-bar phrases are in the tonic, but the harmonic palette is enriched with Neapolitan chords and the chord rhythm is syncopated, causing the tonic chords to fall on weak beats. Schumann deliberately avoids a strong cadence in the main key, thus suggesting that perhaps it is not the main key at all. He upsets the symmetry with a sudden drop to the dominant of C major on the first beat of bar 17, initiating a six-bar phrase (bars 17–22) that arrives – via a powerful, rhetorically 'functional' cadence – in C major in bar 23. The arrival in C major is a parody of the Classical style. The cadence is handled as if it were the concluding cadence in the main (tonic) key. The thematic material that enters here sounds typically transitional and the listener expects a transition to the second tonal area. But in reality the 'contrasting' key has already been reached. The key of C, the relative major (the traditional contrast key when the tonic is minor), will be appropriately and Classically reinforced in bars 63ff., the closing area of the exposition, but not until a reminder of the 'real' tonal argument – A minor vs. F major – has been introduced. After several bars of alternating tonic and dominant chords in C major over a tonic pedal (bars 23–7, a pause on C major, as it were), A minor (bars 28–30) and F major (bars 31–4) are tonicized and harmonies associated with them juxtaposed (bars 35–8) before a sequence of modulations based on a variant of the main theme leads to the vigorous return of C major in bar 63.

In this exposition the presumed tonic (A minor) is exchanged, so to speak, for the new key (C major) just when it should have been unequivocally established. The new key, arrived at harmonically with such great force and drama, is not accorded any comparable thematic interest until the closing area of the exposition, where the 'transitional' figure in quavers that marked its entrance in bar 23 is combined with a variant of the main theme (bars 63ff.). The role of C major in this quartet seems to be as a foil. In the first movement C major had been deliberately diminished in its role as contrast. In the exposition of the finale it attempts to usurp the role of 'main' key. But the unusual way in which the musical material is later recapitulated suggests that it has really served as a stand-in for F major.

Toward the end of a development section in which the aforementioned quaver figure is featured in combination with a variant of the main theme, Schumann again prepares a rhetorical arrival in C (bars 140–8). But this time a measure of uncertainty is introduced since it appears that C will be inflected in its minor mode. However, the resolution is indeed to a C major triad (bar 148), initiating a mysterious, suddenly *piano* passage, rich in altered chords (bars 148–52) that functions as the dominant of F major. At this point the entire second tonal area of the exposition (bars 23–76), which had seen the ascendancy of C major, is recapitulated in F major (bars 152–205). By the time the strong closing area is reached (bars 192ff.) there can be no doubt that F major, a key that appeared only briefly in the exposition, is the key that is recapitulated, and that the C major of the exposition had merely been its surrogate.

Although one may have been puzzled at the tonal treatment of the finale's exposition, when one reaches this juncture in the recapitulation one can only wonder what the tonic key of the movement is. The normal function of a recapitulation is to resolve the tonal conflict of the exposition by presenting in the tonic the material that earlier had been heard in the contrasting key. But in this finale the F major recapitulation, resolving nothing, continues to contribute to the tonal dichotomy of the quartet as a whole. Schumann complicates the matter still further with another grand rhetorical build-up, this time on the dominant of A minor (bars 206–13), and proceeds to recapitulate the principal area of the exposition in its A minor tonic. This is a literal repeat, complete with the equivocal turn toward C, but without the cadence in C. Instead, an eight-bar passage (bars 234ff.) leads conclusively back to A minor. Schumann, however, is not finished. In a coda that begins with a seemingly extraneous Haydnesque/Beethovenian folk-like, hurdy-gurdy tune (actually it is generated from the opening intervals of the quaver figure), he brings the quartet to a 'Classical' close in the affirmative major mode of what we now might be willing to conclude is the tonic: A. But is it?

Opus 41, No. 1 commences a quartet cycle that was conceived as a cycle and ideally should be performed as one. The linkage of Op. 41, No. 1 and Op. 41, No. 2 is especially strong. Schumann's *Haushaltbuch* reveals that the composer began to sketch Op. 41, No. 2 (on 11 June 1842) immediately upon completing the sketch of Op. 41, No. 1 (on 10 June). He wrote out the fair copies in score of both quartets before beginning to sketch Op. 41, No. 3. The autograph of the fair copy of No. 2 (**D-Dühi**, 78.5025) shows that Schumann even considered a direct link between the first two quartets: the last four bars (bars 30–3) of the *Introduzione* to the first movement of No. 1 – a powerful build-up on the dominant of F major that prepares for the *Allegro* in F major – reappear as an introduction to the first movement of No. 2, but were later deleted.[15] (Schumann's sketch of the first movement of Op. 41, No. 2 (**D-B**, Mus. ms. autogr. Schumann 19) does not contain this introduction.)

If Op. 41, No. 2 is viewed in the context of the tonal quandary posed by No. 1, the inconclusiveness with regard to the tonic key of No. 1 would seem to be resolved in favour of the unequivocal F major of No. 2. The role played by C major in both quartets is central and an important part of the linkage. In Classical tonal practice, C major is the traditional contrast key of both A minor (where it is the relative major) and F major (where it is the dominant). How simple and appropriate for Schumann to employ the traditional in this most intellectually rigorous of the Classical genres. And how typical of the composer to invest C major with the power to mislead and detour the tonal argument in the finale of Op. 41, No. 1, only to use it in its most straightforward role – as contrasting key – in both the first movement and the finale of No. 2. The key of C major also links the *scherzo* movements of the two quartets by appropriating the exact centre of each: the *Intermezzo* of the *scherzo* of No. 1 and the *Trio* of the *scherzo* of No. 2. Perhaps most intriguing of all is Schumann's symbolic use of C major in No. 2. In two earlier compositions he had employed C major in a symbolic role as a form of declaration and dedication to Clara ($C = $ Clara): the *Davidsbündlertänze*, Op. 6 and the C major *Fantasie*, Op. 17.[16] (He would later 'dedicate' another C major work to her, the C major Symphony, Op. 61.)[17] At the end of the first movement of the *Fantasie* (bars 295ff.) Schumann includes an unmistakable reference to the Lied 'Nimm sie hin, denn, diese Lieder' ('Take them, then, these songs') from Beethoven's Lieder cycle *An die ferne Geliebte* (*To the distant beloved*). (See Examples 7.1 and 7.2.) He again makes use of this reference in the finale of Op. 41, No. 2, where it forms the second subject, in C major (bars 36ff.; Ex. 7.3a). In Schumann's sketch the melodic line of the theme was originally even closer to that of the Beethoven Lied (Ex. 7.3b). Several years later, in the C major Symphony, Op. 61, a work that has structural ties to Op. 17 and that makes thematic reference to Clara,[18] the theme emerges toward the end of the finale (bars 394ff.; Ex. 7.4) and embodies the tonal and emotional goal of the entire symphony.[19]

Example 7.1 Beethoven, *An die ferne Geliebte*, Op. 98, No. 6, bars 9–10

Example 7.2 Schumann, *Fantasie* in C major, Op. 17, 1st movement, bars 296–7

Example 7.3a Schumann, Quartet in F major, Op. 41, No. 2, 4th movement, bars 36–8

Example 7.3b Schumann, Op. 41, No. 2, 4th movement, bars 36–8, sketch (***D-B***, Mus. ms. autogr. Schumann 19, fol. 16v.)

Example 7.4 Schumann, Symphony in C major, Op. 61, 4th movement, bars 394–7

In 1836, the time of composition of the *Fantasie*, Clara Wieck was indeed Schumann's 'distant beloved'. Her father, Friedrich Wieck, was actively discouraging their relationship. In a letter to Clara of 19 March 1838 Schumann describes the *Fantasie* as 'a deep lament for you'.[20] During the time of gestation of the Op. 41 quartets, Clara Schumann's lengthy concert tour separated the couple for the first time since their wedding. Later in the year, on Clara's twenty-third birthday, 13 September 1842, Schumann's gift to her was the manuscript of the three quartets ('Take them, then, these songs').[21] In December 1845 Schumann sketched his C major Symphony while in the final stages of recovery from a severe mental depression suffered in 1844.[22] This symphony, which was one of Clara Schumann's favourite works,[23]

Example 7.5 Schumann, Quartet in A major, Op. 41, No. 3, 1st movement, bars 1–2

might be considered an offering to her, the beloved made distant by the tribulations of mental illness.

Opus 41, No. 3

The key of A major, appearing for the first time at the end of Op. 41, No. 1, totally absent from Op. 41, No. 2, returns as the tonic key of Op. 41, No. 3. The bright major key does not make an entrance in the theatrical sense at the beginning of the first movement, but rather emerges, or is coaxed, out of an inconclusive recitative-like introduction, *Andante espressivo*, which begins on a minor 7th chord on the supertonic that leads to a deceptive cadence on F sharp minor (the relative minor) (Ex. 7.5). After an additional five bars of similarly deceptive progressions, the exposition, *Allegro molto moderato*, begins with the same chord progression as the introduction, but this time cadencing in the tonic (bar 11). Space does not permit a discussion of this finely wrought movement in the detail it deserves.[24] I shall confine my remarks to the role of this movement and the finale in the overall form of the quartet cycle.

The principal tonal area of the first movement of Op. 41, No. 3 is so short (two four-bar phrases, bars 8–15) that it barely establishes the tonic. The continuation and expansion of the theme in bars 16ff. leads one to expect that Schumann will return to the tonic by means of a perfectly rounded design similar to the 'song form' of the principal tonal area of the first movement of No. 1. This turns out almost to be the case, except that the 'rounding out' with a return to the two opening phrases of the principal theme occurs not in the A major tonic, but in the dominant-of-the-dominant, B major (bars 28–35). In this way – deliberately exploiting the contradiction between the periodicity of the thematic content and the 'wrong' key – Schumann prepares the entrance of the contrasting key, the traditional dominant, E major. The arrival of E major, however, is postponed by a Haydnesque surprise, for Schumann also seizes upon this moment to project the tonal plan of the entire cycle. After the cadence in B major in bar 35, he interjects, *forte*, a strong cadence in C major (bars 36–7) and follows this with a statement of the first phrase of the main theme in C major (bars 38–41). This startling interruption gives way to a short modulatory passage to the second tonal area, E major.

It is most interesting to observe that the interjection of C major does not appear in Schumann's sketch. The passage from bars 36 to 45 is more than twice as long in the sketch and contains no hint of C major, but instead modulates through F sharp minor before arriving at E major.[25] I believe that the 'break-in' of C major in a movement where the tonic key emerges only gradually is Schumann's wonderfully subtle way of linking Op. 41, No. 3 to the two previous quartets in the cycle. The key of C major played an important role in the tonal drama of Nos. 1 and 2. By injecting it into a movement that begins ambivalently, Schumann recalls the role of C major in the tonally equivocal finale of No. 1, and in so doing harks back to the A minor– F major dichotomy of the first two parts of the cycle, suggesting that perhaps it was not a dichotomy at all. Significantly, the key that is interjected at bars 36ff. of the first movement of No. 3 is neither F major nor A minor, but C major, the key that F major and A minor share as their respective 'contrasting' key, and hence the key that unites them. No further reference to the tonal narrative of the first two quartets is needed in this first movement of No. 3. The ambivalent principal theme is not even really recapitulated. In an elision of the end of the development section and the beginning of the recapitulation (bars 146–53) the principal theme returns, but is not permitted to cadence in the A major tonic. Poised over its dominant 7th chord, it is made to serve as the lead-in to the secondary theme, which then takes over the task of affirming the tonic key.

After a variation movement, *Assai agitato*, in F sharp minor (the relative minor of A major) and a slow movement, *Adagio molto*, in the subdominant, D major, the rondo finale of Op. No. 3, *Allegro molto vivace*, completes the task of tonally unifying the three quartets by systematically incorporating their tonalities: A major (No. 3) and the F major– A minor– C major complex (Nos. 1 and 2). This movement, uncompromisingly sectional and stuffed with repetitive phrases and unrelenting rhythms, seems tedious and too long. But when viewed in the context of its tonal function in the cycle, it is clear that its structure is an integral part of the overall plan.

Essentially, the finale is a parallel construction (see Figure 7.1). In Schumann's unique 'parallel' forms of the 1830s, the second half of the structure paralleled and reinterpreted the first half.[26] Here the function of

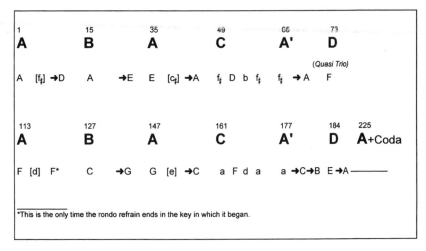

Figure 7.1 Op. 41/3, finale (major keys in capital letters; minor in lower-case).

the second half is less to reinterpret the first part of the finale than to 'review' and conclude the tonal narrative of the quartet cycle. The first half of the rondo, a refrain and two contrasting episodes, presents the A major tonic of Op. 41, No. 3 and its related keys (E major, F sharp minor, D major). A section titled *Quasi Trio* appears midway through the movement. Its key is F major, the first reference in No. 3 to the tonal complex of the two previous quartets since the interjection of C major in the exposition of the first movement. After the *Quasi Trio* the second half of the rondo parallels the first half and is constructed so that the keys emphasized are those of the tonal complex of Nos. 1 and 2: F major, C major, A minor. Finally, a harmonic change near the end of the long parallel (see bars 181–4) leads to a return of the 'quasi trio' beginning in the dominant, E major, and ending in the tonic, thus breaking the parallel and returning to the A major sphere of No. 3.[27]

Schumann's achievement in the Op. 41 quartets, the systematic unification of three otherwise self-contained works by means of a carefully worked out tonal narrative, is impressive and may be unprecedented. Tonal narratives and 'tonal programmes' – narratives carried a step further, such as the symbolic and emotional use of C major as the tonic of all of the movements of the C major Symphony, Op. 61 – as structural underpinnings in large-scale forms are important means to achieving Schumann's aesthetic goal of total unification of the musical material. In the composer's works of the early 1840s the attainment of this goal often seems hampered by his musical language, characterized during this period by a tendency toward rigid phrase structure, fast harmonic rhythm, and harmonic compartmentalization at the phrase level, all traits that carried over from composition by improvisation at the piano. In 1845 Schumann began to compose away from the piano: 'Not until the year 1845, when I began to conceive and work out everything in my head, did an entirely different manner of composition begin to develop.'[28] The works of the late 1840s and early 1850s bear out the composer's observation. The unifying elements that had always been present in Schumann's music – the subtle and not-so-subtle melodic and rhythmic links within and between movements, the contrapuntal combination of themes and motives, the referential use of key – are assimilated into a fluid and powerful ongoing style in which the cyclicism so crucial to the works of every period of the composer's career is intensified. Every detail of the music is absorbed into a synthesis in which everything relates to everything else.

The Op. 41 quartets were Schumann's first and last compositions in the string quartet genre. All of his other large-scale chamber works are for various combinations of strings and piano. The autumn of 1842 saw the composition of two masterpieces: the celebrated Quintet for Piano and Strings in E flat major, Op. 44 (written for and officially dedicated to Clara Schumann: a very 'public' and brilliant work that nonetheless manages to incorporate a private message – the bass theme of Schumann's *Impromptus sur une Romance de Clara Wieck*, Op. 5 appears as the theme of Trio I of the *Scherzo* (bars 45 ff.) and is again embedded in the main theme of the finale (see bars 2–3)), and the equally brilliant but also more intimate Quartet for Piano and Strings in E flat major, Op. 47. In December 1842 Schumann composed a trio in A minor for piano and strings, but as a piano trio this work is so unorthodox in structure that he apparently felt it could not represent the genre. He did not publish it until 1850, and then as *Phantasiestücke*, Op. 88. Schumann would return to the genre of the piano trio in 1847 (Trio in D minor, Op. 63; Trio in F major, Op. 80) and in the autumn of 1851 (Trio in G minor, Op. 110).

1851

Schumann's late style manifests a breadth and continuity not present earlier. Its characteristics include a tendency toward tonal synthesis,[29] dense textures, increased rhythmic flexibility and a marked slowing of the harmonic rhythm coupled with a leaning toward rapidly moving, almost rhapsodic melodic lines. Nine years almost to the day after Schumann presented the Op. 41 quartets to his wife on her birthday, the composer, after a hiatus of four years, turned again to large-scale chamber music to explore a new genre. The 'duo' for pianoforte and violin (Sonata in A minor for Pianoforte and Violin, Op. 105[30]), begun on 12 September 1851, returns to the A minor–F major focus of Op. 41, Nos. 1 and 2. But whereas the Schumann of 1842 examined and ultimately – in Op. 41, No. 3 – resolved the dichotomy between the two keys, the Schumann of 1851 pursues their synthesis from the very beginning. He employs an extremely sophisticated thematic integration together with a familiar structural procedure: de-emphasis of the secondary area of the exposition of a sonata-form movement both tonally and thematically.

In the A minor Sonata, Op. 105, the playing down of the secondary area in both the first movement and the finale highlights the tonal plan of the work as a whole. In the first movement the secondary tonal area of the exposition is the 'traditional' relative major, C. However, Schumann uses many techniques to avoid establishing this key. The exposition is monothematic and features a remarkable continuous expansion of the principal theme; therefore no new theme is present to aid in delineating the new key. The key of C major is arrived at almost by stealth (see bars 35ff.) and a cadence in the key is avoided until near the end of the exposition (bar 59, where the C major chord falls on a weak beat). Furthermore, C major is infused with hints of its subdominant, F major. This has wide-ranging structural ramifications, because the tonal plan of the entire sonata hinges on A minor and F major as two faces of what is essentially one *gesamt* tonality.[31]

It is instructive to see how so many of the melodic, harmonic and expressive details of Op. 105 delineate and confirm the synthesis of A minor and F major, for example: the crescendo to an accented f^1 appoggiatura over an A minor triad and tonic pedal in bar 1 of the first movement (Ex. 7.6a) and, more tellingly, the return of the passage in augmentation in the recapitulation, where the A minor triad is followed by an F major triad (bars 113–15; Ex. 7.6b); the hints at F major in bars 11–13 of the first movement; the build-up on a dominant pedal of F major in the retransition of the first movement (bars 104ff.) culminating in the superposition of the dominant of A minor over the dominant pedal of F (bars 108–9) and a juxtaposition of A minor and F major triads (bars 110–11) that is then repeated at the beginning of the recapitulation (bars 113–15); and the abrupt deceptive cadence to an F major triad at the beginning of the coda of the first movement (bar 177).

In the finale Schumann does not even bother to go through the motions of presenting the secondary area of the exposition in the relative major. The new key *is* F major (bars 31ff.). But in the exposition of the finale F major is not stressed and is not presented as a conflicting key. Significantly, it is almost immediately juxtaposed with A minor (bars 36–41) and, in fact, the end of the exposition reverts to the tonic, A minor, propelling the music, *perpetuum-mobile*-like, back to the beginning of the exposition or forward into the development section. By the time the development section of the

Example 7.6a Schumann, Sonata in A minor for Pianoforte and Violin, Op. 105, 1st movement, bars 1–2

Example 7.6b Schumann, Sonata in A minor for Pianoforte and Violin, Op. 105, 1st movement, bars 113–16

finale is reached, the 'dual-tonal' unity of the sonata is assured. Therefore, the seemingly new, lyric theme that enters in bar 76 after a dramatic build-up is an emotional and highly charged event, all the more so for appearing in the bright key of E major, the dominant (Ex. 7.7). It is the only event in the entire sonata that is so unambiguously prepared. And this preparation, coming after the tonal synthesis and rhythmic homogeneity of the exposition, leads the ear to accept E major and the lyric theme as the true 'second subject', a welcome element of contrast. The new theme, however, is quickly amalgamated into the sonata by being interlaced with previously heard motifs. And

Example 7.7 Schumann, Sonata in A minor for Pianoforte and Violin, Op. 105, 3rd movement, bars 76–82

its relationship to the rest of the sonata is revealed when the principal theme of the first movement appears in the coda of the finale – significantly, over F and A pedals (bars 168ff.). Here the rhythm of the first-movement theme has been altered to evoke the rhythm of the E major theme of the finale (Ex. 7.8). Furthermore, it becomes apparent that the two themes are related intervallically. Thus the E major theme, a seemingly extraneous element in an otherwise totally and carefully unified design, is shown by means of a cyclic recall to be intimately connected with the main thematic idea of the sonata (and, by extension, with its tonal identity).

The A minor Sonata, Op. 105, closely knit in the extreme, is a particularly good example of the undermining of the sonata principle of tonal conflict and resolution in favour of a thematic and tonal unification that can absorb even the most disparate elements. The first movements of the Piano Trio, Op. 110, and the Violin and Piano Sonata, Op. 121, while not as relentlessly

Example 7.8 Schumann, Sonata in A minor for Pianoforte and Violin, Op. 105, 3rd movement, bars 168–71

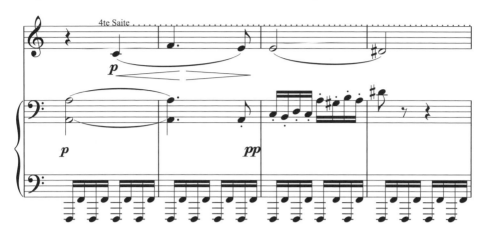

monothematic as the outer movements of Op. 105, also illustrate the prevalence in Schumann's late sonata-based forms of a continuous blending of the thematic elements: a 'secondary theme' is so permeated with elements of the principal theme that the result is one large, fully integrated and continuously expanding thematic complex. In both works this thematic integration is reinforced by de-emphasizing the tonal contrast of the secondary area: strong cadences in the new key are avoided until the last possible moment, and the new key – the relative major in both works – is laced with allusions to its subdominant (in both works the subdominant of the relative major plays an important role in later movements). It may be appropriate to conclude this essay with a discussion of the almost Mahlerian interplay of melodic, rhythmic and harmonic details that, together with a carefully constructed tonal plan, epitomize Schumann's late approach to large-scale composition. The Sonata in D minor for Violin and Pianoforte, Op. 121, will serve as illustration.

In the D minor Sonata, Op. 121, Schumann employs a 'motto' based on the musical letters in the name of the dedicatee, his long-time friend, the violinist Ferdinand David (*DAF* [= v] *D*).[32] The motto appears in block chords at the beginning of the introduction, *Ziemlich langsam* (Ex. 7.9a),[33] and is featured as the 'head motif' of the principal theme (bars 21ff.) of the first movement. It is important to observe that this theme is characterized by the motto's rhythmic pattern as much as by its melodic intervals, if not more so. Example 7.9b gives a few of the melodic variants of the motto that emerge during the course of the first movement. Some of the less obvious appearances of the motto in later movements are also illustrated. (The cumulative impact of the sonata suggests motto linkages that may seem tenuous when isolated in a music example.)

Example 7.9a Schumann, Sonata in D minor for Violin and Pianoforte, Op. 121, 1st movement, bars 1–5

The technique of melodic variation on a characteristic rhythmic pattern is one that Schumann favoured throughout his life. (He employs it with breathtaking effect in the first movement of the Piano Quintet, Op. 44.) In Op. 121 the technique is brought to bear not only on the motto, but on virtually every thematic element in the sonata. The syncopated rhythmic pattern in the fourth bar of the principal theme (bar 24; see the first line in Ex. 7.9b), for example, is of particular importance as a unifying link between the movement's principal theme and second subject (bars 57ff.; Ex. 7.10), where both the violin and piano lines are permeated by syncopated patterns. In the closing area of the exposition and over the course of the development section Schumann gives increasing prominence to syncopation, applying it to the motto of the principal theme and using it to interrelate and to shed new perspective on all of the thematic components of the movement. In bars 84–96, for example, the motto proceeds from its 'straight' rhythm via the syncopated fourth bar of the principal theme to a new, syncopated form (bars 88ff.). Another syncopated form (bars 93ff.) then offers a backward glance to the block chords of the introduction. In a passage near the beginning of the development section, aspects of the second subject meld seamlessly with the syncopated rhythm of the fourth bar of the principal theme (bars 107ff.), which in turn leads into a forceful presentation of the rhythmically 'straight' form of the motto in the bass line (bars 115ff.).

The ongoing connection of the thematic elements in this movement is truly extraordinary and nearly Brahmsian in the respect that it is impossible to separate 'melodic' from 'accompanimental'. Everything heard at any one

Example 7.9b Schumann, Op. 121, "motto" variants.

Example 7.10 Schumann, Sonata in D Minor for Violin and Pianoforte, Op. 121, 1st movement, bars 57–66

time has to be deemed thematic. Consider the opening bars of the exposition (Ex. 7.11). Here (bars 21ff.) the motto in the violin is heard over a syncopated figure featuring semiquavers in the piano that might normally be construed as accompanimental. Syncopation, however, as we have seen, will play a central role in thematically integrating the movement. And here it appears, almost incidentally, in the first bar of the exposition. The 'accompaniment' is transferred to the violin (bar 27), passed back and forth between piano and violin (bars 34ff.), incorporated into the cadential gesture of the principal tonal area (bars 40–3), accorded a leading role in the transition (bars 43ff.), and, with a new melodic shape, made to serve as a lead-in to the second subject (bars 53ff.), which it then pervades (see bars 57ff. in Ex. 7.10).

In Schumann's late style, thematic ideas that may appear incidental and even inconsequential at first often take on increased prominence as a work progresses.[34] The cadential gesture at the end of the principal area of the

Example 7.11 Schumann, Sonata in D minor for Violin and Pianoforte, Op. 121, 1st movement, bars 21–5

exposition (bars 41ff.), for example, seems merely to be a typical cadential formula (see Ex. 7.12a). The succession of four even notes, beginning on a weak beat and ending on a strong beat (marked with + in Ex. 7.12a.), however, will prove to be important in the cyclical unification of the sonata. In the development section of the first movement a powerful rhetorical build-up on the dominant of C minor prepares the entrance of a seemingly new theme in C minor (pianoforte, bars 155ff.; Ex. 7.12b). Not surprisingly, this theme is built on syncopation, but it is syncopation of the barline and the notes are of even value and deployed so as to suggest a series of successions of four even notes beginning on a weak beat and ending on a strong beat. At the beginning of the coda of the first movement the cadence from bar

Example 7.12a Schumann, Sonata in D minor for Violin and Pianoforte, Op. 121, 1st movement, bars 40–3

Example 7.12b Schumann, Sonata in D minor for Violin and Pianoforte, Op. 121, 1st movement, bars 155–7

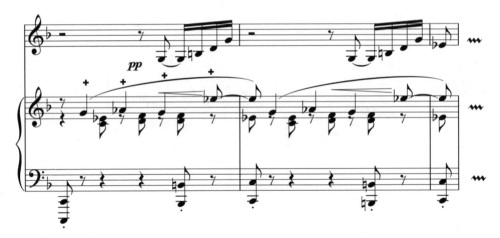

41 reappears expanded and in quasi-sequence, and seems to grow logically out of the chordal form of the motto (bars 261–7).

At the start of the second movement (*Sehr lebhaft*) the four-note pattern becomes an integral part of the theme of the A periods (Ex. 7.13). Note how Schumann emphasizes the pitches with *forte* indications on each of the four notes.[35] (It is no coincidence that in this movement the four notes also happen to be a permutation of the motto.) Toward the end of the second movement the four-note pattern takes on even more prominence as it appears in a climactic role, expanded and with a new melodic line (bars 196–204; Ex. 7.14a). The *forte* dynamic indication, the strong ^ accents in the piano, and the detached staccato in the violin combine to highlight this

Example 7.13 Schumann, Sonata in D minor for Violin and Pianoforte, Op. 121, 2nd movement, bars 2–6

Example 7.14a Schumann, Sonata in D minor for Violin and Pianoforte, Op. 121, 2nd movement, bars 196–200

moment. This apparent climax, however, is only a prelude to the true climax of the movement: a striking new chorale-like theme[36] projected *fortissimo* in B major (the tonic major) on the same rhythmic pattern (Ex. 7.14b). This theme, set in triple metre and totally transformed in character, becomes the theme of the variation movement that follows (*Leise, einfach*). Lest we forget that it, too, derives ultimately from the motto (by way of the melodic and rhythmic connections set up in the second movement), Schumann provides a 'remembrance'. Halfway through the third movement, in a bridge passage that precedes the final, Lied-like variation,[37] two *forte* interjections of the second movement's main theme with its four-note-patterned permutation of the motto (see bars 74ff., 84ff. of the third movement) encircle the 'new', tender transformation of the theme played *pianissimo* on the bridge of the violin (bars 78ff.).

Example 7.14b Schumann, Sonata in D minor for Violin and Pianoforte, Op. 121, 2nd movement, bars 204–8

Example 7.15 Schumann, Sonata in D minor for Violin and Pianoforte, Op. 121, 4th movement, bars 100–2

A striking appearance of the four-note pattern – the penultimate one – occurs in the fourth movement at the end of a development section rich in complex modulations (bar 101; see Ex. 7.15). Here the first three notes of the pattern, confined to a single pitch and thus denied any melodic import, are screamed in triple octaves in the violin over an augmented 6th chord in the pianoforte before resolving, suddenly *piano*, to the tonic chord in second inversion that begins the recapitulation. All that remains is the rhythmic pattern, which, of course, had been the common denominator all along.

The above discussion of Op. 121 offers only a glimpse of the myriad of links that operate continually and on every level within and among the four movements of this complex work. Stylistically and aesthetically this sonata is in perfect harmony with itself. Schumann was a composer with great intuitive strengths. His *œuvre* confirms this. It is interesting to observe, however, that the sketches and drafts of his large-scale works show that "intuitive" connections were often consciously worked out. Many of his composing manuscripts, the draft manuscript of Op. 121 (**D-Dühi**, 74.118) included, reveal that immediate – almost simultaneous – revision was part of his drafting process. In Op. 121 the revisions are unusually extensive,[38] an indication that the sonata, which occupied Schumann for more than three weeks (*c.* 15 October–*c.* 4 November 1851),[39] required a great deal of thought to bring to completion.[40]

* * *

This chapter has attempted not to present a survey of Schumann's chamber music, but to examine in the context of a few selected chamber works the composer's ever innovative approach to large-scale composition. Throughout his life and in all of his music Schumann avoided stereotypical formal designs. His structural innovations have only recently begun to be fully appreciated. Even – especially – when working in the so-called 'Classical' forms, Schumann considered each composition a unique entity with its own laws, manipulating the expectations fostered by the tradition to achieve his own quite different objectives. It is fascinating to observe how he 'invents' the parameters for each work and how works that are vastly different flourish in a milieu of intellectually imposed artifice on the one hand and pure intuition on the other.

Notes

1. Robert Schumann, *Tagebücher*, vol. III, *Haushaltbücher*, ed. Gerd Nauhaus (Leipzig, 1982), p. 571.
2. Robert Schumann, *Gesammelte Schriften über Musik und Musiker*, 5th edn, ed. Martin Kreisig (Leipzig, 1914), vol. I, pp. 430, 461, 463.
3. *Ibid.*, p. 424.
4. Linda Correll Roesner, 'Schumann's "parallel" forms', *Nineteenth Century Music*, 14/3 (spring 1991), 265–78.
5. Robert and Clara Schumann, *The Marriage Diaries of Robert and Clara Schumann: From Their Wedding Day through the Russia Trip*, ed. Gerd Nauhaus, trans. Peter Ostwald (Boston, 1993), p. 53.
6. For example, the G minor Symphony (*Jugendsinfonie*, or *Zwickauer Sinfonie*) of 1832–3, the Piano Quartet in C minor, Op. V (1828–9), and other planned chamber works for piano and strings: see Hans Kohlhase, *Die Kammermusik Robert Schumanns: Stilistische Untersuchungen* (Hamburg, 1979), vol. I, pp. 6–17, vol. II, pp. 1–24, and Wolfgang Boetticher, 'Das frühe Klavierquartett c-moll von Robert Schumann', *Die Musikforschung*, 31 (1978), 465–7. Reinhard Kapp has suggested that much of the piano music Schumann wrote in the 1830s is actually
orchestral music in disguise: *Studien zum Spätwerk Robert Schumanns* (Tutzing, 1984), pp. 31, 39, 47, *passim*.

7. Clara and Robert Schumann, *Briefwechsel: Kritische Gesamtausgabe*, vol. I, *1832–1838*, ed. Eva Weissweiler (Basel and Frankfurt am Main, 1984), pp. 100, 108, 121, 127; Kohlhase, *Kammermusik*, vol. I, pp. 14–17, vol. III, pp. 16–18 (transcriptions of string quartet fragments in *D-B*, Mus. ms. autogr. Schumann 36, nos. 2, 11).
8. For details, see Linda Correll Roesner, 'Schumann', in *The Nineteenth-Century Symphony*, ed. D. Kern Holoman (New York, 1997), pp. 43–77.
9. Linda Correll Roesner, 'Ästhetisches Ideal und sinfonische Gestalt: die d-Moll-Sinfonie um die Jahrhundertmitte', in *Schumann Forschungen*, vol. III, *Schumann in Düsseldorf: Werke–Texte–Interpretationen*, ed. Bernhard R. Appel (Mainz, 1993), pp. 55–71. Excerpts from this article appear below, in English.
10. *Haushaltbuch*, p. 207.
11. Ibid., p. 209.
12. Ibid., pp. 210–16.
13. See his 1842 review of a quartet by Julius Schapler, Schumann, *Gesammelte Schriften*, vol. II, pp. 71–2.
14. *Haushaltbuch*, p. 216. 'Quartett in A Moll angefangen, Satz in F Dur und A moll.' John Daverio detects the influence of Beethoven's Op. 132 in this tonal pairing: *Robert Schumann: Herald of a 'New Poetic Age'* (New York and Oxford, 1997), p. 252.
15. For a facsimile of this page of Schumann's autograph, see Emanuel Winternitz, *Musical Autographs from Monteverdi to Hindemith* (New York, 1955; repr. New York, 1965), vol. II, Plate 114.
16. Roger Fiske, 'A Schumann mystery', *The Musical Times*, 105 (1964), 577–8; Peter Ostwald, *Schumann. The Inner Voices of a Musical Genius* (Boston, 1985), p. 131; Roesner, 'Parallel', pp. 273–6.
17. Linda Correll Roesner, 'Tonal strategy and poetic content in Schumann's C-Major Symphony, Op. 61', in *Probleme der symphonischen Tradition im 19. Jahrhundert*, ed. Siegfried Kross and Marie Luise Maintz (Tutzing, 1990), pp. 303–5. Clara's name as dedicatee appears on the title page of only two of Schumann's works, the F sharp minor Piano Sonata, Op. 11, and the Piano Quintet, Op. 44; see Kurt Hofmann, *Die Erstdrucke der Werke von Robert Schumann* (Tutzing, 1979), pp. 26f., 102f.
18. See Roesner, 'Schumann', pp. 56–7.
19. Anthony Newcomb, 'Once more "between absolute and program music": Schumann's Second Symphony', *Nineteenth Century Music*, 7/3 (3 April 1984), 246–8; Roesner, 'Tonal strategy', pp. 301–5.
20. ' . . . eine tiefe Klage um Dich'. Clara und Robert Schumann, *Briefwechsel*, vol. I, p. 126.
21. Clara and Robert Schumann, *Marriage Diaries*, p. 172. The wrapper of the autograph score (*D-Dühi*, 78.5025) contains Schumann's inscription to Clara: 'Meiner lieben Klara dargebracht am 13ten September 1842.' ('Offered to my dear Clara on 13 September 1842.') Schumann dedicated the published quartets to 'seinem Freunde Felix Mendelssohn-Bartholdy in inniger Verehrung' ('to his friend Felix Mendelssohn-Bartholdy in deep admiration'), see Hofmann, *Erstdrucke*, p. 417.
22. Ostwald, *Schumann. Inner Voices*, pp. 191–201.
23. Berthold Litzmann, *Clara Schumann: Ein Künstlerleben. Nach Tagebüchern und Briefen*, vol. II, *Ehejahre 1840–1856* (Leipzig, 1906), p. 135.
24. See Joel Lester's penetrating analysis of the movement in 'Robert Schumann and sonata forms', *Nineteenth Century Music* 18/3 (spring 1995), pp. 190–5.
25. A diplomatic transcription of all of Schumann's sketches for Op. 41 appears in my dissertation *Studies in Schumann Manuscripts* (New York University, 1973; published on request by University Microfilms, Ann Arbor, MI, 1974).
26. Roesner, 'Parallel', *passim*.
27. Anthony Newcomb discusses this movement as a complete reversal of the 'paradigmatic plot' of the classical rondo: 'Schumann and late eighteenth-century narrative strategies', *Nineteenth Century Music*, 11/2 (autumn 1987), 170–4.
28. Robert Schumann, *Tagebücher*, vol. II, *1836–1854*, ed. Gerd Nauhaus (Leipzig, 1987), p. 402: 'Erst vom Jr. 1845 an, von wo ich anfing alles im Kopf zu erfinden und auszuarbeiten, hat sich eine ganz andere Art zu componiren zu entwickeln begonnen.' The composer's observation apparently dates from 1846 and was written, together with other remarks on the compositional process, for possible inclusion in an autobiography or memoir. See Nauhaus's preface to this volume of the *Tagebücher* (p. 13) and Plate 11 (between pp. 352 and 353).
29. Reinhard Kapp, *Studien zum Spätwerk Robert Schumanns* (Tutzing, 1984), pp. 168–78.
30. Even in its published form the A minor Sonata, Op. 105, is titled Sonata 'for pianoforte and violin', not 'for violin and pianoforte'. See Hofmann, *Erstdrucke*, pp. 228f.

31. The concept of two paired keys functioning simultaneously as tonic is important for the music of the second half of the nineteenth century. Robert Bailey discusses this 'double-tonic complex' in an analytical essay accompanying the Norton Critical Score of the *Prelude and Transfiguration from Tristan and Isolde* (New York, 1985), pp. 116f. Reinhard Kapp perceives a similar 'Bitonalität' in Schumann's late works: Kapp, *Spätwerk*, pp. 175ff.

32. Kohlhase, *Kammermusik*, vol. I, p. 58, vol. II, p. 186.

33. The introduction also incorporates a preview of the tonal compass of the sonata: the chord on the second beat of bar 5, sandwiched between two dominant triads, superposes a minor triad on B (B/D/F sharp) and a dominant 7th chord on G (G/B natural/D/F natural). The keys of the second and third movements of the sonata are, respectively, B minor and G major.

34. The Symphony in E flat major, Op. 97 ('Rhenish'), provides many compelling examples. See the chart in Roesner, 'Schumann', *Nineteenth-Century Symphony*, pp. 62–5.

35. The use of f as an accent is typical of Schumann.

36. Scholars have attempted to identify this melody, but their conclusions vary. See Kohlhase, *Kammermusik*, vol. I, p. 59, n. 49, for a summary.

37. This movement is remarkable for the subtlety of its psychological unfolding. The theme never varies, but the accompaniment does. Gradually the aspect of the music becomes less hymn-like and more Lied-like. The unsettling 'bridge' passage in E minor (*Etwas bewegter*, bars 72–105) leads to the last variation, which Schumann deliberately and nostalgically sets in the style of one of his Lieder of the early 1840s. The autobiographical implications cannot be ignored.

38. Kohlhase discusses these revisions and provides diplomatic transcriptions of them: *Kammermusik*, vol. II, pp. 191–209; vol. III, pp. 91–107. Three pages of Schumann's draft are reproduced in vol. III, Plates VII–IX.

39. *Haushaltbuch*, pp. 574–6: '*Sehr fleißig*' ('hard at work'), Schumann's entry for 15 October, probably refers to Op. 121 (it is his usual way of indicating that he was composing); the entry for 2 November, 'Die 2te Son[ate] ziemlich beendigt' ('the 2nd sonata pretty well finished') suggests that it was not quite finished. In contrast to the amount of time Schumann required to finish Op. 121, the draft of the A minor Sonata, Op. 105, was completed in only five days, and the draft of the G minor Trio in nine days (*Haushaltbuch*, pp. 571–4).

40. In the time since the present essay was submitted for publication the sonatas for violin and piano have appeared in the new historical/critical edition of Schumann's complete works: Robert Schumann, *Neue Ausgabe sämtlicher Werke*, Serie II, Werkgruppe 2 / Bd. 3, ed. Ute Bär (Mainz, 2001).

8 Novel symphonies and dramatic overtures

SCOTT BURNHAM

It is hard to imagine a more dramatic shock at the opening of a symphony than that which occurs moments into Robert Schumann's First Symphony (1841). The movement begins with a brief motto theme in trumpets and horns, assertive in rhythm and timbre, yet slightly unsettling (Ex. 8.1). It is in fact ambiguous as to tonality – it could be G minor, B flat major or even D minor. After a *fermata*, the next iteration of the motto clarifies the tonality as B flat major, with a somewhat odd emphasis of the third, D (it is much more common for the repeated note in an opening figure like this to be the fifth or the tonic).[1] Fuller orchestration (winds and strings), cadential harmony and another *fermata* set this second version of the motto as an orotund, closed-off statement (compare the much more open-ended effect of the initial two *fermatas* of Beethoven's Fifth Symphony). The motto seems to be headed on a progressive course of consolidation: first a brass declamation on a single line, followed by a *tutti*-like confirmation. But then everything falls away, into the suddenly gaping abyss of D minor. Here is the real *tutti*: trombones and timpani join angrily swarming strings; the effect freezes us as in terror. The untoward emphasis on the pitch D in the opening strain proves to have been the only hint that we could possibly find ourselves in this spot.

A move like this at the very outset of the course of a symphony is extraordinary. Beethoven included effects approaching this in several of his slow introductions (think of the lightning bolt of D minor that forms the climax of the introduction to his Second Symphony), but Schumann's D minor abyss opens up before much of anything is established, and with it his symphony crosses a crucial line: when something this arresting happens this early, we are made to hear that Schumann will hold nothing back, keep nothing in reserve. There will be no gauging of thematic material to suit the perceived needs of some long-term narrative, no sense of germinal energy, or of proto-material, no need to be heard to create the world once again. Instead there is a decided concentration of effect, which persists as the introduction continues to trade on dramatically picturesque juxtapositions. We hear the almost regal concision of the opening motto, then the abyss – trombones at full bore, deployed so soon! – followed by all those scattershot brass entrances in bars 8–14, a kind of sonic bursting at the seams. Once the music settles back into B flat, the motto rhythm wafts in the air, peaceably enough. But then a flute cadenza leads to a mysteriously charged pedal point on V/vi,

Example 8.1 Schumann, Symphony No. 1 in B flat major, Op. 38 ('Spring'), first movement, bars 1–6

Example 8.1 (cont.)

Example 8.2 Schumann, Symphony No. 1 in B flat major, Op. 38 ('Spring'), piano reduction of first movement, bars 39–54

which then moves to V, expanding with Beethovenian intensification into the *Allegro*. At the last instant, the horns hasten to announce the arrival of the new tempo.

What kind of *Allegro* has been introduced here? Schumann's theme sets out with predictable regularity (Ex. 8.2). It moves in eight-bar periods, with a stiff rhythmic rhyme every four bars (the rhyme is in fact the climactic point of the line, which draws even more attention to it). Four-bar phrases continue throughout the entire exposition, with one exception (right before the second theme). In fact, this regularity turns out to be something of a signature for all of Schumann's opening allegros that begin with slow introductions: the first themes from his Second and Fourth Symphonies also share this propensity for absolutely regular phrasing. The exposition of the Fourth Symphony tends to double its gestures in two-bar units, creating a distinctly additive effect, whereas the opening *allegro* theme of the Second Symphony is a study in rhythmic saturation – its dotted-rhythm motive persists unaltered through the first sixteen bars. In general, these themes are not differentiated to anywhere near the degree of *allegro* themes in the works of earlier, Classical-style composers.[2]

Related to this lack of differentiation within themes is the additive effect of the frequent sequences in Schumann's thematic process. Both tendencies promote a density of material that can seem cloying at times but can also be heard to create a new kind of musical energy. The relentless, Baroque-style rhythmic texture and motivic saturation, when packed into four-square rhyming phrases with Classical-style harmonic language, make for a compressed and spirited local intensity. One does not hear a steadily flowing (Baroque) texture that runs through cadences and renewed entrances like a waterway changing and diversifying its course, nor an articulated and pressurized (Beethovenian) flow that moves in waves, gathering energy for decisive arrivals. One is aware rather of a sense of constantly checked plenitude, of many full frames; the flow seems to stop and start, and at all points we are made aware of something like shortness of breath, the very sound of excitement.

Critics

Donald Francis Tovey reacted to all this excitement with ambivalence, observing Schumann's 'boyish vein of slow thought and quick expression'.[3] Tovey characteristically captures something vital about Schumann's symphonic style – how it moves in quick, repeated bursts but does not give the impression of covering a lot of ground – though he chooses to present this insight in terms of immaturity. On the other hand, Tovey's reaction is properly Victorian in its faint praise: if you can't be manly, at least be boyish. But how boyish is this music? It clearly does not express the artless, buoyant exuberance of some of Mendelssohn's teenage efforts, but rather exudes the manic devotional energy of someone drawn to excess (like Schumann's beloved Jean Paul), someone unafraid to leap out onto any limb at any time. And when the medium that is thus pushed to be 'quick to expression' is a full symphony orchestra, Schumann's manic energy is heard to push uphill, a situation that brings with it the additional effect of making the listener aware of the orchestra as a massive and intractable sonic medium.

This enhanced opacity of the orchestra as a medium helps nourish one of the most common critical perceptions of this music, exemplified by Gerald Abraham's judgement that Schumann's First Symphony 'is inflated piano music with mainly routine orchestration'.[4] The symphonies written after 1841, on the other hand, are not even granted this much; they are thought instead to suffer from a clumsy heaviness in their scoring.[5] Performances of these symphonies by modern orchestras often evince an indistinct, muffled quality, in which bass lines can be difficult to discern. Consequently, few modern conductors perform these works without lightening the instrumentation. Schumann scholar Jon Finson has convincingly argued that

Schumann's symphonies would be much more transparent if performed with the smaller-scaled orchestra that Schumann himself would have known in Leipzig, and this proposition has been resoundingly corroborated by John Eliot Gardiner's recent recordings of the symphonies.[6]

But orchestration is not the only, or even the primary, problem for mainstream critics of Schumann's symphonies. Simply put, the 'frighteningly excitable temperament' manifest in these works has never been heard as classically symphonic. Paul Henry Lang, in comparing Classical and Romantic symphonic music (with Schumann as the leading exemplar of the latter), warns us to 'guard against mistaking excitement and sequential climaxes for symphonic development . . . [N]o other type of music shows the deep rift between the two styles and musical conceptions so clearly as does the symphony'.[7] Most critics miss in Schumann's symphonies the cogent grandeur of the Viennese Classical style. Lang observed a lack of unity and cohesion in these works, and he also detected a lack of inner tension in their themes, which he felt had more the character of a passive phenomenon than an active force.[8] The high valuation of criteria such as forceful coherence points of course to the presence of the Beethoven symphony as the gold standard of symphonic discourse.

On the other hand, it is not hard to see why the often relentlessly square phrasing in Schumann's symphonies would invite critics to think of the sonata ethos as a Classicistic imposition for Schumann and then to conclude that he did not know how to operate in a truly symphonic fashion. For he seems to have adopted the outward lineaments of the Classical style without absorbing its inner dramatic impulse, locally filling in eight-bar units and globally filling in the sections of sonata form. Tovey referred to Schumann's large instrumental forms as mosaics, or as coral formations, whose individual cells consist of epigrams, though he was generous enough to allow that this should not be held against Schumann: '[I]t is a harsh judgement that forbids the epigrammatic artist to pile up his ideas into large edifices: his mind may be full of things that cannot be expressed except in works on a large scale.'[9] Tovey once again identifies something unique about these works – the paradoxical combination of epigrammatic utterance with large-scale formal setting – and yet he again employs a metaphor that has the effect of a condemnation. For his image of the mosaic clearly invokes a second-rate method of construction, closer to mechanical patchwork than to seamless, organic growth.

Hampering critical motivation to listen for what Schumann achieves rather than what he does not achieve is the fact that Schumann himself invites listeners to hear his symphonies with pieces from the Classical style firmly in mind. It is almost impossible not to hear the opening of the First Symphony, for example, in terms of other openings, to hear Schumann 'measuring up' to the likes of Beethoven and Schubert. Schubert's Ninth rings in his ears, as do several of Beethoven's symphonic introductions. Nor should we forget that Schumann the critic often exhorted his contemporaries to emulate Beethoven's symphonies, though not through the use of literal quotations.[10] In short, we cannot ignore the power or the pervasiveness of such influences. But it does not automatically follow that we should consider these influences as evidence of a lack of artistic *savoir faire* on Schumann's part, as if he were desperately casting around for building materials from other quarries and then failing to produce similarly impressive edifices. Part of our urge to understand these pieces as failures stems from the powerfully attractive view of the history of Western music as a *Problemgeschichte*, in which composition is conceptualized as a search for solutions to compositional problems posed largely by one's position in history. The fact that Schumann turned to the genre of the symphony only after mastering smaller forms reinforces the temptation to view his composition of symphonies as a problem to be surmounted.[11] Carl Dahlhaus's discussion of Schumann's symphonies (in his 1989 book *Nineteenth-Century Music*) is cast entirely in terms of Schumann trying to compensate for problems in his symphonic discourse, problems caused by trying to be Beethovenian without fully understanding the nature of Beethoven's music. Dahlhaus called the undifferentiated nature of Schumann's *allegro* themes 'uniformity without sublimity', contrasting it with the example of Beethoven's Fifth and Seventh Symphonies, in which an ostinato rhythm 'conveyed an impression of sublime uniformity'. Schumann's mistake, according to Dahlhaus, was to make the motivic content of his themes uniform as well.[12]

It is worth following up this observation by making a direct comparison of rhythmic uniformity in Beethoven and Schumann. The *vivace* theme of Beethoven's Seventh Symphony (Ex. 8.3) is a good example of how a motoric *ostinato* rhythm can seem ubiquitous without imparting a sense of static uniformity. After Beethoven establishes the dotted-rhythm *ostinato* in the first four bars, it is enough to suggest it in the rhythm of the tune and in the sparse punctuations of the accompanying strings. Here the rhythmic *ostinato* lurks in the background as a propulsive force, while the theme seems energized by it. The effect is one of buoyancy and power to spare.

By contrast, the opening *allegro* of the Schumann Second Symphony (Ex. 8.4) locks theme and orchestral texture together in a unitary and repetitious rhythmic design, with the result that the melody seems burdened with the weight of the entire orchestra. Such a theme expends much more energy just to keep moving; it is not likely to achieve a sense of lift-off. But to conclude from this that Schumann's procedure is flawed depends largely on the nature of the comparative metaphor. When one employs a mechanical metaphor having to do with power and efficiency – a metaphor that happens to work wonderfully with Beethoven – Schumann's procedure can only

Example 8.3 Beethoven, Symphony No. 7 in A major, Op. 92, first movement, bars 63–74

appear to be wasteful and ineffective. Overlooked in such an assessment, for example, is the breathlessness noted earlier.

Dahlhaus concludes his discussion by observing that Schumann's symphonic discourse founders between lyricism and monumentality: it aspires to Beethovenian monumentality as if in denial of its lyrical *Grundstimmung*. Although such a polar, dialectical pairing is a fundamental aspect of Dahlhaus's critical apparatus and appears in his writing about almost anything, such contradictory pairings abound in the general criticism of Schumann's music. For example, the contradiction felt in his music between

Example 8.4 Schumann, Symphony No. 2 in C major, Op. 61, first movement, bars 50–8

the lyric and the dramatic was noted early on by Brahms: 'The great Romanticists continued the sonata form in a lyric spirit that contradicts the inner dramatic nature of the sonata. Schumann himself shows this contradiction.'[13]

In mainstream music criticism, Schumann's symphonies have always been caught *between* two such poles: between lyricism and drama; between Beethoven and Schubert; and, more recently, between absolute music and programme music.[14] The standing perception that these symphonies lie somewhere between well-established poles indicates that there is something singular going on here, something that escapes easy classification. Unfortunately, a faint but persistent stigma clings to this quality of between-ness, apparent in formulations such as 'neither fish nor fowl', or in the German adjective *zwielichtig*. One cannot trust oneself to put much critical weight onto these symphonies, for they are not securely grounded in the landscape of known quantities.

Unquestioned popularity

Given the critical reservations that have always pestered these symphonies, what could account for their unquestioned popularity? Why do even their stoniest critics stop well short of dismissing them altogether? Several recent writers have argued that, among other things, Schumann was attempting to establish a popular symphonic style that was also viable artistically. For John Daverio, Schumann's Third Symphony (1850) successfully merged a popular style with distinctly artistic aspirations.[15] (This is of course another 'between'-style assessment, but one that is stated positively.)

Schumann had already essayed a more accessible symphonic style in 1841, with his Overture, Scherzo and Finale, Op. 52, as Jon Finson has pointed out in an illuminating study of the work.[16] The absence of a slow movement, like a lack of ballast, already helps ensure that the whole will stay afloat, resisting the pull of unsounded depths. The 'overture' is a masterly example of a smaller-scaled first-movement type of form that is at once charming, dramatic and light on its feet. After a halting, sighing slow introduction featuring a characteristically expressive gapped turn figure (D sharp, E, C, B), a carefree, sunny *allegro* commences, which returns, however, in its second-theme area to the figure from the introduction and its minor-mode inflections. A mock *Sturm und Drang* (Storm and Stress) sequence quickly develops, culminating in a puppet-show version of the harmonic shock from the middle of the first movement of the Eroica Symphony, which then dissipates in a wistful passage. The development section is very brief, almost sonatina-like, and the movement is rounded off with a lengthy coda that introduces new material and a more animated tempo. These proportions indicate that a different kind of sonata ethos is at work here – nothing is probed too deeply, yet the musical argument is pervasively worked out. (For example, Schumann transforms an idea from the coda of the first movement into the theme of the *Scherzo*.)[17] The result is a music that is light but never flimsy, that abounds in closely worked craft but is never lofty and never ponderous. There are few other Germanic symphonies – one thinks first of Beethoven's Eighth – that operate with such assurance in this particular realm. But perhaps because the Overture, Scherzo and Finale has been hard to categorize, both as a genre (Is it a suite? Is it a symphony?) and on account of its hybrid tone, it has endured relative neglect in the concert hall.

Daverio hears the Third Symphony as a kind of popular epic, a formulation that indicates a mix of the popular and the exalted.[18] Each of the symphony's five self-contained movements reflects the rest of the symphony not by assuming an indispensable function in a teleological process but through picturesque contrast. Schumann's movements are more like paintings in a well-appointed gallery than psychologically consequential stages of a multi-movement Classical-style sonata. A walk through the gallery of the Third Symphony leads from the wind and waves of the first movement to a scene of merry rusticity, followed by an engaging yet undemanding *intermezzo*, the antique ceremony of the fourth movement, and the regally jaunty finale, whose coda looks back at the rest of the symphony in a pulsing whirl. Each stage along the way is unburdened with the weight and thrust of the whole and yet each has the heft of a confidently captured image, or *Stimmung*.[19]

Returning to an earlier observation about the way Schumann's *allegro* themes breathlessly fill a succession of four-bar frames, we might now say more globally that the picturesque involves the deployment of musical content that sounds as though it is filling in a space rather than creating a space. We are not compelled to wonder about the shape or extent of the space, but we are free to listen to how it is being filled: the intensive local coherence noted above keeps the listener 'in the frame'. Each movement of the Third Symphony has an appealing self-sufficiency that is never in danger of alienating the rest of the symphony: these are all paintings by the same artist.

Nor have picturesque effects gone unheeded in the other symphonies. Ludwig Finscher, for example, thinks of the middle movements of the First Symphony as *Tagstück* and *Nachtstück*.[20] In the Fourth Symphony, the onset of the *Romanze* seems to step out of the trajectory of the first movement directly into some enchanted nocturnal realm. But the Third Symphony is more relaxed with this way of proceeding; it carries fewer signs of working hard to be a progressive symphony in the great tradition. This sense of staying within itself could answer for the more sanguine critical appreciation of the Third Symphony.

Something like this may also account for the general tendency to consider Schumann's symphonic middle movements to be his most successful, for they are less marked by the dramatic strain of the Classical style than the far more fraught opening and closing movements. Not a small part of the charm that influenced the symphonist in Brahms resides in Schumann's movements of *mezzo caraterre*, such as the A flat movement of the Third. Schumann seems keen to capture oblique moods in these movements, as far from the inward thrust of soul searching as from the outward thrust of dramatic action.

Even when Schumann is intensely dramatic, he is dramatic in a new way. The extrovert drama so abundant in the first movement of the Third Symphony is never heavy-handed or overwhelming but is more closely related to the type of drama found in the Overture, Scherzo and Finale. For one thing, a refreshingly smaller scale becomes apparent with the lack of a repeating exposition. And a complex dramatic effect is achieved when Schumann marks his recapitulation with a so-called 'arrival six-four sonority'. The use of this harmonic topos gives the recapitulation an enhanced dramatic reality as an arrival, but it also means that it will seem smaller-scale than most recapitulations, which usually arrive at the home dominant and then make much ado of resolving onto the tonic as a long-awaited homecoming. The 'arrival six-four' would seem to be too breathless and melodramatic for this important formal juncture, but for a movement on the scale of this one it works well as a way to reproduce the *in medias res* excitement of the opening bars.

The dramatically urgent lyricism of those opening bars belies the ready dichotomy of lyric and dramatic so often invoked in Beethoven-influenced criticism of nineteenth-century music (Ex. 8.5). The melody bursts forth in full sail, billowed by bracing winds that blow across the bar lines. The lack of a portentous slow introduction is an immediate clue that this will be a different kind of symphony. Instead we are pushed immediately into the midst of adventure, in the manner of a nineteenth-century popular novel. Here is excitement of a sort different from the other allegro themes: the melody ramps up through the tonic E flat triad, overshooting the fifth with an irrepressible shout of joyful excitement on the C; it then returns to E flat in a sinuous descent, only to leap back up to C and B flat at the end of the phrase. Hemiola effects reinforce the sense of boisterous enthusiasm. This theme is differentiated in its parts and thus contrasts distinctly with the

Example 8.5 Schumann, Symphony No. 3 in E flat major, Op. 97 ('Rhenish'), first movement, bars 1–17

Example 8.5 (*cont.*)

more typical Schumann thematic construction in which the same motive appears in each bar. The result is a less contained kind of energy and a longer line.

To an even greater degree than the Overture, Scherzo and Finale, Schumann's Third Symphony effectively combines drama, lyricism and the picturesque, resulting in an ambitiously appointed popular style that – miraculously – never condescends.

Example 8.5 (*cont.*)

Overtures and endings

To hear Schumann's most concentrated dramatic writing, however, one must turn to his overtures. The first of these, the 1847 overture to his opera *Genoveva*, is perhaps the most gripping in its dramatic trajectory from doubt to faith, or darkness to light. This trajectory can be conveniently summarized in musical terms as the transformation of the sixth-scale degree from an anguished minor ninth at the very outset to a downright thrilling major ninth near the end. The repeated leaps to this latter ninth, A, from the tonic, C, create one of the most electrifying dramatic effects in all symphonic literature, rivalling the much more famous dénouement at the end of Beethoven's Third Leonore Overture. Throughout, this well-paced overture is rich in dramatically telling details, from the suspensions in its theme to the bass-line drama at the end of the development (the slipping down of the massed F sharps to F at the central hinge of the development is a relaxed version of the celebrated move from F sharp to F in the coda of the finale of Beethoven's Eighth Symphony). The phrasing of themes is less regular, the rhythm more varied than in most of Schumann's other symphonic *allegros*. The major-mode horn call in the second-theme area makes for an extremely effective thematic contrast, one that speaks from within the sonata ethos. In fact, the pacing at both local and global levels puts Schumann's ability to write a dramatic sonata form beyond doubt.

The *Manfred* Overture (1848–9) is easily Schumann's best-known overture, standing out for its concentrated passion and imaginatively deployed dissonance. Throughout much of the overture, Schumann indulges his tendency to double gestures in two-bar units – but here it captures an aspect of Manfred's forever pacing, self-tortured personality, unable to break out, to sing. The harmonic orientation of the overture underscores this portrayal by continually brooding around the dominant. The whole offers a matchless example of maintaining a charged atmosphere of anxiety, and the storms that eventually break out bring no redeeming relief. The somewhat later overture to Schiller's *Bride of Messina* (*Die Braut von Messina*, 1850–1) also features much writhing around the dominant, but without the sharply etched material of *Manfred*.

Two of the overtures, *Faust* (1853) and *The Bride of Messina*, begin with a thrusting upward gesture, like a Romantic shout of the soul, and several begin in the minor and end in the major: *Genoveva*, *Julius Caesar* (1851) and *Faust*. The latter two do not enjoy the same dramatic effect as the *Genoveva* overture, unfortunately, for their themes are less distinctive. Finally, the 1851 overture to Goethe's *Hermann und Dorothea* is essentially a varied treatment of the *Marseillaise* theme (Goethe's epic plays against the background of the French Revolution) and has never made much of a mark in the concert hall.

Three of Schumann's overtures serve as entrées to actual music-theatrical works (*Manfred*, *Genoveva*, *Faust*), but the remaining three are free-standing overtures to literary works by Schiller, Shakespeare and Goethe. These latter overtures make up a compositional project that bears some relation to the literary tone poems of Franz Liszt: namely, an attempt to bear musical witness to canonic works of Western literature (though the works for which

Schumann provides overtures are all dramas, with the exception of Goethe's *Hermann und Dorothea*, which is a kind of bourgeois epic).

Admiration for Schumann's overtures is uneven, and even the most admired among them cannot claim the status of a generally beloved work. On the other hand, critics have not been at pains either to justify them or apologise for them – as a genre less directly consequential to the identity of the great German symphonic tradition, they do not come under the same scrutiny as his symphonies.

As dramatic compositions, the overtures enjoy the advantages of single-movement construction: each has the potential to be heard as a unitary effusion. Schumann's Fourth Symphony aspires to something similar, though on a larger scale, and this ambition is often treated as a progressive feature in his conception of the symphony, relating the Fourth to the First and Second Symphonies, which are also heard as developing a more organically cohesive and progressive kind of cyclical form than has been detected in the more popular orientation of the Third Symphony and the Overture, Scherzo and Finale.[21] There are distinctly tangible thematic transformations between movements in the First and Second Symphonies – but such transformations are more acute and exposed in the run-on, formal design of the Fourth.

For example, the theme from the first movement's slow introduction reappears in a section of the second-movement *Romanze* and is varied in the theme of the third-movement *Scherzo*. The introduction to the finale draws on the turn figure of the first movement's *allegro* theme, while the finale's *allegro* theme brings back the three accented chords that signal the presence of D major toward the end of the first movement (at rehearsal letter L). In addition, neither first movement nor finale recapitulates its opening theme, thus neither enjoys within itself the traditional warrant of closural resolution granted by the so-called 'double return' of Classical-style sonata form.[22] Undercutting the internal self-sufficiency of the outer movements in this way allows Schumann to create a more interdependent symphonic form, in which the four movements lean on each other as four episodes in one large and variegated design. In fact, no single movement save the finale is permitted to close in a traditional fashion: the concluding sections of the first movement recapitulate a lyrical theme from the development, now in D major, crowned with regal double-dotted rhythms; this leads to an arresting D minor chord in the winds signalling the onset of the *Romanze* movement, which ends by pausing on the dominant of the subsequent *Scherzo*, which itself ends unusually with a repetition of the *Trio*, poised on the flat-sixth of the ensuing introduction to the finale. This introduction (often heard as influenced by Beethoven's Fifth and influencing Brahms's First) then moves to a D major *allegro*, which takes up and broadens the D major conclusion of the first movement.

The whole is a complex design: for one thing, though the first movement's exposition is left hanging and unresolved formally, the D major section at the end of the movement concludes with a hurried transfiguration of the opening *allegro* theme. Aspects of the first movement reconvene in the finale, and yet it will not do simply to hear the finale as a recapitulation of the first movement. Linda Roesner thinks of it more as an 'ongoing, joyful expansion' of the first movement, while Mark Evan Bonds hears affirmation rather than resolution, on the grounds that we have already heard the breakthrough to D major in the first movement.[23] Bonds argues convincingly for the symmetry of the outer movements, as opposed to a distinctly teleological design. In this way, Schumann creatively 'misreads' Beethoven's Fifth Symphony – unlike Beethoven, whose finale crowns the entire symphony with an unimpeachable transformation of C minor into C major, Schumann's finale does not take on the burden of resolving the entire symphony.[24] There is no comparable burden at this point in Schumann's conception, for we have already heard a transformation to D major in the opening movement. The finale amplifies the conclusion of the first movement; it does not itself somehow conclude the first movement. This situation allows us to detect a different symphonic ethos at work here, one that is more epic than dramatic: instead of teleology and resolution, we hear symmetry and affirmation.

The very endings of Schumann's symphonic finales also reflect this different kind of weighting. Though the frenetic *stretto* concluding the Fourth Symphony is unmistakably climactic, it does not feel like the fulfilment, or final resolution, of some overarching plot (as happens, say, at the end of the *Genoveva* overture). Instead, a sudden power surge galvanizes the orchestral machine, and we hear a final burst of manic energy, a feverish exaltation both exhilarating and exhausting. The movement – and with it, the symphony – ends not because a teleological process has found its final term, but because there is no greater level of local intensity available.

The one symphony that arguably presents a teleological thematic transformation is the Second, with the 'serenely confident' theme that appears halfway through the finale and holds sway in various permutations from then on.[25] (See Ex. 8.6b.) This theme represents an unclenching, a clarification (or 'Clara-fication', if we are to credit the usual extramusical reading). Such a function is reflected in its discursive shape. Compared to the opening gesture of the finale (Ex. 8.6a), a rocket-like propulsion to the dominant (as if time speeds up here, reaching the dominant in a moment rather than a minute), the symphony's concluding theme makes an easy, almost inconsequential, climb to the tonic (not from $\hat{5}$ but from $\hat{6}$) and then glides from there down to $\hat{3}$, outlining a contented sigh (its underlying line can be construed as a simple descent: $\hat{6}$-$\hat{5}$-$\hat{4}$-$\hat{3}$, as in Ex. 8.6c). In concert with a last word like this one, the orchestra does not get more frenzied toward the end

Example 8.6a Schumann, Symphony No. 2 in C major, Op. 61, fourth movement, bars 1–12

Example 8.6b Schumann, Symphony No. 2 in C major, Op. 61, fourth movement, bars 394–401

Example 8.6c Schumann, Symphony No. 2 in C major, Op. 61, fourth movement, bars 394–7

but seems to solidify and broaden.[26] This is a different sort of narrative culmination, more the sound of sated happiness than of fated triumph.

Novel symphonies

Throughout this chapter, we have observed that Schumann's symphonies ask us to attend primarily to small-scale, local utterance rather than to more overarching rhythms of dramatic development. And yet one does not simply hear additive chains of material; there is an abundant sense that one is in the midst of an expansive and consequential enterprise. The combination of epigrammatic utterance and local intensity with large instrumental forces and large-scale formal design amounts to the creation of a new symphonic manner. Is there a way to construe this new manner that does not automatically invoke an unfavourable comparison to the more firmly established symphonic ethos of Beethoven and Brahms?[27]

Schumann the critic may give us a clue. In his well-known review of Schubert's C major Symphony, he applauds Schubert's vivid proliferation of ideas, enchanting orchestral colours, and acute expression of individual details, all in the service of creating a world of the greatest expanse and purview. Schumann's famous remark about the 'heavenly length' of Schubert's symphony is intended to compare the plenitude of that symphony to the rich diversity of content Schumann finds in the novels of Jean Paul.[28]

Arnfried Edler, in an insightful essay, shows how this valuation of broadly inclusive novelistic diversity finds expression in Schumann's own symphonies. As Edler observes, Schumann's symphonies notably include different characteristic 'tones', such as the conversational, the folk-like (*Volkston*), the sublime, the religious, the elfin mood of Nature (*elfenhafte Naturstimmung*) and the *Romanze*.[29] The sublime is now only one of many possible types of symphonic content (and not even *primus inter pares*). Following Anthony Newcomb's lead, Edler claims that the alternation of these characteristic 'tones' is more decisive for Schumann's symphonic enterprise than the establishment of a network of motivic relations between themes. The technical forms and processes of the classical tradition become a 'fading background' upon which these more essential thematic transformations take shape.[30] This new field of action appropriates the Classical-style symphonic categories of grandeur, unity and relational richness without losing the refined psychological differentiation gained in other intervening genres, such as the Romantic art song or the character piece.[31]

Edler's and Newcomb's insistence on the primacy of the play of characters in these symphonies reverses the usual terms of the debate over Schumann's symphonies. In this view, the classical symphonic tradition becomes a means rather than an end for Schumann: instead of a self-conscious, classicizing and necessarily flawed attempt to emulate the esteemed Viennese school on the part of a composer whose greatest musical gifts are more distinctly manifest in smaller genres, we may now hear the forms and processes of the Classical style as a kind of medium through which Schumann might attain the diverse plenitude he so valued in Schubert and Jean Paul.

In fact, the Classical style is perhaps ultimately more important to Schumann as a historical reality, one that he can refer to along with all the other 'characters' he is keen to include in the world of his symphonies. And this is, of course, not the only such historical reference. In texture and composite

Example 8.7 Schumann, Symphony No. 2 in C major, Op. 61, first movement, bars 1–8

rhythm, as well as through the occasional and always highly marked presence of an archaizing style of counterpoint, Schumann's symphonies also invoke the high Baroque. No one has ever pointed to these latter references as evidence of a failed act of emulation – they are rather conceived as acts of homage. Perhaps we have been too quick to understand the challenge Schumann faced as one of measuring up to his immediate and powerful predecessors. Instead we might ask: what does Schumann get from appropriating these different historical elements?

Critic Michael Steinberg has observed a 'deliciously antiqued' sound in the *Romanze* from the Fourth Symphony, and a general effect of 'antiquing' can be said to apply to much else in Schumann's symphonies.[32] The

Example 8.7 (*cont.*)

atmospheric opening of the Second Symphony is perhaps the most telling concentration of an historical aura (Ex. 8.7). Here Schumann creates a uniquely textured world, whose quietly engaging counterpoint begins *in medias res* with solemn brass declarations and mystically murmuring strings. The reference in the brass to the opening of Haydn's 104th Symphony maintains a wonderful presence here: not exactly in the foreground, not exactly in the background. In this setting, it sounds like the tune of a chorale prelude, except that it appears immediately and is not much of a tune, more a kind of motto, until it eventually becomes a line moving from G to D. Schumann's texture holds these elements together in a kind of suspended flux, free from the usual gravitational requirements of well-defined bass and treble roles. This effect is all the more remarkable when one considers that Schumann has also created a transhistorical counterpoint between Bach and Haydn.

Nor are such references confined to this extraordinary opening. Schumann names Bach in the second trio of his *Scherzo* movement (see the first violin part, seven bars into the *Trio*),[33] and he invokes Bachian counterpoint (as well as that of Mozart's 'armed men' from *The Magic Flute* (*Die Zauberflöte*)) in the B-section of the slow movement.

These instances, as well as the many oblique references to Schubert and Beethoven throughout, mark Schumann's symphonies as among the first to manifest a thoroughgoing intertextual sensibility, a sensibility that reaches across different historical epochs. This sensibility is of a piece with the tendency to include and develop the different 'tones' observed by Edler and Newcomb. These are works that reflect and absorb myriad facets of the world around them, personal and historical. Picturesque, episodic, more spatial than temporal, more epic than dramatic, Schumann's symphonies are above all permeable and open rather than relentlessly and hermetically coherent. Hence, they are much looser in construction globally; they are less about motivic transformation than thematic transformation (which is by nature a looser kind of transformative process). As in the Classical style, contrast is extremely important, but Schumann employs it more as a way to profile his highly characteristic musics than as a dramatic spur, or as something to be transcended with an overmastering resolution. There is, throughout, an emphasis on local materiality rather than long-range instrumentality, on content rather than function.

The fullness of Schumann's symphonic designs is in line with the German Romantics' anti-rational urge to understand (and transform) the world around them through an all-embracing *Poesie*. Toward the end of her study of Schumann's *Dichterliebe*, Beate Perrey cites Novalis's view of the Romantic novel:[34]

> The novel is about life – represents *life* . . . The novel as such does not contain a particular result – it is not an image and a fact of a *sentence*. It is a vivid realization – the realization of an idea. But an idea cannot be captured in one sentence. An idea is an *infinite series* of sentences – an *irrational quantity* – unpositable . . . incommensurable.

Like the Romantic novel so avidly theorized by Novalis and others, the symphony in Schumann's hands became a nearly all-inclusive genre without 'a particular result'. No other instrumental genre could aspire to a similar range nor maintain the same proud station as a grand statement.

By hearing Schumann's symphonies adopt the material grasp and loose flow of the Romantic novel, we find yet another way to understand Schumann as a literary composer, a composer who not only wrote in a high style about music, but who wanted to compose dramatic overtures based on works of literature, and who was often in the business of alerting his listeners to those moments when 'the poet speaks'.[35] (In this, we may somewhat fancifully see him as E. T. A. Hoffmann's opposite: the writing composer over against the composing writer.) But whereas from other Romantic artists and theorists we might expect self-conscious irony, or even world-weary, sardonic sophistication, we are met at every turn with Schumann's brighteyed, feverish ingenuousness. His musical prose is always aroused, always the opposite of phlegmatic. This undisguised intensity belies the notion of Romantic irony, or reaches perhaps another level of irony. Above all, we are made to feel that the material in Schumann's symphonies forms a personal history – he is an artist who relentlessly included everything that affected him in his art. The ubiquitous force of his personality holds his symphonies together, animates these passionate novels of inclusion. For we always feel his presence, bustling us through the vivid scenery of his artist's life.

*

That Schumann's symphonies have hitherto resisted that final elevation, refusing to speak for the German nation or for some other overriding collective, has of course barred them from the highest stream of the symphonic tradition, which runs directly from Beethoven to Brahms. Instead, critics have kept them in a *cordon sanitaire* of condescension. This has allowed us to continue to love them like children, and it may well prove impossible to watch them grow up.

Notes

1. For a fascinating account of the different versions of this opening figure, see Jon Finson, *Robert Schumann and the Study of Orchestral Composition: The Genesis of the First Symphony, Op. 38* (Oxford, 1989), pp. 87 ff.
2. It was not uncommon, however, for Haydn to follow a slow introduction with a theme characterized by a similar degree of rhythmic regularity. See, for example, the opening *Allegros* of Symphonies 93, 102 and 103.
3. Donald Francis Tovey, *Essays in Musical Analysis: Symphonies and Other Orchestral Works* (Oxford, 1989), p. 483, in his essay on Schumann's Fourth Symphony. Compare as well Michael Steinberg on the 'almost frighteningly excitable temperament' in Schumann's Fourth Symphony: Steinberg, *The Symphony: A Listener's Guide* (New York, 1995), p. 520.
4. Gerald Abraham, *The New Grove: Early Romantic Masters 1: Chopin, Schumann, Liszt* (Macmillan, 1985), p. 183.
5. These include the Second Symphony (1845–6), Third Symphony (1850), and final version of the Fourth Symphony (1851). The initial version of the Fourth Symphony was completed in 1841, after the First Symphony.
6. Finson, *Robert Schumann and the Study of Orchestral Composition*, pp. 138–143; John Eliot Gardiner, conductor, with the Orchestre Révolutionnaire et Romantique, *Schumann: Complete Symphonies*, Archiv CD recording, 1997.
7. Paul Henry Lang, *Music in Western Civilization*, with a new foreword by Leon Botstein (New York, 1997), p. 817.
8. *Ibid.*, p. 818.

9. Tovey, *Essays*, p. 170 (in his essay on Schumann's First Symphony). Tovey's sense of mosaic-composition is heightened because of his own sensitivity toward phrase structure – this was how he tended to parse music.
10. Mark Evan Bonds, *After Beethoven: Imperatives of Originality in the Symphony* (Cambridge, MA, 1996), p. 114. In the chapter here cited, Bonds traces Schumann's ambivalence toward the influence of Beethoven's symphonies.
11. Lost in this view is the fact that Schumann sketched his symphonies very quickly; he certainly did not agonize with the original conceptions. See John Daverio, 'Robert Schumann', in *The New Grove Dictionary of Music and Musicians* (London, 2000).
12. Carl Dahlhaus, *Nineteenth-Century Music*, trans. J. Branford Robinson (Berkeley, CA, 1989), p. 159.
13. Cited by Lang, *Music in Western Civilization*, p. 817; originally cited in Oswald Jonas, *Das Wesen des Musikalischen Kunstwerks* (Vienna, 1934), p. 191.
14. Cf. Ludwig Finscher, '"Zwischen absoluter und Programmusik": Zur Interpretation der deutschen romantischen Symphonie', in *Über Symphonien: Beiträge zu einer musikalischen Gattung*, Festschrift Walter Wiora, ed. Christoph-Helling Mahling (Tutzing, 1979), pp. 103–15; and Anthony Newcomb, 'Once more "Between absolute and program music": Schumann's Second Symphony', *Nineteenth-Century Music*, 7/3 (1984), 233–50.
15. John Daverio, *Robert Schumann: Herald of a 'New Poetic Age'* (New York, 1997), p. 465.
16. Jon Finson, 'Schumann, popularity, and the Ouvertüre, Scherzo, und Finale, Opus 52', *Musical Quarterly*, 69 (1983), 1–26.
17. See Daverio, *Robert Schumann*, p. 236.
18. Ibid., p. 466.
19. But it is important to keep in mind Linda Correll Roesner's view of the coda, and consequently, the Third Symphony *in toto*, as a culmination for Schumann of the art of motivic coherence. See Roesner, 'Schumann', in *The Nineteenth-Century Symphony*, ed. D. Kern Holoman (New York, 1997), pp. 43–77.
20. Finscher, 'Zwischen absoluter und Programmusik', p. 111.
21. Linda Correll Roesner's view of the Third Symphony as a culmination of Schumann's art of motivic coherence is written against the grain of the received view of this symphony. See note 19, above.
22. Bonds, *After Beethoven*, p. 132.
23. Roesner, 'Schumann', p. 54. Bonds, *After Beethoven*, p. 132.
24. Bonds, *After Beethoven*, pp. 132 f.
25. The phrase 'serenely confident' is from Anthony Newcomb's path-breaking analysis of the Second Symphony. See Newcomb, 'Once more', p. 247.
26. This effect of broadening is much like the process that occurs at the end of the first movement of Schubert's 'Great' C major Symphony (and there are other marks of that symphony here as well).
27. From the standpoint of musical form, Joel Lester's magisterial review of Schumann's sonata forms goes a long way toward counteracting the received view that Schumann was somehow inadequate as an architect of large-scale form. See Lester, 'Robert Schumann and sonata forms', *Nineteenth-Century Music*, 18/3 (1995), 189–210.
28. Robert Schumann, 'Die 7te Symphonie von Franz Schubert', *Neue Zeitschrift für Musik*, xii (1840), p. 83.
29. Arnfried Edler, 'Ton und Zyklus in der Symphonik Schumanns', in *Probleme der Symphonischen Tradition im 19. Jahrhundert*, ed. Siegfried Kross and Marie Luise Maintz (Tutzing, 1990), p. 194.
30. Ibid., p. 201. Edler cites Newcomb, 'Once more', p. 240.
31. Ibid.
32. Steinberg, *The Symphony*, p. 522.
33. Noted by Finscher, in 'Zwischen absoluter und Programmusik', p. 112. Newcomb finds an additional B–A–C–H citation later in the movement: see 'Once more', p. 247.
34. Beate Julia Perrey, *Fragmentation of Desire: Schumann's 'Dichterliebe' and Early Romantic Poetics* (Cambridge, 2002), p. 219.
35. See also John Daverio's interpretation of Schumann's musical dramas as 'literary opera', and specifically his *Faust* as a 'musical novel'. Daverio, *Robert Schumann*, Chapter 10, pp. 329–87.

9 The concertos

JOSEPH KERMAN

Robert Schumann must be counted among the more prolific composers of concertos; his list of works includes three concertos or *concertante* compositions for piano, two for violin, one for cello and a *tour de force* for four French horns. Concertos and concerto sketches are spreadeagled across his career from the very beginning – even before the beginning – to the very end. Schumann got off to a slow start, however. In his youth he planned several piano concertos without bringing any to a conclusion, and even the wonderful work that he produced at his third serious try, at the age of thirty – the Fantasy for Piano and Orchestra of 1841 – was retired when it went on to greater things as the first movement of the Piano Concerto in A minor, Op. 54.

Various projects are noted in his diary in 1827–8, when he was still vacillating between a career in literature or music – projects, or whims? Piano concertos in E minor, F minor and E flat major that he mentions have left no trace, and only the flimsiest of sketches attest to concertos in B flat major and C minor. He first serious effort was an F major work drafted over several months in 1830–1, along with the *Abegg* variations and *Papillons*, his first opuses. By this time he had decided on a career in music – as a piano virtuoso. That, of course, is why he needed a concerto.

The virtuoso

One movement of the Concerto in F has been largely reconstructed by Claudia Macdonald from the composer's first sketchbook, which transmits the entire solo part of an opening allegro (Schumann never completed the *tuttis*).[1] In some revealing diagrams of the musical form, he tabulated the dimensions of sections of a piano concerto by the popular salon composer Henri Herz, in A major, Op. 34, alongside those of his own work in progress. While he did not always follow the bar-counts of his model – his development section and final *Schlußgruppe* of the exposition go on much longer – he derived many musical details from it, including melodic ideas as well as virtuosic tropes and figuration. The Concerto in F would have been an extremely flashy piece. Songs, polonaises for piano and a piano quartet of the student days likewise rely on models by other composers, and indeed Macdonald has identified another of Schumann's sources, at an earlier stage of composition: the Piano Concerto in A minor, Op. 96, by Johann Nepomuk Hummel. This was a work he greatly admired and performed several times.

The formal plan, routine for concerto first movements of the time, consisted of an opening *tutti*, a solo exposition – the 'first solo' in contemporary parlance, including an orchestral interlude or brief intermediate *tutti* – followed by a central *tutti*; the development section ('second solo'); another *tutti*; the recapitulation ('third solo'); and a final *tutti*. Even after Schumann cut out the third *tutti* in the later stage of composition, this was far from the scheme he would use in most of the concertos he wrote subsequently. In this scheme, a slow introduction is present if the work is in one movement, followed by an exposition, mainly solo but including an intermediate *tutti*; a central *tutti*; development; recapitulation; final *tutti*; and a coda engaging both solo and orchestra.

In a charming diary entry Florestan tells how the *Davidsbündler* responded to his F major concerto-in-progress when he played it for them: 'Probst and Zilia [Clara Wieck] like the second theme very much, Dorn the entire second solo, Master Raro [Friedrich Wieck] the opening, the unknown student the first theme . . . I can't expect a judgement on the whole, for the *tuttis* aren't yet composed. Tomorrow I'll send the first solo to Hummel.' He winced, though, when Dorn and Wieck ascribed 'a Field-like character' to the piece. He considered it 'the first thing in my style that inclines towards Romanticism'.

The critic

Schumann damaged his hand, relinquished ambitions as a virtuoso, and abandoned the F major Concerto. In the *Neue Zeitschrift für Musik* he found himself reviewing concertos and thinking about the genre seriously. In addition to remarks dropped in individual reviews, he came out with a substantial article, 'Das Clavier Konzert', in 1839. These writings, says Macdonald,

> reveal Schumann's historical view of the concerto, and against the background of this view carefully weigh the possible merits and potential hazards of all the new features in form and style that he finds in the works of innovative composers of the time . . . [H]is very much broadened exposure to the literature led to an advocacy of certain particulars of a more modern style. In these arguments he anticipates outright the experimental plan of the 1841 Phantasie for Piano and Orchestra, that is, the piece that has come down to us as the first movement of the Concerto in A Minor, Op. 54.[2]

By 1839 Schumann has turned his back on the kind of music he had emulated in 1830. Herz and even Hummel had come under criticism for their later works. Virtuosity, bravura, have become the enemy. He has come to know the concertos of Bach, Mozart and Beethoven, and they have opened his eyes to the beauties of solo–orchestra interchange – a mannerly battle between the solo and the separate orchestral voices, as he puts it on one occasion. He envisions 'the genius who will show us a brilliant new way of combining orchestra and piano, [able to exploit] his instrument and his skill, while at the same time the orchestra, rather than merely looking on, should be able to interweave its numerous and varied characters throughout the scene'.

As to musical form, sonata structures in concertos should stay solid. The first movement of Clara Wieck's Concerto in A minor, Op. 7, elides a recapitulation before running directly into the second movement; Schumann disapproves. He also disapproves of works strung together out of unrelated parts that are not complete in themselves – exactly what upset him years later when he heard Liszt play his E flat Concerto. On the other hand, a single coherent unit accommodating the characters of different movements was quite another matter. In an astonishingly prescient passage, Schumann the critic – Schumann the theorist, we would say today – envisioned

> the *Allegro–Adagio–Rondo* sequence in a single movement . . . a type of one-movement composition in moderate tempo in which an introductory or preparatory part would take the place of a first *allegro*, the *cantabile* section that of the *adagio* and a brilliant conclusion that of a *rondo*. It may prove an attractive idea. It is also one which we would prefer to realize in a special composition of our own.

Piano Concerto in D minor (draft: 1839) (*Anh.* B5)

The first concerto to reflect any of this theory is one that Robert began writing for Clara in 1839, shortly after publishing his big concerto essay. He completed the full score of most of the first movement, plus one short piano sketch for a *scherzo*, and no more. In a throw-away remark in the essay, Schumann suggested that concertos might incorporate *scherzos* – an idea endorsed by Liszt and Brahms also, of course.

Whatever may have been planned for the later movements, the first was going to be unusually stern as well as compact. Introduced by a brief and pompous orchestral slow introduction – no more than a curtain, if heavily brocaded – the piano plays a forceful phrase in octaves closing on the dominant, repeated by the orchestra closing in the tonic (Ex. 9.1a). This *ouvert-clos* arrangement, to borrow terminology from another era of musicology, also

Example 9.1

served the composer *mutatis mutandis* for both outer movements of the Piano Concerto in A minor, Op. 54.

And in the second subject of the D minor draft, a quiet, ruminative idea speaking like the Poet in *Kinderszenen*, the woodwinds' *ouvert* is answered by the piano – an obvious dry run for the main theme of the later work. That famous tender and tentative opening theme traces its ancestry to a second theme. A 'brilliant new way of combining orchestra and piano' is not much in evidence here, though virtuosity has been drastically reduced and the function of the central *tutti* completely rethought. So far from bravura, in the *Schlußperiode* the piano plays continuous, half-motivic figuration bodying out counterpoint in the strings, and positively slinks into its cadence, where it overlaps an utterly aberrant *tutti* with an agenda all its own. A short modulatory transition built on new material, this *tutti* adds one more strand to a complex of related scale motives (see Ex. 9.1).[3] Next comes a very repetitious development section based on another scale figure (see Ex. 9.1e); and the recapitulation comes as a shock, for a preparatory dominant animated by upward scales brings us to theme 2 (winds and solo, *piano*) ahead of theme 1 (orchestra only, *forte*). An expressive exchange between the piano and a clarinet, exceptional in this piece, forms the briefest of transitions between the themes.

This intriguing score breaks off on an open dominant after theme 1 in the orchestra. While the solo *clos* can no doubt be assumed, whether some version of the bridge and the closing material would have followed, or a slashed recapitulation would have run into a second movement, we cannot know.

Fantasy in A minor for Piano and Orchestra (1841)

Probably Schumann gave up on the D minor draft because he realized he had painted himself into a corner with the recapitulation.[4] Three movements may well have seemed daunting, given his problems with the first. Two years later, when he came to write another concerto for Clara, a Fantasy in A minor ultimately incorporated into the Piano Concerto in that key, he decided to cast it in a single movement, according to the plan that he had already formulated and reserved for implementation when the time was right.

And he refined the plan, so as to bolster 'the *Allegro–Adagio–Rondo* sequence in a single movement' with sonata-form solidity. The *Allegro* (*Allegro affettuoso*) begins in 4/4 time with an exposition and short central *tutti*; followed by a *cantabile* episode (*Andante espressivo*, 6/4); a development back in 4/4; a full-scale recapitulation; a final *tutti*; a written-out cadenza; and a concluding, up-tempo, march-like section to convey the mood, at least, of a rondo (*Allegro molto*, 2/4). To Macdonald, once again, we owe the strong suggestion that Schumann's distrust of dissociated short sections strung together in a concerto led him to adopt a cardinal feature of the Fantasy in the cause of unity, a feature he had *not* advocated in his writings. This is, of course, thematic transformation, which extends to all of its main themes.

The call to order that launches the piece involves more dialogue in the original Fantasy than in its later version in Op. 54 – one of the few salient differences between them[5] – and dialogue is a constant thereafter, as early listeners particularly noted. The bridge and the closing section as well as the themes themselves feature consequential solo–orchestra interchange. The languid *tête-à-tête* of the *Andante espressivo* episode gives way to lively repartee in the development section. Even the formalized *ouvert-clos* of the first theme assumes relational nuance, as we will see in a moment.

Determined not to rely on virtuosity to empower the drive to the central *tutti*, Schumann relies instead on rhythm, or meta-rhythm: after a *ritardando* – *pour mieux sauter*, as it were – the solo starts a new idea mainly in minims, accelerating to *sforzato* crotchets and then to quavers. The effect is always electrifying, at least to me[6] – I think because the triplets that have been running continuously stop at last, and because the quavers retrieve the figure that had launched the earlier *tutti* (Ex. 9.2c) in a hectic transformation.

No doubt writing a good exposition is half the battle. Schumann wrote a very good one and went on to many more famous victories in this piece. Most are too well known and widely admired to require more than a mention: the *calando* at end of the central *tutti*; the tender haven in A flat that it slows down for – another conversation about the first theme between piano and woodwinds; the winding down to the recapitulation; the splendid cadenza with its new figure (not really new) in Bach-like counterpoint; and the concluding march, slightly uncanny, making the final thematic transformation.

Example 9.2

The last page boils theme 1 down to its three initial pitches, C–B–AA, augmented in canon. Overkill, maybe, but perhaps CB[= H]AA spells 'Chiara'.

Excursus 1 Excellent *tuttis*
In Schumann's concerto form the *tutti*, treated so casually by the young composer in 1830, remained the weak link. An exception is the first *tutti* in the Fantasy (and the Piano Concerto). After a dangerously placid opening theme, so unlike a textbook first theme, the momentum picks up at once in a perfect example of Schoenberg's developing variation technique (see Ex. 9.2a–c). At the climax of this dialogue a *tutti* flares up in F major (Ex. 9.2b in F, *forte*) – a highly original move, for this intermediate *tutti* has now lost touch with the first theme and cannot be the second theme either: it is much too terse, and the key is too abruptly prepared and just as abruptly abandoned. What it prepares so carefully, from its subdominant angle, is the luminous apparition of the original first theme in the new key, C major.

A light transformation of theme 1 follows directly as the 'second theme' of the exposition. Then by beefing up Ex. 9.2b as the central *tutti* (Ex. 9.2d), Schumann wrote himself a prescription for dynamic form that would serve him throughout the piece. In the recapitulation, the startling appearance of the intermediate *tutti* in B minor, rather than D major, as expected, works wonders for an otherwise rigid structure.

Schumann had not lost his touch when he wrote *tuttis* for his last piano concerto, the *Conzert-Allegro mit Introduction*, Op. 134, in 1853. In this work the first (intermediate) *tutti* again takes its material from the preceding solo, though in a very different way: Schumann looked back to the action at the analogous point in the Mendelssohn piano concertos and wrote something more powerful. The central *tutti*, on the contrary, introduces all new material, so new that just on the basis of the score one might wonder if it belongs in the same piece at all. It sounds to me just right. Vigorous, sober music, Teutonic in its evocations, and what Germans call *stufenreich* in its harmonic language – dense with primary triads and their dominants – adds dignity and sinew to a composition that definitely needs it.

Piano Concerto in A minor, Op. 54 (1845)

In 1845 Robert expanded the Fantasy to make a full-length vehicle for Clara. One has to marvel at two things: that he could incorporate the original piece with only very minor alterations as the first movement, and that he could complement this member so perfectly with two others (composed, incidentally, in reverse order).

Leon Plantinga has remarked of Schumann's criticism that sometimes the more enthusiasm he tried to convey, the more his prose waxed lyrical, atmospheric, unspecific, and generally unhelpful.[7] The *Intermezzo: Andantino grazioso* of Op. 54 confronts lesser critics with exactly this problem. Call it childlike, call it demure, call it Biedermeier – what we have here is quintessential Schumann at his very best, pure in sentiment and consummate in workmanship. To the unusual propensity for dialogue in the first movement it responds with even more variously nuanced and more pervasive dialogue yet. There is no other movement from the standard concerto repertory that matches it in this respect.

The music breathes with the intimacy of chamber music, yet orchestral sound is of the essence, I feel – more so, paradoxically, in the intermezzo's first large section than in the second, with its full-length cello melody. Nested **A B A′** and **a b a′** units dispense with an introduction or transitions. Think of the **A** section as a conversation between lovers. She seems a little talkative, perhaps; he speaks less, but more emotionally, thanks to expressive ornamentation and minor-mode coloration in **b**, and thanks to a wistful descending-fifth motive in **a′**. (Although this motive furnishes a climax for the piano, idiomatically it belongs to the orchestra, which in fact introduced it almost unnoticed in **a**.) In **B** gender roles will be observed to be more conventional; her answers rephrase some of her utterances in **A**, and his descending-fifth motive puts in a no-longer-wistful appearance.

The modifications in **A′** are exquisite: at the beginning, where a beat is missed, and at the end, where the piano falters and the orchestra cautiously takes up the slack. But it is an insight due to the piano that her initial upward-scale motive can grow into a recollection of the first-movement cadenza motive. This triggers another recall from the first movement, of its terminal gesture, C–B–AA, itself a recollection of theme 1. It may not have been overkill after all.

In a pensive hush aglint with piano arabesques, C–B–AA mutates into C#–B–AA, so that the rondo theme starting with a strong C#–A (and continuing appropriately) presents itself as a final thematic transformation.

Excursus 2 The ownership of themes

In the first movement of the Piano Concerto, the *ouvert* of theme 1 is played by a wind ensemble and the *clos* by the solo, and the difference in texture registers at once – in the warm, tactile piano chords after the heterogeneous texture of the band, and the piano's tell-tale initial grace note. As the music cuts from parade ground to Biedermeier parlour, a public voice is followed by an inward, private one. This theme, as I hear it, belongs to the piano, not the winds. The piano claims it, the winds withdraw.

Sensitized to property issues, we can look in a new way at the finale. Schumann originally entitled it *Rondo* (the final score gives *Allegro vivace*), and while it does not depart from his standard form for fast movements, there is a strong rondo feeling since the *tuttis* take their material from the solo theme. No plain rondo would do, however. The ingenuity with which the refrain is varied, in tonality, extent and distribution between solo and orchestra, can be shown most quickly in a simplified form diagram:[8]

Exposition	TUTTI	Development	Recapitulation	TUTTI	Coda
a^I	(A^V)		(a/A^{IV})	A^I	

Further subtleties include the theme's irregular phrasing, which allows the solo to play both *ouvert* and *clos* without sounding in the least banal; the ingenious and energizing 'pre-entries' of the orchestra prior to the *tuttis*; the send-up in the central *tutti* as the orchestra bites its tongue and whispers a comical *fugato* in C sharp minor; and the way the solo–orchestra dialogue at the recapitulation points up the theme's rhythmic anomaly. The variations have their method, of course. As the orchestra at last gets to play the whole theme, *ouvert* and *clos*, prior to the coda, it dawns on us that the piano has been a cheerful impostor all along. This theme really belongs to the orchestra.

So does the second theme, the *deux-temps* march that vexed Mendelssohn's orchestra in rehearsals for the première. To keep ahead, the piano repeats the theme a fifth higher, in a rather seductive variation, soon slipping back into the continuous quavers that it spins out throughout this finale. They burgeon with seemingly limitless vivacity in the coda.[9]

The professional

Not that any musician who had produced *Dichterliebe* and the Fantasy for Piano, Op. 17, with a list of publications edging up to fifty, could by the wildest stretch of imagination be considered unprofessional. (But Schumann could not extend that list to include the Fantasy for Piano and

Orchestra. Publishers rejected it one after another.) The new direction of his career after his marriage can, however, be characterized as a new, comprehensive commitment to professionalism. In 1841 he composed besides the Fantasy his first two symphonies, and increasingly he weaned himself away from the piano in favour of richer and grander soundscapes. The concertos that he undertook from now on were driven not by virtuosity or theory but by sonority, both as regards the solo instrument and the orchestra.

Thus his next offering for Clara, the *Concertstück*, Op. 92, of 1849, treats the solo much more 'pianistically' than in Op. 54. In the slow introduction she has become an impressionist, in the *allegro* less a companion than a star. The ownership of the first theme lies squarely with the orchestra, leaving the solo free to develop its own stream of idiomatic ideas. Characteristic and attractive pianistic tropes drawn from the composer's rich stock run into one another, as it seems, more and more spontaneously; they resurface at the start of the development section, as though the stream has gone underground during the central *tutti* and now emerges with a new goal in life, namely modulation.

With the other concertos of this period it must have been sonority again, a vision – we have no auditory word – of massed horns and then of a lyrical cello voice that inspired the *Concertstück* for Four Horns and the Cello Concerto. Whether or not this composer wrote as idiomatically for the French horn as some would wish, he certainly revelled in the sounds he actually got, and the Cello Concerto is driven magnificently by song, by the cello as inspired singer. Nothing in the piece impresses more than the grand, wide-ranging melody that launches it – phrase 1 extending over an octave, phrase 2 over two octaves, and the extended phrase 3 over three – with its emotional *crescendo* from fervour, to passion, to transport. Theme 2 offers lyricism again – gentler, this time, and always tending towards the more energetic motion (triplet quavers, in the present case) needed for a closing group. Even the development section starts with a lengthy cello cantilena, more declamatory and improvisational. The Lied-like slow movement taps another lyric vein, nostalgia.[10]

Interaction between the solo and the orchestra becomes a matter of option in the later years. It can sometimes reach a frenzy (in the outer movements of the Horn Concerto) and at other times recede almost completely (the first movement of the Violin Concerto). Orchestration becomes more elaborate, heavier and much more varied than before; as compared to the concertos of 1849–50, the orchestration of the Fantasy and the Piano Concerto looks very innocent. Of course the richer scoring allows, notoriously, for more miscalculations. A distinctive new device is a dreamy *obbligato* in the lower strings (often divided or solo) applied to many lyric melodies; one is shown in Ex. 9.5. The most extensive and poetic of these *obbligatos* comes in the slow movement of the Cello Concerto, with its cello melody tracked by another cello in the orchestra.

Concertstück for Four Horns and Orchestra, Op. 86 (1849)

In Joseph-Rudolph Lewy the Dresden Court Orchestra boasted a hornist renowned for his poetic playing, his virtuosity and his pioneering efforts with the new valve instrument.[11] He and his confrères first performed this *Concertstück* (so called; it is a full three-movement concerto) and it received a good number of other performances – unlike the Cello Concerto, which waited for its première until 1860. For all its bizarre forces, the work stands out amid the music of these years for high spirits and compositional panache.

Its model may have been the Bach *Brandenburg* Concerto for four instruments, No. 2 (also in F) – a remote model, no doubt, yet unquestionably Schumann made use of Baroque *ritornello* form here, and this he would have known through Bach. After an important preface – it introduces a signature fanfare for the horns, insistently emulated by the orchestra – the piece gets going with a concise orchestral period that will punctuate and terminate the form for all the world like a *ritornello* in Vivaldi:

Preface	TUTTI	Exposition	TUTTI	Development	TUTTI	Recapitulation	TUTTI
	A^I	b^I	A^V	b^V	A^I	b^I	A^I

When the horns enter with their modest answer to the 'ritornello', **b**, the little subdominant dip recalls the second *Brandenburg*. And the Schumann piece, like the Bach, is so *busy*, so *packed*... The finale, too, leads off with a complex of *tutti* and solo elements, and this too, even more remotely, may owe something to Bach's complex *ritornellos*, as in *Brandenburg* Concerto No. 4.

The horns are deployed in various ways: as solos and duets, as a rich massed choir, in brassy fanfares and in rather academic counterpoint – one of the many little jokes in a positively manic composition. If this counterpoint would seem too generic to qualify as homage to Bach, the slow movement, a Romance, features an elegant and mellow central episode for two of the horns in strict canon.

In both the first and last movements, episodic developments are announced by sharp jolts to A minor after the central *tuttis* (episodic developments had worked very well in Op. 54). In the first movement, however, figures from the ritornello and the solo seep in; the development section lasts longer than the whole exposition without any flagging of interest. It harkens to a voice from the Romantic forest, a solo horn winding down slowly in F major. There are amusing moments of note-by-note alternation. Fanfares both orchestral and solo snap back on track for a brilliant recapitulation. This is virtuoso music in every sense of the word, music composed and to

183 *The concertos*

be played with the same bravura (a word Schumann actually writes in the score at one point).

Excursus 3 Transitions and trajectories
The last two movements of a Schumann concerto are invariably linked by some kind of dramatic or at least active transitional passage. Beethoven had begun this procedure, of course, as part of his programme to read the sequence of movements in a cyclic composition as a unique emotional or spiritual trajectory. If Schumann's masterpiece, Op. 54, attempts nothing distinctive in this regard, it travels the familiar journey from activity to ebullience, with a respite in the middle, as enthusiastically as if it were the first time. The transition from the intermezzo to the finale in this work is really richer than its model in Beethoven's *Emperor* Concerto, and perhaps even more beautiful.

When Joachim wrote of the later Violin Concerto that the finale 'lacked effortless enjoyment', he may well have had Op. 54 in mind as a standard, whether consciously or not.[12] In the later work the swagger of the violin's polonaise has a frozen quality made almost macabre by the strained transition leading to it from the slow movement.

With the Horn Concerto, the simple transition to the finale matches the work's simple circular trajectory. While the finale is every bit as brilliant as the first movement and packed with new material, texture counts for more than articulation, and it feels similar in mood, gesture, texture and even pace – like an approximate replay of the opening. Unlike the other three-movement cycles, there is no sense of an obligatory teleology from start to finish. This work, which revives, surprisingly, Baroque *ritornello* form, also remotely evokes Baroque *da capo* form.

Only in the Cello Concerto are the first and second movements linked, as well as the second and third (though in the Horn Concerto the Romance follows the first movement directly, after a short pause). The key of A minor, merely wistful in Op. 54, here becomes fraught, and the involuted transitions articulate an emotional trajectory of real originality and pathos. But this proved impossible to sustain in the finale.

Cello Concerto in A Minor, Op. 129 (1850)
Foreshadowing the first movement's cello cantilena, woodwinds play E–A–C in ascending semibreve chords: a Sphinx-like marker for salient points in the coming trajectory (Ex. 9.3a). One thinks of the Brahms Third Symphony. Schumann treats his Sphinx in a more narrative way, Brahms more functionally.

The great rhapsodic cello melody is clearly (to me, at least) under duress, from the halting vamp that precedes it all the way up to its hyperbolic

Example 9.3

cadence. In the intermediate *tutti*, the orchestra tries to ignore this emphatic closure, only to acknowledge it later when responding to another big cello cadence, the C major cadence that closes the exposition. So far from confirming the second key at this juncture, like a regular *tutti*, the instruments enter *subito piano*, on a deceptive cadence pointing back to A minor, and with gestures that sound already developmental. They collapse almost at once in the face of a sudden *forte* outburst – the first of a series of half-articulate cries of warning or alarm that haunt the development section (Ex. 9.3b). All this serves to undercut further developmental initiatives, which involve various rhythmic motives and the first theme struggling to re-establish itself in one distant key after another.

This painful, self-generated narrative – the theme thwarted again and again by its own derivative – appears to resolve in the recapitulation, where A minor returns, with some resignation, after bright periods in G and C major. In fact the movement ends in turmoil. The cello cadence in A major that closes the recapitulation is met by the same non-*tutti* moving back to the minor, with its distressful outcries. The orchestra picks up material drawn from the cello cantilena in the development section – a dramatic but momentary excursion that the Sphinx interrupts, leaving a sense of something not concluded. Abstracted, the solo utters something entirely new in its thematic content, slow tempo and inwardness, *Innigkeit*. The transition to the slow movement is an enigmatic quotation from the Piano Sonata in G Minor, Op. 22, written a dozen years earlier.[13]

A true intermezzo, this slow movement extends no further than five short phrases: a simple melody of great (and in the central, double-stop section, dare I say surplus) tenderness and nostalgia – something of a house speciality with this composer. Yet in the present case there is a special fragility to the nostalgia, it seems to me, as a result of the unsettling transition from the first movement. The continued presence of the Sphinx is not reassuring; we sense that the song will not be able to extend itself.

It still comes as a shock to hear the melody give way to another, more intense drama. Schumann draws his actors from amid the first-movement theme, in a last frenzy of frustration; portions of the second-movement theme; and an impassioned cello recitative that calls to mind another famous A minor work, the String Quartet No. 15, Op. 132, of Beethoven.

Beethoven's impassioned recitative launched his finale in the dark mood of the quartet's first movement. Schumann's introduces a finale whose mood might be described as strenuous jocularity. The first theme has its tricky and humorous side, and the variation of it that turns up as theme 2 runs into an outright parody of the slow movement's descending fifths. Soon afterwards, unfortunately, Schumann succumbed to an obsession that is humourless indeed with a very brief motive, the cello motive with which the opening theme is ventilated. What was originally playful, in its robust way, becomes, on repetition, articulating an almost unbroken succession of two-bar incises, ungainly and coarse.[14]

The escalating pathos of the first two movements might have led to something powerful, even tragic, I would think, yet obviously the trajectory was not sustained. This composition lives on lyricism, and in a finale lyricism would not do. Schumann relied on a pleasantry that the form would not support.

Excursus 4 On citation

In older writings, the citation of themes from one movement of a cyclic work in other movements was confidently held up as evidence of a composer's unifying powers. Critics have to get past the dreary fixation on 'unity' in Schumann before they can begin to assess what his many different kinds of citation or allusion really mean.

Sometimes I think they mean nothing at all – as, for example, in the finale of the Cello Concerto, citations of a few memorable notes from the first movement. In the finale of the Piano Concerto, the numerous citations have the effect of witticisms, wisecracks – the recall of the Intermezzo's descending fifths in the central *fugato*, the jaunty echo of the first-movement cadenza theme just before the *deux-temps* melody (along with a fainter echo of the Intermezzo), the nod to the concerto's very first notes in the episodic development section.[15] When the finale of the Horn Concerto retrieves a rich, close-harmony segment from the preceding Romance, this is an aid to virtuosity, rather than unity. Among other exploits in this piece, Schumann wanted to show off his slow triple-time melody in fast duple time.

In the finale of Schumann's Violin Concerto, allusions to the slow movement feel to me positively uncanny. One of these involves the cello melody that opens the earlier movement, returning with its syncopations desperately rushed under a lyric solo line from another rhythmic universe. For a moment something stirs under the frozen crust of this music. Uncanny in another way is the citation in the finale of an arpeggio motive that threshes around at the slow movement's extended moment of breakdown. Transformed (and conflated with the second theme of the finale), the motive now dances in the very different, buoyant mood of the coda.

Citation plays a major role in the *Concertstück* for Piano and Orchestra, Op. 92: the very striking slow clarinet melody of the introductory *langsam* section returns in the *Allegro*, in double time-values. Although the eloquence of this procedure may be questioned – to take what is essentially a *cantabile* melody and orchestrate it for wind band, grounded by an *alla breve* beat, is to destroy something precious – its functionality certainly cannot be. The melody arrives with great ceremony at the climax of the development section, a grandiose and ethereal chorale, and it arrives once again with a new, extreme harmonic twist in the coda.

Concertstück for Piano and Orchestra, Op. 92 (1849)

Nothing shows Schumann's concern for sonority in these years more vividly than the slow introduction of this *Concertstück*. A gorgeous, diaphanous texture, unlike (I believe) any other in his output, it gives the initial impression of sounds fortuitously overheard. A solo cello, rippling arpeggios by the piano with left pedal, a *pianissimo* low clarinet that sleepily misses the initial note of its melody . . . the melody drifts from instrument to instrument, spun out from two ideas: a cantabile phrase in the clarinet and a horn-call motive. Another voice from the Romantic forest, the latter registers *Sehnsucht* unknown to the Horn Concerto in a single piercing sonority. This detail, the fifth (D) at the peak of the horn-call harmonized as V^9 of ii (E^9), will have to find some confirmation later. The texture falls away, and the piano – entirely solo and *non arpeggiando* – asks a secret question that the strings try but fail to answer (and they too fall away): an enigmatic transition, once again. Following an introduction solidly in G major, the exposition of the *Allegro appassionato* goes from E minor to C, the recapitulation from E minor back to G.[16]

Schumann first withholds the last note of the *allegro* theme so that it does not end, and then keeps bringing it back until it does, interspersed with churning passages of sequential piano writing. Two key facts are established about this work: its rondo quality – the orchestra plays the simple, even simplistic theme six times; it can begin to sound blatant – and the focus on piano sonority. The orchestra and the solo are essentially kept separate, even though initially the piano shares in the playing of the theme; it never does so again (see Ex. 9.4). The principals in this piece hardly ever engage in dialogue. What is primary, instead, is the fluent stream of pianistic ideas. Tovey called it 'one of Schumann's finest specimens of the art of making flowing paragraphs';[17] still, in my view, most of the ideas themselves, while attractive, lack distinction and even definition. It was certainly a good idea to punctuate the second group with echoing horn-calls, Romantic *Wegweiser*

Example 9.4

pointing the solo towards its cadence. Otherwise the orchestra plays a negligible part in this lengthy passage.

One of Schumann's more eventful development sections, culminating in the citation of the introduction melody, plays itself out in a crowded coda. Foregoing a cadenza, the solo gestures to the other star of the day, the French horn. Retracing a sequential move attempted in the development, the horn-calls peak on C and then D, which is pivoted into an evocative B flat (V^7 of ♭VI) chord. What it evokes is that memorable V^9 chord in the introduction. The chorale makes its last appearance prolonging the B flat harmony.

Clara Schumann did not have much success with this determinedly extroverted composition, and critics who talk about it at all tend to bemoan its subsequent neglect. They should also spare some regret for its introverted sibling, the Introduction and Allegro, Op. 134, composed several years later.

Autumn 1853

The Horn Concerto; the *Concertstück*, Op. 92; and the Cello Concerto: each of these works was composed very rapidly, in a few weeks, as was Schumann's way, extending over a period of a year and half in 1849–50, in Dresden and Düsseldorf. He produced his next three concertos, his last, in a *month* and a half – from late August to early October 1853.

Given this schedule, it is less surprising that these late concertos contain some of the composer's most impersonal music – I think of the polka of the Violin Fantasy and the polonaise finale of the Violin Concerto – than to find that they also contain his most personal. The personal work is the Introduction and Allegro, Op. 134, for his own instrument, the piano.

Has there ever been, before or since, a more depressed, retiring concerto or *concertante* composition? To experience a work of art that breaks generic codes as deliberately as this one does, and put out of mind its context in the autumn of 1853, seems to me impossible. Schumann was in a decline that his intense bouts of composing only masked. Gifted to Clara and dedicated to the Schumanns' new discovery, the young Johannes Brahms, the

Introduction and Allegro must be returned to Robert; a self-portrait of the composer *in extremis*, evoking uncertain memories of Florestan and Eusebius, plaintive, half alert, half numb, with fantasies of relief still in the future. Those who hear its first few bars as a recollection of the main theme of Op. 54, going back to the Fantasy written with such confidence in 1841, must find it especially affecting.[18]

Introduction and Allegro for Piano and Orchestra, Op. 134 (1853)
The hushed pizzicato chords promise an operatic recitative, perhaps, but one that we know will bear no tidings of good cheer. After the strings' initial attempt at a *crescendo* sinks down to *pp*, the piano enters with a deep sigh (citing, it seems, the enigmatic transition of the earlier *Concertstück*, Op. 92). Quasi-improvisational solo utterances follow, whose elegance, even extravagance, combines with standard accents of lament: a strange, unusually moving amalgam.

The piano has to struggle to emerge from the shadows, as it will again later. It rebuffs several initiatives from a solo oboe – always a rueful sound in Op. 134 – and then lurches down over the dominant in preparation for a very terse first theme. This preparation is taken over as the start of the intermediate *tutti* mentioned earlier (p. 178), leading to excellently firm chords derived from the original pizzicato chords of the Introduction. The piano re-enters with the sighing motive that they elicited.

The terse, impassioned first theme of this *Allegro* is ignored in the development section and reappears only once, routinely, in the recapitulation. In a sense, the sighing motive takes its place. On the other hand, the almost hopelessly wistful second theme sounds no fewer than eight times (Ex. 9.5. So clear-cut a second theme, so many times repeated, must owe something to the Mendelssohn piano concertos.) And within the second theme a basic motive comes four times, and often the theme itself comes twice, back to back, in the solo and in the orchestra . . . We accept the motivic saturation and find it poignant, I think, because of the theme's structure, the repeated units extending for only three beats, with the remaining space in the standard four-bar phrase filled by echoes and re-echoes in the piano and the oboe. One need only imagine a $3 + 1 + 3 + 1$ arrangement, in place of Schumann's $3 + 3 + 1 + 1$, to see how banality has been skirted.

Theme 2 figures in the development section, the cadenza, the coda and even (beautifully) in the central *tutti*. The development has it in the minor mode – albeit the tonic, D minor! – with restless piano figuration added. In the cadenza, which is written out, of course, and functional in the deepest sense, the theme relocates at last in a relatively remote key, B major.

Here Schumann creates a utopian idyll, withdrawn from such reality as orchestral intervention, dialogue, development and the like may be thought

Example 9.5

to represent. No trace remains of the rueful oboe echo. He can linger in the B major day-dream with new shimmering figurations after having rigorously restricted his keys to D minor and major, F major and just a little G minor (and no A minor). The depressive tonal stasis of the development section, itself a forecast of entropic moments in the Violin Concerto, must have been planned with the upcoming utopian episode in mind.

Theme 2 appears yet again, in D major, under the cadenza's final trill. The wistfulness begins to pall, or appal; yet suddenly the piano transforms the theme into a rousing upward D major arpeggio, which a wholly unanticipated trumpet and trombone (its first appearance) take up in octaves as a sort of valedictory chorale (Ex. 9.6a). Michael Struck hears this as a version of an actual chorale, 'Du meine Seele, singe'.[19] The unusual scoring, with the two brass instruments marked *pp* while *fortissimo* piano arpeggios lap around them, contributes to a compelling sense of muted enthusiasm. The arpeggio flares up again to *forte* in the piano and the strings, but the piece quickly closes before the new experience – an apotheosis, a cure, a conversion? – can be fully absorbed.

If biographical implications in this interpretation strike you as forced or sentimental, read the Introduction and Allegro as a consummate Romantic fragment – both closed and open, coherent in itself yet pointing or rather yearning beyond its boundaries. In another sense it points to Schumann's Violin Concerto, as we shall see.

Violin Concerto in D minor (1853) (WoO1)

Schumann's last concerto is the most ambitious of his essays in the genre, also the most problematic, and the one with the most hectic reception history; see Chapter 13. The impressive orchestral passage at the start presents itself as a species of Classical 'double-exposition' *ritornello*, laying out two ideas, **A** and **B**, that are processed expertly in an ensuing solo exposition (Ex. 9.7).

Example 9.6

In the Classical paradigm, while the solo always engages with the *tutti* at its point of entry, it seldom – if ever, with so fateful and ponderous a partner – trumps the orchestra's first theme as the violin does here, by taking over the basic motive of **A** in triple stops (**a**). The triple stops obviously pay tribute to the Bach *Chaconne*; Schumann had recently been adding piano parts to Bach's solo violin music. One can imagine such a sound forming the germ of the whole composition in his mind.[20]

He will not do a conventional sonata-form exposition. A strange idea interposed after **a** seems to grasp fitfully at one note after another, possessing

Example 9.7

neither the ability nor the ambition to move forward. Once this hurdle is passed and the violin has guided the exposition to its cadence, the following *tutti* **A**^{III} sticks close to **A** – all thirty bars of it, albeit in the major mode. Anyone who is still thinking 'Classical' will be surprised to find first-theme material foregrounded so strongly in a central *tutti*. This feels more Baroque than Classical.

But not as surprised as when **A**^{III} veers back from F to D minor and the form short-circuits. No other key will be established in the nearly ten minutes the movement has remaining. From the tonal standpoint it could be said to have no development section and two recapitulations, for the 'development' proceeds to the irresolute secondary idea and then to **B**, all the while remaining in the tonic.

Matched to the tonal stasis, or stagnation, rhythmic stagnation cuts hard across the dynamics of sonata-based concerto form. The halting idea returns in the recapitulation and stops the action for a third time. Entropy rules at the end of the 'development', to me the most impressive passage in the whole piece; the violin recasts **B** (which is a strained, open-ended relative of the lyric theme from the Introduction and Allegro, Op. 134) in the minor mode and then breaks it down into barely moving fragments. A clarinet materializes to croon a languid theme from the recently completed Violin Fantasy, Op. 131. More instruments step up to join in the trance-like dialogue: an oboe, the violins and a bassoon making painful dissonances against a protracted dominant pedal. Dominant resolves to tonic, but it is a tonic in a different world.

This is a dark and disturbing passage. Parallel to it is a passage in the middle of the slow movement that feels more like a breakdown, an extended moment of stifled rage after the two lyric ideas of this movement have come together (Joachim's *kränkelnder Grübelei,* unhealthy broodings). Schumann draws a remarkable contrast in harmonic vocabulary between these two ideas, between the velvety progressions that support the introductory melody, in the divided cellos, and the texture marked by *appoggiaturas* and pedals that makes the following solo melody so abrasive. The movement is in **A B A** form. Responding to the breakdown, the solo melody returns not in the tonic key, B flat, but in G minor: a bleak effect, if not a black one. Both themes turn bitter.[21]

Schumann draws another sharp contrast between the hard, brilliant polonaise that launches the finale and an almost flirtatious second idea that adheres to it without ever reaching fulfilment. It is unsettling to find among his very last compositions such obvious crowd-pleasers (or intended crowd-pleasers) as this polonaise-finale and the polka of the Violin Fantasy.

But they cannot be written off. The finale sheds light on the first movement – through the lens, once again, of Op. 134. In Op. 134, as we have seen, tonal stasis reinforces the mood of depression and lassitude, and in particular it provides a foil for the appearance of the work's lyric second theme in, finally, the remote key of B major, with its intimations of Utopia. There are no such intimations in the Violin Concerto, certainly. But long after the pervasive tonal stasis of the first movement, B major is heard again at the centre of the finale. Schumann does not go so far as to coordinate this key with a return of the first movement's lyric theme **B**, but he does the next best thing and brings a finale theme that **B** has inspired.

We can also make use of Op. 134 to read the Violin Concerto as regards its conclusion, one of the work's most visionary and at the same time most problematic features. To go back to the first movement: following the last tutti, A^1, the orchestra takes the motive of **B** and stretches it into an almost Mahlerian elegy – **A** has probably been reminding us of Bruckner – merging into gestures of apotheosis, similar to but less definite than those that close Op. 134. They are built from mild, beatific fragments of **A** (Ex. 9.6b). If the form of this movement can be thought of as dialectical rather than teleological in impetus, its ending represents Schumann's attempt at synthesis.[22]

A parallel move (prepared, incidentally, in much the same way) occurs in the finale. Again the orchestra takes over the solo's principal motive and dilates upon it to transcend the world of the polonaise. In both cases the central action in the orchestra works together with buoyant new figuration in the solo. While things are more emphatic and complex in this movement than in the first – the solo adding a new-derived arpeggio figure, wind instruments adding a sort of three-legged march – the apotheosis is still subdued, deliberately precarious. The three thematic elements involved are shown in Ex. 9.6c. This composition, which began so thunderously, ends with more than a minute of quiet music. Just two *sforzandos* signal the close.

Fantasy for Violin and Orchestra, Op. 131 (1853)

To call this Fantasy a pot-boiler would not be very companionable, and unkind, for it has its moments.[23] Beginning in Schumann's *Legendenton*, the orchestra rehearses a serious, far from simple tale of yore as it awaits the bard who will come to declaim it. But on the arrival of this individual with his violin, he turns out to have nothing much to say. Ballads do not interest him. After some self-important declarations and a show of pique he throws off his vatic robe to show us a motley underneath.

An unattractive polka in the *Allegro*, parroted by an intermediate *tutti*; a second group modelled on the second group in the first movement of the Cello Concerto – but Schumann's genius for idiomatic cello lyricism finds no analogue in the violin writing here. Virtuosity in the closing group would not have pleased critic Schumann in the 1830s. A famous stroke at the end of the cadenza in Mendelssohn's Violin Concerto inspired two passages in this Fantasy; it is sobering to see how one great composer can sometimes misconstrue another.[24] Felicitous, at the end of the central *tutti*, is the way in which a reference to the opening ballad lays the ground for a new lyric melody; this can then lead naturally to an actual citation of the ballad, in an atmospheric new scoring. Its *pianissimo* return in the coda – only the last eight bars or so of this Fantasy are *forte* – appears to stab at another subdued apotheosis, as in both of its sibling works from August 1853. But the expressive thrust, as with much else in Schumann's latest music, is hard to make out.

Notes

1. Claudia Macdonald, *Robert Schumann's F-major Piano Concerto of 1831 as Reconstructed from His First Sketchbook* (Ph.D. thesis, University of Chicago, 1996) includes a full-length transcription of the piano part on pp. 462–96. There are also a few preliminary sketches for a rondo finale. Macdonald's work on the early Schumann concertos is foundational, and I draw upon it heavily and gratefully: see Bibliography. Professor Macdonald's *Robert Schumann and the Piano Concerto* (New York: Routledge, 2005), appeared too late for consideration in this chapter.
2. Macdonald, *JM*, 13 (1995), p. 240. Citations from Schumann in this and the next paragraph are taken from the same article, pp. 247–8 and 251–2 (translations slightly modified).
3. Pointed out by Macdonald in *JAMS*, p. 45 (1992) 145–6. These relationships certainly seem schematic, as compared to the lucid, audience-oriented thematic transformations of the Fantasy and the Piano Concerto.
4. With performance in view, the 'reconstruction' of the Draheim edition adds a cadenza prior to theme 2 (64 bars) and a conclusion (19 bars); but see Macdonald's strictures, *ibid.*, p. 150. Recorded by J. Eley, piano, with the English Chamber Orchestra, cond. S. Stone (Koch CD 7197; rec. 1999).
5. 'The piano begins by itself, and the orchestra inserts a quick punctuation mark between its second and third chords' (Steinberg, *The Concerto*, p. 417n). Botched in the appalling edition by Wolfgang Boetticher, this passage is entirely clear in the Op. 54 autograph, our sole, somewhat uncertain source for the Fantasy, though there can be no doubt in this case. See the facsimile in *Documenta musicologica*, 27 (Kassel: Bärenreiter, 1996).
6. I am not sure whether personal interventions are necessary in prose of this kind, or whether they will be accepted in good faith; I put them in to remind readers anyway – as much for my sake as for theirs – of the contingency of critical judgements in texts of all kinds, in my writing in general, and

at the point of insertion in particular. What post-modern critics call the 'mastery scenario' was itself played out relentlessly in not a few 'companion' books of an earlier generation. The essential thing a critic does is clarify his or her perceptions, thoughts and feelings about art; integrity is the ambition, not authority.

7. *Schumann as Critic*, p. 159.
8. Symbols: $\mathbf{a}^I$ = first theme played by the solo – in the tonic; $(\mathbf{A}^V)$ = orchestral playing of only part of the theme – in the dominant; $(\mathbf{a}/\mathbf{A}^{IV})$ = theme shared between solo and orchestra – in the subdominant.
9. Also highly vivacious are the many circling passages of modulation, before and after the second theme in the exposition and recapitulation. Stephan Lindeman traces them to the Chopin E minor Concerto; see Stephan Lindeman, *Structural Novelty and Tradition in the Early Romantic Piano Concerto* (New York: Pendragon, 1999), pp. 160–2.
10. Negative evidence of Schumann's fine sense for the cello emerges from his misguided transcription of the Cello Concerto for violin: *Violin Concertos in D and A Minor*, John Storgaards, violin, and the Tampere Philharmonic Orchestra, cond. Leif Segerstam (Ondine CD ODE 879-2, rec. 1996). Even more of a curiosity is Schumann's piano arrangement of the Horn Concerto: *Konzertstück nach op. 86, Klavier und Orchester*, ed. Marc Andreae, Edition Peters Nr. 8576.
11. Lewy is not in *Grove*: see Steinberg, *The Concerto*, p. 427.
12. 'Kein freies Gefühl frohen Genusses': see Michael Struck, *Robert Schumann: Violinkonzert D-moll* (Munich: W. Fink Verlag, 1988).
13. Irrespective of some probable private reason for the quotation, its pitch-content mediates between the two movements. The Sphinx preceding it, expanded from E–A–C to E–A–D, favours the descending fifth A–D over the rising fourth, and pairs of descending fifths inform both the sonata excerpt and the upcoming cello melody.
14. It should be said that while most critics register some discomfort with this finale, others extoll it: see H. Truscott, 'The evolution of Schumann's last period: Part II', *Chesterian*, 31 (1957), p. 105 – part of a classic and impassioned defence of Schumann's late music as a whole.
15. This nod was more knowing when the concerto was still in its 'first layer' stage: see n. 5. I am indebted to Robert Levin for this observation.
16. Thus illustrating two characteristics of Romantic music that are stressed by Charles Rosen, in contradistinction to Classical: the equivalence of tonic and relative minor and the tendency of compositions to move to the subdominant.
17. *Essays in Musical Analysis*, III, p. 189.
18. See Walker, *Robert Schumann*, p. 248–9.
19. Michael Struck, *Die umstrittenen späten Instrumentalwerke Schumanns* (Hamburg: Verlag der Musikalienhandlung W. A. Wagner, 1984), p. 234. See his exhaustive discussion of the device he calls '"synthetischer Codathema" choralartiger Prägung' in late Schumann – in the violin concertos and other works: Opp. 118; 123; 132, No. 4; 133, No. 4; and the Third Violin Sonata (pp. 591–5 *et passim*). I believe that by far the best use of the device comes in Op. 134.
20. One can also imagine the effect of this concerto on Brahms, who soon after seeing it began the D minor work that would crystallize into his First Piano Concerto. Brahms saves trumping his first theme for the recapitulation, with a power that goes beyond ponderosity. Schumann's triple stops are never developed in their many appearances. Bach is again recalled, as often in late Schumann, by the figuration in bars 79–88, the modulatory bridge passage; see Struck, *Violinkonzert*, p. 38.
21. The melody that came to Schumann in February 1854, on which he and later Brahms wrote variations, is a completely softened version of the concerto's solo melody, in the same key. Schumann's Variation IV is in G minor. On the concerto melody, see Steinberg, *The Concerto*, p. 425n.
22. Pointed out by Struck, *Violinkonzert*, Table I. He notes further derivatives of the concerto's *Kernmotiv* in bars 40–3, as well as in bars 11–12 of the slow movement and even bar 5.
23. Why Schumann called Op. 131 a *Fantasie* rather than another *Concertstück* is hard to say, unless possibly to acknowledge that the introduction is in one key, A minor, and the *allegro* in another, C major. He worked, in any case, to smooth over this anomaly: theme 1 stresses the note A, theme 2 harps on A minor sonorities, and A minor is the key of the central ballad citation. See n. 17.
24. But John Daverio praises Schumann's adaptation (*Robert Schumann*, p. 469). The regrettable transcription by Fritz Kreisler, which is likely to be used for the Fantasy's rare performances today, cuts out the first of these passages and a great deal more.

10 Dramatic stage and choral works

ELIZABETH PALEY

Perhaps more than any other composer, Robert Schumann is known for his lifelong passion for literature. The son of a book dealer, publisher and translator, he earnestly contemplated a literary career during an adolescence focussed as much on poetic as on musical pursuits. 'Poet and composer in one person', Schumann later recalled of himself; he was referring particularly to Lieder he composed in the late 1820s, yet one could also read the epithet as expressing a broader compositional ambition. One regularly finds *belles lettres* paired with music in Schumann's autobiographical comments about his formative years: Jean Paul stood alongside Schubert, Goethe alongside Bach. Music helped feed a burning *Theaterpassion*: between 1823 and 1827 he heard Weber's *Der Freischütz* and *Preciosa*, Cherubini's *The Water Carrier* (*Der Wasserträger*), Rossini's *The Thieving Magpie* (*Die diebische Elster*) and Mozart's *Die Entführung aus dem Serail*, among several other stage works.[1]

Not surprisingly, Schumann's initial compositional forays nourished his literary bent, beginning with some larger choral and orchestral works written in his eleventh year, and soon after 'some numbers for an opera, several vocal pieces, [and] several things for piano'.[2] As a twelve-year-old, he bestowed the distinction of 'Œuvre 1' on a setting of Psalm 150, the vivid timbral imagery of the text realized by an unusual bevy of instruments.[3] When Schumann ultimately decided to follow a career in music, against his mother's wishes that he study law, he expressed his choice in literary terms, equating music with poetry, jurisprudence with prose.[4]

Schumann's instrumental music reverberates with the composer's poetic voice: evidence of literary allusions and narrative strategies abounds in his piano miniatures and chamber works. Yet in the *Musikalische Haus- und Lebensregeln*, compiled in 1850 as an afterword to the *Album für die Jugend*, Schumann admonished musicians to remember that 'the highest expression possible in music comes from chorus and orchestra',[5] and it is in the composer's choral and stage works that we find his literary aesthetic realized on its grandest scale. Monumental compositions such as *Das Paradies und die Peri*, *Genoveva*, *Manfred* and the *Szenen aus Goethes Faust*, with their lush, lyrical gestures, reveal a profound dedication to dramatic integrity and present a mature response to the *Theaterpassion* with which Schumann had burned since his youth.

Reflecting an increasing value placed on music as part of bourgeois education, nineteenth-century Germany saw the rapid rise of predominantly amateur *Singakademien* and *Männerchöre* (choral societies and men's choruses), along with the birth of the music festival. These institutions had social and political as well as educational and musical aims: their social and artistic stature was often a function of the number of musicians, both amateur and professional, involved in their performances. Schumann heard many of the most popular oratorios of the day, including an 1837 performance of Handel's *Messiah* with a chorus of 300 in the Leipzig Paulinerkirche, and an 'imposing and unforgettable' 1838 performance of Haydn's *Die Jahreszeiten* at Vienna's Imperial Winter Riding School with 804 singers and 320 instrumentalists.[6] Following its 1829 revival by the Berlin *Singakademie*, Bach's *Matthäus-Passion* became a model for a new generation of sacred oratorios, including Mendelssohn's *Paulus* and *Elias*. Choral societies and festivals also supported a flowering interest in elevated secular vocal music in the nineteenth century, albeit rarely involving such extensive musical forces as at the Viennese performances of *Die Jahreszeiten*. Schubert, Schumann, Mendelssohn and numerous other composers contributed to a growing partsong repertoire for men's choruses and for mixed voices. The eventual decline of the *Singvereine* was one of the greatest contributing factors to the disappearance of much of this secular repertoire from the canon in the twentieth century.[7]

Schumann responded to the popularity of the *Singakademien* at the beginning of the 'Year of Song' of 1840 with his first pieces for men's chorus, the *Sechs Lieder*, Op. 33, on texts by Mosen, Heine, Goethe and Reinick. The celebrated dramatic oratorio *Das Paradies und die Peri*, Op. 50, for soloists, mixed chorus and orchestra, followed in 1843. *Peri* launched Schumann's international reputation as a composer and was second only to the 'Spring' Symphony in B flat major in frequency of performance during Schumann's lifetime.[8] Two additional volumes of partsongs followed in 1846, both for mixed voices (the *Fünf Lieder* on texts by Robert Burns, Op. 55, and *Vier Gesänge*, Op. 59), but it was not until 1847, when Schumann became an active participant in the *Singakademie* movement as a conductor as well as a composer, that his choral output burgeoned. In a letter of 4 November 1848 to Johann Verhulst, he reported that he had been getting significant practice as a conductor. This was thanks first to having assumed direction of the Dresden *Liedertafel* (men's chorus) in November 1847, after its previous leader, Ferdinand Hiller, moved to Düsseldorf. 'But I gave that up', he wrote to Verhulst, 'because it cost me too much time. And after spending the entire day in musical activity, it was hard to relish those eternal six-four chords of the *Männergesang* style.' More to his taste, Schumann established his own Dresden choral society for mixed voices. It convened for the first time in January 1848, and by November Schumann proudly reported that his *Chorverein* was 'in fullest bloom'.⁹

With a ready laboratory in which to test his own compositions, and with a venue for their performance, it is hardly surprising that the majority of Schumann's choral works date from 1847–53, his time as a professional conductor first in Dresden and then (again following in Hiller's footsteps) as municipal music director in Düsseldorf beginning in the autumn of 1850. This output includes all but fifteen of some seventy partsongs for men's, women's and mixed chorus; four choral 'Lieder' on subjects ranging from sacred to secular (*Adventlied, Nachtlied, Beim Abschied zu singen, Neujahrslied*); scenes extracted from Goethe's *Faust* and *Wilhelm Meister* (the *Szenen aus Goethes Faust* and the *Requiem für Mignon*); the secular cantata *Der Rose Pilgerfahrt*, on a poem by Moritz Horn; four *Choralballaden* based on fairytale plots by Horn, Ludwig Uhland and Emanuel Geibel; and two liturgical works, the *Mass* and *Requiem*, composed for Catholic Düsseldorf. This most fruitful period saw not only an abundance of choral works but also a renewed interest in vocal settings in general, on scales both small and large, with a return to solo song and, at long last, a completed opera, *Genoveva*, Op. 81. Another large-scale literary work, the overture and incidental music to *Manfred*, Op. 115, followed shortly after *Genoveva*, and like the opera is the sole representative of its genre within Schumann's entire output.

Considering the choral and stage works together, an image emerges of Schumann as a composer regularly and self-consciously preoccupied with new ways to present literature through music and, vice versa, music through literature. Especially among the plot-driven compositions, one finds a tendency to experiment with a genre just once before moving on to another. Thus there is only one opera, despite a lifetime of operatic projects. Then Schumann moved on to just one set of incidental music, and more strikingly, just one dramatic oratorio, a genre that, despite the success of *Peri*, Schumann returned to only on a much smaller scale and after an eight-year delay, with the cantata *Der Rose Pilgerfahrt*. *Faust* was another singular, if ongoing, musico-dramatic experiment, its seven tableaux from Goethe's tragedy requiring nearly a decade to complete and in the end not intended for performance as a totality except 'as a curiosity'.¹⁰ Liszt remarked on Schumann's innovative decision 'to compose complete parts of a tragedy, of the most monumental work of our time, *Faust*, without modifying or arranging the text in any way'.¹¹ On a less grandiose musical scale, in Schumann's hands the choral ballad came into its own as a genre, merging choral story-telling, dramatic solos and vivid orchestral imagery in settings of romantic fairytales inhabited by questing adventurers, lovers, minstrels, dragons, mermen, a remarkable number of looming storms and other fantastic marvels.

Further uniting this diverse body of works are thematic connections between the verbal texts that epitomize Romanticism's fascination with the fantastic and the remote. In *Der Rose Pilgerfahrt* we find several of Schumann's favoured threads: supernatural creatures and magical transformations (the fairy queen grants a flower's wish to become a maiden); love as a source of grief (the miller's daughter, dead of a broken heart) but also of unsurpassable personal fulfilment (for Rose herself, as daughter, wife, mother); sacrifice of one's life for another (Rose passes the magic emblem sustaining her human existence on to her baby); and transfiguration (a choir of angels rewards the dying Rose by lifting her up to Heaven). Exchange the German folklorism of *Rose* with exotic orientalism in *Peri* and historicism in *Genoveva*, substitute for *Rose*'s benevolent fairies the sinister supernatural beings in *Faust* and *Manfred*, and the rest of the threads still remain in one form or another.

Sacred and secular works are united by Schumann's fascination with redemption and apotheosis. Spiritual salvation is the motivation of the *Mass* and *Requiem*; it is Christ's gift to Man in the *Adventlied*; for the four boys mourning Mignon's death, it inspires a return to life renewed with hope and light; it rewards Rose, who lovingly yields her life to it, Peri who unfailingly seeks it, and Genoveva who faithfully prays for it; and it even awaits Faust, who does not expect it, and Manfred, who misanthropically spurns it.

One practical feature shared by the plot-driven works in particular is, paradoxically, how little they did for Schumann's reputation as a dramatic composer. In a 1910 re-evaluation of *Genoveva*, Hermann Abert rejected a commonly held explanation for the opera's lack of success in the sixty years since its première: that Schumann was 'a born lyrical composer' for whom 'the portals of the realm of musical drama were simply closed from the start'.[12] Abert's choice of words invites us to broaden our understanding of Schumann as a 'dramatic composer', for it invokes, perhaps with ironic intention, the plot of one of Schumann's most lauded choral compositions, *Das Paradies und die Peri*. Barred from Heaven because of the legacy of her birth, the mythological Peri strives to earn entry through the portals of paradise. After striving without cease, Peri succeeds in her quest; so too did Schumann in his, as the instantaneous triumph of *Peri*, if not *Genoveva*, attests.

The juxtaposition of *Peri* with *Genoveva*, celebrated dramatic oratorio with disfavoured opera, underscores a common bond between Schumann's stage works and many of the large-scale choral compositions: despite the variety of subjects and genres, these pieces embody innovative solutions to the challenge of conveying dramatic, lyric and epic aspects of plot through music. To highlight the diversity of these solutions, and to delve more deeply into a musico-dramatic aesthetic sustained through many of Schumann's literary works, three compositions will guide our way: *Peri*, the first and most successful musical drama; *Genoveva*, the sole experiment in operatic reform; and *Manfred*, the most daring and personal pairing of music with poetry.

Entirely 'absorbed with Peri thoughts' from February to June 1843, Schumann enthusiastically wrote to Verhulst shortly after completing the music: 'I finished my *Paradise and the Peri* last Friday, my greatest work, and I hope also my best ... The story of *Peri* is from Thomas Moore's *Lalla Rookh*, and it is as though it was written for music. The whole idea is so poetic, so pure, that it filled me entirely with enthusiasm.'[13]

Lalla Rookh, published in 1817, was an overnight sensation that nourished romantic cravings for Orientalism. Moore's story follows the journey of Princess Tulip Cheek (Lalla Rookh) from her homeland in Delhi to Cashmere, where her arranged marriage to the King of Lesser Bucharia is to take place. The King has sent the minstrel Feramorz to entertain the princess and her entourage along the way with poetic recitations; Moore weaves Feramorz's four elaborate verse tales into the story's prose framework.[14] 'Paradise and the Peri', the second of the poems, combines lyrical descriptions of exotic lands and characters with a quasi-religious plot of redemption. An ethereal, winged 'child of air', Peri and her race are the progeny of a fallen angel and a mortal. Only by finding 'the gift most dear to Heaven' can Peri earn her entry into paradise. Her first offering is a drop of blood, shed by an Indian youth in battle for liberty; the second, a 'sigh of pure, self-sacrificing love', exhaled by a maiden who perishes with her plague-stricken lover. But it is only the third gift, the repentant tear of a convict, shed when he sees a young boy praying, that redeems not only the prisoner but Peri as well, finally raising the Eternal Gates.

In December 1840, Schumann listed three of Feramorz's four verse poems in his project book, considering 'Paradise and the Peri' and 'The Veiled Prophet of Khorassan' as suitable for opera, and 'The Light of the Harem' as a possible *Concertstück*.[15] Thus he already had the text in mind when Emil Flechsig, a close friend from his Gymnasium and university days, reignited Schumann's interest in the 'Peri' material during a visit to Leipzig in August 1841. According to a study by Gerd Nauhaus, Schumann's annotations in Flechsig's translation show that operatic intentions for *Peri* were abandoned relatively early in his work on the libretto. (Realizing *Peri* as an opera would have required a thorough reworking of the text in order to transform the narrative-lyric prose into dramatic dialogue; moreover, a drop of blood, a sigh and a tear make for less than compelling props on stage.) As Schumann wrote to Karl Koßmaly in May 1843, opera was what *Peri* was *not*: 'at present I am engaged in a great work, the greatest that I have yet undertaken. It is no opera – I believe it is an entirely new genre for the concert hall'.[16]

Schumann's claim to innovation was no idle boast, and reviewers devoted a great deal of press space to the question of genre. The designation on the title page was literary – *Dichtung* [poem] *aus Lalla Rookh von Th. Moore* – though in a letter to Eduard Krüger, Schumann described the composition as 'an oratorio, but not for the prayer room – rather for more cheerful folk'.[17] At that time, the term 'oratorio' typically meant any extensive work for chorus and soloists that relied on texts from Hebrew-Christian tradition and combined narrative, dialogue and emotional reflection in varying degrees. Performances of oratorios regularly took place in concert halls as well as churches, and the works edified listeners as much through their musical artistry as through the morals of their texts. (Indeed, Schumann acknowledged even the *Mass* and *Requiem* as suitable for concert performance.)[18]

By the time Schumann began *Peri*, other composers and critics (including Schumann himself) were already challenging the limits of oratorio as a genre, in terms of the subject matter and the relative balance of epic, lyric and dramatic poetic elements. In his 1840 review of Hiller's *Die Zerstörung Jerusalems*, Schumann declared biblical oratorios a dying genre; the great success of Mendelssohn's *Paulus*, he explained, was an exception that reflected the great achievement of the individual artist. In an 1842 review of Carl Loewe's *Johann Huß* (an oratorio centred on the fifteenth-century Czech religious reformer rather than on biblical subject matter), Schumann's attention turned to questions of poetic expression, noting that 'we still have no good word for this middle genre; as "religious opera" one thinks of something else, nor does "dramatic oratorio" convey the right sense'.[19]

The *Peri* libretto, with its Persian mythology and secular subplots, clearly veered from oratorio tradition. Given its didactic climax celebrating the purity of spiritual redemption, critics most often labelled *Peri* an oratorio, though recurring caveats about the libretto's subject matter reflect anxieties about this classification. As with *Johann Huß*, other compositional choices in *Peri* further complicated the question of genre. 'This is obviously a work that departs from the nature of the oratorio in textual content, conception, style and structure of the single parts', wrote Oswald Lorenz.[20] While Peri's discovery of her three gifts provided motivation for a structural division into three large sections (well within oratorical conventions of the time), Schumann's treatment of the music within each section was less standard. Emulating a feature he had admired in Heinrich Marschner's dramatic cantata, the oriental love story *Klänge aus dem Osten* (1842), Schumann avoided interrupting the musical flow between recitatives, arias and choruses.[21] This technique, which one finds in many of his later works for chorus and orchestra, helped blur distinctions between individual numbers and placed emphasis on dramatic continuity. Again accentuating continuity, Schumann also divided the libretto in a way that maximized dramatic suspense across the musical silences separating each section: sections 1 and 2 end with Peri's discovery of her first two gifts, while sections 2 and 3 begin with her presentation of them to the Angel guarding Heaven's doors.

In his sketches for *Peri*, Schumann designated several numbers 'recitatives', including one described as *recitivischer Gesang*.[22] The near disappearance of these headings in the final score testifies to the *arioso* style of these narrative episodes: only No. 3 remains a recitative, the rest having become simply 'solos'. The musical result is a more graceful flow between recitative and aria than traditional oratorio style permitted, while still providing musical distinctions between narrative, reflective and dramatic portions of the text. Some years later, Schumann wrote to Franz Brendel, his successor as editor of the *Neue Zeitschrift für Musik*, asking for an opinion on 'two rebukes' from critics: 'the shortage of [simple] recitatives, and the continuous stringing together of the musical pieces'. Rather than viewing these as problems, Schumann considered them 'the true advantages of the work', and formal advances.[23] Brendel had previously described the oratorio in the pages of the journal as 'rich in content and musical innovation' but lacking 'unity of style and character'.[24] As will become more apparent shortly in the discussion of *Genoveva*, Brendel cultivated a generally ambivalent reception of Schumann's music in the *Neue Zeitschrift* during his tenure as editor (from 1845 until his death in 1868). Trained as a philosopher whose view of music past, present and future was steeped in Hegelian dialectical principles, Brendel would emerge as a strong advocate for the music of Wagner, Liszt and others of the 'New German' school.

Although Schumann discarded operatic plans for *Peri*, his most significant changes to Moore's poem reveal a dramatic conception for the composition, one in which the music vividly depicts characters and locations without the visual stimulus of theatrical staging. To achieve this, Schumann turned much of the narrative into dramatic and instrumental dialogue. In some cases this simply involved requiring a character to speak directly rather than through a narrator. The most obvious example is the role of the Peri: in *Lalla Rookh*, Feramorz mediates all of her thoughts, whereas Schumann's oratorio centres on Peri's own voice. Other portions of the text underwent greater reworking, such as the battle scene in section 1. Whereas Moore's Feramorz narrates the entire scene, Schumann gives individual voice to 'Gazna, fierce in wrath' (bass), the Indian youth (tenor), and the armies of conquerors (bass voices accompanied by low strings and a grumbling ophicleide, all in unison) and defenders (heroic tenors, supported by brass fanfares). A fearsome janissary march brings Gazna's ruthless invasion to life, with clashing cymbals, squealing piccolos, pounding bass drums and ornamented quaver scales in the strings. Solo narrators and chorus fill in descriptive details that music and direct dialogue cannot. Thus we learn that the youthful Indian warrior, 'blood gushing from his many wounds', valiantly shoots his last arrow against the tyrant. A portentous grand pause accompanies the arrow's flight – and Gazna lives. Entering in a dissonant cascade of thirds, a chorus of female voices mourns the fall of the hero.

Schumann's second significant alteration to the libretto was to add his own newly written verse texts. While these do little for the advancement of the plot, they highlight as a group the theme of redemption and Schumann's proclivity for mystical characters and oriental imagery, musically realized through an array of mimetic orchestral effects. With airy texture and articulation reminiscent of the fairy music in Mendelssohn's overture (and later incidental music) to *Ein Sommernachtstraum* and Weber's opera *Oberon*, a chorus of Nile Genies (No. 11) evokes the river's creatures in nimble waves of rippling semiquavers and sparkling pizzicato in the strings. Less spritely but equally delicate are the *tremolo* strings and *staccato* arpeggiation of the winds in the quartet of Peris (No. 22), whose desire to enter Heaven with the protagonist adds to her burden. Opening the third section of the oratorio is the Houris' song (No. 18), in which rhythmic strumming of open fifths in the bass, the dissonant drone of a tonic pedal, and the janissary timbres of the great drum, cymbals and triangle suggest an 'oriental' dance as the graceful Houris, bedecking the steps of Allah's throne with flowers, remind Peri of the heavenly reward that awaits her. Focussing on Peri's quest and redemption are two other additions: beginning pensively with Peri's dismay at still being cast out of paradise, No. 20 ('Verstossen!') soon strikes a joyous turn as Peri renews her determination; and whereas Moore's poem ends with Peri's declaration, 'Joy, joy forever! – my task is done – / The Gates are passed, and Heaven is won!', Schumann confirms her redemption with a lengthy, rondo-form Chorus of the Blessed Spirits (No. 26) that welcomes her into paradise.

Schumann's use of reminiscence motives in *Peri*, while less extensive than in the stage works, reveals a keen sensitivity to details of the text. Of particular interest are short motives introduced in Peri's first aria (No. 2, the strophic 'Wie glücklich sie wandeln') and the Angel's response (No. 3, 'Der hehre Engel, der die Pforte'), for these both establish Peri's quest and allude to the gift that seals her redemption. Example 10.1 shows the opening of Peri's strophic, binary-form aria, in which she exclaims 'how happy are the holy spirits who wander [in Heaven]'. In No. 9, as Peri seizes on her first gift, the drop of blood she hopes will end her exclusion from paradise, the motive

Example 10.1 *Peri*, No. 2, 'Wie glücklich sie wandeln', bars 1–4

[How happy are the holy spirits who wander there]

Example 10.2 *Peri*, No. 9, 'Die Peri sah das Mal der Wunde', bars 16–20

[Be this, my gift]

Example 10.3 *Peri*, No. 3, 'Der hehre Engel', bars 36–9

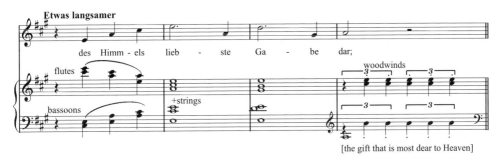

[the gift that is most dear to Heaven]

is sweetly recalled in major mode and augmented rhythms (Ex. 10.2). In section 2, No. 11, when Peri must resume her quest, the original melody returns intertwined with the rising arpeggios of the Nile Genies, as she mourns with words newly added by Schumann, 'Ah Eden, how my heart longs for you, / Oh when will your gates be open to me?' Though the composer henceforth abandons the melody, another motive, originating in No. 3, will link Peri's quest with her final gift.

When the Angel who guards Heaven's gates hears Peri's plea and reveals that 'the Peri yet may be forgiven', a rising arpeggio leads to the movement's melodic climax (Ex. 10.3) to highlight 'the gift that is most dear to Heaven!'

Example 10.4a *Peri*, No. 13, "Die Peri weint," mm. 49–51

[that such a spirit weeps for man]

Example 10.4b *Peri*, No. 13, bars 61–5

[For there's a magic in each tear]

This cadential gesture recurs at crucial points in the plot, always marked by a three-beat anacrusis, the progression from cadential six-four to dominant seventh, and a pair of descending melodic leaps that ends on the leading-tone prior to the tonic arrival (musical closure perhaps anticipating eventual closure in Peri's quest). Variations of the motive (Ex. 10.4) cap off two imitative passages in the No. 13 quartet ('Die Peri weint'). 'There's magic in each tear, / Such kindly spirits weep for man!', the narrators explain, as Peri's own tears foreshadow the convict's tear of remorse that will become her successful offering. Making another parallel between Peri and the mortals she observes, Schumann reuses the 'ist Zaubermacht' ('there's magic') variation from No. 13 to end the mezzo-soprano narrator's description of the praying boy in No. 23: Peri is like that 'stray babe of Paradise, / Lost upon the earthly plain / And seeking for his home again'.[25] Linking gift, tears and quest, when Heaven's gates finally open for Peri at the end of No. 25, the cadential motive returns in glorified form (Ex. 10.5): the tenor begins the motive with the three-note anacrusis, soon taken over by adamant unison winds and horns. Delaying the dominant-seventh resolution of the prolonged cadential six-four is Peri's interjection, 'Joy, joy for ever! My task is done –.' Labelled 'q' in

Example 10.5 *Peri*, No. 25, 'Es fällt ein Tropfen', bars 145 ff.

[TENOR: ...that soon opened Heaven to her!
PERI: Joy, joy forever! my task is done-- /
The gates are pass'd, and Heaven is won!]

Ex. 10.5, the phrase in turn is derived from the B section of No. 2, bringing Peri's quest full circle.[26]

With the advantage of hindsight, we could consider *Peri* as Schumann's trial run for an opera. Indeed, critics hungry for a new national style of German opera anticipated as much long before Schumann achieved a staged drama. In his lengthy 1845 review of *Peri*, Krüger suggested that Schumann was striving 'from his earlier songs through instrumental works and oratorio towards opera as his true goal', and suspected *Faust* would be the subject, knowing that Schumann had already begun working on music for Goethe's tragedy in 1844.[27] His intuition that Schumann's dramatic impulses were heading toward opera would be borne out not by *Faust* but by Schumann's next large-scale dramatic composition, *Genoveva*.

With *Genoveva*, Schumann finally brought to fruition his long-held aspiration to compose a stage work. As early as 1830, he had been in 'fire and flame' over a grand opera on Shakespeare's *Hamlet*, but left off with just eight bars of a 'Sinfonia per il Hamlet'. A decade later, he wrote to Clara about his next serious subject, E. T. A. Hoffmann's novella *Doge und Dogeressa*. He was worried about the poetic quality of Julius Becker's in-progress libretto, yet vowed to forge through, feeling 'sufficient dramatic talent within me' (work on the opera halted shortly thereafter).[28] In 1842, he wrote to Koßmaly declaring his 'morning and evening artist's prayer' to be for '*German opera*. That's where a contribution can be made!', and shortly after completing *Peri* in June 1843, he wrote in the *Tagebuch* that 'the next thing shall be an opera, and I'm fired up about it'.[29] Nothing materialized until late the following June, when he turned to Byron's verse epic *The Corsair*. After composing an opening chorus and a fragment of an aria, he abandoned that project too, in order to continue work on the first of his *Faust* scenes – a story he had originally conceived of setting as an opera. All told, Schumann contemplated over fifty subjects for opera before settling on the legend of Saint Genevieve.[30]

Genoveva was Schumann's answer to a 'deeply rooted need for a new German opera', an attempt to forge a path away from what he considered the annoying trivialities of foreign influences toward a style distinctly German.[31] In a scathing 1837 review of *Les Huguenots*, Schumann accused Meyerbeer of using cheap plot gimmicks, orchestral excesses, vapid melodies and bleating rhythms in order 'to dumbfound or titillate' his audiences. In his subsequent critique of Reißiger's grand opera *Adèle de Foix*, he again denounced composers who seemed to write only with the goal of pleasing the public, and who criticized the excesses of Italian and French composers while imitating their styles. Schumann held the colossal success of *Der Freischütz* partly to blame for this trend, even though he considered Weber's operas the most meaningful German operas of the time.[32]

Responding to his own call for 'a strong artist' who could 'lead the way and awaken emulation and courage',[33] in April 1847 Schumann selected the subject of Saint Genevieve, primarily as told in Friedrich Hebbel's play *Genoveva* (1841) and Ludwig Tieck's *Leben und Tod der heiligen Genoveva* (1799). He assembled the libretto himself, after an unsuccessful collaboration with Dresden poet and painter Robert Reinick. Hebbel, who considered *Genoveva* one of his weaker plays, rebuffed Schumann's requests for assistance. The libretto, 'after Tieck and Hebbel', was drafted by the end of 1847. Composition of the music occupied Schumann until August 1848.

Set in the eighth century, the opera centres on two characters: Genoveva, whose husband Count Siegfried joins Charles Martel's campaign against Arab invasion at the beginning of the opera, and Golo, the knight who remains behind to protect her. Like Hebbel's Golo, Schumann's is a conflicted man who struggles to contain his amorous feelings toward Genoveva. She spurns his increasingly aggressive advances, finally crying 'stand back, infamous bastard!' Golo vows revenge and, egged on by the witch Margaretha, accuses Genoveva of adultery. Siegfried is preparing to return home when he receives false word of his wife's infidelity, and he orders her executed. Just as she is to be killed, Genoveva is saved by a remorseful Siegfried, who has learned of Golo's treachery. Added to the mix: a stolen kiss, a murder, a magic mirror, a ghost and, on a rocky cliff, a hidden cross whose divine rays illuminate Genoveva as she clings to it for deliverance. Missing from Schumann's libretto is a more poignant side to the legend, of larger epic proportion: Genoveva gives birth to a child (aptly named Schmerzenreich, literally meaning 'rich in pain') and wanders with him in the woods for seven years before a repentant Siegfried finds her again.[34] While Schumann surely intended Genoveva's loyalty to husband and cross to be uplifting, his libretto featured many extravagances of the sort he criticized in grand opera.

Yet as the chosen subject for operatic reform, one finds much in *Genoveva* that must have appealed to the composer. The story derived from a well-known French legend that, despite its origins, was popular in Germany. For Schumann at least, its heroine portrayed an ideal of German womanhood. In a line much berated by critics, the departing Siegfried tells Genoveva, 'you are a German wife, so do not weep!' (She faints instead.) As a character type, she resembles the protagonists in *Frauenliebe und -leben* and *Der Rose Pilgerfahrt*: a self-sacrificing woman, pure of heart, living a fantasy of good wifeliness. Like Gretchen in *Faust*, Genoveva also redeems. Enveloped in the rosy light of the cross, she begs a final wish from her would-be executioners: 'when my husband returns, tell him this: that however harshly he treated me, I forgave him all before I died'. This capacity to forgive, combined with her faith in God – her refusal to abandon the cross – is her salvation.

In addition to its heroine, the story offered other features to appeal to romantic audiences, including the medieval setting, with its Gothic halls and knights in shining armour, and the painterly natural landscapes (one easily imagines a Caspar David Friedrich rendering of the scene in which Genoveva is to be killed, with its cross, rocky cliff and looming thunderstorm).[35] Schumann found opportunities to borrow from German sacred and folk music in the plot-motivated songs, which include an opening chorale, 'Erhebet Herz und Hände', reminiscent of 'Ermuntre dich'; Genoveva and

Golo's strophic duet, 'Wenn ich ein Vög'lein wär'' (No. 9), the text of which is borrowed from *Des Knaben Wunderhorn*;[36] and Siegfried's lusty strophic solo, 'Bald blick' ich dich wieder, mein Heimatschloß' (No. 14).

The libretto offered Schumann another opportunity to explore the supernatural, and it is striking that the only character who stands out as having a unique musical voice is the witch Margaretha, her jagged melodies routinely accompanied by strident piccolos and high-pitched flutes. (George Bernard Shaw called her music 'vulgar and trivial' with a tendency toward squawking.)[37] She has an uncanny ability to transform herself musically in order to manipulate her victims. Thus in No. 7 ('Sieh da welch' feiner Rittersmann!'), she suddenly abandons her increasingly chromatic debate with Golo in favour of a reassuringly lilting, square folk melody that successfully persuades him that Genoveva returns his affections. In the Act 3 Finale (No. 15, 'Ich sah ein Kind im Traum'), the rumbling bass *tremolos* and whirling *staccato* arpeggios that accompany her recollection of murdering her infant daughter instantly disperse when Siegfried arrives: the orchestra effects a cunningly effortless modulation from F sharp minor to the distantly related E flat major, and Margaretha warmly welcomes the count to her room. Later in the opera, Schumann mingles the supernatural with the divine by using offstage choruses both for the threefold conjuration of false images in Margaretha's magic mirror and the angelic assurances of 'peace' during Genoveva's prayers at the cross.

Franz Brendel, who was more vociferous than Schumann in his call for a new direction in German opera, recognized *Genoveva* as a clear attempt at reform, though one that missed its mark. Like most critics, Brendel reserved his harshest criticisms for the libretto, which must have caused Schumann some consternation given the genesis of the text. Brendel found *Genoveva*'s characters too one-sided to be excused simply on the basis of 'historical representation': the maltreated heroine was too pitiable, Golo and Margaretha too evil, and Count Siegfried too much a *Dummkopf* of a husband. Having the aged steward Drago hide in Genoveva's bedchamber on the premise of vindicating the countess, and allowing 'drunken rabble to judge the chastity of their Lady' were in poor taste; and finally, the appearance of Drago's ghost and the flames and spirits that spring from the floor to chase Margaretha were, for Brendel, unmotivated bits of fantasy.[38] He felt that it was imperative for libretti to speak to 'the people's consciousness'; *Genoveva*, with its unsympathetic characters and lack of justice for evil-doers, did not. The ideal Brendel set forth was the *Nibelungen* saga, a German legend that could appeal to a 'united fatherland'.[39]

Musically, Schumann fared better, for *Genoveva* followed a principle already practised in *Peri* and vital to Brendel's vision of new opera, that dramatic continuity requires musical continuity. It is in the music, if not the libretto, that Schumann avoided the excesses he so harshly criticized in grand opera. Like *Peri*, *Genoveva* features smooth transitions from one movement to the next, as well as a flexible range of singing styles from recitative to song. Neither technique was revolutionary to opera, but both were taken to new extremes in *Genoveva*, where a declamatory singing style placed new emphasis on the text. In this sense, *Genoveva* anticipated the arioso declamatory style of Richard Wagner's later operas. Thus, Brendel observed, in place of simple recitative Schumann employed a 'recitative-in-beat [*Recitativ im Takt*], as one could call it', creating a 'smooth and lively flow' from one dramatic event to the next. Coupled with the avoidance of traditional numbers, this enabled Schumann to abandon the older 'dead and rigid' schemes of recitative and aria.[40] (It is especially startling, then, when stark silence ruptures this continuous musical flow for the pivotal deed of Golo's downfall: the kiss he steals from the unconscious Genoveva.)

Despite the opera's compositional innovations, critics objected to a lack of musical differentiation between characters. Hanslick noted that throughout one hears 'the same song style in which *Peri* and *Rose Pilgerfahrt* are told – an epic tone that is the main reason why we are practically never sympathetic with *Genoveva*'.[41] Brendel advocated acts in which the music progressed as 'one finale in uninterrupted flow', changing according to the dramatic situation, yet felt that Schumann treated every part of the libretto with equal intensity, so that the music suffered from a 'lack of light and shadow' and came across as monotonous.[42] An anonymous reviewer in the *Neue Zeitschrift*, most likely Krüger, explained that 'the entire opera is a continuous recitative' lacking 'genuine, flowing, hard as rock, evergreen melodies that get memorized and passed on from mouth to mouth'.[43] Or as another musician privately observed, 'Schumann has forgotten that *singing* is the main point in opera.'[44]

While listeners today would perhaps disagree with these assessments – for as modern audiences are coming to appreciate, *Genoveva*'s music is rich in variety and beauty – Schumann's opera was long heard as a 'negative', offering neither the melodic thrills of grand opera nor the thematic development of leitmotivic composition. As in *Peri*, Schumann used reminiscence motives less to identify individual characters than to link different dramatic ideas, creating intricate if sometimes obscure connections between portions of the text. Consider, for example, the complementary uses of a theme from Act 4 (see Ex. 10.6): when Golo uses the melody in No. 17, it is to claim control over Genoveva's fate; when Genoveva uses the same melody in No. 18, it is to yield her fate to God. A more prominent motive introduced in Act 1 similarly juxtaposes contrasting dramatic elements. Example 10.7a shows Margaretha's sarcastic assessment of Golo: 'see there, what a fine knight!' (No. 7). The motive recurs in the following number, in the midst of the

Example 10.6a *Genoveva*, No. 17, 'Kennt Ihr den Ring', bars 63–5

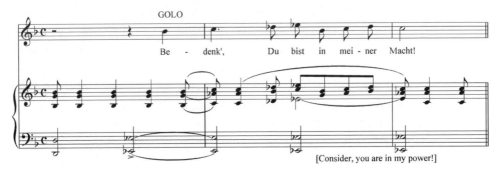

Example 10.6b *Genoveva*, No. 18, 'Weib, heuchelt nicht im letzten Augenblick', bars 28–30

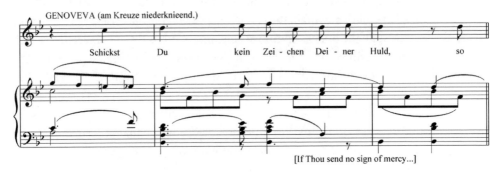

offstage song of the drunken vassals. Scored for piccolos and clarinets, it betrays Margaretha's presence before Golo confirms it verbally. Golo subsequently uses the characteristic pattern of the motive's first four notes when he accosts Genoveva (No. 9), demanding 'into my arms, woman! In my embrace!' (Ex. 10.7b), and Golo and Margaretha trade the motive back and forth as they plot Genoveva's downfall in No. 10. Rather than clearly representing either Golo or Margaretha, the motive is more generally emblematic of evil. Yet fragments of the motive occur in more positive circumstances in Act 1: Drago also uses the melodic kernel of Ex. 10.7b in his duet with Golo (also No. 10) when he vows to clear Genoveva's name, and Genoveva herself claims the same music in No. 3 when she promises Siegfried that 'even when parted' ('Ob auch getrennt'), a sacred bond will unite them. Going back further, the motive derives from the chorale (No. 1) that frames the opera, in turn foreshadowed in the overture's ominous opening bars and triumphant fanfare closing off its coda. The chorale, sung by knights, squires and commoners, provides religious motivation for the military action, though the words also prefigure Genoveva's willingness to die if that be God's plan. Anticipating the salvation of the cross, the chorale asks, 'what harm should befall us when He is by our side?' (Ex. 10.7c). Thus the

Example 10.7a *Genoveva*, No. 1, 'Erhebet Herz und Hände', bars 17–20

Example 10.7b *Genoveva*, No. 9, 'Wenn ich ein Vöglein wär,' bars 135–8

Example 10.7c *Genoveva*, No. 1, 'Erhebet Herz und Hände', bars 17–20

network of motives generates a complicated bond between the sacred and the sinister: Golo's lust is the harm that befalls Genoveva; Genoveva's faith in God is her salvation.

The premiere of *Genoveva* took place in June 1850 in Leipzig, under Schumann's direction, following a delay due to competition with Meyerbeer's latest opera, *Le Prophète*. This must have caused Schumann particular chagrin, given his low opinion of Meyerbeer and *Les Huguenots*. The partisan climate in which the opera debuted played as much a role in the opera's lack of success as did the music itself; one disenchanted out-of-town observer noted much discussion 'pro and contra' regarding *Genoveva* as operatic reform, but found that in the musical press 'one does not dare to censure [the opera] and speaks thus about a masterpiece, the beauties of which may not be realized till after repeated hearings'.[45] Subsequently, Schumann's sole attempt at operatic reform would compete with – and lose out to – Wagner's leitmotivic solution in the urge for a distinctly German opera.

If *Genoveva* and *Peri* were both experiments in musical drama, *Manfred*, which occupied Schumann from July to November 1848, was a far more radical exercise. Corresponding with Liszt about the possibilities of a staged performance, Schumann wrote 'the whole must be presented to the public not as an opera or *Singspiel* or melodrama, but rather as a "dramatic poem with music". It would be something entirely new and unheard of'.[46] Byron himself never intended the poem for the stage, and while Schumann conceived of the music for the theatre, he also understood staged performances would be rare. Unlike the *Szenen aus Goethes Faust*, the individual numbers in *Manfred* lend themselves poorly to concert performance apart from the rest of the work. Shortly after completing the music, Schumann therefore began work on a set of *Zwischenreden*, or incidental texts, that could be recited in a concert setting.[47]

The supernatural characters and diverse assemblage of Eastern deities in *Manfred* are far more sinister than those in *Peri*, and the brooding hero Manfred is akin to Faust (though Byron denied being influenced by Goethe's tragedy). Byron's psychodrama centres on the efforts of its melancholic hero, Count Manfred, to find relief from guilt over the death of his beloved Astarte. Alike in 'lineaments' and 'lone thoughts', Manfred and Astarte shared familial blood. Their unspoken sin, presumably incest, transforms this into the blood of Astarte's sacrifice. Having already rejected humanity, Manfred does not turn back to it for solace after her death but rather delves deeper into a menacing supernatural domain. Conjuring one spirit after another, he ultimately descends into the realm of Arimanes, sovereign of chaos and destruction, to summon the phantom of Astarte. Rather than giving Manfred the forgiveness he seeks, her ghost tells him only that he shall die the following day. Preparing for his death, Manfred receives a visit from an Abbot, who urges him to repent, and a demon, who arrives to claim Manfred's soul. Manfred's victorious mental battle with the demon shatters his physical strength; taking the Abbot's hand, he mutters 'Old man! 'Tis not so difficult to die', and expires.

Known to audiences today primarily through its tumultuous overture, *Manfred* also includes one *entr'acte* and fourteen incidental movements. Separated by lengthy expanses of dialogue, these are more closely related motivically than the music in either *Peri* or *Genoveva*. Three are songs: the first emanates from the invisible spirits introduced at the beginning of the drama,[48] the second is their *Geisterbannfluch* (spirit's curse) condemning Manfred to eternal restlessness, and the third is a fearsome hymn sung by Arimanes's demons. When Manfred refuses to prostrate himself before Arimanes, the demons spit out two angry *Chorsätze*, or choral phrases, the first just four bars, the second half that. But the most remarkable feature of *Manfred* is that the remaining nine musical episodes are all melodramas – spoken declamation with musical accompaniment.

The invention of melodrama is generally attributed to Rousseau, whose 1770 *scène lyrique* 'Pygmalion' alternated spoken phrases with music newly composed for the text by Coignet. In Germany, the technique took hold with Brandes and Benda's well-received 1775 collaboration *Ariadne auf Naxos*. Melodrama sparked the imaginations of Mozart, Beethoven, Weber, Schubert and numerous other composers who incorporated it into operas, incidental music and other stage genres. This blossoming tradition compelled one reviewer to declare, in an 1829 edition of the *Berliner allgemeine musikalische Zeitung*, that despite melodrama's philosophical origins, Germans 'have always taken this genre of artwork more seriously' than the French.[49]

German critics were divided on melodrama's merits. Its supporters argued that the synergistic combination communicated inexpressible feelings that neither poetry nor music could alone, while its detractors objected that superimposing the two arts prevented listeners from attending to either.[50] Whereas song binds poetic and musical expression, allowing music to emanate from the voice as well as from accompanying instruments, in melodrama the voice is no longer a source of music, nor does it clearly motivate accompaniment. Because listeners often found this disjunction between declamation and music disconcerting, composers frequently reserved melodrama for representations of the supernatural, as in the Wolf's Glen scene in Weber's *Der Freischütz* and the dream sequence in Beethoven's incidental music for Goethe's *Egmont*. As one critic explained, melodrama is ideally suited for such uses precisely because the music does not derive from the actor's voice: 'in Egmont's dream melodrama, we interpret the music as the language of the spirit world opening up to him; thus music could generally sound in a spoken drama as the language of the spirit world entering into the lives of men'.[51]

In *Manfred*, Schumann took advantage of melodrama's division between music and text to depict Manfred's eerie interactions with the spirit realm. Melodrama is an emblem for spiritual autonomy: the demons controlled by Manfred sing, but Manfred himself, ranking with the mightiest spirit rulers, speaks. While music lends Manfred's monologues an epic stature,

Example 10.8 *Manfred*, No. 10, 'Beschwörung der Astarte', bars 12–14

[By the power which hath broken the grave which enthralled thee, speak to him, who hath spoken, or those who have call'd thee!]

the count's inability to engage with music is symptomatic of his difficulty coping with the world. Contemplating suicide high atop the *Jungfrau* mountain, Manfred hears the sound of a distant alphorn (represented in No. 4, *Alpenkuhreigen*, by pensive phrases in the solo English horn), and wishes he could *be* music: 'Oh, that I were / the viewless spirit of a lovely sound, / A living voice, a breathing harmony, / A bodiless enjoyment – born and dying / with the blest tone that made me!' Indeed, for Manfred the absence of Astarte is the absence of music itself – she is 'the voice that was my music'. Seeing her ghost is insufficient: Manfred insists on hearing her as well. In No. 10 (*Beschwörung der Astarte*), one of the most spine-tingling of all Schumann's compositions, muted *pianississimo* strings meander in rhythmically disorienting accompaniment to the whispery incantation that makes Astarte's phantom visible. The spell succeeds, and we 'hear' the phantom of Astarte rise before Manfred as *pianissimo* woodwinds displace the gloomy E flat minor cadences in the strings with a shimmering E flat major sonority. Borrowing the second phrase of the conjuration music for the incantation to make Astarte speak (Ex. 10.8), the next melodrama stops short: leaving the music hanging, the final cadence fails to resolve when the ghost meets Manfred's demand for sound with an unexpected, chilling silence.

In the midst of music, Manfred dies in silence. Even if the Abbot knows not where Manfred's soul has flown, the music enlightens its listeners. In the most significant change Schumann made to Byron's text (in German translation by Karl Adolph Suckow), a requiem heard from a distant cloister accompanies the scene of the count's death. Voices and organ quietly sound in E flat minor during Manfred's final exchange with the monk, halting as Manfred gives his icy hand to the Abbot. Immediately after Manfred's death, the chorus re-enters, faster, suddenly *forte*, now in E flat major, for a four-bar *et lux perpetua* before receding again into the background. The shift from minor to major echoes the same modal shift accompanying Astarte's apparition in No. 10. Moreover, woven into the final part of the requiem is

Example 10.9 *Manfred*, Overture, bars 54–7

Example 10.10 *Manfred*, Overture, bar 1

a fragment transposed from the second thematic group of the sonata-form overture. In the overture, this sinuous, chromatic theme has traditionally been associated with Astarte (Ex. 10.9), and its echo in the requiem links Manfred's deliverance with his feminine counterpart. Despite Manfred's own ambivalence about death, Schumann's added requiem thrusts salvation upon him;[52] and Astarte, who appears so briefly in *Manfred* that she can barely be considered a character independent of Manfred's reminiscences, joins the ranks of Genoveva and Gretchen as both a love object and a feminine vehicle for the redemption of the male protagonist.

Like the *Sphinxes* of *Carnaval*, Op. 9, there are more 'viewless spirits of lovely sounds' to *Manfred* than meet the ear. The overture immediately pits sight against sound, opening with three loud syncopated chords segregated from the subsequent slow introduction (Ex. 10.10). The syncopation is less a gross 'miscalculation'[53] than a message clear to the eye but not the ear. Likewise in the conjuration and disappearance of the *Alpenfee*, at the beginning and end, respectively, of No. 6, Schumann again incorporated gestures so absent of all rhythmic context that the syncopations cannot be heard. The same is true for the appearance of the Spirit of Evil Genius at the beginning of No. 14, where Manfred even urges us 'look there . . . and steadfastly'; but no matter how hard we 'aurally peer' at the Spirit, the accompanying syncopations remain hidden. These contrasts between the visible (the score) and the invisible ([in]audible sound) mimic the apparitional transitions enacted on stage.

'Never before have I devoted myself to a composition with such love and energy as to *Manfred*', Schumann told W. J. Wasielewski, who once observed Schumann become so distraught while reciting the poem that the composer broke down in tears and was unable to continue.[54] Richard Pohl watched Schumann conduct the overture in March 1852 and later recalled that, 'totally immersed in the score, completely oblivious to the public, and paying little attention even to the musicians, he lived in the tones, molding them to his mission: he himself became Manfred'.[55] Both Wasielewski and Pohl deemed the *Manfred* music and Schumann's intense identification with Byron's melancholic protagonist to be symptoms of the composer's impending mental decline. Indeed, *Manfred* has played a prominent role in what Peter Kivy has termed 'biographical description', wherein the music is heard to convey not only the tragic tale of the doomed count, but also the autobiographical mental thrashings of its tortured Byronic composer.[56]

Franz Liszt conducted the stage premiere of *Manfred* in Weimar in June 1852, a performance Schumann could not attend owing to illness. Three years later, after Schumann had been committed to Endenich, Liszt also directed a Weimar production of *Genoveva*, an opera for which he professed great admiration.[57] In a series of articles published in the *Neue Zeitschrift* around the same time that he was working on *Genoveva*, Liszt applauded Schumann's central role as a uniter of 'authorship and music', a composer who tied 'the history of music more closely to that of poetry and literature'.[58] The order of Liszt's compositional evidence for this literary aesthetic is revealing: cantatas and oratorios first, then instrumental music and lastly Lieder. Posterity has cast Schumann primarily as a composer of piano music and songs, a 'born lyrical' composer who supposedly lacked the technical skills and epic vision necessary to compose for larger forces. Yet Liszt's inventory reminds us of the contrary, for Schumann's large-scale choral works rank among the literary musician's most expressive achievements.

Notes

1. Georg Eismann, ed., *Robert Schumann: Ein Quellenwerk über sein Leben und Schaffen*, 2 vols., vol. I (Leipzig: Breitkopf & Härtel, 1956), p. 18.
2. Eismann, *Robert Schumann*, pp. 15, 17.
3. The piece is now lost except for the title page. See Robert Schumann, *Tagebücher*, 4 vols., vol. II, ed. Gerd Nauhaus (Leipzig: Deutscher Verlag für Musik, 1987), p. 402. The text of Psalm 150 includes, 'Praise Him with trumpet sound; praise Him with lute and harp! Praise Him with timbrel and dance; praise Him with strings and pipe! Praise Him with clanging cymbals; praise Him with loud clashing cymbals!' The setting was for soprano and alto voices accompanied by piano, two violins, two flutes, two oboes, two trumpets, viola, horn, bassoon and timpani.
4. Eismann, *Robert Schumann*, p. 60.
5. Robert Schumann, *Gesammelte Schriften über Musik und Musiker*, 4th edn, vol. II (Leipzig: Breitkopf & Härtel, 1891), p. 480.
6. Schumann, *Tagebücher*, vol. II, pp. 46, 80.

7. See Carl Dahlhaus, *Nineteenth-Century Music*, trans. J. Bradford Robinson (Berkeley: University of California Press, 1989), pp. 160–8, and Howard E. Smither, *A History of the Oratorio*, 4 vols., vol. IV: *The Oratorio in the Nineteenth and Twentieth Centuries* (Chapel Hill: University of North Carolina Press, 2000), pp. 29–40.

8. Gerd Nauhaus, 'Quellenuntersuchungen zu Schumanns "Paradies und die Peri"', *Robert-Schumann-Tage*, 10 (1985), 69.

9. Robert Schumann, *Robert Schumanns Briefe: Neue Folge*, ed. Gustav Jansen, 2nd edn. (Leipzig: Breitkopf & Härtel, 1904), p. 294.

10. Wilhelm Joseph von Wasielewski, *Robert Schumann: Eine Biographie* [1857], 4th edn (Leipzig: Breitkopf & Härtel, 1906), p. 434; cited in John Daverio, *Robert Schumann: Herald of a 'New Poetic Age'* (New York: Oxford University Press, 1993) p. 369. Schumann began the *Szenen aus Goethes Faust* in 1844 with the Apotheosis scene, continued to work intermittently on the composition from 1847 to 1850, and finally rounded out the scenes with an overture in 1853. The first section (*Abtheilung*) sets three scenes from Part 1: Gretchen and Faust in the garden, Gretchen before the picture of the *Mater dolorosa* and Gretchen's remorseful scene in the *Dom*. The second section also sets three scenes: the twilight scene opening Part 2, Act 1; and from Act 5, the midnight dialogue with Want, Guilt, Care and Necessity, and the scene of Faust's death. The culminative third section, divided into seven subsections, is dedicated to Faust's transcendence. On a much smaller musical and literary scale, the *Requiem für Mignon* is drawn from the exequiem scene from *Wilhelm Meister*, Book 8, Chapter 8. Included as a silent prelude to the published score is Goethe's text describing the position of Mignon's bier, the four boys looking on, and the hidden choruses in the Hall of Remembrance. The *Requiem* was published together with nine *Lieder und Gesänge* for soprano and bass with piano accompaniment, Op. 98a, on poems from the same novel.

11. Franz Liszt, 'Robert Schumann' [1855], trans. John Michael Cooper, Christopher Anderson and R. Larry Todd, in *Schumann and His World*, ed. R. Larry Todd (Princeton: Princeton University Press, 1994), p. 350.

12. Hermann Abert, 'Robert Schumann's *Genoveva*', *Zeitschrift der Internationalen Musikgesellschaft* 11/9 (1910), p. 277. Abert also rejected a second explanation – that the composition suffered from the composer's impending insanity – but conceded a third point, that some of the blame might lie with the libretto. He suggested that the main reason for *Genoveva*'s failure was that the libretto was better suited to an oratorio in the style of *Das Paradies und die Peri* than to a staged opera (p. 282).

13. Schumann, *Tagebücher*, vol. II, p. 197, and letter dated 19 June 1843, in Schumann, *Robert Schumanns Briefe*, p. 229.

14. The princess, smitten by Feramorz's poetry, finds to her dismay that she has fallen in love with the minstrel by the time she arrives in Cashmere. All ends joyously, if predictably, on her wedding day when the doting bridegroom is revealed to be none other than Feramorz himself, and the couple live happily ever after.

15. Gerd Nauhaus, 'Schumanns *Das Paradies und die Peri*: Quellen zur Entstehungs-, Aufführungs- und Rezeptionsgeschichte', in *Schumanns Werke-Text und Interpretation*, ed. Akio Mayeda and Klaus Wolfgang Niemöller (Mainz: B. Schott, 1987), p. 134.

16. Schumann, letter dated 5 May 1843, *Robert Schumanns Briefe*, p. 226.

17. Schumann, letter dated 3 June, 1843. *Ibid.*, p. 228.

18. Daverio, p. 471, and Smither, pp. 3–7.

19. Schumann, *Gesammelte Schriften*, vol. II, pp. 399–400.

20. Oswald Lovenz, *Allgemeine musikalische Zeitung*, 45 (27 December 1843), col. 954. For a detailed discussion of *Peri*'s performance and reception history, see Nauhaus, 'Schumanns *Das Paradies und die Peri*', pp. 143–6.

21. See Schumann's review in 'Drittes Abonnementconcert, den 22 October', *Gesammelte Schriften*, vol. II, p. 288.

22. Nauhaus, 'Schumanns *Das Paradies und die Peri*', pp. 146–8.

23. Schumann, letter dated 20 February 1847, *Robert Schumanns Briefe*, 267.

24. Franz Brendel, 'Robert Schumann with reference to Mendelssohn-Bartholdy and the development of modern music in general' [1845], trans. Jürgen Thym in *Schumann and His World*, ed. Todd, p. 331.

25. In Moore's English, the stray babe is not 'lost' but rather has 'just lighted upon that flowery plain'.

26. The melody is harmonized two ways in No. 2. The phrase in No. 26 echoes the first of these but substitutes a different inversion of the dominant seventh. The second harmonization is used in No. 3 for a rhythmically altered version of the same melodic descent, when upon hearing Peri's sad song, 'a tear-drop glistened / Within [the Angel's] eyelids' ('entsinkt ihm eine Thräne').

27. See Eduard Krüger, 'Robert Schumann: Das Paradies und die Peri. Op. 50', *Allgemeine musikalische Zeitung*, 47 (20 August 1845), col. 562, and Schumann's letter to Eduard Krüger, October 1844, in *Robert Schumanns Briefe*, 244. Krüger's largely negative review, published in the AmZ in four instalments (20 August–10 September), took *Peri* as evidence that Schumann was a better instrumental than vocal composer.

28. On *Hamlet*, see Daverio, p. 99, and Schumann's letter to his mother, 12 December 1830, in *Jugendbriefe von Robert Schumann*, 4th edn (Leipzig: Breitkopf & Härtel, 1910), 133. On *Doge und Dogeressa*, see Daverio, p. 192, and Schumann's letter to Clara, 15 May 1840, in *Jugendbriefe*, p. 314.

29. Schumann, letter dated 1 September 1842, in *Robert Schumanns Briefe*, 220, and Schumann, *Tagebücher*, vol. II, p. 270.

30. On *Faust* as an opera, see Schumann, *Tagebücher*, vol. III: *Haushaltbücher*, Part 1, ed. Gerd Nauhaus (Leipzig: Deutscher Verlag für Musik, 1982), pp. 366–8. According to Wasielewski, Schumann 'was long undecided as to a subject. In his book of hints he marked the following, one after another: Faust, Till Eulenspiegel, El Galan (Calderon), Hanko (Beck), Nibelungenlied, The Wartburg War, The Bridge of Mantible (Calderon), Abelard and Héloise, The False Prophet (from *Lalla Rookh*), The Last Stuart, Kunz von der Rosen, Atala (Chateaubriand), The Noble Bride (König), The Pariah, The Corsair (Byron), Maria Stuart, Sacontala (Gerhard's translation), War of the German Peasants (Kolhas), Saranapalus (Byron), The Robbers of the Bell (Mörike), The Stone Guidepost (Immermann), The Smith of Gretna Green, and The Dead Guest (L. Robert).' See Joseph Wilhelm von Wasielewski, *Life of Robert Schumann* [1871], trans. A. L. Alger, Detroit Reprints in Music (Detroit: Information Coordinators, 1975), p. 152.

31. Review of Ferdinand Hiller, *Die Zerstörung Jerusalems* [1841], in Schumann, *Gesammelte Schriften*, vol. II, p. 309.

32. On *Les Huguenots*, see ibid., p. 61. On *Adèle de Foix*, see ibid., p. 391. For Schumann's opinion of Weber, whom he considered the successor to Mozart and Beethoven, see the reviews of Marschner's *Der Templer und die Jüdin* and Hummel's studies for pianoforte in *ibid.*, p. 474 and vol. I, p. 61, respectively.

33. See the review of Hiller, *Die Zerstörung Jerusalems*, in Schumann, *Gesammelte Schriften*, vol. II, p. 61.

34. Hebbel's play ends gruesomely with the retributive murder of Golo after Genoveva has been abandoned to wander in the woods. In 1851, he added an epilogue wherein Genoveva and Siegfried are reunited.

35. For a brief discussion of the influence of contemporary painting on *Genoveva*, see Linda Siegel, 'A second look at Schumann's *Genoveva*', *The Music Review*, 36/1 (1975), 40–1.

36. *Des Knaben Wunderhorn* was a collection of German folk songs and poems, edited by Achim von Arnim and Clemens Brentano and published in three volumes between 1805 and 1808.

37. George Bernard Shaw, *Music in London, 1890–94*, 3 vols., vol. III (London: Constable, 1950), pp. 109, 110.

38. Franz Brendel, 'R. Schumann's Oper: Genoveva', *Neue Zeitschrift für Musik*, 33 (2 July 1850), 2–3. The nationalist call for a new German opera became more prominent in the pages of the *Neue Zeitschrift* after Franz Brendel assumed editorship of the journal in 1845. He began his tenure with a lengthy essay entitled 'Opera – past, present, and future', published in instalments between July 1845 and February 1846; many of the main points are repeated in his review of *Genoveva*. For a discussion of Brendel's operatic vision, see Jürgen Thym, 'Schumann in Brendel's *Neue Zeitschrift für Musik* from 1845 to 1856', in *Mendelssohn and Schumann: Essays on Their Music and Its Context*, ed. Jon W. Finson and R. Larry Todd (Durham: Duke University Press, 1984), pp. 21–36.

39. See Brendel, 'Genoveva', p. 2 n, and Thym, 'Schumann in Brendel's *Neue Zeitschrift*', pp. 24, 28–9.

40. Brendel, 'Genoveva', p. 3.

41. Eduard Hanslick, *Die moderne Oper: Kritiken und Studien* (Berlin: Hofmann, 1875), pp. 258–9. Hanslick was not alone in suggesting *Genoveva* would have been better off as an oratorio: see also Abert, 'Robert Schumann's *Genoveva*', p. 282.

42. Brendel, 'Genoveva', p. 3.

43. 'Musik für das Theater. Opern im Clavierauszug. Robert Schumann, Op. 81. Genoveva', *Neue Zeitschrift für Musik*, 13 (28 March 1851), p. 130. Thym concludes the reviewer was Eduard Krüger based on the style of writing (Thym, 'Schumann in Brendel's *New Zeitschrift*', p. 29).

44. From the diary of Norwegian composer Halfdan Kjerulf, who was studying in Leipzig when *Genoveva* premièred. See Dag Schjelderup-Ebbe, 'Some recollections by two Norwegian artists of German musical life in the 1850's', *Studia musicologica norvegica*, 2 (1976), p. 127.

45. Kjerulf in *ibid.*, p. 127.
46. Schumann, letter dated 5 November 1851. *Robert Schumanns Briefe*, pp. 349–50.
47. Richard Pohl, 'Reminiscences of Robert Schumann' [1878], trans. John Michael Cooper, in *Schumann and His World*, ed. Todd, p. 246. The first published *Zwischenreden* for *Manfred* were written by Pohl ('Reminiscences', p. 265, n. 38).
48. Representing air, water, earth and fire, Schumann reduced the four spirits from the seven in Byron's original.
49. M., 'Ueber das Melodrama; bei Gelegenheit vom Doktor Johannes Faust, Volksmelodrama von Karl v. Holtey. Musik von Karl Blum [Schluss folgt]', *Berliner allgemeine musikalische Zeitung*, 6/4 (25 January 1829), p. 28.
50. See, for example, D. F. Reiberstorffer, 'Ueber Ouvertüren und Entr'actes zu Trauer-, Schau-, und Lustspielen', *Wiener allgemeine Musik-Zeitung*, 8 (11 April 1848), p. 178, and Otto Gumprecht, 'Berliner Musikbericht: Schumanns Musik zu Byrons "Manfred". Unkünstlicher Charakter der melodramatischen Behandlungsweise. Aufführungen zum Gedächtniß Ludwig Spohr's: "Jessonda", "Faust", Hubert Ries'sches Concert', *Monatsschrift für Theater und Musik*, 6 (11 July 1860), p. 432.
51. M., 'Ueber das Melodrama; bei Gelegenheit vom Doktor Johannes Faust, Volksmelodrama von Karl v. Holtey. Musik von Karl Blum [Schluss]', *Berliner allgemeine musikalische Zeitung*, 6/5 (31 January 1829), p. 38.
52. While the rate of declamation in the melodramas is generally left to the performer, Schumann set portions of the spoken text metrically, though still unpitched, in No. 14 (Manfred's battle with the Spirit of his Evil Genius) and No. 15 (the *Schluß*-Scene with the *Requiem*). The Spirit and the Abbot also engage in this metred dialogue. Perhaps, as he approaches death, Manfred succumbs to some musical control, straddling both spirit and mortal realms.
53. Gerald Abraham, 'The dramatic music', in *Schumann: A Symposium*, ed. Gerald Abraham (London: Oxford University Press, 1952), p. 262.
54. Wasielewski, *Robert Schumann: Eine Biographie*, p. 398.
55. Pohl, 'Reminiscences', p. 250.
56. Peter Kivy, *Sound Sentiment: An Essay on the Musical Emotions, Including the Complete Text of The Corded Shell*, ed. Joseph Margolis (Philadelphia: Temple University Press, 1989), p. 3. Some critics also offered Schumann's impending illness as an explanation for *Genoveva*'s shortcomings.
57. Liszt's opinion of *Genoveva* became substantially less enthusiastic after Schumann's death and as Liszt became increasingly involved with Wagner's music dramas. See Siegel, pp. 33–4.
58. Liszt, pp. 348–9.

PART III

Reception

11 Schumann in his time and since

REINHARD KAPP

The image takes shape

The reactions of his immediate circle to the musical exploits of the young Schumann, from domestic music-making to performances in the school context, are known to posterity almost entirely in the form of later reminiscences: we see him in his social environment but learn little that is specifically musical. We have rather more precise information about his progress and setbacks in his study of the piano, as well as about the appearances as a soloist in Zwickau, Schneeberg and even Heidelberg. The primary source is Schumann himself, but at least he collected the opinions voiced in Heidelberg and compiled a unique list in his diary of various views (possibly edited or touched up, but clearly representative). There are no reports of the occasional performances of his music during his childhood, in private or semi-public contexts, all under his personal supervision and with his own participation, but he profited by even such modest exposure. What is clear from these events is that Schumann grew up in an environment where music was not only loved but also eagerly discussed.

After his first lessons with Kuntsch, who may have been a provincial musician but was by no means deficient in judgement or understanding, Schumann turned to various professional musicians with a reputation extending beyond Saxony in his search for a formal course of study. Carl Maria von Weber responded affirmatively to an enquiry from August Schumann, but was prevented from taking his son as a pupil: Robert suffered the deaths of potential musical fathers (Weber, 1826; Beethoven, 1827; Schubert, 1828) as well as his birth father (1826) one after another in close succession. The opinions of the teachers he then chose, or half-heartedly considered choosing, communicated as little as the compositions he sent them. At a later date he published, without attribution, the assessment of the Lieder composer Gottlieb Wiedebein as one that he could accept as fair comment. Hummel was unable to form any very clear impression from the fragment of a piano concerto (in a somewhat Hummelish style) submitted to him. Only with Friedrich Wieck, a systematic but also volatile teacher, did Schumann pursue, from 1830, a programme of study to some extent worthy of the name. Wieck oversaw and commented on Schumann's development as a pianist and also on his early essays in large-scale forms (C minor Piano Quartet, Toccata, G minor Symphony).

With his first publications, Schumann began to make his name almost simultaneously as a writer on music and a composer of piano music – to begin with both media were substitutes for the larger-scale works he planned to compose. The journalist became known more quickly. Even so, the responses of the growing circle of readers must have been hard to gauge at first: they tended to be reactions primarily to the *Neue Zeitschrift für Musik* in which his work appeared – the movement the journal represented, or the type of information and opinions it conveyed – rather than to the personality of the editor or author (often hard to identify amid the bewildering proliferation of pseudonyms and monograms). The new form of the reviews, the semi-fictional members of the *Davidsbündler*, aroused interest and curiosity; as he built up a team of co-writers, Schumann succeeded in spreading something of the spirit of his undertaking and even in finding imitators[1] – one of the ways by which to restore 'the poetry of art' to a position of honour.[2]

Schumann the composer had a harder time of it, partly because of the unconventional elements of the works (which observers saw primarily, and with some justification, as reaching out towards a hypothetical future), partly because he was unable to give the virtuosic performances that would have made them known and established a performing tradition for them. He was reluctant, too, to publicize them in his own journal to any significant extent. We need to recognize how unusual his career as a composer was in being promoted entirely through publication, the championship of other, well-disposed pianists and above all private performances. The major exception in Schumann's keyboard period – the public performances of movements from the G minor Symphony in Zwickau, Schneeberg and Leipzig (and these were neither rehearsed nor directed by the composer) – failed to arouse any more significant reactions. Since putting himself in the public eye, therefore, Schumann achieved his ends indirectly: he theorized, he took no personal active part in the occasional performances of his compositions, and thirdly he created works that in a certain sense did not stand on their own feet. All of this had an enduring effect on how he was received. At the same time, the mysterious incognito made the composer, distancing himself from every form of praxis, pre-eminently the representative and spokesman of the Romantic movement.

Some musicians among those closest to him became acquainted with the early works soon after they were written: Clara Wieck (at first with her father's backing) is inseparable from any account of Schumann's life, a permanent and decisive factor in his development, in all her many roles. She played his music in private circles to begin with; the first piece she played in public was the Toccata, followed by smaller pieces or selections but nothing bigger than the Piano Quintet. Although she did not venture to perform many of the larger-scale piano works in public until much later, it was she who would make Schumann's piano music known across half Europe and determine its reception until almost the end of the nineteenth century. Schumann's friend and almost exact contemporary Louis Schuncke also played the Toccata, although not on his concert tours: any further engagement with Schumann's music was halted by his early death, which lost it the championship of a well-disposed virtuoso. Schumann's relationships with these two pianists, his first interpreters, are among those 'situations' in which repeatedly he entered into close productive collaboration with contemporaries. Similar situations, which have not yet received the attention they merit, would recur: with Bennett, Berlioz, Brahms, Gade, Heller, Henselt, Hirschbach, Joachim, Liszt, Mendelssohn and Wagner. In every one of these cases the influence was mutual. It is hard to think of another composer whose orientation was so interactively effective.

Already some sympathetic reviews appeared, from the pens of Moscheles and Liszt, both admittedly acquaintances of Schumann as editor and of their fellow-pianist Clara Wieck. Little is known, even now, about the dissemination of the early piano works among contemporaries in general. Clearly, Schumann understood from an early age how to interest individuals in himself and his aspirations, but the attention of the wider public was harder to gain. The cryptic elements in the works themselves went hand in hand with their reception in closed circles. There is relatively little testimony from outsiders, those who came to know the works exclusively from the printed editions (Rellstab, von Seyfried, Gottfried Weber). Reviewers recognized the originality; Schumann was accepted as an aspiring though perhaps rather over-ambitious votary of art. If the pieces seemed obscure, muddled, it was at first attributed to the composer's evident youth, seen as grounds for sympathetic treatment – although Schumann continued to be thought of in such terms for rather a long time. But his development reveals that he was aware of it. His ever wakeful self-criticism, often published in the form of reviews of other people's music, had to make up for the absence of greater public attention, but criticism of his own works, whether oral or printed, was carefully noted and considered and the reception had an effect on his production. At this stage, when Schumann was still wide open and his position not yet stabilized, he was at the centre of an extensive process of evolution of ideas, partly initiated by himself, but into which also he was drawn by others, and in this process the works too were an element.

Gradually the word began to spread. Johann Peter Lyser's 1838 essay 'Robert Schumann und die romantische Schule in Leipzig'[3] was an attempt to prepare the ground in Vienna. Julius Becker's 'musical novel' *Der Neuromantiker* (Leipzig, 1840) contains a chapter entitled 'Über Compositionen von Florestan und Eusebius'. Schumann found it necessary to defend himself against the charge of being 'a Romantic'. Georg Kastner, in the profile he published in 1840 in the *Revue et gazette musicale*,[4] spoke already of Schumann's growing influence and advised him to pursue orchestral composition as his true *métier*. As he emerged from writing purely for the piano and turned to genres that the authorities of the musical world rated as more significant and less subjective (Lied, symphony, chamber music, oratorio), a wider public did indeed become more aware of Schumann as a composer. This is the real starting point of a reception history as the history of reactions to a compositional trajectory as it stabilized. Greater clarity of musical thought and more immediately comprehensible musical messages were speedily followed by acclaim. It must be said, also, that this recognition was coloured in advance by the 'romantic' (in the other sense) tale of the composer's fight to win the hand of Clara Wieck, an extension of the poetic life of the *Davidsbündler* into real life. This kind of poeticization helped now to make the piano works more accessible, with their characteristically fragmentary, many-layered and playful qualities; what had at first been regarded as signs of immaturity were now taken as modern, interesting, witty and intelligent. Another reason for the increased understanding and acceptance was probably that the greater variety in Schumann's output gave him a more clearly distinguishable public profile. The Lieder would help to advance Schumann's recognition: listeners were no longer in any sense bereft of words. The first commercial success in Schumann's career also came at this stage, borne on the back of a surge of mass feeling: his was the umpteenth setting of Nikolaus Becker's patriotic *Rheinlied*. The First Symphony made the round of the concert halls relatively quickly after its première in the Leipzig Gewandhaus. While the relationship with Wieck and his daughter (Liszt, too) could count as personal, it was as established fellow-musicians that Mendelssohn and Ferdinand David took up Schumann's music. If the symphony ranked still as a surprise, a lucky fluke, the first chamber compositions and above all *Das Paradies und die Peri* earned Schumann the respect also of those who had been inclined until then not to take him entirely seriously as a composer. Faced with the growing technical mastery and inner assurance of his composing, colleagues now took Schumann into the repertory: Gade, Hiller, Liszt (as Kapellmeister in Weimar), Rietz, Spohr, Taubert.

Schumann's own conducting appearances also helped to make his name better known. He directed not only his own works (starting with *Peri*) but also those of others as a choral conductor in Dresden and Düsseldorf. In this capacity he appeared in public in his own right (no longer merely the husband of the celebrated pianist), and gradually an 'image' formed of the artist that was an odd mixture of charm, authority and nonconformity.

Schumann's reputation as a composer also spread outside the borders of Germany during his lifetime (preceded, as in his homeland, by his editorial activities). It would be inaccurate, however, to picture knowledge and fame growing and spreading steadily and evenly: rather, a kind of underground career coexisted with occasional recognition by the musical authorities. France was perhaps the country where Schumann's influence was first noticed and also proved most enduring. Kastner wrote of 'des partisans zélés parmi les artistes' already in the 1830s. Berlioz, for example, became acquainted with the piano music through Liszt, who, having cautiously tested the water in his recitals, confined himself to private and publicizing initiatives, while Alkan first heard it played by Clara Schumann. The further dissemination of the music during the 1840s was brought about partly by the championship of personal acquaintances: Kirchner in Switzerland,[5] Gade in Denmark, Norman in Sweden, Anton Gehrke in St Petersburg, and possibly Hiller, too, in Italy.[6]

Schumann's journeys abroad helped both the music and the composer personally to become better known. He made a great impression when he and his wife visited Russia together in 1844. Not only were some of the more important works performed but he also made contact with leading lights on the Russian musical scene: Henselt, L'vov, Wielhorski; and by chance the fourteen-year-old Anton Rubinstein, later one of the most important interpreters of Schumann, heard the Piano Quintet. The journey to Vienna in 1846 was unsuccessful insofar as Clara Schumann failed to build on her earlier triumphs – but at least, rather as literary figures responded positively to Wagner in Paris at a later date, reactions were aroused in the writers Eichendorff and Stifter. This visit does not appear to have been the occasion of Schumann's contact with Hebbel, who later (despite the disastrous experience of *Genoveva*) may have sought closer collaboration with him.[7] It was only in the 1850s and later that Schumann's music found a more sympathetic audience in Vienna. However, in Berlin (where he conducted *Peri*), Prague (where the Piano Concerto was performed, as well as other works) and Zwickau (in what amounted to a Schumann festival), he was welcomed by enthusiasts who had already formed groups of 'Schumannianer'. The long-planned concert tour of England did not take place, despite Mendelssohn's personal recommendation of *Peri* and Queen Victoria's interest in Schumann's music. On the other hand, when Schumann visited the Netherlands early in 1854, where Verhulst had been busy, he found a more broadly based reception already awaited him and his triumphal tour made him feel that his music was almost more at home there than in his homeland.[8]

One index of the recognition on a professional level and the spread of Schumann's reputation is the dedication of compositions to him. This rested more or less on knowledge of his *œuvre* but should not be read as the token of especial veneration in every case. Clara dedicated three published works to Schumann (Opp. 3, 11, 20) and more in private. Sometimes dedications were a matter of returning a compliment: the case of Clara Wieck's Op. 3 and Robert Schumann's Op. 5 is similar to that of Schuncke's dedication of his *Grande Sonate*, Op. 3, of about the same date as Schumann's *Toccata*, Op. 7. Other composers who responded in kind to dedications from Schumann were Bennett, Chopin, Gade, Henselt, Liszt, Moscheles and Reinicke. Brahms, the dedicatee of the *Conzertallegro*, Op. 134, composed his Schumann Variations, Op. 9 (1854), as a token of friendship and sympathy for Clara Schumann; while the Sonata, Op. 2, was dedicated to her, he did not dare as yet to place Robert Schumann's name at the head of one of his works, he told Schumann in a letter (mid January 1855). Numerous younger composers, whether actual pupils or not, dedicated compositions to him as a sign of their respect: Bargiel, Dietrich, Heller, Carl Ritter,[9] Smetana, Verhulst,[10] Julie von Webenau.[11] Kirchner's *Grüße an meine Freunde*, Op. 5 (1855),[12] was perhaps already an expression of his veneration of Schumann, and a whole series of posthumous works (*Neue Davidsbündlertänze*, etc.) certainly were. Private *Albumblätter* should also be taken into account,[13] and even poems, by Böttger, Hebbel and others. Such dedications are very informative, especially the fact that the majority of them were of sonatas,[14] none of salon music or virtuoso pieces: this demonstrates the significance and standing Schumann had acquired, as well as showing that his views had become well known and respected.

It is now, as a composer to reckon with, that Schumann's position in history becomes a subject for consideration. After Mendelssohn's death he can be reckoned a national institution: the closing scene from *Faust* was performed in Weimar, Dresden and Leipzig in 1849 as part of the celebration of Goethe's centenary. First in Germany and then elsewhere in western Europe, Schumann's standing as the leading representative of 'pure' music, the heir of Beethoven, was unchallenged, even by the adherents of Wagner, for some time to come. Official honours confirmed his position.[15] Furthermore, Schumann now had a growing consciousness of working for the public arena and a tangible audience. Works of 'applied' art, music composed for political or pedagogical motives, show that he calculated effects and listeners' expectations, and also that he was sufficiently in command of his music to be able to choose varying degrees of difficulty, demands and means. When he put himself in the position of a recipient of his own music and undertook alterations and augmented orchestrations, or revised earlier works for new editions, he concerned himself with accommodation as well as technical improvements. Works such as the *Clavierstücke [Album] für die Jugend* (1848) or *Waldscenen* (1850) were very successful with a wide spectrum of the public. But whenever he turned to the project of promoting the *große Form* (and with it the *große Musik*) the broader public showed no great willingness to follow him.

The addition of more and more new genres to his œuvre meant that its reception multiplied and polarized: the piano pieces were regarded as either the equals of the works for chamber and orchestral ensembles or as promising prospects, sometimes even as the truly interesting category, when compared with the apparent conservatism of the later works. While some thought a period of mastery had begun, others had doubts about the aesthetic and technical foundations; while many welcomed the consideration given to practical requirements, there were some to whom the new works represented an unwelcome diversion. The New Germans, at bottom not a school at all, could not agree on their attitude to Schumann: was he a progressive or not? 'His' *Neue Zeitschrift für Musik* became a battleground, even more so than the field of composition itself. Despite his growing fame, Schumann in his last years found himself under attack on three sides: not only by the rising Wagner–Liszt party but also, still, by the Classicists (perhaps also by the political right in Germany), and thirdly by the critics who had followed his path with sympathy but did not like the late works. It is unlikely, however, that Schumann's own view would have been that composers of his own age, or younger, were catching up with or overtaking him by means that he had helped to develop but they now used to greater effect;[16] the crucial thing is that he was still considered worth arguing about. With the rallying cry of *Neue Bahnen* Schumann sounded one more well-timed fanfare, then the *Gesammelte Schriften* in 1854, two years before his death, appeared like a posthumous publication. His mental collapse added a new dimension to the reception – and where renewed romanticization did not celebrate madness, all questions remained open for the foreseeable future.

Did Schumann found a school?

Very gradually the circle of Schumann's influence widened. The programme insofar as it was felt to be representative, the innovations in his music, the quality of his work (this must not be overlooked even when focussing on sociological and psychological motivation) combined to make him a trend-setter, a teacher despite himself, a focal point for analogous aspirations, an authority. He had manifested early a talent for friendship, for attracting those of like mind (despite not being particularly extrovert by nature): schoolfriends, fellow-students, the network of colleagues growing up around the journal; the circle of friends of both Schumanns, who kept open house, which led to more activities in the wider community; the choirs and *Kränzchen* that Schumann conducted, the artists' colonies, pupils and disciples in Leipzig, Dresden and Düsseldorf. The *Davidsbündler* were to some extent an idealization of a loose-knit circle that really existed, but it also served as a model for real associations, bringing together individuals in small, conspiratorial groups in Schumann's name: Schumann himself got to hear of meetings of such informal bodies in Berlin, Hanover (the *Kaffernbund*, or 'League of Bumpkins'), Paris and Prague. In Weimar, the *Davidsbündler*'s declaration of war on the Philistines was interpreted as an honourable early phase in the campaign of the New Germans. The role of the Philistines in this was assigned to a ubiquitous 'association of mediocrities'. The foundation of the Neu-Weimar-Verein in 1853, with 'Murls' such as Cornelius, Joachim, Bülow and Raff among its members, forms a link between the *Davidsbündler* and the Wagner societies that followed in due course.

Doubt is sometimes expressed as to whether Schumann was a particularly gifted teacher, but he had a talent for imparting instruction and the capacity for empathy. His institutionalized teaching activity at the Leipzig Conservatory (1843–4) does not appear to have been attended by any outstanding success, but throughout his life he exerted influence by example and suggestion on people of his own age at first, on younger adherents later – a school where regular instruction was the exception although a series of private pupils came to him regularly. There were pupils who later turned away from him, while others remained loyal; some in whom Schumann's influence amalgamated with that of others and some whom he rendered immune to other influences; finally, there were some in whom the influence does not reveal itself at first sight. But of none could it be said that his influence had no effect at all.

He gave formal lessons to Dietrich, Ehlert, Meinardus, Reinecke and Carl Ritter. Kirchner seems to have been profoundly marked by the personal association (it began when he was very young), to his detriment.[17] But none of these had a particularly forceful personal voice. Reinecke continually adopted Schumannesque turns of phrase and preferred the genres that were also Schumann's favourites. Ritter later fell under Wagner's spell and abandoned composition for literature. Other influences – Liszt's, among others – mingled in Meinardus. Clara Wieck-Schumann passed through several stages: for all her independence of judgement she turned into something very like a pupil and as a composer she remained so. From 1840 onwards no clearcut distinction can be made between her influence and her husband's: possibly pupils were attracted by her, but obtained things from him as well through the sheer proximity. Albert Dietrich remained a Schumannianer, even when he thought he was moving in step with Brahms. Close ties, verging on a pupil–teacher relationship, existed with Bargiel, Brahms, Eduard Franck, Grimm, Joachim, Louise Japha-Langhans and Heinrich von Sahr. The band of followers embraced a whole series of other fellow musicians, of Schumann's own age and younger. Isolated encounters could have lasting consequences, as in the cases of Cornelius, Louis Ehlert and Smetana.[18] There was never any personal contact with Heller, a devoted adherent, but letters were exchanged intermittently, with enthusiasm on Heller's side at least.

Many writers, from the 1830s onwards, were convinced of the existence of a School of Schumann, for good or ill. The epithet 'Schumannianer' might be used as a mark of approval or disapproval. Brahms was long described as one, and not just because of *Neue Bahnen*. He declared brusquely, in one of his misanthropic fits and probably in response to a silly question, that all he had ever learnt from Schumann was how to play chess, but he also said something very similar about his revered teacher Marxsen. Brahms maintained a close and lifelong relationship with Schumann, and with his wife and widow. As composer, performer and co-editor of the Gesamtausgabe, he remained permanently involved with Schumann's music. As a general rule, he later carefully avoided direct reminiscences, but the association revealed itself at many times on different levels. The first of Schumann's *Märchenerzählungen* seems to prefigure Brahms – Brahms played it in public. The two serenades contain clear traces of Schumann. The D minor Piano Concerto relates to Schumann in a number of ways; *Ein deutsches Requiem* plainly commemorates not only the composer's mother but also Schumann.

Contemporaries take sides

Admiration for Schumann also united composers who did not have any direct contact with him. His contemporaries found much to debate in the Schumann phenomenon, matter both for applause and for rejection. Of the older generation, Berlioz remained largely unmoved, despite several encounters, whereas Meyerbeer could not be indifferent after Schumann's review of *Les Huguenots*. Just how far the close attention he paid to contemporary music included Schumann remains to be examined. The string quartets won the respect of the Thomaskantor Moritz Hauptmann. Spohr conducted the First Symphony and at least considered mounting a production of *Genoveva*, but he was alarmed by the dissonances in Schumann's later compositions. Moscheles was a declared admirer and even Schumann's work of the 1850s held his interest.

Of course, the debate began in Schumann's own generation during his lifetime. Norbert Burgmüller (born 1810) died too soon to take any note of Schumann's early compositions. Camille Stamaty (1811) went to Leipzig in 1836 to study with Mendelssohn but he associated with Schumann too; the consequences of his stay can be observed in his pupil Saint-Saëns, at the latest. Hermann Hirschbach (1812) was a collaborator on Schumann's journal and strove to outdo Schumann both as composer and as musical commentator. Chopin appears to have remained largely uncomprehending, perhaps under the influence of a 'Parisian' aesthetics; it is not clear how much Schumann impinged on him as either critic or composer.[19] He did not live to witness the first phase of more general reception of Schumann in France. Mendelssohn's case was different in every way. Something like a friendship developed, despite his reservations about the journalist, and he belongs with others of his generation – Ferdinand David, Henselt, Hiller[20] – among those who helped Schumann's music become better known. Already an established figure himself, Mendelssohn gave the premières or early performances of several of Schumann's orchestral works, was involved in the *Variations*, Op. 46, took an active part in the rehearsals for *Peri* and played the Piano Quintet in private. He was probably acquainted with much more, but perhaps felt like Schumann's mentor rather than anything else. His influence on Schumann is often mentioned, but it is hard to say whether the opposite also holds good: that is, whether Schumann's music could be said to have impressed Mendelssohn in a way that took effect in his own music: it is another of the 'situations' that have yet to be investigated. That the completion and publication of the 'Scottish' Symphony can be traced back to the success of his own First Symphony was more than a figment of Schumann's imagination, at all events. Later, when the dispute between the Schumannites and the Mendelssohnians began to dissolve under the impact of Wagner, the influences of the two composers sometimes merged.

Schumann outlived Mendelssohn and Chopin by just long enough to make it possible to rank him with the 'moderns'. Yet after his death, it seems as if Wagner, Liszt and Verdi belonged to a later generation altogether, though they were scarcely any younger. General reception of Schumann set in when those three embarked on a development into the unknown, in which Schumann – in the nature of things – could take no part. The 'star-blessed friendship' Pfitzner imagined between Schumann and Wagner might have been realizable in the heavens, but on earth there could be no meeting of temperaments (at the very least). *Das Paradies und die Peri* probably made a real impression on Wagner – he seems to have been drawn to the motive of redemption, the atmosphere and certain technical aspects. Schumann the conductor repelled him, however, and he probably found the personality antipathetic too. The more the Wagnerian position became fixed as a historical one, the more it excluded other composers' aspirations towards the same ends – this applied to Liszt, Mendelssohn and Verdi; only to Chopin, who composed solely for piano and moreover picked the right time to die, did Wagner do justice, within limits.[21] There are two passages in the Singers' Contest in Act II of *Tannhäuser* that can be related musically to Schumann – but they are the contributions of Wolfram, whose style of lovesong is mocked by Tannhäuser as insipid and feeble. Whereas Mendelssohn's style was already formed when he became aware of Schumann, Wagner's style in the 1840s was still unstable. He seems to draw close to Schumann in the sketches for *Siegfrieds Tod*, and in a short essay (1852) on Wilhelm Baumgartner's songs, a (local-)political polemic targeted against Franz Abt, he approves Schumann's direction, even though he does not expressly name him. Wagner called Schumann's orchestral music uninteresting (he owned a copy of the Second Symphony, at least), unlike Mendelssohn's, he saw no more in it than something that followed in Beethoven's footsteps without a Beethovenian purpose. On several occasions he ruled against performing any of it and refused to be swayed by the arguments of Schumannianer in his circle (Cornelius, Kienzl, Kirchner, Liszt, Schemann).

Liszt's generosity of spirit had exactly the opposite effect: his sympathy for the New German programme did not entail any prejudice against Schumann. However much the personality amused him, Liszt was convinced of his artistic stature. Although in his glory days as a virtuoso pianist he made only halfhearted attempts to champion the music in performance, for all his talk of Schumann as one of the very few new figures who interested him, he appears to have wanted to make the omission good later. As ducal Kapellmeister in Weimar, Liszt conducted Schumann's major works and even staged performances of *Manfred* and *Genoveva*. Furthermore, he vigorously promoted Schumann's music in his writings (among other things he translated the *Haus- und Lebensregeln*), his transcriptions and his teaching activities.

After Schumann's death

The 1850s witnessed the slow spread of Schumann's reputation outside the immediate circle of his influence. The successive appearance of a number of works (some of major importance), either sent to press by himself or published after his death, created rather the same impression as if he had been still active. Much of the 'music of the future' appeared on the scene shoulder to shoulder with Schumann's music;[22] it was possible at this period for him to be claimed for the New German school (which also sought to recruit Brahms and Joachim) or to be rejected with it.[23] Personal initiatives played an important role: personal friends of Schumann and newly won friends of his music alike were active as propagandists throughout half Europe (and revealed his influence in their own work). As well as those already named, there was Louis Ehlert in Berlin, Erkel in Budapest, Herbeck in Vienna, Eduard Langer in Moscow, L'vov (and Anton Rubinstein) in St Petersburg, Smetana in Gothenburg; there were performers on the international stage such as Hiller, Joachim, Lind, Rubinstein, Stockhausen; and some journalists: Ambros, Bagge, Hanslick. More substantial accounts of Schumann's life and work began to circulate at this time. Lobe, who published an inadequate biography at the time of his leaving the *AMZ*, was followed by Riccius in 1850, Neumann in 1855, Müller von Königswinter in 1856 and Wasielewski in 1858, as well as the first major assessments of his achievement *in toto*: by Liszt in 1855; Ambros, Bagge, Debrois van Bruyck in 1858. Already by the end of the decade the first monographs on individual works appeared, on *Peri* and *Faust*. Graf Laurencin hailed Schumann as one of the great composers of the new era, implying in an 1859 essay, intended as a riposte to Hanslick, that the resistance of Viennese musicians to Schumann was still considerable. In the same year, however, Bagge reported that Schumann was at the zenith of his popularity in Vienna.[24] Still in Vienna, Robert Volkmann (born 1814) showed the first signs of Schumann's influence in the 1850s – having managed to resist it during his time as a student in Leipzig. Not much later the first clear signs appeared in the work of contemporaries elsewhere: Kirchner, Baumgartner and Joseph Carl Eschmann in Switzerland; Alkan, Gounod, Lalo and Saint-Saëns in France. Still in the 1850s, the youthful Massenet (born 1842) happened upon some of Schumann's piano pieces, but when he played them his listeners were dismayed. The prior influence of Mendelssohn was necessary to prepare Gounod for that of Schumann's music, but the signs can be seen in *Faust* (1852–9) and *Roméo et Juliette* (1867). Around 1860 Schumann was still not acceptable to the general public, however: in 1861, while Clara marvelled at how well Parisian musicians knew his works, a performance of the Third Symphony was hissed there.[25] Only during the following decade did that change.

A whole group of musicians of Brahms's generation were excited to some degree by Schumann's music. Hans von Bülow (born 1830), who knew Schumann as a young man, was later one of the many swayed by Wagner's critique, but he never completely renounced his youthful enthusiasm for Schumann.[26] In the case of Ludvig Norman (born 1831), who had also known Schumann and been encouraged by him, reminiscences became apparent already in 1850, while he was a student in Leipzig. Bernhard Scholz (born 1835), champion of Brahms and composer of *Golo*, an opera on the same subject as *Genoveva*, was also active on Schumann's behalf in

Frankfurt – he succeeded in gaining Clara Schumann for the Hoch Conservatory. The 'Order of the Black Cat' founded by him in 1862 was in the tradition of the *Davidsbündler*. Adolf Jensen (born 1837) had hoped to study with Schumann, but although he came under the spell of Schumann's music only in the mid 1850s, it lasted for the rest of his life. Max Bruch (born 1838) was too young to benefit from Schumann's personal acquaintance;[27] like Reinecke he was one of the eclectics who never abandoned the foundations of Mendelssohn and Schumann conjoined. Schumann was one of the mainstays of his repertory as a conductor and reminiscences are encountered everywhere in his work.

By the end of the decade the frontier between New Germans and Schumannianer was clearly marked. *Neue Bahnen* was already defensive against the rising clamour of the New Germans' publicists, although it was perceived by its writer in other respects as a rallying call rising above party differences. The 1860 *Erklärung* of the four arch-Schumannianer, Brahms, Grimm, Joachim and Scholz, should have attracted a larger circle of signatories (Ehlert, Radecke), some of them members of the Schumann societies that have been mentioned above, and it might have succeeded in stimulating a public discussion, but once it had been prematurely leaked it was tainted by its being perceived as a reactionary manœuvre. For Wagner, who saw himself as a contender for the position of sole original genius of his age, the debates with Schumann's supporters became increasingly irksome. He found some tortuous and grudgingly approving phrases for Schumann's gifts in his essays, but adopted the conviction of some individual Schumannianer that Mendelssohn had had a detrimental influence on their idol and thereafter circulated, by word of mouth and in writing, the formulas that his own followers would make their own. What was intended as the *coup de grâce* was delivered by Wagner's protégé Joseph Rubinstein, whose article 'Über die Schumannsche Musik' published in *Bayreuther Blätter* in 1879 took care of dissent even in the Wagner camp. Humperdinck[28] reported a remark of Wagner's from 1882, in which he summarized his personal relations with Schumann: 'Justice impossible, odious stickwagger'[29] – a definitive dismissal of any kind of association with the outmoded concept of 'absolute music'.

To the world outside Wagner's personal fiefdom, these were minor squabbles of no general significance. The crop of books about Schumann that sprang up in the 1860s – Reissmann, Reimann, Wasielewski (the second edition of the biography, *Schumanniana*) – bore witness to the growing general interest. Schumann's works were now to be found throughout Europe, carried on a tide of editions,[30] reissues with new title-pages, licensed editions and arrangements: Schumann entered the repertory. Contrary to the opinion later voiced by Nietzsche, Schumann was already a figure of European importance by now. Nietzsche's musical horizons were not European, for all his enthusiasm for *Carmen*. At first, he was as much in thrall to Schumann as he later was to Wagner, but he came to believe that parting from Schumann showed him to be not only older but wiser, casting off his little-German perceptions. Other commentators (Ehlert, Tchaikovsky) were in no doubt, however, that it was Schumann who stamped his impression on his age, even the remainder of the century. At all events, the 1860s can be termed the age of Schumann, just as the 1870s are the age of Wagner.

Yet there was something undemanding and old-fashioned about the Schumann of the committed Schumannianer when placed in the vanguard of opposition to the New Germans. By this time the Romantic revolution looked like a new Classicism, no longer the newest thing on the musical scene.[31] Adherents of Schumann, in Germany at least, determined the academic climate. Whether or not they would have marginalized themselves without assistance is uncertain. It is possible to speculate that the loss of Schumann was the reason for this state of affairs, while the leaders of the New Germans were still alive and continuing to develop. Brahms, himself trapped as a Schumannianer to some extent (and therefore perceived by many as a better substitute for Schumann), was not a natural leader. Now, if not earlier, a 'right' and a 'left' emerged in Schumann reception: one a line through Reinecke–Brahms–Bruch–Pfitzner–Schoeck, the other sustaining a decidedly non-imitative relation to Schumann and embracing such as Musorgsky, Debussy, Mahler and Berg. These groupings are not intended to denote movements or parties. *Leipzigerisch*, already in Schumann's lifetime, was used combatively by the New Germans as a synonym for unprogressive – and certainly the conservatism of Leipzig grew more entrenched the longer it lasted. Yet Leipzig was the place to hear the music of Mendelssohn, Schumann and Gade, and since students from every nation under the sun were drawn to the Leipzig Conservatory from 1843 onwards the city was in effect an entrepot of the greatest importance. As the man on the spot, Schumann represented modernity to all those who returned home from Leipzig, until Wagner arrived on the scene: indeed, in some places he and Wagner continued to be regarded as equally modern for some time to come. As a whole, however, his music was gradually absorbed into the general fund of musical language and form, constituting the *lingua franca* of the nineteenth century.

When composers took up Schumann now, it was indirectly or for indirect reasons: reception was a matter of free choice. The Schumann tradition did not impinge on the musical education of Cornelius (born 1824) but he showed a lifelong interest in the music, even finding merit in *Genoveva*. Schumann was the reason why Cornelius was able to resist surrendering himself body and soul to Wagner. Nureddin's first scene in *Der Barbier von Bagdad* is pure Schumann. Cornelius's exact contemporary Bruckner performed several pieces when he was a choirmaster in Linz. His studies with Kitzler introduced him to Schumann as well as to the modernism of Mendelssohn and Wagner. He mentioned 'Kind im Einschlummern' in his lectures on account of the non-resolution at the end; and individual passages that can be traced back to Schumann are found throughout his work, from Psalm 146, through the F minor Symphony and the G major Overture, to the finale of the Seventh Symphony. If Bruckner called Schumann's symphonies *Sinfonietten* (rather than *Sinfonien*) and felt that they lacked a true *adagio* character, it must surely be traced back to Wagner and his followers. It did not prevent him from looking to Schumann in his search for answers to the problem of the finale. Hermann Goetz (born 1840) was a more wholehearted Schumannianer, as his Piano Trio, Op. 1, of 1863 reveals.

In France, Louise Japha-Langhans played the chamber music in the 1860s, Clara Schumann resumed her recital-giving and the conductor Pasdeloup included Schumann in his concert programming. The greater general interest in the music was reflected in the press coverage (Scudo, Kufferath). From this period onwards, some composers were active in editing and arranging Schumann: Bizet, Chevillard, Debussy, Delage, Dubois, Fauré, Gevaert, Godard, Saint-Saëns. Pieces 'alla Schumann' began to appear, traces can be discerned everywhere, in Bizet, Fauré, Widor – even in César Franck (born 1822), albeit that his major works, in which the influence of Schumann is explicit, date rather from the 1880s. Schumann figured prominently in Franck's composition teaching, and Schumannianer were still to be found among his pupils (those of Brahms's generation, that is): Lacombe (born 1837), de Castillon (1838). Writers, musicians and musical amateurs united in the *culte Schumannien*. Even Wagner reception in France acknowledged the presence of Schumann in the background, up until the 1880s.[32]

The other country where Schumann made a major impact was Russia. Interest boomed during the 1880s, the decade of the first Russian symphonies. The compositions of two Westernizers, Anton Rubinstein (born 1829) and Tchaikovsky (born 1840), reveal the consequences of an intense preoccupation with Schumann's music. Tchaikovsky also frequently wrote about Schumann and translated the *Musikalische Haus- und Lebensregeln* into Russian (for the second time, following Stasov's version), and he orchestrated two of the Symphonic Etudes and the *Ballade vom Haideknaben*, Op. 122, No. 1. Schumann had a bearing on the innovators, too. Not one of the national schools can be imagined without its relationship to the German musical tradition; what they claimed as their heritage was something that had been learnt in Germany (notably in Leipzig). Schumann himself registered the rise of young musicians all over Europe and recommended the study of folk songs. Stasov apostrophized the Mighty Handful itself as a Russian League of David. Rimsky-Korsakov recalled that the musical and artistic taste of Balakirev's circle inclined towards Glinka, Schumann and Beethoven's late quartets, but while Liszt rated mention Wagner scarcely ever did. And so the signs of Schumann's influence are often to be found in Borodin, Cui, Musorgsky and Rimsky-Korsakov. An edition of Schumann's piano music appeared in the late 1860s, edited by Balakirev and Nikolay Rubinstein; Herman Laroche referred in his review to Russia's having its own Schumann cult. Eventually Wagner reception set in, leading to an aesthetic division, but Schumann continued to play a significant role for many Russian composers for many years to come.

By the end of the century Schumann reception had gone through analogous phases in every country in Europe and on the North and even South American continents. Local differences – whether the efforts of Antonio Bazzini (born 1818), who had known Schumann in Leipzig, to acquaint Italian audiences with German instrumental music, or the number of English and American composers who studied in Germany – do not amount to any essentially new phenomena. It would undoubtedly be enlightening to up-end the history of music in the second half of the century, and look for the traces Schumann's music undoubtedly left behind in those countries (despite the dominance of opera in Italy and the unassailable position of Mendelssohn in England).

Setting aside the epigones and eclectics who are to be found everywhere and at all times, the generation born in the 1860s (with the possible exception of Sibelius) started out as the last almost directly connected with Schumann, before it progressed to *Gründerzeit* Modernism, Im- and Expressionism and 'New Classicality', and consigned Schumann to history. The evidence of early close attention is not wanting. This is the generation that witnessed Schumann's gradual transformation into a 'classic', his canonization in a *Gesamtausgabe* and the definitive end of the division between 'New German' and 'absolute' musicians. Now, if not earlier, Schumann's music in general filled the role of an ontogenetic stage in the evolution of a composer or a stylistic period distinct from everything new or merely specific. Richard Strauss's recoil from the 'Classicist' positions of his youth proved not to be definitive – any more than his New German position did. Mahler made his debut as a pianist with Schumann, played the chamber music in private, and still returned to him regularly in his maturity. He set great store by his revised orchestration of the four symphonies and the *Manfred* Overture, and from the early songs onwards his own compositions frequently reveal allusions and reminiscences of Schumann.[33] The early songs of Hugo Wolf likewise follow in Schumann's footsteps: he inherited Schumann's literary sensibilities and set the same poets, sometimes in conscious rivalry. Pfitzner's passion for Schumann emerges not only in the numerous echoes:[34] he was also a Schumann conductor of the first rank (as the surviving recordings demonstrate). He did not go in for re-touching, but he did devise an orchestral accompaniment (with instrumental interludes) for some of the choral works for female voices. He reworked a number of romantic operas, both musically and dramaturgically, but decided after mature reflection that it would be impossible in the case of *Genoveva*.

The style of the titles Satie gave his works honoured Schumann's tradition; without making any direct allusions, his deployment of evocative sonorities brings Schumann to mind. In the case of Debussy, besides echoes in the early Piano Trio, we should recall the arrangements of the Studies in canonic form, Op. 56, for two pianos, and of 'Am Springbrunnen' (one of Impressionism's primal images) from Op. 85; perhaps the enthusiasm for Russia can also be seen as an indirect contact with Schumann's music. Anton Arensky's Piano Trio, Op. 32 (1894), for instance, is peppered with Schumannisms. The form of Glazunov's reception provides evidence that Schumann had become the yardstick for Classicists. There are reminiscences of Schumann up until the Fifth Symphony. Glazunov orchestrated part of *Carnaval* and considered re-orchestrating the symphonies. Isaac Albéniz often played Schumann's concerto and his own First Piano Concerto contains Schumannesque traces. The young Busoni made arrangements of Schumann's Concert-Allegro, Op. 134, for two pianos, and of 'Abendlied' from Op. 85, for clarinet quintet (perhaps at the request of his father, a clarinet player), and it is clear that Schumann's contrapuntal works made an impression on him.

The last Schumannianer from the mid nineteenth century survived into the twentieth (Bruch, Reinecke). While certain pieces had long been absorbed into the domestic repertory or drifted down to the level of light entertainment, Schumann gradually vanished from the view of creative artists. He can be taken for granted as a predecessor for Reger (born 1873) – although his point of departure was in Brahms. 'Der Himmel hat eine Träne geweint', Op. 35, No. 2, retraces the outline of a song by Schumann (though not the setting of the same poem in the Heine *Liederkreis*). Like many other conductors, he re-touched Schumann's symphonies for his own performances.

In the eyes of the Viennese School Schumann did not belong to the canon as Schubert and Brahms did, for example, because he did not offer them any contact points either in his language (like Schubert) or in his technique (like Brahms).[35] Alexander Zemlinsky (born 1871) made a four-hand piano reduction of *Peri* and performed the *Scenes from Faust* in Prague. Webern was involved in the rehearsals of the latter, and later in his career conducted Schumann in Mahler's re-touched versions. Schoenberg (born 1874), however, was roused to ire not by Schumann's 'poor' orchestration but by the failure to examine the conventional opinion that it was poor.[36]

The ghost of Schumann certainly haunts some of his early songs.[37] As a teacher, Schoenberg claimed to have liberated Berg from his inveterate habit of thinking instrumentally and cited Schumann as an example of a composer whose work was always songlike[38] – perhaps an autobiographical hint. In fact, Berg is the real Schumannianer of the Viennese School: the surviving juvenilia include two fragmentary cycles of variations on themes of Schumann, and the echo-reprise of the Carinthian folk song in the Violin Concerto evokes the second 'Wie aus der Ferne' in the finale of the *Davidsbündlertänze*. Perhaps this is the reason why Berg liked the Schumannesque First Symphony of Borodin. In the controversy with Pfitzner, the other Schumannianer among contemporary composers, Berg took a decidedly progressive stance compared with Pfitzner's worn-out Romanticism. His pupil Adorno orchestrated pieces from *Album für die Jugend* (*Kinderjahr* 1941, a typical exile's work) and wrote the afterword for an Insel-Verlag edition of the Eichendorff *Liederkreis* as late as 1960. Edward Steuermann, in the year of his death (1964) started a set of variations on a Schumann theme for two pianos. According to Adorno he had an especially high regard for *Kreisleriana*. Rudolf Kolisch remarked on instrumental peculiarities of Schumann's chamber music (playing on the bridge) and campaigned against the distortions in American editions of the violin sonatas.

Schoenberg's contemporary Novák (born 1870) began with Schumanniana: *Variations on a Theme of Schumann* and *Ballad on Byron's Manfred*, Op. 2, for piano. Déodat de Sévérac (born 1873) opened his nostalgic collection of 'petites pièces romantiques' *En vacances* (1912) with an 'Invocation à Schumann'. Ravel orchestrated parts of *Carnaval* as well as Musorgsky's *Pictures at an Exhibition* – itself decidedly in the line of descent from Schumann; and Ravel is yet another whose earliest compositional essays include some Schumann variations. As composer, Artur Schnabel (born 1882) belonged to the *avant-garde* but his inventive performance directions are in the Schumann mould. Always labelled a 'late Romantic', Othmar Schoeck (born 1886) was another pronounced Schumannianer: some of the songs contain direct allusions – and demonstrate that the musical language was no longer actually usable. By contrast, the take on Schumann of Modernists such as Bartók, Hába and Prokofiev shows a transforming power. At all events, in Bohemia and in France,[39] in Switzerland and in Hungary, in Russia and in Italy, the effect of Schumann was felt well into the twentieth century.

Schumann was not forgotten: his music was heard in the concert hall, the home, the conservatory. At times pieces like *Träumerei* seemed to be ubiquitous, but journalism and literature, the existence of Schumann societies (even in America), Schumann monuments and Schumann museums also bore witness. This was all a matter of respectful preservation of a tradition, of course. Publication of posthumous works not included in the *Gesamtausgabe* served to consolidate his position in history. The 'anti-Romantic' mood of the 1920s caused a breach in reception. In the 1930s Schumann was suddenly hailed as a national hero and the Romantic artist was exhumed – both labels serving to cover all manner of deceit and distortion. Schumann's love of his German homeland was presented as his essence, his critique of Meyerbeer was placed in the foreground, his closeness to Mendelssohn was partly dismissed as unimportant, partly denied. Just as Handel's oratorios were aryanized, so too *Peri* was de-Christianized, to end not with the repentant sinner but with the youth's blood-sacrifice in the cause of national freedom. The process of revision and reinterpretation culminated in the bombastic Berlin world première of the Violin Concerto in 1937: it marked the official severance of Schumann from Mendelssohn in that the piece was substituted for Mendelssohn's now suppressed concerto.

Schumann today

The misuse of Schumann by the National Socialists made a certain reserve understandable after the war, at least in Germany. In certain regions reception evolved only cautiously. It took decades for academia to work off the burden left by the moral and musicological catastrophe that became associated with the name of Wolfgang Boetticher. The series of previously unpublished works continued to appear, and from time to time tentative steps were made to see Schumann in a clear, objective light.[40] Renewal of academic interest was spurred by various anniversaries (especially 1956), with emphases falling differently in the eastern and western halves of Germany, in the nature of things. There is no mistaking the upswing that began in the 1970s, which was connected with new assessments. After the relative stagnation fostered by the 'objective' approach of the post-war period, the way was open for a rediscovery of the composer, along with the music and aesthetics of the nineteenth century as a whole. Popular prejudices could be swept away and the late works, in particular, could at last be rated as they deserved. Since then research has expanded, in the USA as well as in Europe. Substantial special studies, source studies and editions of sources, the *Neue Gesamtausgabe* now in progress (in addition to several 'Urtext' projects) have stimulated interest in fragments and sketches as well. A major biography has yet to be published, the new image of Schumann has yet to be consolidated. As ever, reception is still of two kinds: the regressive, conservative and conservationist, and the progressive, 'Schumann-our-contemporary' tendency, and both are found in academic and in popular writing, in performance and in composition. Performance now goes as a rule, it is almost safe to say, hand-in-hand with musicology, and complete recordings of whole segments of the œuvre have brought back to life pieces that had become neglected, and others that had never entered the repertory. Earlier versions of canonic works have become acceptable alternatives. The period-performance movement has put the question of Schumann's orchestration on a new level.

Composers, too, have been able to approach Schumann again,[41] but on completely new terms. When Hindemith (incognito) adapted the solo part of the Violin Concerto to make it 'more rewarding' for the 1937 première, it was in response to a commission from the soloist, Kulenkampff, and the performance was entirely within the bounds of early twentieth-century conceptions of making a big effect. When he conducted the Mass, among other things, after the war, it was an act of creative curiosity. If the discovery of Schumann's 'revolutionary' side ties in with the reappraisal of the avant-garde in the early twentieth century, the reassessment of the late work belongs in the context of a specific interest in the complex, the physical, the material – and perhaps also the spiritual. The approaches are as varied as the compositional ventures: the common factor is that nostalgia and reheated Romanticism scarcely play a part any more; rather, a modernity is perceived in Schumann and is emphasized: reflectiveness, multi-layeredness, intertextuality, ambivalence, fragmentation, awkwardness, extremism.

At the present time, general interest in Schumann seems somewhat overshadowed by the marketing of Clara Schumann – with consequences that remain to be seen.

Conclusion

From vague impressions to a shaping of the conception of music, from altered perception to provision of models, Schumann delivered everything that could be expected of significant music. His music changes imperceptibly and reveals different aspects according to different readings, interpretations, and forms of actualization. A historical pattern emerges from the *trouvailles*, references or usages. The stages in the history of Schumann reception run parallel to stages in the historical development of composition, music and culture, to changes in the aesthetic paradigms. The confrontation takes place everywhere: in composition, performance and acceptance by the public, editing and publication, lastly in writing about music and the successive 'new media', and the process is always affected, of course, by whether the image is formed from the music on the printed page, from performance, recordings, musicological studies, journalism or literature, or from visual media, as well as by whether the impression is at first, second or third hand. Schumann is not one of those composers with whom confrontation seems inevitable, such as Bach, Beethoven, Wagner or Schoenberg; no work of his inflames or overwhelms of itself: the recipient must make an active contribution. But precisely because he has not been consistently included in the canon of the greatest masters but has always been an object of individual passion, he has been rediscovered with astonishment again and again – more than Bach, Mozart, Beethoven, even Wagner or Brahms, Schumann's stock, like Berlioz's, has always been subject to fluctuation. Individual segments of his total œuvre vary more in the general estimation than is the norm, the points at which sections of the public latch on to him vary more than usual, every new movement discovers a Schumann to suit it: Beethovenian and New German, Romantic and Realist, Classicist and Progressive, Impressionist and Expressionst, Constructivist and Post-serialist.

As it affects composers, reception, as a rule, is not confined to explicit statements, verifiable personal contacts, study, experience of performance, unambiguous reminiscences (comparable motivic material, harmonic progressions, compositional idiosyncrasies, formal situations or structures); an influence may be more general or it may be entirely concrete, rather than direct borrowing it can take the form of an overall alteration in a composer's attitude. Context, the stage of stylistic evolution, can play a determinant role in the various kinds of reception but so can historical distance (permitting or preventing direct incorporation in the recipient composer's own musical language), and purely conceptual confrontation centres on the positions held by the protagonists on questions of aesthetics or music history – in Schumann's case the key terms might be diatonicism, integration, construction of variants, poeticization. Reception was at first made easier and more enticing for other composers by the fact that Schumann over time developed a 'style' that invited imitation. If a composer makes history by the dissemination of personal stylistic characteristics then Schumann was an important figure in the history of music. Additionally, other composers have taken themes by Schumann as the basis for sets of variations (some have already been named), or arranged and transcribed works by him (a form of close study in itself); an innumerable throng of direct *hommages* (reflected in titles and subtitles such as 'alla Schumann', 'Andenken an Schumann', 'Schumanniana' etc.) continued to be composed until well after the turn of the century, and references taking many forms picked up again in the second half of the twentieth century. A catalogue with any pretensions to completeness would be extremely long.

Schumann's not directly generic titles sparked further stylistic development, mostly on account of their 'poetic' quality. The forms were either directly adopted (intermezzo, humoresque, fantasy, novelette, sketch) or adapted in some way. Schumann's example doubtless led to titles of the type 'Overture, Scherzo and Finale' or 'Something Scenes' becoming fashionable, even in the case of specific titles such as *Papillon* (Fauré) and *Davidsbündlertänze* (Kirchner), or combinations such as John Ireland's *Leaves from a Child's Sketchbook*. Schumann served as a model for other composers in virtually every genre he wrote in (with the exception of opera), and not just in those he invented. This influence lasted longer in some genres than in others. It is strongest in the Lied (Arthur Seidl proclaimed Schumann the forefather of the Lied in the modern age),[42] in the lyrical piano piece and in cycles of small forms of that type (including *Liederspiele*, *Rose*), but the Piano Quintet, music for young players, smaller choral works with orchestral accompaniment (especially the ballads) all left their mark. Even Schumann's Latin church music seems to have been studied. And other composers realized some of Schumann's projects: a German requiem (Brahms), an oratorio about Luther (Meinardus, *Luther in Worms*), a textless opera (Hiller, *Operette ohne Text*), and his idea of a series of overtures to, or about, the great dramas of world literature – was taken up by many a composer.

Many of Schumann's achievements were recognized to have a wider significance, and contributed decisively to the aspirations of his time; along with specific details of his musical language other composers adopted principles and tendencies that he had discovered or invigorated: a song-like quality informing structural building blocks, the lyric piece transferred to chamber music, the solo concerto redefined, the folk-like recognized as a poetic characteristic, music designed to appeal to children (not just easier pieces for use as teaching material), the secular oratorio and the secularization of church music. All this can be regarded as already entailed in the idea of 'poeticization', which emerges even more distinctly with respect to literature, in the greater integration in the relationship between words and music (taking the texts more seriously and seeking a specific music for the specific atmosphere of a Byron, an Eichendorff, a Heine and so on) and in meeting the challenge of 'big' subjects. Then there are certain 'tones' in Schumann's music that were not entirely new but came to exert a special influence: nature and its moods, melancholy, nostalgia, exoticism. Poetry also informs the 'scenes', 'pictures', 'tales', as they are actually called. Poetry is the key word in the overall conception of music – but the new status of music as an equal partner, rather than an attractive aid to identification, also had consequences; ambiguity was poetic; the play with quotations, ciphers, inner voices, subtexts was poetic; and so was the 'music for the eye' in the appearance of the music on the page, and the 'paratexts' of published editions.

Poeticization, finally, has formal consequences: through-composition in opera and oratorio, fusion and hybridization between genres, the amalgamation of *adagio* and *scherzo* characteristics in the intermezzo[43] (a movement included in cyclic structures by countless composers since Schumann's day); the one-movement symphony (Hermann Hirschbach thought of writing one[44] but Schumann influenced Arensky, Mahler,[45] Mangold, Nicodé, Schoenberg, Strauss; and Liszt's piano concertos and some of his symphonic poems can be mentioned here as well).[46] The French symphony, or *sonate cyclique*, owes its existence to Schumann's new conception of the symphony with cyclic organization of the movements. Motivic combination, innovations in thematic disposition: changing the focus of attention in the development section, introduction of new ideas after the exposition, 'synthetic coda themes',[47] two different trios in the scherzo. In harmony: rejection of academic rules (taking lessons in counterpoint from Jean Paul Richter); liberalization and broadening of range in tonal organization; expansion of dissonance in the diatonic context (chromaticism as a means of adding spice to diatonicism); greater prominence for ninth and eleventh chords; stabilization of passing notes as chord notes. Typical consequences: secondary dominants (e.g. the II then III degrees) above dominant pedal points, emancipation of the progression V–IV, discovery of the subdominant.

Other composers' reception of Schumann is shown in other ways besides their own music. Large numbers of them[48] have also expressed their responses to him in literary forms, from miscellanies and reviews to poems, single chapters in symposia, and entire monographs. In Schumann's own work, writing was one facet of his overall programme of poeticization. There are examples of direct imitation of his style of journalism, but there is also the line, leading first from Hoffmann's *Serapionsbrüder* to Schumann's *Davidsbündler*, and from there onwards to Liszt's *Baccalaureus der Tonkunst*, Debussy's Monsieur Croche and Satie's many masks.[49]

Even composers who did not belong to any particular party found reasons to criticize Schumann. For example, his approach to certain subjects was repeatedly found to fall short in significance, encouraging the critic to produce a more powerful treatment of his own in order to show how Schumann should have done it. This happened with *Faust*, *Manfred*,[50] *Des Sängers Fluch*, *Julius Caesar*, and settings of Eichendorff, Goethe, Heine and others. The criticism, too, took not only musical form but also verbal (usually among the followers of Wagner: Bruckner, Draeseke), even literary. The arguments were not always very carefully chosen. When Bülow spoke of 'Schumann's intervallic howling', at least he referred to an actual trait of the music, pinpointing a specific harmonic loading of large intervals in late Schumann.[51] But composers, too, have sometimes merely repeated received ideas without testing them, as when Boulez dismisses the fughettas as merely imitative – which is the last thing they can be called.

The reception of Schumann by other writers on music was always simultaneously the reception of his own writing and his aesthetics. From the first, he was much read, cited and also much imitated by the critics. To this day, Schumann's judgements serve as a reference point at every level of writing about music. He made music itself a subject for reflection but never reduced it to the merely aesthetic or technical: when professional critics are influenced by literature it is revealed in the significance given to the form of a review and in the materialization of the literary aspect in concrete technical conditions. As time passed, changes in attitudes were reflected in the journalism. The chapter on Schumann in the history of criticism is a sorry tale: composers acquit themselves scarcely any better than journalists (save for usually having something they want to say). While Schumann was still alive, he was already being accused of hair-splitting and brooding. The unworldly, impractical aspects of his character seemed to match the eccentricity, fantasy and ineffectuality of some of his later compositions – both these having a tragicomic or perhaps lovable side to them. At the same time, however, the arguments were still concerned with tangibilities. The news of Schumann's mental illness seemed to allow a period of grace to ensue. After his death all inhibitions vanished: now everyone 'knew' that the later works betrayed the signs of a clouded mind, the loss of faculties. The early, inspired, audacious (and so on) Schumann was played off against the exhausted, dried-out, later composer – the dividing line being set arbitrarily. Writers varied between over-meticulous assessment, sceptical prejudice and simple wholesale dismissal. Besides the late-work syndrome, writers fell back regularly on references to the insanity, some embarrassed or dismissive, some impressed or even fascinated. Before long, Schumann was the 'schoolboy of musical history', to be patronized and treated more roughly than possibly any other composer. An endless series of condescending verdicts offers more material for students of the psychology of reviewing than for musical analysis. An anthology could be compiled of the daftest and diametrically contradictory opinions on Schumann, uttered about every single work but also about his character. Generalizations such as: the children's composer, the singer of lovesongs, the intrinsically lyrical temperament and so on, are supported by spontaneous reactions or mere hearsay rather than by any reasoned argument based on thorough investigation. The unexamined acceptance and re-use of such clichés still permeates comments on Schumann, from academic writing via journalism, the broadcast media and teaching, to fiction.[52]

Among musicologists, the gathering of biographical information (the editions of Wasielewski's life, Jansen's and Erler's editions of the letters) and the study of sources (from 'DAS' to the *Gesamtausgabe*, variant readings of material in the *Gesammelte Schriften*) have always served to reinforce a general picture. Research has reflected contemporary concerns: positivism and the 'great man' school of biography, sociology and psychology, structuralism and cultural studies have all made their appearances in turn in musicology as elsewhere. The decisions taken in the old *Gesamtausgabe*, for instance (which pieces to include, and in which versions), rested on aesthetic dogmas that had developed gradually and were not to be overthrown by editorial principles. But composers, interpreters, teachers and musicologists have worked on editions of Schumann's music for more than 150 years, comparing variant readings, implementing different criteria, inserting supplementary material, taking textual decisions, and thereby they have underpinned the aesthetic preferences and idiosyncrasies of their own day.

The living presence of Schumann's music in performances has followed analogous conceptions over the years, and here too constant change can be observed. The number of interpreters involved in this process grew as the music became more widely known, including numerous composers – Britten, Holliger and Maderna in the second half of the twentieth century, for example, to say nothing of the pianists among them. It seems likely that the two activities – performing and composing – had an effect on each other, as is the case generally with performance and composition in any given period. The state of performance history is already illustrated by the fluctuations in the repertory themselves, the variations in opinions as to the quality of individual pieces: Op. 52, for example, once a favourite with audiences, later almost disappeared from the concert hall; or Op. 133, hitherto neglected, but now discovering admirers. Today, however, as a general rule, even stock that has gathered dust for years has found its way on to recordings if nowhere else, and recordings also enable an airing to be given to such relatively impractical works as the original version of the Andante and Variations for two pianos, Op. 46, with the accompaniment of two cellos and horn. Certain pieces or genres seem to have been of paradigmatic importance in the development of Schumann interpretation: at first the Piano Quintet and Piano Concerto and certain songs; the piano music contributed to a 'poetic' style of playing the piano, just as the song collections assisted in the development of a dramaturgy for song recitals. In the latter part of the nineteenth century it was the symphonies and oratorios, and the fate of the Violin Concerto in the second half of the twentieth may be said to reflect the alterations both in views of the late work and in performance practice as it affects Schumann's music.

The effect made by a piece by Schumann has always depended on the version being performed. Both in the composer's lifetime and since, the process of revision (re-touching, new arrangements, re-orchestration) has never ceased. Like the performance statistics, these versions also show that the separate sectors of the œuvre have not been equally popular at all times. The most popular piece by Schumann in the nineteenth century was probably *Abendlied*, which circulated in countless arrangements – Joachim's may have done most to make it popular but Busoni, Raff, Saint-Saëns, Svendsen and Wilhelmj all played their part. *Träumerei* replaced *Abendlied* in the twentieth century as the *pièce de résistance*, in every conceivable scoring.[53] Arrangements are a means of becoming better acquainted with Schumann's music not only for the arrangers but also for music-lovers and 'users' of all kinds. They make manifest the changing of pieces to meet the altered needs of one age after another. In its successive new guises, *Träumerei* has determined the image of Schumann and the conception of music for generations – and, vice versa, its new clothes have been tailored according to those changing conceptions. It seems characteristic that *Träumerei* today does not enjoy the prominence it did a hundred years ago (unless resistance to the more flowing motion appropriate to the piece points to some deep psychological fixations).

With regard to the re-touching of original orchestrations, it is hard to separate admiration for Schumann from criticism as the motive. Anton Rubinstein and Elgar both considered doing it; Mahler, Reger, Szell, Weingartner and others all did it. The Third Symphony was rescored by both Glazunov[54] and Frederick Stock.[55] Acting in good faith, interpreters have allowed themselves interventions that they did not always own up to, in the interests of richer colouring or emphasizing what each regarded as the essential – or they have decided independently to perform 'original' versions (Pfitzner, Bernstein). The principles justifying the versions have corresponded to the maxims governing the other aspects of the interpretation. Frequently the size of the hall has been a consideration, but all too often it has been a matter of simple falsification, as in the case of attempts to treat Schumann *à la* Beethoven (Furtwängler's well-known recording of the Fourth Symphony), Weber, Spohr (giving the last movement of the Violin Concerto *alla polacca* rather than as a slow *polonaise*), or Wagner (tempo modifications and rubato). Today the guidelines of historical performance practice (which also entails restoring the original sound) have extended their reach as far as Schumann. The growing ambition to complete works left unfinished by their composers, on the other hand, is creating a climate in which the ideal of authenticity has been so far dispelled that currently gradual distinctions are emerging between original and new versions (sometimes, as in the case of Mahler's re-orchestrations, the 'new' version is regarded as historical in its own right).

The general public's image of Schumann is a mixture of first impressions and simple habit, their own attempts to play his music and experiences in the concert hall, good and bad performances, admired performers and their identification with the music, aesthetic commonplaces, fashion, marketing, early teaching and adult classes, programme notes, biographies, portraits, films and television programmes. This does not apply exclusively to Schumann, however – any more than it is possible to judge the extent of the public's contribution to reception history.

In view of all this, Schumann was one of the most influential composers in the history of Western music. It is to Schumann (his works or only a particular image of him) that we refer but if we try to pin down his influence he breaks into thousands of facets, sinks into the sand, and the reception of Schumann in particular becomes impossible to separate from that of Western classical music in general. Of course the works can be brought out for inspection once again; it all depends on who does it whether they sound as fresh as on the very first occasion, as they always do, or as they never have before; whether they have nothing new to say or reveal completely unexpected aspects, demonstrate their indisputable historical importance or rest on their reputation as cultural heritage. The 'children's composer' makes the first impression many receive; he really does lay the foundations for their musical education, now as in the past. He is moreover one of those composers from whom all of us, whatever our age, can learn what music is.

Notes

This essay is indebted to numerous earlier studies; here I will mention only the chapter on reception in Arnfried Edler's book on Schumann and the reports from the Arbeitstagungen in Zwickau.

1. See Bonnie Lomnäs *et al.*, *Auf der Suche nach der poetischen Zeit. Der Prager Davidsbund* (Saarbrücken, 1999).
2. Robert Schumann, *Gesammelte Schriften über Musik und Musiker* (Leipzig: Breitkopf & Härtel, 1854; reprint ed. Witt epilogue, Gerd Nauhaus, 2 vols. (Wiesbaden: Breitkopf & Härtel, 1985); 'Einleitendes'.
3. In Saphir's *Humorist*, 171, 20 October 1838.
4. Pp. 345ff.
5. Kirchner involved himself in first performances of Schumann in Switzerland from his arrival there in 1844. The Piano Quintet was an instant success and other major works followed in quick succession. Schumann was to be a dominant figure in Swiss concert halls during the second half of the century.
6. The earliest impressions of Schumann in Italy are reflected in the *Dodici studi*, Op. 15 (1843) of Stefano Golinelli (1818–91), dedicated to Hiller.
7. Alois M. Nagler, *Hebbel und die Musik* (Cologne, 1928).
8. Letter to Strackerjan, 17 January 1854 *Robert Schumanns Briefe. Neue Folge*, ed. Gustav Jansen (Leipzig: Breitkopt & Härtel, 1904), pp. 390–1.
9. Sonata, Op. 5, 'in memory of his immortal teacher'.
10. String Quartet, Op. 12 – *before* Schumann's dedication to him of his Op. 52.
11. Heinrich von Sahr's Piano Trio in C minor, Op. 7, which Schumann heard in 1852, might also be listed, but it was not published until 1860.
12. Reinhold Sietz, *Theodor Kirchner. Ein Klaviermeister der deutschen Romantik*, Studien zur Musikgeschichte des 19. Jahrhunderts, 21 (Regensburg, 1971), pp. 100f.

13. For example, Sechter's *Fuga* or a *Konzert-Adagio* by Wilhelm Immanuel Schüler.
14. Including the dedication by the publisher, Haslinger, of the first edition of Schubert's last sonatas.
15. See Kapp, 'Schumann nach der Revolution. Vorüberlegungen, Statements, Hinweise, Materialien, Fragen', in Bernhard B. Appel, ed., *Schumann-Forschungen 3: Schumann in Düsseldorf. Werke – Texte – Interpretationen* (Mainz, London: Schott, 1993), pp. 315ff.
16. Helmut Kirchmeyer, 'Robert Schumanns Düsseldorfer Brahms-Aufsatz *Neue Bahnen* und die Ausbreitung der Wagnerschen Opern bis 1856. Psychogramm eines "letzten" Artikels' (= *Abhandlungen der sächsischen Akademie der Wissenschaften zu Leipzig, Philologisch-historische Klasse* 73/6) (Berlin, 1993), on a first version of this article see [note 14], pp. 329f., 338ff.
17. He declared, at the Schumann Festival in Zwickau in 1860, without being contradicted, that 'of all those present I loved Schumann the most faithfully and am also closest to him in spirit'; quoted here from Sietz, *Theodor Kirchner*, p. 137.
18. The young Anton Rubinstein has already been mentioned.
19. The well known letter to Tytus Woyciechowski (12 December 1831) about a review of his Op. 2 does not concern the article by Schumann but a much longer one by Friedrich Wieck.
20. Hiller embraced Schumann not only as a friend but also as a composer; he created professional opportunities for him and also conducted the première of the Piano Concerto and the first complete performance of the *Scenes from Faust*.
21. See Werner Breig, 'Wagner und Chopin', in Wulf Konold, ed., *Deutsch-polnische Musikbeziehungen* (Munich, Salzburg, 1987), pp. 54ff.
22. See, for example, Richard Stern *Erinnerungsblätter an Julius Stern* (Leipzig, 1886), pp. 158ff., 181ff.
23. Franz Brendel, 'Alfred von Wolzogen, Musikalische Leiden der Gegenwart', *Augsburger Allgemeine Zeitung*, 1857.
24. 'im Vollglanze seiner Beliebtheit'. Reinhold Seitz, *Aus Ferdinand Hillers Briefwechsel* (Beiträge für rheinische Musikgeschichte, 28), p. 143.
25. *Ibid.*, p. 176.
26. His *Königsmarsch* for Munich (1880), despite some Lisztian flourishes, is a late testimony to his Schumannesque foundations.
27. He may have heard him as a boy in Cologne, conducting a symphony in 1852.
28. The Witch in *Königskinder* has a passage towards the end of Act 1 reminiscent of the witch Margaretha's 'Du läßt die arme Frau allein' in the first finale of Schumann's *Genoveva*.
29. 'Gerechtigkeit unmöglich, widerwärtiger Stockmusikant'; see H. J. Irmen, ed., *E. Humperdincks Briefe* (Kölin: Volk, 1975–), 2, 118.
30. Including the first 'critical edition', by DAS (Dr Adolf Schubring).
31. This applies generally to Classicism in entertainment music, operetta etc.
32. Adolphe Jullien wrote, in *Richard Wagner. Sa vie et ses œuvres*: 'Schumann, que tout le monde musical reconnaît actuellement comme le plus grand musicien symphoniste après Beethoven'. (Paris, 1886), p. 304.
33. Reinhard Kapp, 'Schumann-Reminiszenzen bei Mahler', in *Musik-Konzepte Sonderband Gustav Mahler*, pp. 325ff.
34. The opening of the opera *Die Rose vom Liebesgarten* is reminiscent of the opening of *Der Rose Pilgerfahrt*.
35. Nevertheless, the pianist and writer on music Rudolf Réti, who was very close to the Viennese School at times, published a series of satirical sketches in *Musikblätter des Anbruchs* in its first year (1919) under the title 'Neue Davidsbündler'.
36. 'New music, outmoded music, style and idea', in *Style and Idea. Selected Writings*, ed. Leonard Stein (London, Boston, 1984), pp. 113ff.
37. Postlude of Op. 1/2, modelled on the postlude of *Dichterliebe*; 'Erwartung' from Op. 2, an echo of *Vogel als Prophet*.
38. In a letter to Emil Hertzka, 5 January 1919.
39. In France, Schumann remained one of the models for young musicians to follow: see Olivier Messaien, *Vingt leçons d'harmonie* (Paris, 1939).
40. Karl Heinrich Wörner, *Robert Schumann* (Zurich, 1949).
41. See Kapp, 'Schumanns Aktualität', *Correspondenz. Mitteilungen der Robert-Schumann-Gesellschaft e.V. Düsseldorf*, 12 (1991); Wolf Frobenius, 'Schumann in der Musik nach 1950', in Frobenius, ed., *Robert Schumann: philologische, analytische, sozial- und*

rezeptionsgeschichtliche Aspekte, Saarbrücker Studien zur Musikwissenschaft, n.F. 8 (Saarbrücken, 1998); and Jörn-Peter Hiekel's contribution to the present volume.

42. *Moderner Geist in der deutschen Tonkunst*, Deutsche Musikbücherei, 5 (Regensburg, 1912), pp. 159f.

43. Christian Gottlieb Müller may have contributed to the idea; see *Briefe und Gedichte aus dem Album Robert und Clara Schumanns*, ed. Wolfgang Boetticher (Leipzig, 1979), p. 141.

44. *Ibid.*, p. 87 (1838).

45. Part II of the Eighth Symphony.

46. Liszt orchestrated Schubert's *Wanderer Fantasy*, one of the models for Schumann's D minor Symphony, but there was a special reason for Liszt's dedication of his B minor Sonata to Schumann (apart from responding to Schumann's dedication of the Fantasy, Op. 17, to himself): Liszt had taken part in the concert at which the first version of Schumann's D minor Symphony was performed for the first time.

47. In Michael Struck's phrase.

48. Ambros, Berg, Boucourechliev, Cornelius, Cui, Dukas, Ehlert, Flothuis, Gál, Grieg, Haas, Hiller, Holliger, von Holstein, Jemnitz, Kienzl, Killmayer, Knab, Koechlin, Leibowitz, Liszt, Moscheles, Pfitzner, Pousseur, Reinecke, Réti, Rihm, Rubinstein, Ruzicka, Schoenberg, Tchaikovsky, Weingartner.

49. It would be interesting to compare Berlioz's criticism with Schumann's and describe the interaction between them.

50. Only with Tchaikovsky's *Manfred* Symphony was confrontation with Schumann not the primary motive.

51. Whereas Wagner's disciple Joseph Rubinstein found fault with Schumann's notorious two-bar phrasing – a characteristic he shared with Wagner, among others.

52. A very recent example is Eva Weissweiler's 'biography' of Clara Schumann, in which speculation is unimpeded by any factual knowledge.

53. K. Csipak and R. Kapp, '*Träumerei*', *Musica*, 35 (1981), 438ff.

54. His version is lost.

55. See Walter Damrosch, *My Musical Life* (New York, 1937), p. 361.

12 The compositional reception of Schumann's music since 1950

JÖRN PETER HIEKEL

Schumann: a model case

As a composer, Robert Schumann was particularly conscious both of the necessity and of the difficulties of a creative engagement with the music of earlier times. This explains his famous saying that history, because of the examples it holds up to the present, is an 'Angel of Death'. While he occasionally seems to have been driven almost to despair by his predecessors, he nevertheless also trained himself by an intensive study of their works. The exemplary intellectual alertness that this demonstrates is something of which later composers who find themselves responding to his music should be aware.

This chapter will focus on concepts that aim to illuminate one particular aspect of the past and bring out its most fascinating features, or the specific questions it raises. Following a few general remarks, we shall look at a series of paradigmatic works that, insofar as they are marked by an engagement with Schumann, show in an exemplary way how he was seen as so inspiring by other composers even in the second half of the twentieth century. This influence was particularly due to his compositions, but it also stemmed from his life and thought. Schumann's own Bach reception anticipates key aspects of the examples I have selected: for more recent composers, Schumann functions as a catalyst, as well as helping them to become more self-aware and more sure of their own creative powers.

Nowadays, when it comes to the influence of Schumann's work on contemporary composers, we find hardly any of those aesthetic concepts that (especially when prompted by fortuitous occasions such as anniversaries) might tend towards a reverential homage and thus perpetuate the obsolete idea of the 'great man' theory of history. Nietzsche, who categorized such ideas as 'monumental' history, rightly stated that 'an excess of history is detrimental to life'.[1] In comparison to the celebrations that marked the 200th anniversary of the death of Bach or the 100th anniversary, in 1928, of Schubert's death, there were, characteristically, no attempts to embrace Schumann and turn him into a cultural monument in 1956, on the hundredth anniversary of his own death.[2] However, the reasons for this are not only to be found in the music: it also reflects the fact that times have changed.

In addition to the examples on which this essay will focus, it must be admitted that there can always be types of influence that go beyond any explicit reference to Schumann. The importance that Schubert's music had for Morton Feldman is a striking case. But any search for traces of influence is difficult when we do not have at least some verbal indications pointing to such relationships. However, tracking these influences down would be well beyond the scope of this study. This also means of course that any delineation of compositional reception will always remain inconclusive. There are however a few significant phenomena that might help to form an initial, provisional overview.[3]

Abstinence and contrived rapprochement

Perspectives on the history of influence and the reception of a composer or of a compositional trend can be all the more significant when, instead of a specific presence, there is evidence of a conscious avoidance.[4] In the 1950s, it became almost normal among many European composers to renounce musical Romanticism. Although Bernd Alois Zimmerman's stage music to William Saroyan's play *Sam Ego's House* (1953), which quotes from Schumann's Piano Concerto might seem to be the one notable exception to this rule, it was also, significantly enough, a relatively unimportant work in the composer's overall output.

The widespread avoidance of Romanticism at that time coincided, at least in German-speaking circles, with a general feeling that 'it appears worse than anachronistic to invoke the spirit of Romanticism in music', as Willibald Gurlitt, one of the most influential German musicologists, stated in his 1950 lecture 'Robert Schumann und die Romantik in der Musik'.[5] He suggested that the use of the term 'Romantic' had started to carry 'an aftertaste of disapproval, indeed disparagement', while also emphasizing 'the continuing musical supremacy of Germany in our century' and a 'German movement in music' that 'reaches from Schumann, Brahms and Reger to Paul Hindemith'.[6] Despite its intention to open itself up to the present, it becomes clear how much this text remains imprisoned in 'great man' historiography when the author demands, in closing: 'Think of the quiet heroism of today's composers, those young unknown musicians in search of new paths, and the future of German music, which lies in its artistic efforts alone.' Precisely in the connections he makes with the present, Gurlitt's lecture appears retrospectively as a desperate effort to summon up and salvage a continuity that was already on the point of dissolution.

Of course, this kind of thinking found less and less resonance among the middle-aged and younger generations of composers, even if the rallying call for 'new paths' was itself an acknowledgement of a sense of heroism. One of the main reasons for the often strict avoidance of any connection with Romanticism was probably the idea of a fundamentally new aesthetic beginning, perceived by many (as never before in musical history) as an absolute necessity. Sometimes, the exaggerations of reception history have a certain plausibility. Thus the widespread reservations regarding genuine Romanticism were, at least in part, a reaction against the frequent distortions to which the music of the nineteenth century had been exposed, most significantly as a result of the disastrous extravagances of ideology and nationalism. (It was precisely the 'German' aspects of Romanticism, stressed by Gurlitt and linked to Schumann, that were for obvious reasons no longer particularly highly prized.)

For a time, such ideas were radicalized, particularly in the centres for the newly emerging, internationally significant musical avant-garde – the Darmstadt summer courses, for example. Yet rather than this being a watershed, a 'year zero' as the legend has it, people were still in fact reacting to earlier music. But it was the structural aspects of this music that were emphasized, rather than the expressive ones. The most prominent example of this is the reception of Anton Webern's music, in which the strongly post-Romantic colourings were to a great extent underplayed and the numerous progressive elements were accentuated. In retrospect, this was, at least in part, a misunderstanding, albeit a productive one. However, such misunderstandings in the reception history of earlier art by later artists should, generally speaking, never be underestimated.

What is important for us here is a further significant change of perspective in the aesthetics of music during the twentieth century: a remarkably high number of works dating from the 1970s established connections with works by composers of the nineteenth and the beginning of the twentieth centuries, in order to reflect and elaborate on aspects of these works. Especially with regard to this last point, the preoccupation with Schumann has to be seen as part of a wider development that included the compositional reception and critique of Beethoven, Schubert and Mahler. It is not just from today's perspective that compositions that were more or less explicitly 'music *about* music' came to be understood as responses to a one-sided and rigid exclusion of tradition. It was already customary for critics of the 1950s avant-garde to emphasize the markedly anti-historical attitude that had come to fruition in the idea of serial music. Evidently, in some cases another particular emphasis came to the fore: the tendency – certainly not always justified – to associate an inflexible denial of tradition with almost totalitarian motives.[7] Those who did return to Romanticism were granted the psychological reward of being able to retrieve what had been to some extent ignored.

What is most interesting in this situation, from a music-historical point of view, is – retrospectively speaking – not so much the polemical controversy over the relevance and acceptance of an often consciously ahistorical avant-garde. More important is the recognition that different circumstances had cleared the path for composers to create a kind of music that succeeded in productively developing a number of substantial approaches inspired by their musical predecessors. 'Productive' here means, first and foremost, escaping from the conservative reverence afforded the 'heroes of music history'. Yet 'productive' also means that contemporary approaches to earlier music consciously aimed to avoid picking up on musico-historical truisms – and thus endorsing what Walter Benjamin had called the 'crippling' weight of continuity – and instead emphasized specific aspects that had remained unnoticed up to that point. Typically, there was less interest in relatively unproblematic works such as Schumann's 'Rhenish' Symphony.

One thing that is certain is that, since the above-mentioned 'change of direction in reception history'[8] (at whatever precise point we may consider it to have begun), there have been many works that do indeed reflect aspects of Romanticism, but do so without a polemical tone – perhaps even without the feeling of being taboo. This attitude is only mentioned since it was evident among a few decidedly conservative composers, mostly of German origin, to whom the undeniably vague label *Neue Einfachheit* (New Simplicity) was quickly applied. At this time, the terrain of Romantic art, in the stricter sense of the term, still seemed for many to be associated with the lure of the 'forbidden', for even in 1971 (i.e. roughly at the time of this 'change of direction'), Hans Werner Henze indicated (in the guise of the quotations from Schumann in his second Violin Concerto) his distance from Romanticism: in this gesture, the aforementioned purism of the post-war years still clearly resonates. The theatrical texture of the work aims to represent a Romantic virtuosity in the solo part that projects passages from Schumann's *Bunte Blätter* so as to distance itself from this foreign element. In his commentary, Henze clearly emphasized the inauthenticity of his reference: 'The virtuoso appears exactly as Romanticism saw him: as magician and tragic wizard.'[9]

The perceptible effort of development

'What is different about Schumann's music?'[10] asked the German composer Wolfgang Rihm in 1984 after having intensively explored Classicism and Romanticism and their aura in his own works from the 1970s – something that put him consciously at odds with the aims and goals of the

Darmstadt avant-garde. One of the most significant compositional results of this preoccupation with an earlier repertoire is a cycle for string trio in three parts of 1982–4. Its title, *Fremde Szenen* (*Foreign Scenes*), seems to suggest a distancing from history. However, the pieces under this title follow a dialectical process, typical of Rihm, which succeeds in obscuring this 'distancing' at certain points. In those of Rhim's works that allude to Romanticism, the composer aims at referring to, reconstructing or reflecting the emphatic idiom of Romantic chamber music and its urgent, persistent, intense elements, as well as its 'big' gestures. What is essential for Rihm's compositional procedures is that these elements will in many places in his compositions take on much more weight and force than would have been conceivable in the nineteenth century, to the extent of producing an almost manic expressive concentration.

Rihm's three *Foreign Scenes* emulate the ambience of Schumann's three piano trios. But nowhere do they suggest that Schumann's music represented an idyllic world that many longed for. On the contrary, this world in itself represents a degree of conflict. Characteristic for such aesthetics of conflict are the abrupt changes between seemingly lyrical and fleeting, elegiac or euphoric soundscapes on the one hand, and energetic outbursts on the other. Rihm's music is torn between form and formlessness. It establishes motivic connections and their development but then allows these to fall apart. There are several obvious resonances with Schumann's music in all three parts of the cycle. However, these have been introduced through the back door, so to speak, as can be heard at the beginning of the closing piece. As if peeping from behind a curtain, these Schumannesque resonances emerge as if by stealth, and become concrete enough to produce a consciously disorientating dialectic between the foreign and the familiar, between the immediately graspable and the unattainably distant: we get the impression that these isolated 'Romantic' components belong to a reservoir of references that are familiar and yet taboo. What also becomes clear is that a complete restitution of their expressive potential has long become completely impossible and absurd.

It is characteristic of Rihm's intensification of 'Romantic' elements that they often disrupt, erase or cancel continuity – itself often tenuous to begin with. This is a response to what Rihm sees as achieved or at least hinted at in Schumann's own music. The cycle *Foreign Scenes* in particular is closely related to views Rihm has expressed in various texts about Schumann. In answering his own question as to what distinguishes Schumann's music, he writes: '[It is] music whose efforts are palpable . . . It is different from music where we can follow a clear trajectory with a goal and a purpose. This music is difficult to "place" or "situate" (more in terms of its development than its style). Thus Schumann's music, especially in his late works, is rather difficult even for the previously initiated musical mind ((*Vor-*) *Verstand*). He prefers concrete artistic reality (*Zuständlichen in der Kunst*) to academic consistency.'[11]

We can see how Rihm's approach negates the traditional reservations about the structure of some of Schumann's works; but he also reinterprets their core – their seeming inconsistency and intrinsic interruptions – thereby offering new interpretative perspectives. It is also true that the quality Rihm is indicating, the increasingly significant notion of 'reality' in music, seems to be opening up new paths in Schumann's music. As is the case with comparable compositional procedures in Schubert's œuvre, these can be analysed as a conscious alternative to more teleological or linear and discursive conceptions.[12]

Rihm's own Schumann pieces emphasize a certain aimlessness but also a certain rootedness – to such an extent that even those tonal passages that *do* allude to Romantic chamber music (without directly quoting them) never seem like someone nostalgically flicking through the faded pages of a photo album. This differs significantly from many other compositions of recent decades by various composers who have also experimented with elements of the Romantic aura, but in such a way that the ghosts they summoned up could never again be dismissed. In contrast, Rihm's Schumann-related works exhibit an ambivalence that turns aside from some higher (imaginary) position. This indirectness, however, sits squarely in the tradition of Romantic irony in general, and, more specifically, of Schumann's preference for ambiguity. At the same time, in works like these, the Rihm who is in some sense committed to Adorno's idea of a *musique informelle* is also paying tribute to the aesthetic of the Romantic fragment. In addition to adopting Schumann's initiatives, Rihm radicalizes them even in works that do not refer explicitly to the Romantic repertoire.

Rihm's aesthetic views entail his conviction that only music after 1950 was capable of sensitizing and alerting listeners to Schumann as a role model. 'Our ears have been sharpened to perceive rapid shifts of densities, states of mind and soul, different types of movement (in the musical sense), the juxtaposition of clarity with darkness, and the kinship between places of ill repute and lofty aspirations (*verrufene Stellen und Aufschwünge*); we can hear the agonizing battles between musical ideas, and how the music is paralysed or else drills deep into the ground; we can perceive the melancholy gaze and the sense of going round in circles.'[13] Here Rihm's image of Schumann coincides with that of Roland Barthes, who emphasizes, in similarly unacademic and exaggerated terms, how Schumann's music depends on bodily expression: he also foregrounds its fragmentary nature, its intermezzo-character, its non-discursiveness, the way it is full of surprises and often seemingly obsessive: 'In Schumann's *Kreisleriana*... I actually hear no note, no theme, no contour, no grammar, no meaning, nothing that would permit me to reconstruct an intelligible structure of the work.'[14]

The intrinsic fragmentariness of Schumann's music is central to Rihm's assertions about the significance of Schumann for contemporary composition. Schumann's partial deviations from conventional formal patterns associated with the Viennese Classics can be seen to parallel Rihm's own attitude toward a number of tendencies in the musical avant-garde. Rihm's Schumann-related music is often in search of a kind of expressivity that the 1950s shift of aesthetic paradigms had marginalized.

It should also be noted that Rihm is perfectly aware of the conservative ethos emanating from his choice of instrumentation;[15] yet he has been able to transcend it through his dialectical zeal. This indeed lies at the core of Wolfgang Rihm's musical thinking, even beyond any specific references to Schumann. And this is an important strand of contemporary European composition.

Poetic miniatures

'Strange pirouettes by Kapellmeister Johannes Kreisler' is the title of the first, miniature-like movement of György Kurtág's *Hommage à R. Sch.* composed in 1990. It is in this work consisting of six movements for clarinet, viola and piano that Kurtág most explicitly follows in Schumann's footsteps. The first movement, which one might call the impulse for the whole work, was conceived during a period when Kurtág was preoccupied with Romantic chamber music, in this case Schumann's chamber piece *Märchenerzählungen*. Kurtág had used this approach once before for a different work, the *Kafka-Fragmente* of 1985–7, of which one section is called 'Hommage à Schumann'.

We can indeed find analytically verifiable motivic correspondences between Kurtág's *Hommage à R. Sch.* and Schumann's own music, especially in relation to the *Fantasiestücke*, Op.12.[16] But more important is the expressive intensity by which Kurtág, whose music (like Rihm's) has found real resonance among younger composers all over Europe, is linked to Schumann's world. Schumann's notion of a 'poetic music' filled with curious, marvellous elements distanced from strict Classical formal models is particularly relevant here. Although one can find a great number of connections to earlier composers in Kurtág's work, none is as substantial and aesthetically significant as the connection to Schumann. Again and again, Kurtág writes lyrically dense, miniaturist, character pieces that are the very antithesis of more discursive processes and for which Schumann can be seen as one of the progenitors. Apart from Johannes Kreisler, the poetic focus of Schumann's *Kreisleriana*, Kurtág's *Hommage à R. Sch.* contains other concrete points of reference: Florestan, Eusebius and Master Raro, the three scintillating *Davidsbündler* characters in whose name Schumann articulated, and actually composed, his artistic vision. They reappear in the titles of single movements in Kurtág's work.

Kurtág, like Schumann, composes music of poetic hues that alludes to moments of existential significance while being counteracted by accents pointing in the opposite direction. The *Davidsbündler* often speak, as Schumann himself emphasized, with a humorous and ironic edge. Likewise, Kurtág's fragmentary constructions are often able to embrace similar, slightly disorientating effects. In the smallest space they can contain feverishly tempestuous tones as well as subdued, almost resigned, ashen tones. But constant interruptions and flashes of doubt give none of these basic elements sufficient room to consolidate or elaborate. This is directly comparable with the intentional breathlessness of some of Rihm's compositional reflections on Schumann, although in this case without the need for pseudo-citational allusions mentioned earlier. After five movements characterized by Kurtág's brevity and succinctness, the final movement lasts a whole six minutes. This is a calm and twilit *adagio* movement ending with the clarinettist playing a bass drum. The end, like a deliberately heterogeneous, curiously surreal death-blow, sounds like a response to the earlier fugitive and tentative moments of virtuosity and vigour, which themselves allude to Schumann's fascination with Paganini. That Schumann's Master Raro is introduced in connection with Machaut in the last movement can also be associated with the fact that this figure in Schumann's semi-fictional critical writings pleads for more differentiated dealings with the old masters. Kurtág has written a *Passacaglia* that refers to Machaut and Schumann at the same time – as well as to Bach! However, if Kurtág tracks Schumann and other composers in this way, it is not in the spirit of monumentalism, but rather in order to explore poetic ideas at the heart of which lies an internal contradiction.

Insecurity and quest

At the première of György Kurtág's *Hommage à R. Sch.* in 1990, there was surely no-one, among either composers or critics, who would have judged Kurtág's references to Romanticism to be out of kilter with present times: thirty or forty years earlier, the composition would most certainly have been received quite differently in most parts of Europe. Meanwhile, however, it had become perfectly natural, even for an ex-representative of the Darmstadt avant-garde such as Luigi Nono, to associate himself openly with Schumann. His remark from 1980 is particularly striking in this respect: 'I have developed the technique of serialism not in the light of Webern, but through the study of the Netherlands school (Ockeghem) as well as a composer such as Schumann.'[17] On the one hand, this comment is typical of the later Nono who aimed to distance himself from the conceptual narrow-mindedness of the 1950s. On the other hand, it shows how Schumann, even among avant-garde composers, was not exclusively perceived (at least privately) as a representative of his epoch and its specific aura. But Nono also intimates where his fascination with Schumann lies and this, as it happens, coincides with Wolfgang Rihm's views: 'Today it is more important for me to present material from a number of different aspects, to derive new properties from it, than to compose closed forms. To choose a historical example: Schumann, rather than Brahms.' Various of Nono's works of the 1980s, such as *Prometeo* (1984) und *La lontananza utopica futura* (1988/9), refer directly to Schumann's work. In *Prometeo*, the key work from Nono's last creative phase, the beginning of Schumann's incidental music *Manfred* is quoted altogether nine times. Nono explores here, via subtle links with material from Schumann's *Prometheus*,[18] aspects of Byron's poetry as well as aspects of Schumann's music. Interestingly, it is the lack of metrical clarity at the beginning of this overture that becomes Nono's reference-point – as a conscious gesture of insecurity. Furthermore, it may not be entirely coincidental, from an ideological viewpoint too, that Nono here returns to Schumann: throughout his life, he always favoured artists of all kinds who could be identified as in some way 'rebellious'. As far as the emphasis on moments of vacillation is concerned, Nono's Schumann reception obviously corresponds with that of Kurtág and Rihm. At the same time, this aspect in Nono seems also to relate to the central notion of his 'late work', and all that that implies: 'searching' and 'wandering', in a figurative as well as a political sense. For Nono, Schumann is, among various other literary and philosophical influences, one of the few spiritual and conceptual ancestors in the musical field.

In the footsteps of madness

It has often been observed that the aesthetics of works of art may not always coincide with the modes of thinking that prevailed at the time they were created. While art may well seem to be in advance of its own time, the problem may in fact be that aesthetic discourse cannot measure up to the substance of contemporary artistic issues. Conversely, one could ask if, and to what extent, art works manifest a perceptible change in the basic beliefs of *scholarly* discourse. This is particularly relevant with regard to music that reflects on already existing music. In the case of the composition reception of

Schumann after 1950, this question focusses on whether the change (evident to specialists, at least) in the assessment of Schumann's music – and in particular his puzzling late work[19] – finds an echo in the trends of those contemporary compositions that concern themselves with Schumann. The response to this question is clearly 'yes', and especially in relation to Schumann's last creative phase, which was marked by severe psychological problems and to which more attention has recently been paid.

Someone who has addressed this issue thoroughly is the Swiss composer and renowned oboist Heinz Holliger.[20] The following remark about Schumann's reception history characterizes Holliger's position well: 'Bearing mental illness like the mark of Cain, Schumann, more than all other composers, is susceptible to misunderstanding. On the one hand, certain works of his early and middle period are praised to the skies, while on the other hand a pious veil of silence obscures the more sober, austere and concentrated works of the late period.'[21] This interest in the late Schumann, i.e. the Schumann who was under immense mental stress, recalls the reception history of the German poet Friedrich Hölderlin. The image of Hölderlin spending close to forty years in his Tübingen tower has become a symbol of the artist's fate on the edge of madness. There is indeed a whole range of composers who have adopted this 'new' Hölderlin reception, one that considers the poet's late work to be of particular artistic value, and they have reflected this view in their compositions. Concurrently, in the reception of Schumann, too, a number of related topics have attracted special interest in recent years, namely the way one can suffer from the world, go mad (in appearance or reality) or collapse in the confrontation with it.

For Heinz Holliger, drawing the parallel between Hölderlin and Schumann became the very stimulus for one of his works reflecting both artists: the *Gesänge der Frühe* of 1987 for choir, orchestra and tape. It contains some of Hölderlin's late poems signed with the imaginary name 'Scardanelli', as well as the harmonization of a chorale from Schumann's own *Gesänge der Frühe* for piano, written in 1853, to which Holliger adds the text of one of Hölderlin's poems about the seasons. Holliger's composition also contains extracts from the medical reports on Schumann, comments taken from letters by the poet Bettina von Arnim about the mental illness of both artists, and extracts from Schumann's diary. Thanks to the diary, we know that the composer originally intended to call his *Gesänge der Frühe* 'Diotima' – the name of Hölderlin's beloved who has become the symbol of a highly individualized kind of poetry and who is the most famous of his dedicatees. What characterizes this piece by Holliger is its alternation between collage-like and highly complex multidimensional sonorous planes, its striking anti-Romantic sobriety and the singers' and instrumentalists' heightened expressivity. The composition's main message is clear from its opening, thanks to a quotation from a letter by Bettina von Arnim, to whom Schumann dedicated his *Gesänge der Frühe*: 'We use the word madness, I realize, to denote that which finds no resonance in someone else's spirit. It does, however, find a resonance in me. In fact, rather than being merely a concept, it resonates in me to the innermost depths of my spirit. In my soul it is as in the thundering mountains where one echo awakes another; and it is in this way that the madman's words will forever resonate in my soul...'[22] Those passages of Holliger's work that lead away from the analytical sobriety of its spoken text seem to represent the strongest argument for the thesis that apparent madness is, in truth, an exemplary condition of authentic art. This idea – highly contentious, given that Schumann's mental illness is undeniable – reflects controversies of the last few decades, notably represented by Michel Foucault's famous *History of Madness in the Age of Reason* with its core thesis that light can only shine in the 'darkness of madness'. In the Schumann literature a link has often been made between the composer's assumed madness and the unusual and disturbingly anticlassical moments in his music. Charles Rosen, for example, concludes in *The Romantic Generation* that Schumann had been 'the composer who achieved the most powerful musical representations of pathological states of feeling before Wagner [...] Schumann can effect a kind of shock denied to Wagner and Verdi.'[23] Rosen was here particularly referring to the suspension of traditional musical logic as, for example, in Schumann's famous *Toccata*, and to the manic quality of some of its rhythmic patterns.

Other examples of the compositional reception of Schumann's music from a similar perspective are Wilhelm Killmayer's much noticed chamber-music piece *Schumann in Endenich* (1972); Peter Ruzicka's *Annäherung und Stille* (Moving Closer and Silence) of 1981 with the sub-title *Vier Fragmente über Schumann* (Four Fragments about Schumann), associating Schumann with the poet Paul Celan; and Aribert Reimann's *Sieben Fragmente für Orchester (in memoriam Robert Schumann)*, (Seven Fragments for Orchestra (in memoriam Robert Schumann)) of 1987/8. The main trait of Killmayer's piece, historically among the first to undertake this kind of approach to Schumann's music, is its marked austerity. In contrast to Holliger's piece, which combines passages of great sobriety and economy with passages full of pathos, *Schumann in Endenich* shows the composer as the ancestor of a mysterious kind of simplicity that consciously renounces the riches of compositional means – offering a rather convincing interpretation of Schumann's late work. Endenich, the place where Schumann spent his last few years in a mental asylum, has become his *Tower of Tübingen*, as it were. As Killmayer explains: 'Schumann exemplified the conflict between inner and outer world. He saved himself – but as a broken man.'[24]

Schumann as poet (too)

The tendency to take into account not only Schumann's compositions but also his artistic profile as a whole is an approach shared by various other composers. In Mauricio Kagel's Lied-opera *From Germany* of 1977–80, for example, the aim was to reflect German Romanticism in general. At the work's centre lies the question of identification with Romanticism, and Kagel uses idiosyncratic means such as ironic reflection and dramatic, occasionally twisted exaggeration to reflect the 'seductive' pull of Romanticism as developed on various levels involving sound and text. The yearning for death – *Todessehnsucht* – which in this work is synonymous with the yearning for Romanticism, is therefore an important motive. As Kagel sketches his picture with reference to Schumann's famous song cycles based on poems by Heinrich Heine or Eichendorff, he conjures up the Romantic world (including that of Schubert's song cycles) by throwing some of its defining features into relief: features such as contradiction, iridescence of tone and colour, *Ungemütlichkeit* (a feeling of unease), mystery and menace. Such an appearance of the unfamiliar in a seemingly familiar context becomes an ironic commentary on today's post-Romantic, and sometimes indeed anti-Romantic, sensibility, and the line between cliché and reality is obscured, often deliberately. No doubt such procedures point more to Romanticism in general than to Schumann, yet they allude to a number of prejudices, much discussed in philosophical, historical and literary circles, with which this period of intellectual history in the twentieth century has often been confronted. It is in this more indirect way that the reference-points in Kagel's composition are of significance for the reception of Schumann's music.

Kagel's *Mitternachtsstük* (Midnightpiece) of 1980–1 and 1986, for four vocal soloists, speaking choir and instruments, is conceived with a similar perspective, but focusses even more directly on Schumann. It is a musical setting of four fragments from Schumann's diary, first published in 1971. The piece explores, as its title indicates,[25] the eeriness of midnight, its disturbing as well as magical quality. It evokes, by using particularly modern compositional techniques (a speaking voice, unusual ways of playing instruments and *musique concrète*), the spooky experiences of Selene, a character described by Schumann in a diary entry of November 1828. The literalism and realism in Kagel's shaping of sound thus seems to be raised at the same time to the level of surrealism. By means of an unusual dialectical move, both distance and proximity in relation to Romantic sentiment are simultaneously appreciable, so that Schumann appears to be Jean Paul's direct heir. The composer's intriguing psychological situation also seems to resonate here. As Kagel writes in the preface to the score: 'This interpretation may perhaps express those "psychic dreams" that preoccupied Schumann so much.' In hearing, in Part IV of *Mitternachtsstük*, something of the magical powers of music as well as its distorted reflections ('suddenly it seemed like a tone spoken in a broken voice, as if in slumber'), we are led to look out for similar fissures in Schumann's original music. We almost automatically associate Kagel's work not only with Schumann's words but with his music too. As Kagel's composition uses both of the latter, the implication is to proceed similarly in our own attempts at interpreting Schumann, and not to underestimate the richness of his many-faceted verbal utterances. After all, Kagel himself, as a director of film and radio plays as well as other kinds of text-centred works, can hardly be seen as fulfilling the usual role of classical composer, but rather should be considered in this regard as one of Schumann's direct descendants.

Playfully serious dreamwork

In a post-modern age, the techniques of collage or montage no longer attract as much attention as they did in the 1960s. At the same time, a more playful aspect has come to the fore. Luciano Berio's famous *Sinfonia* (1968–9), however, is an example of how such playfulness occasionally surfaced even as early as the end of the 1960s, however deeply embedded in a network of philosophical ideas it may be. This work presents a small but important new perspective on Schumann in that one of its main sections, the *Scherzo* from Mahler's Second Symphony, itself reflects the Schumann Lied 'Das ist ein Flöten und Geigen' from his song cycle *Dichterliebe*. Since Mahler's *Scherzo* is itself based on the song 'Des Antonius zu Paduas Fischpredigt', there is a fascinating chain of alternating quotation and invention. This tells us something about the potential resilience of music in general, and Schumann's in particular, especially in its acute sense of futility. Mahler knew how to intensify through orchestral means the generally bitter and bizarre tone of Schumann's Lieder.[26] This is what is radicalized by Berio. Biting irony, based on Schumann's reference to a wedding ball, is deepened through a further quotation from the second movement, the 'ball', of Berlioz's *Symphonie fantastique*.[27] It is this network of quotations that makes this passage from Berio's *Sinfonia* a model for a creative approach to history. Once again, Schumann's role is that of the inspiring initiator whose own approach passes, thanks this time to Mahler, into the music of the present.

Such procedures continue to be at work in *Dichterliebesreigentraum* of 1991–2 by Henri Pousseur who, like Berio, was a member of the Darmstadt avant-garde. Here again, the above-mentioned Lied from Schumann's *Dichterliebe* re-surfaces at different moments in the piece and invariably succeeds in transmitting its original atmosphere, even if surrounded by contrasting musical material opening up yet other perspectives from *Dichterliebe*. In comparison to the various hands through which these perspectives had already passed, Pousseur's deviations are no doubt the most pointed and poignant.

Pousseur's *Dichterliebesreigentraum* is a work for singers, chamber choir, two pianos and chamber orchestra that, in its complexity and dissolution of linear continuity, reminds one of his music-theatre work, *Votre Faust*. In *Dichterliebesreigentraum* each song from Schumann's *Dichterliebe* becomes the focal point of an accumulation of curiously de-familiarized elements that overlie the original songs. They remain intermittently recognizable, but often only sketchily so, and as if seen through a distorting mirror. Identities are dissolved because both musical and, especially, textual elements taken from different songs are filtered into each number of Pousseur's work. The aim here is to reflect the idea of unity in *Dichterliebe* dialectically, in other words to reflect both its coherence and its non-linear, non-homogeneous structure. While composing this piece Pousseur wrote a lengthy analytical essay in which he offers his particular reading of Schumann's *Dichterliebe*.[28] Here he emphasizes – apart from somewhat forced systematizations[29] – the quality of freedom in Schumann's music. For Pousseur, Schumann's shunning of linear continuity is a 'chief factor in the achievement of freedom'[30] and initiates a historical development leading from Schumann to Webern and beyond. This can be interpreted as an instance of reconciliation between the reception of Webern's music by the Darmstadt avant-garde and a newly created Schumann image. Pousseur's *Dichterliebesreigentraum* is an attempt to demonstrate this thesis. Both essay and composition converge further in that Schumann's biography, with all its discontinuities, represents an important point of reference here. As a result, the conspicuous incongruity of *Dichterliebesreigentraum* can be read as a compositional commentary on it.

The word *Reigen* in the title of Pousseur's 'composed interpretation'[31] *Dichterliebesreigentraum* is characteristic of a playful tendency that determines various constellations, like kaleidoscopes, in this work. These constellations contain emphatic, sentimental, but also, at all levels, curiously contradictory moments. The word *Traum* (dream) points towards a rather surreal quality in the work as a whole that is heightened by the miniaturism of some of its elements. Those who know Schumann's song cycle well will find themselves constantly thrown off the scent, but they will also come to discover new, unexpected potential connections. At times, by way of a kind of role-play, the dialogical quality of Schumann's original music is conveyed and intensified. Following in Schumann's footsteps means for Pousseur aiming for a playful approach that captures and perpetuates the seriousness and intensity of Schumann's music. Above all, however, it means making use of the vitality of his music, pitted with breaks and fissures as it may be, a music that is often pure exuberance and triumphant joy, but that is also, in its own strange way, often full of doubt and pain.

Notes

1. See Friedrich Nietzsche, *Unzeitgemäße Betrachtungen II: Vom Nutzen und Nachteil der Historie für das Leben*, in *Kritische Studienausgabe*, ed. Giorgio Colli and Mazzino Montinari, 15 vols., vol. I (Munich, 1980), p. 258.
2. On Schumann's Bach reception and reception history more generally see Martin Zenck, 'Bach reception: some concepts and parameters', in *The Cambridge Companion to Bach*, ed. John Butt (Cambridge, 1997), pp. 218–25.
3. See also Wolf Frobenius, 'Schumann in der Musik seit 1950', in *Robert Schumann: philologische, analytische, sozial- und rezeptionsgeschichtliche Aspekte*, ed. W. Frobenius, Saarbrücker Studien zur Musikwissenschaft, N. F., 8 (Saarbrücken, 1998), pp. 199–218.
4. Cf. Carl Dahlhaus, 'Problems in reception history', in *Foundations of Music History*, trans. J. B. Robinson (Cambridge, 1983), pp. 150–65.
5. W. Gurlitt, 'Robert Schumann und die Romantik in der Musik' (1950), in *Musikgeschichte und Gegenwart*, ed. Hans Heinrich Eggebrecht, Beihefte zum Archiv für Musikwissenschaft, vol. I, part 1 (Wiesbaden, 1966), pp. 182–97. Quotation here pp. 182–3.
6. *Ibid.*, pp. 195 and 197.
7. Cf. Helmut Lachenmann, 'Zum Problem des Strukturalismus', in *Musik als existentielle Erfahrung. Schriften 1966–1995*, ed. Josef Häusler (Wiesbaden, 1996), pp. 83–92.
8. Cf. Thomas Schäfer, *Modellfall Mahler. Kompositorische Rezeption in zeitgenössischer Musik*, Theorie und Geschichte der Literatur und der schönen Künste, 97 (Munich, 1999), p. 16.
9. Hans Werner Henze, *Musik und Politik. Schriften und Gespräche* (Munich, 1984), pp. 164–5.
10. W. Rihm, *Fremde Blätter (über Robert Schumann)*, in *Ausgesprochen. Schriften und Gespräche*, ed. Ulrich Mosch (Winterthur, 1997), 2 vols., I, pp. 229–33 (p. 230).
11. *Ibid.*, pp. 230–1.
12. Cf. *Abschied in die Gegenwart. Teleologie und Zuständlichkeit in der Musik*, ed. Otto Kolleritsch Studien zur Wertungsforschung, 36 (Wien-Graz, 1998).
13. Rihm, *Fremde Blätter*, p. 229.
14. Cf. Roland Barthes, 'Rasch', in *The Responsibility of Forms*, trans. Richard Howard (New York: Hill and Wang), p. 299.
15. He speaks of 'crowded instrumentation' in the commentary to his own work in Mosch, ed., *Schriften und Gespräche*, vol. II, p. 333.
16. Cf. Friedrich Spangemacher, 'Hommage: György Kurtág und die Musik Robert Schumanns', in Frobenius, ed., *Robert Schumann: philologische, analytische, sozial- und rezeptionsgeschichtliche Aspekte*, pp. 219–27.
17. Quoted after F. Spangemacher, *Ein Arbeitsgespräch mit Luigi Nono, September 1980*, unpublished manuscript, p. 5.
18. Cf. Lydia Jeschke, *Prometeo. Geschichtskonzeptionen in Luigi Nonos Hörtragödie*, Beihefte zum Archiv für Musikwissenschaft, 42 (Stuttgart, 1997), pp. 143–55.
19. See John Daverio on Schumann's late work in this volume.
20. In this respect he resembles Hans Zender, who in his *Schumann-Phantasie* for orchestra, composed in 1997, demonstrates the benefit of his experience as a conductor of Schumann's music.
21. Quoted from *Düsseldorfer Symphoniker Tonhallemagazin*, Düsseldorf: 1998, p. 438.
22. See Holliger's score (Mainz, 1988).
23. Charles Rosen, *The Romantic Generation* (Cambridge, MA, 1996), p. 648.
24. Quoted from Norbert Linke and Gustav Kneip, *Robert Schumann. Zur Aktualität romantischer Musik*, Materialien zur Didaktik und Methodik des Musikunterrichts, 4 (Wiesbaden, 1978), p. 5.
25. Note the deliberately archaic spelling of '-stük' in the title *Mitternachtsstük*, instead of the usual spelling '-stück'.
26. See Beate Julia Perrey, *Schumann's 'Dichterliebe' and Early Romantic Poetics: Fragmentation of Desire* (Cambridge, 2002).

27. Cf. Schäfer, *Modellfall Mahler*, pp. 144–5.
28. H. Pousseur, 'Schumann ist der Dichter. Fünfundzwanzig Momente einer Lektüre der *Dichterliebe*', in *Robert Schumann*, ed. Heinz-Klaus Metzger and Rainer Riehn, Musik-Konzepte, Sonderband 2 (Munich, 1982), pp. 3–128.
29. See the commentary by Peter Jost, 'Komponieren mit Schumann. Henri Pousseurs *Dichterliebesreigentraum*', *Musiktheorie*, 15 (2000), 121–36.
30. Pousseur, 'Schumann ist der Dichter', p. 4.
31. This term, 'composed interpretation' (*Komponierte Interpretation*), has originally been used by Hans Zender in his arrangement of Schubert's *Winterreise*.

13 Songs of dawn and dusk: coming to terms with the late music

JOHN DAVERIO

> In the history of art, late works are the catastrophes.
> THEODOR ADORNO 'BEETHOVEN'S LATE STYLE' (1934)

In his review of the 1888 première in Vienna of Brahms's 'Double' Concerto for violin, cello and orchestra, Op. 102, Eduard Hanslick concluded that, unfortunately, the work did not belong 'in the first rank' of his old friend's creations. The first movement in particular struck a sour note, seldom breaking free from 'its half-defiant, half-depressed mood, or from its A minor tonality. Daylight rarely shines through its many suspensions, syncopations, rhythmic jolts, and its augmented and diminished intervals. We are almost reminded of Schumann's late manner.'[1] In the 1880s, to ascribe the stylistic features of Schumann's 'late manner' to a musical work was tantamount to delivering the kiss of death, and despite the efforts of a small band of revisionists, received opinion of the music of Schumann's later years remains largely negative over a century later. Sounding a typical refrain, a reviewer of a 1978 recording of Schumann's Violin Concerto describes the slow movement of that work as music 'with so much insanity in its innards that it's frightening'.[2] Sympathetic critics, fearful that their remarks will be met with scepticism, feel compelled to go on the defensive. Joseph Kerman, for instance, prefaces his thoughtful remarks on the 'visionary' cadenza near the end of Schumann's *Concert-Allegro mit Introduction* for piano and orchestra, Op. 134, with the reminder that even though it is 'a late work, composed shortly before [Schumann's] commitment', it should 'by no means . . . be dismissed on that account'.[3]

Critical commentary on Schumann's late music – or on the late music of any composer, for that matter – is bound up with the larger topic of late style in general. According to one view, traceable to Winckelmann's *Geschichte der Kunst des Altertums* (1756–62) and later espoused by Hegel, lateness is synonymous with cultural decay or decline. An alternative outlook was adumbrated by Goethe, who lent a metaphysical flavour to the prevalent organicist notion of late style in his own late writings. As he famously (and cryptically) put it in his *Maximen und Reflexionen*, 'old age' is the 'gradual withdrawal from appearance', a conceit that would allow subsequent thinkers, including Thomas Mann and the cultural critic Georg Simmel, to view late style as the transcendence of time and place that great artists achieve at the end of their careers.[4] Many of the current theories of late style are themselves inherently dualistic. In his essays and fragments on Beethoven, Theodor Adorno claimed that the essence of the composer's late music lay in its unmediated polarization of bare 'monody' and dense 'polyphony'; of eccentric flights of fancy and conventional, formulaic gestures; of intense expression and cool detachment.[5] Troping on Adorno, Carl Dahlhaus has defined the concept of a composer's late work – a category he associates primarily with Bach, Beethoven and Liszt – as a configuration comprising both 'archaizing and modern elements'.[6] More recently, the composer Alexander Goehr has offered a sensitive definition of artistic lateness as an enigmatic blend of curtailment (the creator, in his final years, having 'jettisoned' some aspects of his earlier work) and 'syntactical complexity'.[7]

Evaluations of an artist's late works are obviously dependent on the spin given to the apparently negative elements – withdrawal, lack of mediation, eccentricity, archaism, curtailment – that inform all late styles to varying degrees. For Adorno, 'failure' to achieve aesthetic harmony becomes 'a yardstick of success',[8] a difficult conclusion to swallow unless one happens to share Adorno's unflinching dialectics. More to the point, there is no foolproof method to determine whether we are dealing with 'majestic weariness' (Mann's phrase) or exhaustion, compressed utterance or lack of invention, introspection or solipsism, spiritual fragmentation (to paraphrase Adorno) or incoherence.[9] The first term in each of these pairs is an emblem of transcendence, the second of decline. The former elements have been linked with the canon of 'great' late works of Goethe and Ibsen, Da Vinci and Picasso, Bach, Beethoven and Stravinsky; the latter qualities turn up with numbing regularity in descriptions of Schumann's late music. There seems to be a curious double standard at work here. While, for example, the transformed recurrence of a four-note motive in Beethoven's string quartets Opp. 130, 131 and 132 is viewed as a token of the inner unity of the composer's late œuvre, the similarities between the main idea of the slow movement of Schumann's Violin Concerto and the E flat major theme upon which he was writing variations in February 1854, just days before his suicide attempt, have been interpreted as a symptom of his waning powers of invention. Why the discrepancy?

Before addressing this question we should consider what in fact constitutes Schumann's late output. Nearly all commentators agree that the quite sizeable body of instrumental music dating from the year or so before he was remanded to the asylum in Endenich in March 1854 belongs in this category. Many writers also include the sacred music of 1852, the large-scale secular compositions for vocal and orchestral forces of 1851–3, the chamber works of 1851 and the orchestral music of 1850–1 – in short, nearly the whole of the substantial body of works composed during Schumann's tenure as Municipal Music Director in Düsseldorf. At the same time, it would be an error to take an arbitrary biographical marker, such as the Schumanns' move to Düsseldorf in September 1850, as the catalyst for a shift in stylistic orientation. Moreover, not all of Schumann's late works in the strict, chronological sense are 'late' from the point of view of aesthetics – a paradox they share with the music of Beethoven's final period.[10] The Cello Concerto, Op. 129, composed in October 1850, displays many of the features of late style: introspection, motivic and formal concentration, and textural transparency. In contrast, the 'Rhenish' Symphony, Op. 97, completed just a few months afterwards, bears relatively few of the signifiers of lateness, apart from the self-consciously archaic character of its penultimate movement.

Keeping these qualifications in mind, we may now consider some of the factors that have conspired to exclude so much of Schumann's later output from the canon. In the first place, a significant portion of this repertory has been adversely affected by decisive shifts in musical-institutional structure: specifically, by the decline of what might be called the 'choral culture' that nurtured a number of Schumann's late works. Although the (amateur) choral society is still alive and well in a number of American and European centres, the choral concert and the symphony orchestra concert have more or less gone their separate ways. In Schumann's day, this split had not yet occurred; the appearance of his Düsseldorf chorus and orchestra on the same programme was an expectation – not a special event. This, in turn, was the background against which Schumann conceived one of the more imposing projects of his last years: a cycle of four ballades for vocal and orchestral forces, all but the third loosely based on texts by Ludwig Uhland (*Der Königssohn*, Op. 116; *Des Sängers Fluch*, Op. 139; *Vom Pagen und der Königstochter*, Op. 140; and *Das Glück von Edenhall*, Op. 143). Of all the genres of nineteenth-century music, none has fared less well in the modern concert hall than those involving chorus and orchestra. The disappearance of Schumann's ballades and oratorios from the standard repertory is thus part of a larger trend.

Changes in the nature of musical institutions may also be linked with an important shift in nineteenth-century aesthetics, namely, the growing conviction that 'dramatic' modes of artistic expression were superior to their 'epic' cousins.[11] This trend has also exercised a negative impact on the reception of Schumann's later music, which, as a number of nineteenth-century writers observed, displayed an increasing affinity with the epic genres in form, content and character. 'As important as Schumann is in his lyric works', Adolf Schubring wrote in 1861, 'he is at his greatest in his epic works – not the effete religious epic but the modern, romantic one, which has found its proper form in the romance, ballade, legend, novella, novel, and *Märchen* [fairy tale]'.[12] The prominence of several of Schumann's late works for vocal and instrumental forces on Schubring's list of examples – the musical *Märchen* of 1851, *Der Rose Pilgerfahrt*, Op. 112 and two of the late ballades, *Der Königssohn* and *Vom Pagen und der Königstochter* – affirms the connection between choral culture and epic posture, a connection that has proven detrimental to the survival of these works on the concert stage.[13]

The reception of late Schumann is bound up with another aesthetic debate, this one a more purely musical affair: the conflict between the proponents of the progressive 'New German' school and their adversaries, which polarized German musical criticism in the second half of the nineteenth century. Schumann failed to appease either of these camps; too radical for the conservatives, he was seen by the New German faction as a deserter from the cause of musical progress. In a review of a concert held at the Leipzig Gewandhaus in 1856 and devoted to Schumann's later music, Richard Pohl claimed that Schumann 'acted contrary to his own inclinations' by aligning himself with 'the Mendelssohn school', the musical products of which 'border on weakness'. Furthermore, a number of works on the programme (including the *Adventlied* for chorus and orchestra, Op. 71; the 'Rhenish' Symphony; and the *Phantasie* for violin and orchestra, Op. 131) dated from 'the unfortunate master's most disagreeable period, a time when he had already overtaxed himself and succumbed to a morbid craving to produce'.[14] It is odd, to say the least, that Pohl would construe a perfectly natural desire – a composer's need to produce – as a pathological urge. And with this, we arrive at another theme in the negative reception of Schumann's late music: the relationship between creativity and illness.

Schumann is not the only composer whose late output has been viewed as a lapse into senility. Writing in 1914, the French critic Jean Chantovoine claimed that signs of Wagner's 'exhaustion and decrepitude' were clearly apparent in *Parsifal*.[15] Neither is he the only composer who spent the final years of his life in the throes of mental illness and physical decline; indeed, there are uncanny parallels between Schumann's tragic dénouement and that of Hugo Wolf. Yet neither Wagner's nor Wolf's posthumous reputations as artists have suffered to the same extent as Schumann's. In part this may be the result of Schumann's steady rate of production well into the period when the symptoms of his final illness began to emerge with alarming clarity. Given that he had weathered a number of depressive (and downright neurotic) spells much earlier in his career, it is tempting to view his entire output as an emblem of the madness that he managed to keep in check in the 1830s and 1840s but that spun hopelessly out of control in February 1854. At the same time, the dispassionate critic of Schumann's late music is faced with a paradox. Just as John Rosselli has written of the 'draining of Eros' from Mozart's late works,[16] so too can we recognize a draining of madness from Schumann's. There is little or nothing in his late music to compare with the quirky outbursts in earlier works such as *Carnaval*, the *Concert sans orchestre* or *Kreisleriana*. If lateness implies curtailment, then it is precisely the madcap element that Schumann purged from the music of his final period.

It should also be stressed that our understanding of Schumann's late music is in no way furthered by the sensational theories on the circumstances surrounding his final illness that have plagued Schumann biography almost since its inception. One of the more recent of these hypotheses appears in the writings of Eva Weissweiler – a noxious brew of innuendo, distorted facts and out-and-out fiction that has been transmitted in the English-language literature, albeit in modified form, by Eric Frederick Jensen. According to Weissweiler: Clara Schumann conspired to have her husband locked away in Franz Richarz's asylum in Endenich so that she would be free to pursue her career as a concert artist and her liaison with Brahms; while not actually 'mad' at the time of his commitment, Schumann was driven to that state by the horrible mistreatment he received at Richarz's clinic; finally, in a gesture of protest he committed suicide by self-starvation despite the attempts of his doctors to feed him by force.[17]

This twisted tale feeds directly into a mythic image of Schumann. The hapless pawn of a conniving wife and the defenceless victim of sadistic doctors, he appears here as a quixotic dreamer who, through a desperate act of Promethean defiance, manages to escape from the clutches of his foes. As a first step toward making an impartial assessment of Schumann's late creativity, it might be better to concede that he was neither Don Quixote nor Prometheus – but merely human, all too human.

The reception of Schumann's late music is a wide-ranging topic that cannot be addressed fully in a brief essay. The following comments, therefore, aim merely to trace some of the main strands in the reception of this repertory, focussing alternately on various types of 'receivers', including critics and scholars, creative artists and performers. While there is considerable overlap among these groups, examining them in turn will at least provide a framework for a subject that still remains fraught with controversy.

All of the leitmotifs of the traditional view of Schumann's late works were already present in the first major monograph on the composer, the 1858 biography of Joseph Wilhelm von Wasielewski, who had served briefly as the concertmaster of Schumann's Düsseldorf orchestra.[18] Wasielewski was hardly unsympathetic to Schumann's later creative efforts, calling attention, for example, to the 'rich fantasy' and 'depth of thought' in the larger chamber works of 1851: the sonatas for violin and piano in A minor, Op. 105 and D minor, Op. 121; and the Piano Trio in G minor, Op. 110. At the same time, Wasielewski felt that all three pieces projected a fundamentally 'gloomy mood' (*verdüsterte Stimmung*), and therefore bore traces of Schumann's 'physical indisposition'.[19] While he marvelled at Schumann's ability to continue producing compositions of significant scope, such as the *Missa sacra*, Op. 147, and *Requiem*, Op. 148, of 1852 and the *Faust* Overture of 1853, Wasielewski found these to be 'uneven' works that, despite their 'many isolated beauties', displayed an 'atrophy of formative power' (*Schwinden der Gestaltungskraft*) and a 'striking intellectual exhaustion' (*auffallende geistige Ermattung*). The less said about the late music the better, for 'Why should we tarnish the lofty image of the radiant master that we carry within us through a detailed analysis of creations that no longer attain to the high level of his earlier endeavours?'[20]

Among the pieces that Wasielewski passes over in silence is the Violin Concerto, composed in the autumn of 1853 as a vehicle for the twenty-two-year-old virtuoso Joseph Joachim. In light of the parallels that Wasielewski (and many subsequent writers) drew between Schumann's increasingly melancholy disposition and the affective quality of his later music, it is interesting to observe that for the composer himself the play of moods in the Violin Concerto was motivated by the character of the performer who inspired it. Informing Joachim of its completion in early October 1853, Schumann noted that the new work 'will perhaps suggest to you an image of a certain seriousness from behind which a cheerful mood often peeks out. While I was writing [the concerto], you were often present in my imagination, and this probably contributed to the mood of the work.'[21] Conceived in the spirit of the young violinist's motto, 'Frei aber einsam' ('Free but lonely'), the concerto eventually came to be viewed by Joachim as a portrait of Schumann's troubled psyche. Responding to Andreas Moser's request for information on the manuscript of the concerto in a letter of 5 August 1898, Joachim offered an assessment that echoes Wasielewski's critique of the late works as a whole point for point. Withheld from publication because it was 'not equal in rank to [Schumann's] many splendid creations',[22] the Violin Concerto displayed 'a certain unmistakable quality of exhaustion [*Ermattung*]'. While some passages, like the 'gentle' second theme of the first movement, were 'genuine Schumann', others, including much of the slow movement and the transition to the finale, gave way to 'sickly brooding' and 'dull reflection'. The last movement gets off to a promising start, but grows 'monotonous' with the elaboration of the main theme, generating 'tiresome repetitions' instead of 'joyful flights of fancy'.[23]

The rhetoric of fatigue in Joachim's letter resonates not only with Wasielewski, but with Hanslick, who reviewed a number of Schumann's late works during his long and auspicious career as a music critic. None of them comes off well. Invoking by now familiar phrases, Hanslick wrote of the 'already exhausted power of invention' in the *Julius Caesar* Overture, Op. 128, and of the 'martyr-like, gloomy and obstinate' character of the *Phantasie* for violin and orchestra. As for the choral-orchestral ballades, *Des Sängers Fluch* was 'feeble and laborious', *Vom Pagen und der Königstochter* 'sick and shadowy', and *Das Glück von Edenhall* 'tortured and dull', representing a clear descent into 'Indian summer'.[24] The same litany of adjectives recurs with the monotony attributed to the succession of ideas in Schumann's late music.

According to Michael Struck, the early reception of Schumann's late works was marked by a curious reversal. Initially viewed in a rather positive light, the late music became the object of critical censure with the increase in public awareness of Schumann's mental decline. Commenting on the *Phantasie* for violin and orchestra, Struck observes that the enthusiastic response to Joachim's première of the work in January 1854 (as one critic wrote: 'there are few compositions of this type that we would recommend with such utter conviction of their artistic value') gave way within only a few years to highly negative critiques (Pohl, for instance, noted its 'insignificance in terms of inner musical worth').[25] A similar change of heart is evident in reactions to the Violin Concerto; while Joachim and Clara Schumann were at first favourably disposed toward the work, they both began to voice doubts over its musical value as early as 1857.[26] The conclusion seems clear: thoughts of Schumann's final illness and death had a decidedly negative influence on the reception of his late works.

The situation, however, is somewhat more complicated. Even before Schumann's commitment, some of his later works were criticized for their 'gloominess' (the opera *Genoveva*) and lack of invention (the A minor Violin Sonata)[27] – features that were subsequently ascribed to his deteriorating physical and mental state. On the other hand, the reviews of Schumann's late works that appeared soon after his death were not unremittingly negative. In a lengthy critique of his choral-orchestral ballades, Peter Lohmann maintained that these works, despite their shortcomings, represented 'the spiritual highpoint of Schumann's productivity'.[28] Likewise, Selmar Bagge, in an appreciative though not uncritical review of the *Missa sacra*, praised Schumann for having 'grasped the essence of genuine old church music' and 'translated' it into 'the language of modern music'.[29]

In any event, the positive voices were clearly in the minority. By the late nineteenth and early twentieth centuries, Schumann's late music had more or less disappeared from the critical radar screen, many writers assuming, like Wasielewski, that the best approach was to ignore it.[30] Others simply repeated the old mantras, many of which have proven to be remarkably resilient. Invoking the widespread notion that Schumann's late works were autobiographical statements of his depressive condition, Walter Dahms described the *Gesänge der Frühe* in his 1916 biography of Schumann as pieces reflecting 'the hoar-frost of resignation, that can no longer rejoice at the longed-for sun, but must rather dry the tears of night secretively and greet the daylight with forced composure'.[31] Though lacking the purple prose of Dahms's description, Kathleen Dale's account of the same piano pieces also treads over well-worn ground, criticizing Schumann's 'inert' part-writing, 'frequently awkward and ineffective' textures and 'greatly disorganized' harmonic schemes.[32] And while Charles Rosen concedes that the first of the *Gesänge der Frühe* is one of the 'undeniable masterly successes' of Schumann's last period, he concludes that 'recent attempts to re-evaluate [Schumann's] late works' and 'the orthodox judgment that there was a falling off in the last decade' are 'both correct'. In Rosen's opinion, the chief technical flaw of the late music has to do with Schumann's difficulty in 'sustaining momentum' – in other words, with the 'exhaustion' that many writers before him associated with Schumann's late style.[33]

The attempts at re-evaluation to which Rosen refers did not get into full swing until the early 1980s, though the initial stirrings of a revisionist movement occurred somewhat earlier. Commenting on the recently unearthed Violin Concerto in a letter of 25 September 1937 to *The Times* of London, Tovey wrote that, popular opinion notwithstanding, 'there is nothing morbid about any elements of Schumann's latest style. On the contrary, if we look for morbid elements we shall find them where we least wish to cavil, in the best-loved early works...'.[34] Implicit in these remarks is a critical attitude that refuses to recognize a necessary connection between Schumann's musical productivity and his psychological state, an attitude that also underlay the sporadic attempts at a critical reappraisal of the late works during the mid twentieth century. Focussing their attention on the musical substance of these pieces, revisionist critics stressed two factors: the motivic economy of Schumann's late style, and its prefiguration of subsequent developments in the musical language of the nineteenth century. Both factors were underscored in an important article published in 1957 by Harold Truscott, who traced the growth of long-breathed, lyrical paragraphs from taut motivic gestures in a number of the instrumental works of 1853 (the *Faust* Overture, the *Concert-Allegro* for piano and orchestra and the Violin Concerto), concluding that these compositions represent 'studies for something that was to come'.[35] The progressive thrust of Schumann's late works was also a leading theme in two essays published in 1981 by Helmuth Hopf and Norbert Nagler, who argued that this music points not only to the sonorous world of Bruckner and the harmonic experiments of Liszt and Reger, but even to the radical products of the Second Viennese School.[36]

The most probing inquiries into the nature of Schumann's late style, however, were undertaken in the mid 1980s by Michael Struck and Reinhard

Kapp. Though approaching the issue from rather different angles, both scholars agree that the putative decline in quality in the music of Schumann's later years is nothing more than a myth.[37] Proceeding from a close analysis of the instrumental works of 1853, Struck argues that Schumann's late style was a logical outgrowth of the 'poetic' tendencies of his earlier music, both with regard to its varied affective palette and its exploitation of subtle thematic relationships. According to Struck, Schumann's final illness does not represent the 'hidden meaning' of the late music, but should rather be viewed as the stroke of fate that brought his productivity to an abrupt halt. In a stunning reversal of received opinion, Kapp sees Schumann's late style as the apex of his artistic development, the culminating phase in a process of objectification that led him to exchange the hyper-expressivity of the lyric genres for the sober detachment of the epic mode. For Kapp, Schumann's last creative period was a time of intense exploration – of the outer limits of diatonicism, of the mystical powers of sheer sonority, and of the potential of the tiniest motive for infinite elaboration (Kapp's single-paragraph, twenty-three-page analysis of the motivic relations in the orchestral exposition of the first movement of the Violin Concerto is a strong candidate for mention in the *Guinness Book of Records*).[38] A number of the points raised by Struck and Kapp have been developed further in monographs by Irmgard Knechtges and Gerhard Dietel on the 'poetic' character of the late keyboard music, and in Markus Waldura's study of 'monomotivicism' in Schumann's sonata forms.[39] To round out this admittedly incomplete sketch of the revisionist literature, mention should also be made of Dagmar Hoffmann-Axthelm's reading of the Violin Concerto – a rather more sophisticated exercise in psycho-criticism than earlier efforts along similar lines. Interpreting the work as a 'mirror of a highly endangered psyche', Hoffmann-Axthelm emphasizes that in order to give artistic expression to psychic anguish, one must be in command of one's senses.[40]

For the revisionists, Schumann's music embodies the entire complex of features that have been associated, at one time or another, with the 'great' late styles of Beethoven and other creative artists. From the revisionist perspective, the monomotivicism of Schumann's late sonata-form movements is a marker of brevity and concision; the intimations of future developments in harmony and sonority in the late instrumental music are signifiers of incipient modernity; Schumann's adoption of an 'epic' stance in the ballades for chorus and orchestra speaks to a process of objectification; and, finally, the visionary, 'poetic' quality of the late music is an emblem of transcendence.

What remains to be studied more closely is the dialectical interaction of these elements. Consider, for instance, the first of the five pieces assembled in the *Gesänge der Frühe*. Conceived as an evocation of the chorale style, it opens – to borrow Adorno's terms – by juxtaposing 'monody' (a two-bar

Example 13.1 Schumann, *Gesänge der Frühe*, no. 1, bars 1–9

gesture presented in bare octaves) with 'polyphony' (the block-chordal harmonization of the gesture's continuation: see Ex. 13.1). The archaic character of the texture, however, is belied by the 'modern' flavour of the harmonies, especially in bars 6–8, where Schumann decorates an underlying progression in parallel fifths with 2–3 suspensions, passing tones and neighbour notes in the inner voices that together produce a succession of parallel seconds between the upper two parts. Adding to the conflict is the dissociation of the 'tenor' from the other voices: the F sharp and E in bars 6 and 7, respectively, arrive one beat too soon, thereby anticipating the harmony on the downbeats of the following bars. The resultant clash with the passing tones in the upper parts creates a blurring effect, an imitation of the overlapping of discrete sonorous units in a vast, reverberant space. But even when performed in the concert hall, the piece conjures up the atmosphere of the most intimate of spaces: the bourgeois music room or salon. Finally, an analyst of motivic relationships would have little trouble in showing how the entire thirty-nine-bar composition evolves from its initial four-bar gesture. Yet in a sense the piece is not developmental at all, consisting rather of a series of free variations on a chorale-like phrase. Opening *pianissimo*, it builds toward a climax (at bar 27) of intense expression, only to fade away into nothingness. Future critics of Schumann's music might well give some thought to unriddling the meaning of the polarities – between archaic and modern, vastness and intimacy, development and stasis, detachment and expressivity – that inform not only the first of the *Gesänge der Frühe* but the late music as a whole.

Needless to say, it is impossible to prove the aesthetic worth of Schumann's late music. Even the most painstaking motivic analysis will not convince the sceptical listener that what he or she hears as lack of invention is in fact a manifestation of the compressed utterance that characterizes most late styles. In other words, evaluations of Schumann's late works are very much dependent on the personal taste of the beholder. Without question, however, this music has inspired some of the more discerning members of the community of listeners – beginning perhaps with Johannes Brahms.

In a letter of January 1873 to Friedrich Heimsoeth, Brahms wrote: 'The memory of Schumann is sacred to me. That noble, pure artist has constantly been my model.'[41] While the significance of Schumann's earlier music for Brahms's development has been widely acknowledged,[42] the controversial late works were equally as important for the evolution of the younger composer's creative sensibility. Predictably enough for this most taciturn of nineteenth-century composers, Brahms's documented comments on the music of Schumann's final years are few and not especially revealing. One remark, however, made in response to a question about Schumann's output in general, is more suggestive than it at first seems. When asked late in his life what he learned from Schumann, Brahms is supposed to have replied: 'Nothing, apart from how to play chess.'[43] With this typically ironic rejoinder, Brahms was saying that Schumann (or rather, his music) had taught him quite a bit about compositional strategy. Compelling evidence for the truth of the claim can be found in Schumann's late music.

One strategy that Brahms derived from late Schumann – or at least refined through his study of the late music – involves sonata form. In a series of recently published articles, Peter Smith has provided a convincing rationale for one of Brahms's more notable deviations from conventional sonata-form paradigms, namely, his tendency to blur the interface between development and recapitulation, both by prolonging harmonic instability well past the reprise of the main theme, and by presenting that theme in augmented note values. Having withheld the moment of definitive return from its expected location, Brahms generally reserves it for a later point in the form, thus creating what Smith calls a 'continuous linear evolution' from one end of a movement to the other, a process exemplified in the opening movements of the String Quartet in C minor, Op. 51, No. 1; the Cello Sonata in F, Op. 99; and the Fourth Symphony, Op. 98.[44] Brahms would have found ample precedent for this strategy in Schumann's later sonata-form movements, many of which also undercut the articulative force of the thematic return at the point of reprise by coupling it with an unstable harmony.[45] Schumann's merger of developmental and recapitulatory functions in the first movement of the Violin Sonata in A minor is particularly noteworthy, for here we find firmly in place all of the markers that distinguish Brahms's

279 *Songs of dawn and dusk: the late music*

Example 13.2 Schumann, Sonata for piano and violin in A minor (Op. 105), first movement, bars 108–15

approach to the technique: the gradual dismantling, through repetition, of a motivic fragment from the first theme (bars 108–9), the return of the first theme over unstable harmony (the tonic chord in first inversion: bar 110) and rhythmic augmentation (bars 110–13, 113–15: see Ex. 13.2). The suppression of clearcut articulation at this juncture makes the assertion of tonic harmony at the very end of the movement all the more powerful, imparting to the design that 'continuous linear evolution' that Smith observed in Brahms's sonata forms.

Another area of elective affinity with Brahms can be detected in Schumann's works for instrumental soloists and orchestra. Apart from a number of unfinished youthful projects, a concerto movement in D minor, and the well-known Piano Concerto in A minor, Op. 54 (1841/45), most of Schumann's *concertante* works were clustered in the last four years of his creative life: the *Concertstück* for four horns and orchestra, Op. 86 and the *Introduction und Allegro appassionata* for piano and orchestra, Op. 92, both composed in 1849; the Cello Concerto of 1850; and the *Phantasie* for violin and orchestra, the *Concert-Allegro with Introduction* for piano and orchestra and the Violin Concerto, all dating from 1853. The last three of these pieces must have had especially personal connotations for Brahms, calling up memories of the heady days in the autumn of 1853 when he first entered the Schumann circle. Indeed, his arrival in Düsseldorf on 30 September nearly coincided with Schumann's completion of the Violin Concerto. Moreover, he was almost surely on hand when Joachim read through the concerto and performed the *Phantasie* with the Hannover court orchestra in late January 1854. If the pieces for violin and orchestra 'belonged' to Joachim, there was a sense in which Brahms could call the *Concert-Allegro* his own: during a visit to the ailing composer at Endenich in January 1855, he received the dedication of the work, a gesture he cherished deeply. In his letter of thanks to Schumann, dated 30 January 1855, Brahms reported that he and Joachim had often discussed the *Phantasie* and the *Concert-Allegro*, attempting to determine 'which might be our favorite' – though without being able to decide.[46] Twenty years later, he and Joachim collaborated on a performance of the *Phantasie* during Brahms's last season as director of the concerts of the Gesellschaft der Musikfreunde in Vienna, and it is difficult to imagine that piety alone led him to encourage Joachim to play the same work for the 1880 concert in commemoration of the unveiling of the Schumann monument in Bonn.[47]

In all of his works for soloists and orchestra, Schumann confronted a problem he had articulated in an 1839 review-essay, namely, the need for the serious concerto composer to mediate between technical brilliance, on the one hand, and musical substance, on the other. While conceding that 'the opportunity for flashy display . . . should not be excluded from a concerto', Schumann nonetheless gave the final word to '*Music*, [which] should stand above everything else'. This attitude extended to every aspect of the *concertante* genres, including 'the old cadenza', which 'now rests on much sounder principles, and might even be put to good use today'.[48] Not surprisingly, Schumann's efforts to allow the soloist sufficient scope for display without compromising the aesthetic integrity of the whole are clearly evident in the cadenzas and cadenza-like passages of his *concertante* works. The written-out cadenza toward the end of the first movement of the Piano Concerto, for instance, is less a site of virtuosic exhibitionism than a protracted moment of reflection on the thematic ideas presented earlier in the design. Schumann's desire to integrate the cadenza into the ongoing

281 Songs of dawn and dusk: the late music

Example 13.3a Brahms, 'Double' Concerto, first movement, bars 5–7

Example 13.3b Schumann, Cello Concerto, first movement, bars 5–8

argument is equally prominent in his late *concertante* works. In the Cello Concerto, this tendency emerges in the impassioned recitative for soloist and orchestra that links the second and third movements, and in the ruminative accompanied cadenza of the finale. If the terminal cadenza in the *Phantasie* for violin and orchestra attempts a rapprochement between the style of a Paganini caprice and that of a Bach sonata *senza basso*, its counterpart in the *Concert-Allegro*, to quote Kerman, functions as 'a vision of Utopia',[49] a dreamy rhapsody on the work's lyrical second theme.

These lessons were not lost on Brahms. But whereas, for Schumann, the 'old cadenza' provided the opportunity for reflection on past events, in Brahms's hands it became an agency of premonition, or even of presentation. The Second Piano Concerto, Op. 83, for instance, opens with a wistful exchange between orchestra and soloist, and a brief but urgent cadenza that fulfils two related functions: the introduction of a dotted motive that will have a long and fruitful career in the subsequent discourse, and preparation for the orchestral exposition proper. Similarly, Brahms fashioned a double cycle of orchestral calls and soloistic responses in the first movement of the 'Double' Concerto as a means of introducing *two* soloists. While the cello's recitative-like response to the orchestra's emphatic call elaborates the head-motif of what will become the movement's first theme, the violin takes off from an arching gesture that spans the centre of the second theme. As if to confirm that the initial paragraphs of this movement were conceived in the spirit of Schumann, Brahms distantly echoes an affective gesture from the latter's Cello Concerto in the first of the two recitative-cadenzas, the cello opening with an oblique reference to the dip into the nether regions that lends a sombre hue to the first theme of Schumann's work (cf. Exx. 13.3a and b).

The parallels between Schumann's and Brahms's violin concertos are even more explicit, demonstrating that even if Brahms may have considered his mentor's last work for soloist and orchestra to be flawed in some way, he was still able to learn something from it.[50] Schumann introduces the violin in the first movement of his concerto in an altogether striking manner. After opening with a bravura variant of the main theme in sonorous quadruple and triple stops, the solo violin proceeds with a declamatory passage that leads to a powerful statement of the main theme, now at its original pitch level. This series of events may well have been the template for the corresponding passage in the first movement of Brahms's concerto, where the soloist enters with a rhapsodic, minor-mode variation of the head-motif of the main theme, engages in a heated, recitative-like exchange with the orchestra, and then, after a long passage of ornamental filigree, presents the main theme in something more closely akin to its original form. It was probably parallelisms of this kind that led Yehudi Menuhin to describe Schumann's concerto as 'the historically missing link of the violin literature' and 'the bridge between the Beethoven and the Brahms concertos, though leaning more toward Brahms'.[51]

With Schumann's Violin Concerto, we arrive at a work that both refutes and confirms one of Dahlhaus's observations on late works in general. Noting the 'gap' between the time when they were written and the age during which they were assimilated, Dahlhaus concludes that 'their afterhistory is discontinuous'.[52] If the impact of Schumann's Violin Concerto on Brahms was more or less immediate, there is no denying that the piece was not absorbed into concert life until nearly a century after it was composed – a process in which Menuhin, quoted above, played a leading role. Having received a photocopy of the autograph early in 1937 from Wilhelm Strecker, then the editor-in-chief at Schott-Verlag, he was invited by the publishing firm to première the concerto later in that year. Political circumstances, however, prevented him from garnering that distinction. Displeased that the world première might be given by a foreigner, let alone a Jew, the authorities at the Nazi Reichskulturkammer, headed by the propaganda minister Joseph Goebbels, arranged a first performance with the German violinist Georg Kulenkampff, and Karl Böhm leading the Berlin Philharmonic on 26 November 1937. Menuhin, therefore, had to settle for the American première(s): with piano on 6 December 1937 in New York, and with orchestra (the St Louis Symphony under Vladimir Golschmann) on 23 December of the same year.[53]

Schumann's Violin Concerto assumes two rather different forms in the renderings of Kulenkampff and Menuhin. A far cry from Schumann's original, the violin part that Kulenkampff played was a highly doctored arrangement prepared by Hindemith (a fact left unmentioned at the time of the German première). No doubt this adaptation was made in response to a still prevalent myth, according to which a significant portion of the original

Example 13.4a Schumann, Violin Concerto, first movement, bars 117–19 (autograph, Staatsbibliothek zu Berlin, Mus. ms. autogr. 22)

Example 13.4b Schumann, Violin Concerto, first movement, bars 117–19 (copy, Staatsbibliothek zu Berlin, Mus. ms. autogr. 22)

Example 13.4c Schumann, Violin Concerto, first movement, bars 117–19 (from Gustav Lenzewski's arrangement of the violin part in Georg Schünemann's *Klavierauszug*, Schott 1937)

solo part is either unplayable or poorly conceived for the instrument, thus reflecting Schumann's imperfect grasp of violin technique. An influential source for this view lies within the Schumann circle itself: in his 1898 letter to Moser, Joachim claimed that both the first and last movements of the Violin Concerto contained many passages that were 'difficult to play [*schwer spielbar*] without being effective [*wirkungsvoll*]'.[54]

Joachim's criticism is a lame one. In fact, there are only two brief passages in the first movement – comprising a total of four bars – that are genuinely impracticable from a technical point of view: bars 117–19 in the solo exposition and the analogous spot, bars 306–8, in the recapitulation. Since the problem is essentially the same in both instances, we will focus briefly on the passage in the exposition. Elaborating the lyrical second theme in double stops, the soloist is required to play both the sustained melody and an accompaniment in undulating semiquavers – a device that would have been familiar to Schumann from Paganini's Caprice No. 6 and the slow movement of Mendelssohn's Violin Concerto. The realization of this effect, however, obviously caused him some difficulty, as will be apparent from a look at the versions of the passage as transmitted in the autograph (see Ex. 13.4a) and the professionally prepared copies of the violin–piano arrangement and score, which include emendations to the solo part in Schumann's hand (see Ex. 13.4b).[55] The problem in the autograph version comes on the first beats of bars 117 and 119, where the simultaneous rendering of melody and accompaniment necessitates a painful stretch between the third finger, on

Bb′ and the fourth, on G″. The emended version, as entered into the copies, is even less successful, though now the technical difficulties occur on the middle beats of bars 117 and 119. While perfect fifths on the violin should generally be taken with the same finger, here, in order to accommodate the upper note and measured *tremolando* figuration, the fifth between D‴ and G″ must be played with the fourth and third fingers respectively, forcing the left hand into a claw-like shape in which it is nearly impossible to play in tune. But again, it should be emphasized that these measures and their analogues in the recapitulation are the *only* passages in the concerto that approach unplayability. Otherwise, Schumann usually demands much less of the soloist than Brahms does in his concerto, not to mention Tchaikovsky or Sibelius in theirs. Moreover, we can assume that if Schumann had seen the concerto through to performance and publication, he would have arrived at a more grateful solution. The one supplied by Gustav Lenzewski in Georg Schünemann's 1937 edition of the concerto (in violin–piano arrangement) is perfectly acceptable (see Ex. 13.4c).[56]

Hindemith's adaptation extended far past the brief passages we have just considered. In an attempt to make the violin part at once more brilliant and more easily playable, he transposed entire melodies and/or portions thereof up one and sometimes two octaves, added double stops, chords, trills and other ornaments, and in some cases – especially in the finale – replaced Schumann's original passagework with entirely new material. The result, of course, represents an extreme departure from the original conception, often transforming Schumann's mellow alto into a *coloratura* soprano, and forcing his sometimes quirky figuration into the straitjacket of considerably less interesting patterns. Alterations in the technical domain frequently obscure the musical logic of the original as well. At the soloist's entrance in the first movement, for example, Hindemith takes the melodic line up to a high F‴, thus pre-empting the effectiveness of the moment about twenty bars later where Schumann's violin part catapults to the same pitch (cf. Exx. 13.5a–c). Likewise, Hindemith's version of the passage beginning from bar 275 of the finale – a wholesale rewrite involving octave transposition and the elimination of repeated notes, double stops and double-stop trills – sacrifices the idiosyncratic bravura of the original for a tamer gesture that destroys the falling curve of the melodic line.[57]

In a letter written soon after he received a photocopy of the autograph of Schumann's concerto, Menuhin allowed that anyone 'who realizes the greatness of the work' was free to play it, but insisted that 'it must, *it must*, remain pure *Schumann*, exactly as it left the hands and soul of the great master, no hyphens, no mutilations'.[58] Although Menuhin's live and recorded performances of the concerto were far closer to what Schumann had in mind than Kulenkampff's, they did not present the work 'exactly as it left the hands'

Example 13.5a Schumann, Violin Concerto, first movement, bars 54–8 (Hindemith's version)

Example 13.5b Schumann, Violin Concerto, first movement, bars 54–8 (autograph)

Example 13.5c Schumann, Violin Concerto, first movement, bars 78–9 (autograph)

of the composer. Taking the autograph as his point of departure, Menuhin did not incorporate into his reading the revisions that Schumann entered into the copies, presumably in response to Joachim's trial run(s) with the Hannover court orchestra in January 1854.[59] At the same time, to strive for an absolutely 'pure' reading of the concerto is tantamount to chasing after a will-o'-the-wisp. While the text of the work was nearly fixed at the time of Schumann's death, the chances are that he would have continued to make minor adjustments in response to the performances that failed to materialize during his lifetime. In any event, one thing is certain: Menuhin's championing of the concerto in what he believed to be the *Fassung letzter Hand* had a profound effect on the reception of the work in the second half of the twentieth century. Of the many instrumental works composed during the last years of Schumann's creative life, the Violin Concerto is one of the very few that has carved out a niche for itself in contemporary concert life. In the decades after Menuhin introduced the concerto to American audiences, major artists such as Henryk Szeryng and David Oistrakh added it to their repertoires, and since then it has become an attractive vehicle for interpreters including Ulf Hoelscher, Gidon Kremer and Joshua Bell.[60]

Sharing his enthusiasm for Schumann's Violin Concerto with Vladimir Golschmann in a letter of 22 July 1937, Menuhin wrote: 'Here is a score as romantic, heroic, supplicating, and tender as when it was not yet dry.'[61] Light years removed from the references to exhaustion and waning creativity in much of the previous literature on Schumann's late works, the rhetoric of Menuhin's assessment is apt to strike us as overblown. Yet one of the more remarkable aspects of Schumann's late music is its power to evoke similarly passionate reactions from a small though dedicated band of performers. Commenting on the late violin music, Gidon Kremer has observed that its 'naked ideas or naked impulses are so brilliant that they are sometimes more powerful than the most carefully composed piece of music by Brahms'. For the cellist Steven Isserlis, 'those who criticise [the Cello Concerto] have simply failed to understand that it takes us deeper into the inner life of its creator than virtually any other concerto (for any instrument)'. Similarly, Andras Schiff, who attributes his interest in late Schumann to the Swiss composer Heinz Holliger, has described Schumann's last major creative effort – the Variations on a Theme in E flat for piano – as 'one of the most moving documents in music'.[62] Currently engaged in recording Schumann's complete Lieder on the Hyperion label, the collaborative pianist Graham Johnson is more circumspect. Uncertain whether Schumann 'is attempting to lead us to a magical place as yet undreamed-of, or if he is merely a confused guide taking us down the garden path', Johnson arrives at an eminently sensible conclusion: 'Much of the responsibility lies with the performer.'[63]

To a large extent, the afterlife of musical artworks is sustained by those who have no professional stake in attending concerts, reading concert reviews, buying CDs and enjoying music at their leisure in the privacy of their homes, either as players or listeners – that is, by amateurs. An amateur in the best sense of the word, at least when it came to Schumann, the French critic Roland Barthes offered a suggestive comment on one of Schumann's late works in an unlikely place: a series of vignettes on photography collectively entitled *Camera Lucida*. Eager to explain the profound effect of a photo of his deceased mother taken when she was only a child, Barthes compares the faded snapshot to the first of Schumann's *Gesänge der Frühe*, which for him embodies both his 'mother's being' (described earlier in the book as the 'assertion of a gentleness') and his 'grief at her death'.[64] Insistent gentleness and grief: the qualities of Schumann's character piece are also inscribed in the photo of the author's mother. The remainder of Barthes's book (roughly half of its 120 pages) comprises a meditation on this 'winter garden' photo (so named because it was taken in a glassed-in conservatory) and what it reveals about the essence of photography. For Barthes, the photographic portrait is an emblem of the fragility of human relationships (leading him to realize that 'it is love-as-treasure which is going to disappear forever')[65] – and, even more importantly, a powerful reminder of the viewer's own mortality. 'Photography is a certain but fugitive testimony', Barthes writes, that 'by giving me the absolute past of the pose . . . tells me death in the future'.[66]

Barthes's observations on the ambiguous essence of the photograph have something significant to tell us about Schumann's *Gesänge der Frühe* – and, by extension, about his entire late œuvre as well. Often translated as 'morning' or 'dawn', *Frühe* was a rather more ambivalent concept for Schumann, a designation for the shadowy realm between darkness and light, resignation and hope, death and rebirth. As he put it to the publisher Friedrich Arnold in a letter of February 1854, the *Gesänge der Frühe* 'portray the sensations engendered by the approach and gradual emergence of morning, more from the perspective of an expression of feelings than of tone-painting'.[67] Poised between dawn and dusk, the *Gesänge der Frühe*, like the winter garden photo in Barthes's *Camera Lucida*, bring us face to face with our own death. And it is probably for this reason, the insight of an amateur, that Schumann's late music will continue both to allure and to disturb for some time to come.

Notes

1. Eduard Hanslick, *Aus dem Tagebuche eines Musikers. Der 'Modernen Oper' VI. Theil* (Berlin, 1892), p. 266.
2. Thomas Rübenacker, review of Schumann, Violin Concerto in D minor, performed by Susanne Lautenbacher and the Orchestra of Radio Luxembourg, Cond. Pierre Cao (reissued in *Schumann: Complete Works for Solo Instrument and Orchestra*, VoxBox CDX5027, 1991), in *HiFi Stereophonie Schallplattenkritik* 1978, p. 112; quoted in Michael Struck, *Die umstrittenen späten Instrumentalwerke Schumanns*, Hamburger Beiträge zur Musikwissenschaft, 29 (Hamburg, 1984), p. 366.
3. Joseph Kerman, *Concerto Conversations* (Cambridge, MA and London, 1999), p. 77.
4. For a lucid exposition of these points of view and their bearing on the reception of Wagner's final music drama, see Anthony Barone, 'Richard Wagner's *Parsifal* and the theory of late style', *Cambridge Opera Journal* 7/1 (1995), 37–54.
5. Unresolved dualism is a recurrent theme in the comments on late style that Adorno intended to flesh out in his projected (but never completed) book on Beethoven. All of the preliminary materials for the study have been published as: Theodor Adorno, *Beethoven: The Philosophy of Music*, ed. Rolf Tiedemann, trans. Edmund Jephcott (Stanford, CA, 1998). See especially 'Beethoven's late style', a brief essay written in 1934 (pp. 123–6), the 1966 radio talk with the same title (pp. 186–93), and the 1957 essay 'The alienated *magnum opus*: On the *Missa solemnis*' (pp. 141–53).
6. Carl Dahlhaus, *Ludwig van Beethoven: Approaches to His Music*, trans. Mary Whittall (Oxford, 1991; originally published as *Beethoven und seine Zeit* (Laaber, 1987)), p. 219.
7. Alexander Goehr, 'The ages of man as composer: what's left to be done?', *Musical Times*, 140 (summer 1999),19.
8. Adorno, 'The alienated *Magnum Opus*', p. 152.

9. See Thomas Mann, 'The sorrows and grandeur of Richard Wagner' [1933], in Mann, *Pro and Contra Wagner*, trans. Allan Blunden (Chicago, 1985), p. 95; and Adorno, *Beethoven: The Philosophy of Music*, p. 189.
10. According to Adorno, the first movement and *Scherzo* of the Ninth Symphony, for instance, were essentially 'middle-period' Beethoven. See Adorno, 'Beethoven's late style', p. 192.
11. For an account of drama's displacement of the epic as the 'highest' of the poetic genres – a process that can be traced through the critical writings of A. W. Schlegel, Novalis, Hegel, Wagner, Victor Hugo and James Joyce – see Gérard Gennette, *The Architext: An Introduction*, trans. Jane E. Lewin (Berkeley and Los Angeles, 1992; originally published as *Introduction à l'architexte* (Paris, 1979)), pp. 41–4.
12. Adolf Schubring, 'Schumanniana No. 4: the present musical epoch and Robert Schumann's position in music history', trans. John Michael Cooper, in *Schumann and His World*, ed. R. Larry Todd (Princeton, 1994), p. 1.
13. Further nineteenth-century accounts of the epic quality of Schumann's late music include: Franz Liszt, 'Robert Schumann' (1855), trans. John Michael Cooper, in *Schumann and His World*, p. 350; and Peter Lohmann's review of the four choral-orchestral ballades, in *Neue Zeitschrift für Musik* (hereafter *NZfM*), 53 (1860), 4–5, 9–11, 17–18, 26–8.
14. *NZfM*, 45 (31 October 1856), 198–200. Writing here under the pen-name 'Hoplit', Pohl had collaborated with Schumann a few years before on the text of *Des Sängers Fluch*.
15. See Barone, 'Richard Wagner's *Parsifal*', p. 53.
16. John Rosselli, *The Life of Mozart* (Cambridge, 1998), p. 137.
17. See Eva Weissweiler, 'Nachtasyl eines Komponisten: Robert Schumanns letzte Lebensjahre in der psychiatrischen Klinik Bonn-Endenich', *Frankfurter allgemeine Zeitung für Deutschland* (1 February 1986, No. 27/5D, *Bilder und Zeiten* section), p. 4; and *Clara Schumann: Eine Biographie* (Hamburg, 1990), pp. 303–41. See also Eric Frederick Jensen, 'Schumann at Endenich: buried alive', *Musical Times*, 139 (March 1998), 10–18; and *Musical Times*, 139 (April 1998), 14–23. Jensen echoes Weissweiler's account on matters including Clara's desire to resume her concert career, her lack of interest in her husband's condition, the debilitating effects of Richarz's therapeutic methods, and Schumann's hunger strike.
Presented without clear references to the pertinent documents, Weissweiler's 'findings' have been widely dismissed by scholars in Germany and the United States. See the reviews of her biography of Clara Schumann by Dietz-Rüdiger Moser, in *NZfM*, 152 (1991), 27–9; Joachim Draheim, in *Musica*, 46 (1992), 48–9; and Friederike Becker, in *Musiktheorie* 8/1 (1993), 74–7. See also Nancy Reich, '"Kunst, Kinder, und Freunde": recent publications on Clara Schumann (Part 2)', *American Brahms Society Newsletter*, 17/2 (Autumn 1999), 5.
On the basis of Richarz's medical diary, excerpts from which were first published during the late 1990s, we can be all but certain that Schumann suffered from syphilis. This, together with severe depression, was the cause of the disintegration of mental and physical powers that culminated in his death on 29 July 1856. See Franz Hermann Franken, 'Robert Schumann in der Irrenanstalt Endenich', in *Robert Schumanns letzte Lebensjahre: Protokoll einer Krankheit; Archiv Blätter 1* of the Stiftung Archiv der Akademie der Künste, Berlin (Berlin, March 1994), entry of 12 September 1855, p. 21.
18. Joseph Wilhelm von Wasielewski, *Robert Schumann* (Dresden, 1858). Future citations are from the fourth, expanded edition, ed. Waldemar von Wasielewski (Leipzig, 1906).
19. *Ibid.*, p. 469.
20. *Ibid.*, p. 476.
21. Letter of 7 October 1853 from Schumann to Joachim, in Johannes Joachim and Andreas Moser, eds., *Briefe von und an Joseph Joachim*, 3 vols. (Berlin, 1911–13), vol. I, p. 84.
22. The decision not to include the Violin Concerto in the *Gesamtausgabe* of Schumann's works was probably made jointly by Joachim, Clara Schumann and Brahms in the mid 1880s. See Michael Struck, *Robert Schumann: Violinkonzert D-moll (WoO 23)* (Munich, 1988), p. 19.
23. Joachim and Moser, eds., *Briefe von und an Joachim*, vol. III, pp. 486–8.
24. See *Hanslick's Music Criticisms*, trans. and ed. Henry Pleasants (New York, 1988), p. 80; Eduard Hanslick, *Am Ende des Jahrhunderts. Der 'Modernen Oper' VIII. Teil* (Berlin, 1898), p. 256; Hanslick, *Concerte, Componisten und Virtuosen der letzten fünfzehn Jahre, 1870–1885* (Berlin, 1886), p. 74; and Hanslick, *Aus dem Concert-Saal: Kritiken und Schilderungen aus den letzten 20 Jahren des Wiener Musiklebens* (Vienna, 1870), pp. 200, 347. The choral-orchestral ballades also receive harsh criticism in Dietrich Fischer-Dieskau, *Robert Schumann – Words and Music: The Vocal Compositions*, trans. Reinhard Pauly (Portland, OR, 1988; originally published as *Robert Schumann: Wort und Musik – Das Vokalwerk* (Stuttgart, 1981)), pp. 197, 209.

25. Cf. the unsigned review of the première in *NZfM*, 40 (20 January 1854), 42, and Richard Pohl's review in *NZfM*, 45 (31 October 1856), 199. See also Struck's commentary in *Robert Schumann: Violinkonzert*, p. 17.

26. See in particular Clara's letter to Joachim of 27 November 1857: 'Recently I was reminded of how bitter it is when a blemish is found on something that one loves above all. This will help to explain my tears . . . over Robert's [Violin] Concerto. Have you given any thought to [revising] the last movement?' Joachim and Moser, eds., *Briefe von und an Joseph Joachim*, vol. I, p. 465.

Apparently, Joachim did not undertake this task. See Struck, *Robert Schumann: Violinkonzert*, pp. 14–16.

27. See Eduard Krüger's review of *Genoveva* in *NZfM*, 34 (28 March 1851), 129, and Theodor Uhlig's review of the A minor Sonata in *NZfM*, 37 (17 September 1852), 119–20. As Uhlig wrote: 'We are not unjustified in attributing the insignificant passages in this sonata, as well as those in Schumann's other recent compositions, to incessant scribbling [*Vielschreiberei*] . . . Indeed, Schumann is already past his prime, and can only save himself from shallowness by moderating his rate of productivity.'

28. Peter Lohmann, 'Robert Schumann's *Balladen*', *NZfM*, 53 (1860), 5.

29. Selmar Bagge, 'Messe von Robert Schumann', *Allgemeine Musikalische Zeitung*, Neue Folge, 1. Jahrgang (21 January 1863), cols. 61–2. Then the editor of the *Allgemeine Musikalische Zeitung*, Bagge was not equally receptive to Schumann's other late compositions. The *Missa*, he wrote, 'is distinguished by many praiseworthy qualities that cannot be attributed to most of the other works of [Schumann's] late period' (col. 68).

30. See, for example, Hermann Abert, *Schumann*, 4th edn (Berlin, 1920). Abert has nothing at all to say about the late piano music and Lieder, and gives scant attention to the late choral, chamber and symphonic music.

31. Walter Dahms, *Schumann* (Berlin and Leipzig, 1916), p. 300.

32. Kathleen Dale, 'The piano music', in *Schumann: A Symposium*, ed. Gerald Abraham (London and New York, 1952), p. 70. Cf. Dieter Schnebel's comments on the Violin Concerto's 'droning, powerless' melodies and 'circular, crumbling' forms, in 'Postscriptum zu Schumanns Spätwerken', *Musik-Konzepte Sonderband: Robert Schumann II* (December 1982), 367.

33. Charles Rosen, *The Romantic Generation* (Cambridge, MA, 1995), p. 689.

34. Quoted in Alfred Niemann, 'The concertos', in *Robert Schumann: The Man and His Music*, ed. Alan Walker (London, 1972), p. 271.

35. Harold Truscott, 'The evolution of Schumann's last period', *The Chesterian*, 31, No. 189 (1957), p. 111. Eduard Melkus makes a similar point in 'Zur Revision unseres Schumann-Bildes', *Österreichische Musikzeitschrift*, 15 (1960), 189–90.

36. See Helmuth Hopf, 'Fehlinterpretation eines Spätstils am Beispiel Robert Schumann', in Julius Alf and Joseph A. Kruse, eds., *Robert Schumann: Universalgeist der Romantik. Beiträge zu seiner Persönlichkeit und seinem Werk* (Düsseldorf, 1981), pp. 238–49; and Norbert Nagler, 'Gedanken zur Rehabilitierung des späten Werks', *Musik-Konzepte Sonderband: Robert Schumann I* (November 1981), 303–46.

37. See Michael Struck, *Die umstrittenen späten Instrumentalwerke Schumanns* (1984); and Reinhard Kapp, *Studien zum Spätwerk Robert Schumanns* (Tutzing, 1984).

38. Kapp, *Studien zum Spätwerk*, pp. 79–101.

39. Irmgard Knechtges, *Robert Schumann im Spiegel seiner späten Klavierwerke* (Regensburg, 1985); Gerhard Dietel, *'Eine neue poetische Zeit': Musikanschauung und stilistische Tendenzen im Klavierwerk Robert Schumanns* (Kassel, 1989), pp. 432–87 (on the *Gesänge der Frühe*); and Markus Waldura, *Monomotivik, Sequenz und Sonatenform im Werk Robert Schumanns* (Saarbrucken, 1990), pp. 317–37, 343–6, 358–66 (on the Cello Concerto, the Piano Trio in G minor, the Violin Sonata in D minor and the posthumously published 'Third' Violin Sonata in A minor).

40. Dagmar Hoffmann-Axthelm, *Robert Schumann: 'Glücklichsein und tiefe Einsamkeit'* (Stuttgart, 1994), pp. 167–73.

41. Johannes Brahms, *Briefwechsel*, 16 vols., vol. III (Berlin, 1908), p. 121.

42. See, for example, Hermann Danuser, 'Aspekte einer Hommage-Komposition: Zu Brahms' Schumann-Variationen op. 9', in *Brahms-Analysen: Referate der Kieler Tagung 1983*, ed. Friedhelm Krummacher and Wolfram Steinbeck (Kassel and Basel, 1984), pp. 91–106; Constantin Floros, *Johannes Brahms: 'Frei aber einsam' – Ein Leben für eine poetische Musik* (Zurich and Hamburg, 1997), pp. 145–65; and Oliver Neighbour, 'Brahms and Schumann: Two Opus Nines and Beyond', *Nineteenth Century Music*, 7/3 (1984), 266–70.

43. Max Kalbeck, *Johannes Brahms* (Berlin, 1912–21), 4 vols., vol. I, p. 125.

44. See Peter Smith, 'Liquidation, augmentation, and Brahms's recapitulatory overlaps', *Nineteenth Century Music*, 17/3 (1994), 237–61; and 'Brahms and Schenker: a mutual response to sonata form', *Music Theory Spectrum*, 16/1 (1994), pp. 77–103.

45. Examples from the late instrumental works include the first movements of the Cello Concerto, the 'Rhenish' Symphony, the Violin Sonata in D minor and the Piano Trio in G minor. Schumann first invoked this technique in the 1840s in the *Finale* of the *Ouverture, Scherzo und Finale* (Op. 52) and the opening movement of the String Quartet in A (Op. 41, No. 3); it also appears in the third movement of the Second Symphony (Op. 61), the first and last movements of the Piano Trio in F (Op. 80) and the *Genoveva* Overture (Op. 81).

46. *Johannes Brahms: Life and Letters*, selected and annotated by Styra Avins, trans. Josef Eisinger and Styra Avins (Oxford and New York, 1997), p. 84. See also Brahms's letter to Clara Schumann of 23–4 February 1855, in which he wrote out the dedication of the *Concert-Allegro* as Schumann had notated it for him (*Brahms: Life and Letters*, p. 560).

47. The Viennese performance took place on 10 January 1875; see Robert Hirschfeld, *Geschichte der K. K. Gesellschaft der Musikfreunde in Wien. 2. Abteilung: 1870–1912* (Vienna, 1912), p. 305. See also Brahms's letter to Joachim of 5 April 1880 in Eisinger and Avins, trans., *Brahms: Life and Letters*, p. 560.

48. Schumann, 'Das Clavier-Concert', *NZfM*, 10 (4 January 1839), 5–6.

49. Kerman, *Concerto Conversations*, p. 79.

50. That Brahms had reservations about the quality of Schumann's Violin Concerto can be inferred from his role in the disposition of the Schumann *Gesamtausgabe*. See Struck, *Die umstrittenen späten Instrumentalwerke Schumanns*, pp. 252, 305.

51. Letter of 22 July 1937 from Menuhin to Vladimir Golschmann; quoted in Struck, *Robert Schumann: Violinkonzert*, p. 87.

52. Dahlhaus, *Beethoven*, p. 219.

53. Both violinists recorded the concerto: Kulenkampff in December 1937, with Hans Schmidt-Isserstedt and the Berlin Philharmonic, and Menuhin in February 1938, with Sir John Barbirolli and the Philharmonic Symphony Orchestra of New York. Both renditions have also been reissued on CD: Kulenkampff's on Dutton CDEA 5018 (1998) and Menuhin's on Biddulph LAB047. For an account of the extraordinary events leading up to the publication and first performances of the concerto – a tale whose strangest chapter tells how Jelly d'Aranyi and Adili Fachiri, nieces of Joachim and both violinists, were commanded by the spirits of Schumann and their uncle to bring the purportedly lost work to light – see Struck, *Robert Schumann: Violinkonzert*, pp. 19–23.

54. Joachim and Moser, eds., *Briefe von und an Joachim*, vol. III, p. 487.

55. For a thorough discussion of the sources, see Struck, *Die umstrittenen späten Instrumentalwerke Schumanns*, pp. 367–8, 392–7, 404–6 and 422–3.

56. Schünemann (the director of the music division of the Staatsbibliothek Preußischer Kulturbesitz in Berlin, now the Staatsbibliothek zu Berlin) edited the full score and the violin–piano arrangement of the concerto, both published by Schott (Mainz) in 1937.

57. The concerto was not the only one of Schumann's late violin works to undergo radical surgery at the hands of a twentieth-century arranger. In his edition of the A minor Violin Sonata, published by Schirmer in 1945, Harold Bauer transposed roughly 30 per cent of the original violin part up an octave, added (or altered) double stops, often assigned the violin line to the right hand of the piano and vice versa, and eliminated many of the doublings between violin and piano. Motivated, in Bauer's words, by a desire to revive 'public interest' in a 'grand' work that had 'practically disappeared from concert programs', these alterations transform the mellow blend of sonorities of the original into a sound-world characterized by sharp contrasts.

58. Quoted in Struck, *Die umstrittenen späten Instrumentalwerke Schumanns*, p. 341.

59. See *Ibid.*, pp. 367–8. Apart from Schumann's unsuccessful attempts to address bars 117–19 and 306–8 in the first movement, the major revisions in the solo part involved a passage in double stops from the recapitulation of the first movement (bars 302–3) and two bars of figuration near the end of the exposition of the finale (bars 124–5). Schumann's autograph also served as the primary source for Schünemann's editions, in which the emended readings from the manuscript copies are relegated to a bare-bones critical report. Moreover, the piano arrangement in Schünemann's violin–piano edition of the concerto bears no relation to Schumann's own reduction of the orchestral accompaniment as transmitted in the autograph and the copies.

60. A recent issue of the *R. E. D. Classical Catalogue: Master Edition 1* (London, 2000) lists eight currently available recordings. At least five more have been released since the mid 1960s, by Susanne Lautenbacher, Václav Snítil, Juliet Kang, Henryk Szeryng and Ulf Hoelscher.

291 Songs of dawn and dusk: the late music

61. Quoted in Struck, *Die umstrittenen späten Instrumentalwerke Schumanns*, p. 342.
62. See the liner notes to Kremer's 1994 recording of the Violin Concerto with Nikolaus Harnoncourt and the Chamber Orchestra of Europe (Teldec 4509-90696-2), and *Steven Isserlis Plays Schumann* (RCA Victor/BMG Classics 09026-6880-2; recorded 1996–7). Schiff's remarks are quoted in John C. Tibbetts, 'Andras Schiff: the focus is on Schumann', *American Record Guide* (September/October 1998), 48.
63. Graham Johnson, liner notes to *The Songs of Robert Schumann – 1* (Hyperion CDJ33101; recorded 1995), p. 7.
64. Roland Barthes, *Camera Lucida: Reflections on Photography*, trans. Richard Howard (New York, 1981; originally published as *La chambre claire*, 1980), pp. 69–70.
65. *Ibid.*, p. 94.
66. *Ibid.*, pp. 93, 96.
67. Quoted in Wolfgang Boetticher, *Robert Schumann: Einführung in die Persönlichkeit und Werk* (Berlin, 1941), p. 219. For a thought-provoking discussion of Schumann's understanding of *die Frühe*, see Markus Waldura, 'Zitate vokaler Frühgesänge in Schumanns *Gesängen der Frühe* op. 133', in *Schumann in Düsseldorf: Werke – Texte – Interpretationen. Bericht über das 3. Internationale Schumann-Symposium am 15. und 16. Juni 1988* (Mainz, 1988), pp. 51–3.
Another Schumann lover, the psychoanalyst Michel Schneider, also touches on the duality in Schumann's understanding of *die Frühe*. The *Gesänge der Frühe*, he writes, give voice 'neither to evening nor to night-time', but rather to 'the night of the night, when night wanes', that is, to 'dawn, the blanching of a sorrow already nearly eclipsed'. See Michel Schneider, *La tombée du jour: Schumann* (Paris: Editions du Seuil, 1989), p. 73.

Select bibliography

Barthes, Roland, 'Loving Schumann', *The Responsibility of Forms: Critical Essays on Music, Art, and Representation*, trans. R. Howard (Berkeley: University of California Press, 1985), 293–8.
Bonds, Mark Evan, *After Beethoven: Imperatives of Originality in the Symphony* (Cambridge, MA: Harvard University Press, 1996).
Boucourechliev, André, *Schumann*, trans. A. Boyars (New York: Grove, 1959).
Daverio, John, *Nineteenth-Century Music and the German Romantic Ideology* (New York: Schirmer, 1993).
  'Sounds without the gate: Schumann and the Dresden revolution', *Saggiatore musicale*, 4 (1997), 87–112.
  Robert Schumann: Herald of a 'New Poetic Age' (New York: Oxford University Press, 1997).
  '"Beautiful and abstruse conversations": the chamber music of Schumann', in *Nineteenth-Century Chamber Music*, ed. S. Hefling (New York: Schirmer, 1998), 208–41.
  Crossing Paths: Schubert, Schumann, and Brahms (New York: Oxford University Press, 2002).
Downes, Stephen, 'Kierkegaard, a kiss, and Schumann's Fantasie', *Nineteenth Century Music*, 22/3 (1999), 268–80.
Edler, Arnfried, 'Ton und Zyklus in der Symphonik Schumanns', in *Probleme der Symphonischen Tradition im 19. Jahrhundert*, ed. Siegfried Kross and Marie Luise Maintz (Tutzing: Hans Schneider, 1990).
Eismann, Georg, *Robert Schumann: A Biography in Word and Picture*, trans. Lena Jaeck (Leipzig: VEB Verlag, 1964).
Ferris, David, *Schumann's Eichendorff "Liederkreis" and the Genre of the Romantic Cycle* (Oxford: Oxford University Press, 2000).
Finscher, Ludwig, ' "Zwischen absoluter und Programmusik": Zur Interpretation der deutschen romantischen Symphonie', in *Über Symphonien: Beiträge zu einer musikalischen Gattung* (Festschrift Walter Wiora), ed. Christoph-Helling Mahling (Tutzing: Hans Schneider, 1979), 103–15.
Finson, Jon, *Robert Schumann and the Study of Orchestral Composition: The Genesis of the First Symphony, Op. 38* (Oxford: Clarendon Press, 1989).
Finson, Jon, 'Schumann, popularity, and the "Ouverture, Scherzo, und Finale", Opus 52', *Musical Quarterly* 69 (1983), 1–26.
Finson, Jon and Larry Todd, eds, *Mendelssohn and Schumann: Essays on Their Music and Its Context* (Durham, NC: Duke University Press, 1984).
Hoeckner, Berthold, 'Schumann and romantic distance', *Journal of the American Musicological Society*, 50 (1997), 55–132.
Jensen, Frederick, 'Explicating Jean Paul: Robert Schumann's program for Papillons, op. 2', *Nineteenth Century Music*, 22/2 (1998), 127–43.

Kerman, Joseph, *Concerto Conversations* (Cambridge, MA: Harvard University Press, 1999).

Kramer, Lawrence, '*Carnaval*, cross-dressing, and the woman in the mirror', in *Musicology and Difference: Gender and Sexuality in Music Scholarship*, ed. R. A. Solie (Berkeley: University of California Press, 1993), 305–25.

Lester, Joel, 'Robert Schumann and sonata forms', *Nineteenth Century Music*, 18/3 (1995), 189–210.

Macdonald, Claudia, 'Schumann's earliest compositions and performances', *Journal of Musicological Research* 7 (1986–8), 269–71.

Marston, Nicolas, 'Schumann's monument to Beethoven', *Nineteenth Century Music*, 14 (1990–1), 247–64.

Schumann: 'Fantasie', op. 17 (Cambridge: Cambridge University Press, 1992).

Moore, Gerald, *Poet's Love: The Songs and Cycles of Schumann* (London: Hamilton, 1981).

Musgrave, Michael, 'Symphony and symphonic scenes: issues of structure and context in Schumann's "Rhenish" Symphony', in *Analytical Strategies and Musical Interpretation: Essays on Nineteenth- and Twentieth-Century Music*, ed. C. Ayrey and M. Everist (Cambridge: Cambridge University Press, 1996), 120–48.

Muxfeldt, Kristina, '*Frauenliebe und Leben* now and then', *Nineteenth Century Music* 25/1 (2001), 27–48.

Newcomb, Anthony, 'Once more "Between absolute and program music": Schumann's second symphony', *Nineteenth Century Music* 7/3 (1984), 233–50.

'Schumann and late eighteenth-century narrative strategies', *Nineteenth Century Music* 11/2 (1987), 164–74.

Ostwald, Peter, 'Florestan, Eusebius, Clara, and Schumann's right hand', *Nineteenth Century Music*, 4 (1980–1), 17–31.

Schumann: Music and Madness (London: Gollancz, 1985). [Also available as *Schumann: The Inner Voices of a Musical Genius* (Boston: Northeastern University Press, 1985).]

Perrey, Beate Julia, *Schumann's 'Dichterliebe' and Early Romantic Poetics: Fragmentation of Desire* (Cambridge: Cambridge University Press, 2002).

Plantinga, Leon, *Schumann as Critic* (New Haven: Yale University Press, 1967).

Reich, Nancy, *Clara Schumann: The Artist and the Woman*, revised edn (Ithaca, NY: Cornell University Press, 2001).

Roesner, Linda Correll, 'Schumann's "parallel" forms', *Nineteenth Century Music*, 14 (1991), 265–78.

'Schumann', in *The Nineteenth-Century Symphony*, ed. D. Kern Holoman (New York: Schirmer, 1997), 43–77.

Rosen, Charles, *The Romantic Generation* (London: HarperCollins, 1996).

'Secret codes: Caspar David Friedrich, Robert Schumann', in *Romantic Poets, Critics, and Other Madmen* (Cambridge, MA: Harvard University Press, 1998).

Schumann, Robert, *On Music and Musicians*, ed. Konrad Woolff, trans. Paul Rosenfeld (London: Dennis Dobson, 1947).

Schumann, Clara and Robert, *The Complete Correspondence of Clara and Robert Schumann: Critical Edition*, ed. E. Weissweiler, trans. H. Fritsch and R. Crawford (New York: Peter Lang, 1994).

Schumann, Robert and Clara, *The Marriage Diaries of Robert and Clara Schumann*, ed. Gerd Nauhaus, trans. with a preface by Peter Ostwald (London: Robson, 1994).

Steinberg, Michael, *The Symphony: A Listener's Guide* (New York: Oxford University Press, 1995).

Todd, Larry, ed., *Schumann and His World* (Princeton: Princeton University Press, 1994).

Index

Abegg, Pauline Comtesse d' 71–2
Abert, Hermann 198–9, 217, 218, 289
Abraham, Gerald 152, 219
Abt, Franz 233
Adorno, Theodor W. 24–6, 60, 240, 257, 269, 287, 288
Albéniz, Isaac 239
Alkan, Charles-Valentin 227, 234
Allgemeine musikalische Zeitung 26–7
Ambros, August Wilhelm 234
Andersen, Hans Christian 18, 106
Appel, Bernhard 84
Aranyi, Jelly d' 290
Arensky, Anton 239, 245
Arnim, Achim von 218
Arnim, Bettina von 261, 262

Bach, Johann Sebastian 8, 21, 28, 112, 196
  Mendelssohn and 8, 55–6, 196
  RS and 8, 13, 21, 28, 48, 55–8, 60, 84, 94, 170, 172, 175, 178, 182, 190, 194, 195
Bach-Gesellschaft 56
Bagge, Selmar 234, 274
Bailey, Robert 147
Balakirev, Mily 237, 238
Barbirolli, John 290
Bargiel, Woldemar 228, 231
Barthes, Roland 36, 70–1, 83, 91, 121, 122, 257–8, 286–7
Bartók, Béla 240
Bauer, Harold 290
Baumgartner, Wilhelm 233, 234
Bazzini, Antonio 238
Becker, Julius 206, 226
Becker, Nikolaus 226
Beckett, Samuel 102, 111
Beethoven, Ludwig van 55, 60, 153, 213, 288
  RS and 7, 8, 21, 25, 48, 49, 50–1, 52, 55, 58, 59, 60, 84, 123, 124, 146, 148–51, 153–7, 163, 165, 170, 172, 175, 183, 185, 223; (quoted) 7, 52–3, 54–5, 82, 120, 128–9
Benda, Georg 213
Benjamin, Walter 80–1, 255
Bennett, William Sterndale 225, 228
Berg, Alban 236, 240
Berger, Ludwig 67
Berio, Luciano 264
Berlioz, Hector 27, 42–3, 70, 225, 227, 231
Bernstein, Leonard 248
biography 4, 5–6, 26
Bischoff, Bodo 48

Bizet, Georges 237
Boetticher, Wolfgang 84, 193, 241
Böhm, Karl 282
Bonds, Mark Evan 165, 172
Borodin, Alexander 238, 240
Böttger, Adolf 228
Boulez, Pierre 246
Brahms, Johannes 8, 18, 31, 58, 80, 175, 231, 233, 236, 239
  and Clara Schumann 18, 31–2, 228
  and RS 31, 33–4, 99, 159, 164, 194, 225, 228, 231, 235, 236, 244, 278–82, 288, 290
  on RS 157
  RS and 31, 61, 183, 187, 225, 229, 231
Brandes, Johann Christian 213
Brendel, Franz 30, 40, 88, 201, 208–9, 218
Brentano, Clemens 218
Britten, Benjamin 247
Bruch, Max 235, 236, 239, 250
Bruckner, Anton 236–7, 245
Bruyck, Debrois van 234
Bülow, Hans von 230, 234, 245, 250
Burgmüller, Norbert 232
Burns, Robert 18, 114, 196
Busoni, Ferruccio 239
Byron, George Gordon, Lord 6, 18, 42, 106, 206, 212, 214–15

Carlyle, Thomas 41
Castillon, Alexis de 237
Celan, Paul 262
Cervantes, Miguel de 6
Chamisso, Adalbert von 110–14
Chantovoine, Jean 271
Cherubini, Luigi 195
Chevillard, Camille 237
children's books 74
Chiroplast 11, 12
Chopin, Frédéric 48, 72, 75, 194, 228, 232, 233, 250
choral societies 196–7
Chua, Daniel 60
ciphers and encipherment 71–5, 84
Collin, Heinrich Joseph von 39
Cone, Edward T. 120
Cornelius, Peter 230, 231, 233, 236
cryptography 73–4, 79–80
  see also encipherment
Cui, César 238
Czerny, Carl 57

Dadelson, Georg von 57, 58
Dahlhaus, Carl 154–7, 269, 282
Dahms, Walter 274–5
Dale, Kathleen 275
Daverio, John 24, 35, 36, 37, 52, 58, 59, 60, 89,
    90, 100, 101, 103–4, 120n., 146n., 157,
    158, 172n., 194n., 217, 218, 266
David, Ferdinand 56, 137, 226, 232
Davidsbündler 13–16, 24, 31, 72, 74, 76, 86,
    174, 224, 226, 230, 235, 259
    see also Florestan and Eusebius
Debussy, Claude 236, 237, 239, 245
dedications 13, 32, 69, 72, 84, 100, 128, 133,
    137, 146, 187, 228, 249, 250, 251, 261,
    262, 280, 287, 291
Delage, Maurice 237
Dietel, Gerhard 276
Dietrich, Albert 228, 230
Doppelgänger 7, 13–14
Dorn, Heinrich 10, 13, 42, 56, 174
Downes, Stephen 85
Draeseke, Felix 245
Draeske 25
Dresden Court Orchestra 182
Dubois, Théodore 237

Edler, Arnfried 167, 170
Ehlert, Louis 230, 231, 234, 236
Eichendorff, Joseph von 18, 97, 227
Einstein, Alfred 71
Elgar, Edward 248
encipherment 71–5, 84
    see also cryptography
Endenich 33–5, 262
Erkel, Ferenc 234
Eschmann, Joseph Carl 234
Eusebius *see* Florestan and Eusebius

Fachiri, Adila 290
Fallersleben, Hoffmann von 100
Fauré, Gabriel 237, 244
Feldman, Morton 253
Field, John 71, 93, 174
Finscher, Ludwig 158, 172
Finson, Jon 152, 157
Fischer-Dieskau, Dietrich 288
Flechsig, Emil 7, 13, 39, 199
Florestan and Eusebius 13, 27, 69, 72, 80,
    86–7, 174, 188, 226, 259
    see also Davidsbündler
Foucault, Michel 262
Franck, César 237
Franck, Eduard 231
Fricken, Ernestine von 69, 72
Furtwängler, Wilhelm 248

Gade, Niels 225, 226, 227, 228
Gardiner, John Eliot 153

Gehrke, Anton 227
Geibel, Emanuel 197
Gerstmeier, August 103
Gevaert, François-Auguste 237
Glazunov, Alexander 239, 248
Gleim, Johann Wilhelm Ludwig 39
Gluck, Christoph Willibald von 60
Godard, Benjamin 237
Goebbels, Joseph 282
Goehr, Alexander 269
Goethe, Johann Wolfgang von 6, 7, 18, 56, 97,
    106, 195, 212, 268
Goetz, Hermann 237
Golinelli, Stefano 249
Golschmann, Vladimir 282
Gounod, Charles 234
Grabbe, Dietrich 42
Grimm, A. L. 74
Grimm, Julius Otto 231, 235
Gurlitt, Willibald 253–4

Hába, Alois 240
Handel, George Frideric 60, 84, 196, 241
Hanslick, Eduard 30, 209, 234, 268, 273–4
Haslinger, Tobias 84, 250
Hauptmann, Moritz 231
Haydn, Joseph 60, 124, 125, 169–70, 171,
    196
Hebbel, Friedrich 30, 96, 206, 207, 218, 227,
    228
Hegel, Georg Wilhelm Friedrich 268
Heine, Heinrich 9, 18, 42, 106, 107, 110,
    114–19, 120
Heller, Stephen 225, 228, 231
Henselt, Adolf 225, 227, 228, 232
Henze, Hans Werner 255
Herbeck, Johann von 234
Herder, Johann Gottfried von 7
Herz, Henri 45, 71, 173, 175
Hetsch, Louis 59
Hildesheimer, Wolfgang 105
Hiller, Ferdinand 48, 196, 197, 200, 218, 226,
    227, 232, 234, 244, 250
Hindemith, Paul 242, 282, 284
Hirschbach, Hermann 59, 225, 232, 245
Hoeckner, Berthold 85, 88, 89, 99
Hoffmann, Ernst Theodor Amadeus 14, 90,
    95, 98, 171, 206, 245
Hoffmann-Asthelm, Dagmar 276
Hölderlin, Friedrich 261
Holliger, Heinz 247, 261–2, 286
Hopf, Helmuth 275
Horn, Moritz 197
Hugo, Victor 42
Hummel, Johann Nepomuk 71, 174, 175,
    223
Humperdinck, Engelbert 235
Hünten, Franz 45

Ireland, John 244
Isserlis, Steven 286

Jamison, Kay 104
Jankélévitch, Vladimir 94
Japha-Langhans, Louise 231, 237
Jean Paul (Johann Paul Friedrich Richter) 7,
    14, 40–2, 72, 152
    RS and 7, 9–10, 40–2, 49, 50, 51, 69, 72, 90,
    98, 167, 195
Jensen, Adolf 235
Jensen, Eric 97, 272
Joachim, Joseph 230, 233
    and RS 31, 33, 34, 225, 231, 234, 235, 273,
    274, 280, 283, 288
    on RS 183, 191
Johnson, Graham 286
Jullien, Adolphe 250

Kagel, Maurizio 263–4
Kalkbrenner, Frédéric 45
Kaminsky, Peter 84, 99
Kapp, Reinhard 37, 83, 145, 146, 147, 190, 276
Kastner, Georg 226, 227
Keller, Hans 121
Kerman, Joseph 60, 268, 281, 288, 291
Kessler, Joseph Christoph 67
Kienzl, Wilhelm 233
Killmayer, Wilhelm 262
Kirchner, Theodor 227, 228, 230, 233, 234, 244
Kistner, Friedrich 72
Kitzler, Otto 237
Kivy, Peter 216
Kjerulf, Halfdan 218
Klüber, Johann 73, 79–80
Knaben Wunderhorn, Des 208, 218
Knechtges, Irmgard 276
Komar, Arthur 108–9
Kosegarten, Ludwig Gotthard 39
Koßmaly, Carl 48, 53, 68, 94, 95
Kramer, Lawrence 111, 119
Krebs, Harald 76, 100
Kreisler, Fritz 194
Kremer, Gidon 286
Kristeva, Julia 95
Krüger, Eduard 205–6, 209, 217–18, 289
Kufferath, Maurice 237
Kulenkampff, Georg 242, 282, 284, 290
Kuntsch, Johann Gottfried 223
Kurtág, György 106, 258–9, 260

Lacombe, Paul 237
Lalo, Edouard 234
Lang, Paul Henry 153
Langer, Eduard 234
Laroche, Herman 238
Laube, Heinrich 96
Laurencin, Ferdinand Peter, Graf 234

League of David *see Davidsbündler*
Leipzig Conservatory 236
Lenzewski, Gustav 284
Lester, Joel 61, 172
Lewy, Joseph-Rudolph 182
Lindeman, Stephan 194
Liszt, Franz 201, 219, 230, 232, 233
    and RS 98, 216, 225, 226, 227, 233, 234,
    245, 251
    on RS 90, 92, 175, 197, 216, 219, 225, 288
    RS and 75, 175, 212, 225, 228
Litzmann, Berthold 37
Lobe, Johann Christian 234
Loewe, Carl 59, 200
Logier, Johann Bernard 11, 12
Lohmann, Peter 274, 288
Lorenz, Oswald 200
L'vov, Alexey 227, 234
Lyser, Johann Peter 74, 76, 84, 225

McClary, Susan 121
Macdonald, Claudia 84, 173, 174, 177, 193
Maderna, Bruno 247
Mahler, Gustav 236, 238, 239, 245, 248, 264
Mahlert, Ulrich 120
Mangold, Carl 245
Mann, Thomas 268, 269
Marschner, Heinrich 200
Marseillaise 7, 163
Marston, Nicholas 60, 68, 83, 85
Marxsen, Eduard 231
Massenet, Jules 234
Meinardus, Ludwig 230, 244
Melkus, Eduard 289
Mendelssohn, Felix 55–6, 93, 152, 196, 232,
    233, 241
    and RS 180, 225, 226, 232
    RS and 13, 48, 51, 56, 60, 146, 178, 188, 193,
    202, 225
    RS on 200
    Wagner and 233, 235
Menuhin, Yehudi 282, 284, 290
Messiaen, Olivier 250
Meyerbeer, Giacomo 206, 211, 231, 241
Mintz, Marie Luise 48
Möbius, Paul 26
Moore, Thomas 18, 199–200, 201–2
Moraal, Christine 100
Moscheles, Ignaz 43–4, 70, 71, 72, 84, 225,
    228, 231
Moser, Andreas 273
Mozart, Wolfgang Amadé 105, 122, 213, 272
    RS and 6, 60, 84, 124, 170, 175, 195
Müller, Christian Gottlieb 251
Müller von Königswinter, Wolfgang 234
Müller, Wilhelm Christian 48, 58
musicology, ideology and 110–14, 121
Musorgsky, Modest 236, 238, 240

Nagler, Norbert 275
Nauhaus, Gerd 35, 36, 37, 46, 58, 59, 145, 146, 199, 216, 217, 218, 249
Nazi Germany 241, 282
Neue Zeitschrift für Musik (NZfM) 13, 26–7, 45, 74, 224
    RS and 13, 26–7, 45, 48, 201, 224, 229; (RS's article 'Neue Bahnen') 61, 229, 231
    under Brendel 201, 209, 218
Neumann, William 234
'New Germans' 229, 230, 233, 235–6, 238, 271
Newcomb, Anthony 167, 170, 172
Nibelungen saga 208
Nicodé, Jean Louis 245
Nietzsche, Friedrich 235–6, 252
Nono, Luigi 259
Norman, Ludvig 227, 234
note names, German 84
Novák, Vítežslav 240
Novalis (Friedrich von Hardenberg) 42, 94, 103, 170

Ostwald, Peter 36, 104, 120

Paganini, Niccolò 11, 25, 72, 73, 75–9, 85, 86, 87
Palestrina, Giovanni Pierluigi da 28
Pasdeloup, Jules Etienne 237
Paul, Jean *see* Jean Paul
Perrey, Beate 36, 101, 103, 120, 170, 172, 266
Pfarrius, Gustav 96
Pfitzner, Hans 232, 236, 238–9, 240, 248
Phillips, Adam 16, 35
Plantinga, Leon 105, 179
Pohl, Richard 104, 120, 216, 219, 271, 274, 288
Pousseur, Henri 264
Prokofiev, Serge 240
Proust, Marcel 80
puzzles *see* encipherment *and* rebuses

Raff, Joachim 230
Ravel, Maurice 240
rebuses 74–5, 84
Reger, Max 239, 248
Reimann, Aribert 262
Reimann, Heinrich 235
Reinecke, Carl 228, 230, 235, 236, 239
Reinick, Robert 206
Reißiger, Karl Gottlieb 206
Reissmann, August 235
Rellstab, Ludwig 225
Réti, Rudolf 250
Reynolds, Christopher 97
Riccius, A. F. 234
Richarz, Franz 34, 37, 288
Richter, Johann Paul Friedrich *see* Jean Paul
Ries, Ferdinand 55
Rietz, Julius 226

Rihm, Wolfgang 255, 258, 259, 260
Rimsky-Korsakov, Nikolay 237, 238
Ritter, Carl 228, 230
Roesner, Linda Correll 61, 99, 165, 172
Romanticism 3, 5, 19, 24, 27, 36, 226, 253–4, 255–8, 263–4
Rosen, Charles 58, 87, 98, 99, 106, 194, 262, 275
Rosselli, John 271
Rossini, Gioacchino 195
Rothe, Heinrich 46
Rousseau, Jean-Jacques 213
Rübenacker, Thomas 287
Rubinstein, Anton 227, 234, 237, 248
Rubinstein, Joseph 235, 251
Rubinstein, Nikolay 234, 238
Rückert, Friedrich 106
Ruzicka, Peter 262

Sahr, Heinrich von 231, 249
Saint-Saëns, Camille 232, 234, 237
Sams, Eric 73, 79–80, 115, 120
Samuels, Robert 100
Satie, Erik 239, 245
Schapler, Julius 146
Schemann, Ludwig 233
Schenker, Heinrich 59
Schenkerian analysis 108–9
Schiff, Andras 286
Schiller, Friedrich von 6, 7, 39
Schindler, Anton 55
Schlegel, August 42
Schlegel, Friedrich 42, 68, 93
Schmidt-Isserstedt, Hans 290
Schnabel, Artur 240
Schnebel, Dieter 289
Schneider, Michel 119, 291
Schoeck, Othmar 236, 240
Schoenberg, Arnold 104, 106, 111, 239–40, 245
Scholz, Bernhard 234–5
Schott-Verlag 282
Schubert, Ferdinand 27, 36, 44, 45, 47, 51
Schubert, Franz 106, 213, 239, 257
    RS and 24, 27, 48, 49–52, 54, 55, 58, 84, 121, 154, 157, 170, 172, 195, 223; (promoting performance) 51, 52, 55; (writings) 27, 44–5, 49–50, 51, 60, 167
Schubring, Adolf 250, 270–1
Schüler, Wilhelm Immanuel 250
Schulze, Ernst 39
Schumann, August (RS's father) 6, 7, 18, 22, 38–9, 223
Schumann, Clara (Clara Wieck) 3, 4, 5, 10, 13, 16, 17, 18, 19, 20, 21, 22, 24, 30, 31, 32, 33, 35, 36, 37, 46, 52, 56, 59, 66, 69, 71, 79, 80, 81, 82, 83, 84, 85, 86, 87, 89, 90, 94, 99, 100, 101, 103, 107, 114, 115, 118, 119,

120, 123, 124, 128, 129, 133, 145, 146, 165, 169, 174, 175, 177, 179, 181, 182, 193, 202, 206, 218, 224, 225, 226, 227, 228, 230, 234, 235, 237, 242, 251, 272, 274, 289, 290, 291
  Brahms and 228
  portrait of 17, 23
  relationship with RS: as performer 18, 224–5, 227, 237; RS's works and 17–18, 23, 69, 83, 86, 87, 89–90, 99, 118–19, 128, 146, 165, 274, 288; *see also under* RS
  RS's fictional versions of 13, 72
  on RS's works 24, 123–4, 174
  works 21–2, 23, 81, 82, 175; RS and 175, 228
Schumann, Eduard (RS's brother) 95
Schumann, Emil (RS's son) 28
Schumann, Emilie (RS's sister) 7
Schumann, Julie (RS's daughter) 34, 99
Schumann, Robert
  and aesthetics 3, 7, 8, 13–16, 23–6, 38–45, 48–9, 58, 72, 93–4, 98, 108, 112, 132, 195, 199, 216, 246, 271, 278, 280
  autobiographical writing 4, 5, 133, 146
  character 3–4, 8, 18, 22, 30–1, 246; *see also his* mental states
  and his children 20
  on his compositional methods 133
  conducting 30, 56, 196–7, 226–7, 232
  critical writing *see his* music criticism
  diaries, notebooks etc. 4–5, 9–10, 19–20, 21–2, 35; editions of 46
  family background 6, 7, 18, 38–9
  health issues: final illness 31–5, 216; hand injury 3, 11–13, 16, 65, 174; syphilis 288; *see also his* mental states
  and history / older music 8, 48–9, 55–6, 115, 167–70, 252
  and humour/irony 41–2, 71–2, 87, 99, 106, 171, 259
  importance of writing for 21
  life 3–37
  literary writing 9–10, 13–14, 40, 103, 115, 120, 206, 214–15, 288
  and literature 6–7, 21, 38–44, 96–8, 171, 195; *see also* texts chosen *under his works below*
  marriage diaries 21–2
  mental states 3, 4, 9–10, 14, 15, 16, 26, 30, 31–5, 36, 37, 98; and depression/manic-depression 3–4, 26, 104–5, 271; final illness 31–5, 216; imaginary multiple personalities and 13–16; and reception of his music 35, 229, 246, 261–2, 271, 272; and schizophrenia 14–15, 26; self-perception 19–20
  music criticism 13–14, 26–8, 30, 31, 40, 42–5, 48–9, 54–5, 59, 61, 67–8, 86, 174–5,
179, 200, 206, 224, 229, 231, 241, 246; and his own music 69–71, 75, 90, 123, 154, 167, 175, 224, 225, 280
  musical training 6, 10, 11, 49–50, 56
  Musikalische Haus- und Lebensregeln 195, 237
  pseudonyms and imaginary personalities 13–16, 27; *see also* Florestan and Eusebius
  relationship with Clara 3, 10, 11–13, 16–23, 30, 31–2, 33–4, 103, 128–30, 226; *see also his* marriage diaries; *see also under* Schumann, Clara
  self-criticism 225
  suicide attempt 33
  as teacher 22, 230–1, 236
  and teaching material 56, 60, 195
  writing *see his* literary writing *and his* music criticism
  WORKS
  dynamics in 142, 147
  editions of 18, 98, 193, 231, 235, 238, 240, 241, 247, 284, 288, 290
  formal aspects 23–4, 69, 93–4, 123, 125–8, 145, 172, 185–6, 245, 278–9
  harmonic aspects 102, 107, 109, 113, 115–18, 121, 122, 245
  intertextuality 170
  metrical dissonance in 76–9, 91–2, 100
  orchestration 152–3, 188, 189
  other composers' reorchestrations, revisions and arrangements of 237, 238, 239, 240, 247–8, 284, 290
  other composers' works based on / responding to 240, 243–4, 245, 253, 260, 261–6
  performance history 98–9, 224–5
  performance practice and 152–3, 247
  phrasing 151–2, 153, 158, 163, 251
  piano music as orchestral and vice versa 145, 152
  quotation/reminiscence in 7–8, 53–5, 59, 86, 88, 99, 185–6, 188, 189, 191
  reception history and influence 229–49, 261, 268–82; *see also under other composers*
  recordings of 171, 194, 248, 284, 286, 290
  relationship with Clara and *see under* Schumann, Clara
  relationship to earlier music 8, 48, 62, 115, 167–70, 252; *see also under other composers*
  reviews of 205–6, 209, 212, 217–18, 225, 274
  revisions of 98, 228
  rule-based decision-making in 8
  Schenkerian analysis of 108–9
  sketches and drafts 11, 65, 66, 68, 76, 81, 84, 85, 87, 124, 128, 129, 131, 145, 146, 171, 201

Schumann, Robert (cont.)
  stylistic development and late style 24–6, 35, 133, 268–82
  texts chosen 110–19, 201–2
  themes derived from letters/names 71–5, 137, 178
  titles 43–4
  tonality in 128–30, 134, 146, 148–51, 186, 189, 194
  words (indications etc.) on 69, 86–7, 89–90
Abegg variations (Op. 1) 11, 16, 52, 66, 68, 69, 71–5, 80, 84, 173
'Abendlied' 248
accompaniments to Bach solo string works 56, 57–8, 190, 252
Album für die Jugend (Op. 68) 56, 60, 74, 84, 195, 229
Albumblätter (Op. 124) 53, 66, 67
Allegro (Op. 8) 66, 75, 79
Andante and Variations (Op. 46) 232
Arabeske (Op. 18) 93
Ballades 197–8, 270, 274, 288
'Beda' 75
Blumenstück (Op. 19) 92–3
Bride of Messina Overture 163–4
Carnaval (Op. 9) 11, 16, 50, 52, 53, 68, 69, 71, 72–5, 78–9, 80, 84, 86, 87, 95, 98, 99, 215
Cello Concerto (Op. 129) 25, 29, 182, 183–5, 187, 193, 270, 281, 289; arrangement for violin 194
Choralballaden 197–8, 270, 274, 288
Clavierstücke (Op. 32) 57, 60
Concert Allegro with Introduction (Op. 134) 178–9, 187–9, 192, 228, 268, 280, 281
Concert sans orchestre 16, 69, 79, 81, 87
Conzertstück for four horns and orchestra (Op. 86) 181, 182–3, 185, 187; arrangement for piano 194
Conzertstück for piano and orchestra (Op. 92) 181, 186–7, 188
Davidsbündlertänze (Op. 6) 14, 15, 68, 76, 86–9, 92, 97–8, 99, 128
Dichterliebe (Op. 48) 8, 18, 24, 36, 97, 101, 102, 105–10, 120, 121, 170, 172, 180, 250, 264–6, 267
Eight Polonaises 51, 65, 68
Etuden in Form freier Variationen über ein Beethovensches Thema 52–3, 68
Etudes after Caprices by Paganini (Op. 3) 11, 76–9
Etudes after Caprices by Paganini (Op. X) 76
Etudes symphoniques (Op. 13) 16, 52–3, 57, 68, 69
Fantasie (Op. 17) 7, 54–5, 60, 68–9, 82–3, 85, 128–9

Fantasiestücke (for clarinet and piano, Op. 73) 29
Fantasiestücke (for piano, Op. 12) 88, 90, 94, 98, 258
Fantasiestücke (for piano trio, Op. 88) 133
Faschingsschwank aus Wien (Op. 26) 7, 98
Faust see Szenen aus Goethes Faust
Frauenliebe und -leben (Op. 42) 7, 105, 109–14, 119, 121
Fünf Lieder (Op. 55) 196
Geistervariationen 32, 99
Genoveva (Op. 81) 28, 197, 198–9, 205–12, 216, 217, 219, 227, 231, 233, 236, 239; overture 162–3, 165, 290
Gesänge der Frühe (Op. 133) 33, 275, 276–7, 286
'Hamlet' symphony (sketches) 65
Hermann und Dorothea overture 30, 163–4
Humoreske (Op. 20) 87, 94–5, 98
Impromptus sur une Romance de Clara Wieck (Op. 5) 60, 68, 69, 81, 87, 133
Introduction and Allegro (Op. 134) see Concert Allegro with Introduction
Julius Caesar Overture 163–4
Kinderszenen (Op. 15) 43, 57, 86, 92–3, 95, 98, 121, 240, 248
Kreisleriana (Op. 16) 8, 60, 71, 86, 87, 92, 95, 98, 121
Lieder (Op. II) 65
Lieder und Gesänge aus Wilhelm Meister (Op. 98a) 104, 120, 217
Lieder-Album für die Jugend (Op. 79) 100, 104, 120
Liederkreis (Op. 24) 18, 102, 121
Liederkreis (Op. 39) 8, 18
Liederreihe (Op. 35) 57
Manfred (Op. 115) 28, 197, 198, 199, 212–16, 233; overture 163, 215, 238
Märchenbilder (Op. 113) 30
Märchenerzählungen (Op. 132) 33, 231
Mass (Op. 147) 30, 197, 200, 242, 274
Myrthen (Op. 25) 18, 114–19
Nachtstücke (Op. 23) 90, 95–6
Novelletten (Op. 21) 69, 90, 92, 98
other projected works 206, 218
Overture, Scherzo und Finale (Op. 52) 157–8, 159, 161, 164
Papillons (Op. 2) 11, 13, 41, 50, 51, 53, 68, 71, 87, 99
Das Paradies und die Peri 196, 197, 198–205, 209, 212, 217, 226, 227, 232, 234, 239, 241
Phantasiestücke see Fantasiestücke
Piano Concerto in A minor (Op. 54) 173, 174, 176, 177–80, 181, 183, 185, 193, 247, 250, 280
Piano Concerto in D minor (draft) 175–7, 193
Piano Concerto in F (drafts) 65, 173–4, 193

Piano Quartet in C minor (Op. V) 51, 59, 65, 224
Piano Quartet in E flat (Op. 47) 54, 59, 133
Piano Quintet in E flat (Op. 44) 60, 133, 138, 146, 225, 227, 232, 247, 249
Piano Sonatas: No. 1 in F sharp minor (Op. 11) 11, 68, 69, 70, 81–2, 103, 146; No. 2 in G minor (Op. 22) 68, 103, 184; No. 3 in F minor (Op. 14) *see Concert sans orchestre*
Piano Trios: No. 1 in D minor (Op. 63) 133; No. 2 in F (Op. 80) 54, 60, 133; No. 3 in G minor (Op. 110) 30, 123, 124, 133, 136–7, 147, 289; *see also Fantasiestücke* (Op. 88)
Psalm 150 65, 195
Rebus 74, 84
Requiem (Op. 148) 30, 197, 200
Requiem für Mignon 217
Der Rose Pilgerfahrt 197, 198
Sechs Fugen über den Namen BACH (Op. 60)
Sechs Gesänge (Op. 89) 120
Sechs Gesänge (Op. 107) 248
Six Intermezzi (Op. 4) 11, 68, 69, 71, 76
Sechs Lieder (Op. 33) 196
Sonatas for Violin and Piano: No. 1 in A minor (Op. 105) 30, 123, 124, 133–7, 147, 278; No. 2 in D minor (Op. 121) 30, 123, 124, 145, 289; No. 3 in A Minor 33
String Quartets (Op. 41) 133, 134, 231, 290
Studien für den Pedal-Flügel (Op. 56) 57
Studies after Caprices by Paganini (Op. 3) 11, 76–9
symphonies 159, 166–71, 238; No. 1 ('Spring') (Op. 38) 124, 125, 152, 158, 164, 196, 226, 231, 232; No. 2 (Op. 61) 7, 28, 128–30, 151, 154, 164, 165–6, 168–70, 171, 233, 290; No. 3 ('Rhenish') (Op. 97) 29, 57, 147, 157, 158–61, 164, 171, 172, 234, 248, 255, 270, 289; No. 4 (Op. 120) 30, 124, 125, 151, 158, 164–5, 168, 171, 248; unfinished in G minor 11, 52, 53–4, 60, 65, 224
Szenen aus Goethes Faust 28, 97, 99, 172, 197, 198, 205–6, 212, 217, 218, 228, 234, 239, 250; overture 163
Thema mit Variationen (Geistervariationen) 32, 99
Toccata (Op. 7) 11, 79, 224, 225, 228, 262
'Träumerei' 240, 248
Vier Fugen (Op. 72) 56, 60
Vier Gesänge (Op. 59) 196
Violin Concerto 33, 99, 181, 183, 185–6, 187, 189–92, 241, 242, 247, 248, 268, 269, 273, 274, 275, 280, 281–6, 288
Violinphantasie (Op. 131) 33, 187, 191, 192, 193, 194, 274, 280, 281
Waldszenen (Op. 82) 29, 96–8, 99, 229
Zwölf Gedichte aus Rückerts Liebesfrühling (Op. 37) 23
see also 66–7
Schumann societies 230
'Schumannianer' 227, 231, 235–6
Schünemann, Georg 284, 290
Schunke, Louis 225, 228
Scott, Walter 6
Scudo, Pierre 237
Sechter, Simon 250
Seidl, Arthur 244
Sévérac, Déodat de 240
Seyfried, Ignaz von 55, 225
Shakespeare, William 18, 206
Shaw, George Bernard 208
Sibelius, Jean 238
Simmel, Georg 269
Smetana, Bedřich 228, 231, 234
Smith, Peter 278
Solger, Karl Wilhelm Ferdinand 42
Solie, Ruth 110–14, 115, 119, 121
Spitta, Philipp 114
Spohr, Louis 226, 231, 248
Stamaty, Camille 232
Stasov, Vladimir 237
Steinberg, Michael 168, 171
Steuermann, Edward 240
Stifter, Adalbert 227
Stock, Frederick 248
Stockhausen, Julius 234
Strauss, Richard 238, 245
Stravinsky, Igor 58
Strecker, Wilhelm 282
Struck, Michael 189, 274, 275–6
Suckow, Karl Adolph 214
Szell, George 248

Tadday, Ulrich 102n.
Taubert, Wilhelm 226
Tchaikovsky, Pyotr Ilyich 236, 237, 251
Thibaut, Anton Friedrich Justus 10
Tieck, Ludwig 206
Töpken, Anton 71, 84
Tovey, Donald Francis 152, 153, 172, 186, 275
Truscott, Harold 194, 275

Uhland, Ludwig 197
Uhlig, Theodor 289
Uhlrich, Karl 56

Verdi, Giuseppe 232, 233
Verhulst, Johannes 227, 228
Victoria, Queen of England 227
Vieuxtemps, Henri 85
Volkmann, Robert 234

Wagner, Richard 105, 201, 212, 232, 236, 248, 251, 271
  Liszt and 219
  and RS 209, 225, 232–3, 235
  RS and 225
Wagner Societies 230
Waldura, Markus 276
Wasielewski, Joseph Wilhelm von 20, 216, 234, 235, 272–3, 274
Webenau, Julie von 228
Weber, Carl Maria von 6, 60, 84, 195, 202, 206, 213, 223, 248
Weber, Gottfried 225
Weber, J. J. 74, 84
Webern, Anton 239, 254, 265
Wegeler, Franz Gerhard 55
Weingartner, Felix 248
Weissweiler, Eva 251, 272, 288
Werner, Zacharias 39
Widor, Charles-Marie 237
Wieck, Clara *see* Schumann, Clara
Wieck, Friedrich 10–11, 13, 16–18, 22, 49–50, 129, 174, 223–4, 226, 250
Wiedebein, Gottlieb 223
Wieland, Christoph Martin 7
Wielhorski, Michail 227
Winckelmann, Johann Joachim 268
Wolf, Hugo 238, 271

Zemlinsky, Alexander 239
Zender, Hans 266
Zimmerman, Bernd Alois 253

Cambridge Companions to Music

Topics

The Cambridge Companion to Blues and Gospel Music
Edited by Allan Moore

The Cambridge Companion to the Concerto
Edited by Simon P. Keefe

The Cambridge Companion to Conducting
Edited by José Antonio Bowen

The Cambridge Companion to Grand Opera
Edited by David Charlton

The Cambridge Companion to Jazz
Edited by Mervyn Cooke and David Horn

The Cambridge Companion to the Lied
Edited by James Parsons

The Cambridge Companion to the Musical
Edited by William Everett and Paul Laird

The Cambridge Companion to the Orchestra
Edited by Colin Lawson

The Cambridge Companion to Pop and Rock
Edited by Simon Frith, Will Straw and John Street

The Cambridge Companion to the String Quartet
Edited by Robin Stowell

The Cambridge Companion to Twentieth-Century Opera
Edited by Mervyn Cooke

Composers

The Cambridge Companion to Bach
Edited by John Butt

The Cambridge Companion to Bartók
Edited by Amanda Bayley

The Cambridge Companion to Beethoven
Edited by Glenn Stanley

The Cambridge Companion to Berg
Edited by Anthony Pople

The Cambridge Companion to Berlioz
Edited by Peter Bloom

The Cambridge Companion to Brahms
Edited by Michael Musgrave

The Cambridge Companion to Benjamin Britten
Edited by Mervyn Cooke

The Cambridge Companion to Bruckner
Edited by John Williamson

The Cambridge Companion to John Cage
Edited by David Nicholls

The Cambridge Companion to Chopin
Edited by Jim Samson

The Cambridge Companion to Debussy
Edited by Simon Trezise

The Cambridge Companion to Elgar
Edited by Daniel Grimley and Julian Rushton

The Cambridge Companion to Handel
Edited by Donald Burrows

The Cambridge Companion to Haydn
Edited by Caryl Clark

The Cambridge Companion to Liszt
Edited by Kenneth Hamilton

The Cambridge Companion to Mendelssohn
Edited by Peter Mercer-Taylor

The Cambridge Companion to Mozart
Edited by Simon P. Keefe

The Cambridge Companion to Ravel
Edited by Deborah Mawer

The Cambridge Companion to Rossini
Edited by Emanuele Senici

The Cambridge Companion to Schubert
Edited by Christopher Gibbs

The Cambridge Companion to Schumann
Edited by Beate Perrey

The Cambridge Companion to Sibelius
Edited by Daniel Grimley

The Cambridge Companion to Verdi
Edited by Scott L. Balthazar

Instruments

The Cambridge Companion to Brass Instruments
Edited by Trevor Herbert and John Wallace

The Cambridge Companion to the Cello
Edited by Robin Stowell

The Cambridge Companion to the Clarinet
Edited by Colin Lawson

The Cambridge Companion to the Guitar
Edited by Victor Coelho

The Cambridge Companion to the Organ
Edited by Nicholas Thistlethwaite and Geoffrey Webber

The Cambridge Companion to the Piano
Edited by David Rowland

The Cambridge Companion to the Recorder
Edited by John Mansfield Thomson

The Cambridge Companion to the Saxophone
Edited by Richard Ingham

The Cambridge Companion to Singing
Edited by John Potter

The Cambridge Companion to the Violin
Edited by Robin Stowell